C

C

Problem solving and programming

KENNETH A. BARCLAY

Napier College, Edinburgh, Scotland

Prentice Hall

New York   London   Toronto   Sydney   Tokyo

First published 1989 by
Prentice Hall International (UK) Ltd,
66 Wood Lane End, Hemel Hempstead,
Hertfordshire, HP2 4RG
A division of
Simon & Schuster International Group

Printed and bound in great Britain by
A. Wheaton & Co. Ltd, Exeter.

Library of Congress Cataloging-in-Publication Data
are available from the publisher.

British Library Cataloguing in Publication Data

Barclay, K. A. (Kenneth A.), *1947–*
    C: problem solving and programming.
    1. Computer systems. Programming languages:
    C language
    I. Title
    005.13'3

ISBN 0-13-115510-5

---

1 2 3 4 5   93 92 91 90 89

0-13-115510-5

Contents

Preface   xi

1 The C programming language   1

2 The essentials of a C program   3

     2.1   A first program   3
     2.2   Compiling and running   8
     2.3   Summary   9
     2.4   Exercises   9

3 Types, operators and expressions   11

     3.1   Integer constants   11
     3.2   Floating point constants   13
     3.3   Character constants   14
     3.4   String constants   15
     3.5   Identifiers   16
     3.6   Variable declarations   17
     3.7   Integer qualifiers   18
     3.8   Arithmetic expressions   19
     3.9   Type conversions   22
     3.10   The assignment operator   25
     3.11   The compound assignment operators   27
     3.12   The increment and decrement operators   28
     3.13   The type cast operator   30
     3.14   The comma operator   31
     3.15   Summary   31
     3.16   Exercises   32

4 Input and output   34

     4.1   Access to the standard library   34
     4.2   Formatted output   35
     4.3   Formatted input   39
     4.4   The functions getchar and putchar   41
     4.5   Summary   44
     4.6   Exercises   44

5   Program structure   45

5.1	The structure of a function	45
5.2	Multifunction programs	49
5.3	Automatic variables	54
5.4	Function values	57
5.5	Function arguments	61
5.6	Function argument agreement and conversion	66
5.7	Pointers and function arguments	69
5.8	The C preprocessor	75
5.9	Mathematical functions	78
5.10	Summary	79
5.11	Exercises	80

6   Flow of control   84

6.1	Relational operators and expressions	84
6.2	Equality operators and expressions	86
6.3	Logical operators and expressions	88
6.4	The conditional operator	89
6.5	The while statement	90
6.6	The for statement	100
6.7	The do statement	103
6.8	The if statement	108
6.9	The switch statement	123
6.10	The break statement	133
6.11	The continue statement	136
6.12	Summary	137
6.13	Exercises	138

7   Programming in the large   142

7.1	Systematic data design	143
7.2	Designing into C	145
7.3	Storage classes	147
7.4	Storage class auto	147
7.5	Storage class extern	151
7.6	Storage class static	158
7.7	Storage class register	160
7.8	Summary	161
7.9	Exercises	162

8   The C preprocessor   164

8.1	Simple macro definitions	164
8.2	Macro arguments	166
8.3	Macro expansion	168
8.4	Redefining and undefining macros	169
8.5	File inclusion	170
8.6	Conditional compilation	170
8.7	Line numbering	174

| 8.8 | Summary | 177 |
| 8.9 | Exercises | 178 |

9 More on data types — 179

9.1	The typedef statement	179
9.2	Enumeration types	182
9.3	Summary	185
9.4	Exercises	186

10 Recursion — 187

| 10.1 | Summary | 191 |
| 10.2 | Exercises | 192 |

11 Arrays and pointers — 193

11.1	Declaring and referencing arrays	193
11.2	Multidimensional arrays	197
11.3	Arrays as function arguments	199
11.4	Array initialization	202
11.5	Pointers and arrays	204
11.6	Functions returning pointers	208
11.7	External array referencing	209
11.8	Arrays and typedef declarations	209
11.9	Summary	220
11.10	Exercises	220

12 Character strings — 223

12.1	String comparisons	226
12.2	Character string input	227
12.3	Standard library string handling functions	231
12.4	Conversions between strings and numerics	241
12.5	Arrays of pointers	243
12.6	Pointers to pointers	248
12.7	Command line arguments	249
12.8	Initializing pointer arrays	254
12.9	Summary	260
12.10	Exercises	261

13 Storage management — 264

13.1	Implementation	265
13.2	Summary	281
13.3	Exercises	281

14 Files — 283

14.1	File access	285
14.2	The functions fgetc, feof and fputc	287
14.3	The functions fscanf and fprintf	291

viii   Contents

14.4   The functions fgets and fputs   293
14.5   Stdin, stdout and stderr   296
14.6   The function exit and error treatment   297
14.7   Direct access   306
14.8   Summary   310
14.9   Exercises   310

15   Structures, unions and bit fields   312

15.1   Members   313
15.2   Name overloading   316
15.3   Internal storage of structures   316
15.4   Structures and functions   317
15.5   Pointers to structures   322
15.6   Initializing structures   326
15.7   Array members of structures   326
15.8   Arrays of structures   327
15.9   Nested structures   331
15.10 Files of structures   333
15.11 Unions   342
15.12 Bit fields   345
15.13 Summary   347
15.14 Exercises   348

16   Dynamic data structures   349

16.1   The linear linked list   350
16.2   List processing   354
16.3   Binary trees   367
16.4   Binary tree processing   371
16.5   Summary   383
16.6   Exercises   384

17   Operations on bits   385

17.1   Bitwise operators and expressions   385
17.2   Summary   396
17.3   Exercises   396

18   Advanced topics   398

18.1   Generic program units   398
18.2   Pointers to functions   402
18.3   Functions as arguments   407
18.4   The goto statement   413
18.5   Summary   417
18.6   Exercises   417

Appendices   418

A   Hardware characteristics   418
B   ASCII character set   419

C   **Reserved keywords**   422
D   **Identifiers**   423
E   **Operators**   424
F   **The standard C library**   426

   F.1   Character functions   426
   F.2   String processing   429
   F.3   Storage management functions   430
   F.4   Standard I/O functions   431
   F.5   Mathematical functions   447

G   **Compiling under UNIX**   449

   G.1   Lint: a C program checker   451
   G.2   Make: maintaining computer programs   452
   G.3   SCCS: source code control system   453

H   **ANSII standard C**   455

Index of symbols   459

General index   461

Preface

This book provides a comprehensive introduction to the C programming language and is suitable for use both by novice programmers and by those with a knowledge of other programming languages. The complete language is described and fully illustrated. More general programming principles, consistent with current methods of abstraction, structured programming and stepwise refinement, are also featured.

In addition to a full study of the C programming language, the important principle of 'programming *into* a programming language, not *in* it', is emphasized. In general, this principle deals with data and its representation, as well as commands. There is, therefore, a strong emphasis on structured problem solving. 'Program refinement' is now well established and is present in many modern programming texts. 'Data refinement' has, however, not received the same attention. This concept is concerned with data structures which match the problem space. Once a correct program design has been developed, the data structures are refined to make them more efficient and implementable in the chosen programming language. In both cases the relevant C language features in support of this principle are described.

Presently, the C programming language is not supported by any standard. The definition to which I have adhered is that found in the *C Reference Manual* [*The C Programming Language*, B. Kernighan and D. Ritchie, Prentice Hall, 1978]. Two accepted extensions to that definition, namely, enumeration types, and functions with structure arguments and functions returning structures, are included. Further, due cogniscence has been taken of the proposed standard from the X3J11 subcommittee of the American National Standards Institute.

Considerable effort has been taken to present the topics in a clear and concise manner. With the exception of Chapter 2, 'The essentials of a C program', the material is presented in learning order. Chapter 2 introduces a small number of the features of C, and provides an introduction to the detailed studies of the later chapters.

Chapters 3 to 6 present four fundamental aspects of programming: data types, operators, program flow control and program design. In particular,

Chapter 5 provides a full exposition of the C function. The function is one of the pivotal concepts in structuring large software systems. For this reason, it is introduced early in the text and is reinforced through continual use.

Chapter 7 addresses the problem of 'Programming in the large', using the concept of a *program unit* to maintain a clear separation of the definition and use of a resource from its implementation. These divisions are supported by the *storage classes* of C. The scope rules and the proper use of each class are discussed.

Within this general model, subsequent chapters participate in the evolution of the concept of the *abstract data type*. For a number of standard types, specifications are developed, external representations are defined, implementations are programmed and practical applications are illustrated.

A particular feature of the book is the inclusion of a number of major case studies. They are used to illustrate various aspects of the C language, fundamental computing algorithms and systematic program design, in a relevant context, not otherwise achievable with small programs. Where appropriate, each chapter includes many complete programs. All program listings are reproduced directly from the computer and should execute correctly on any machine supported by a standard C compiler.

A short list of the major issues raised in each chapter is repeated as a summary at the end. Most chapters include a set of exercises. The exercises include the construction of new programs as well as modifications and extensions to the given examples. Solutions to a selection of these exercises are given under separate cover.

Acknowledgements

My special thanks go to Dr John Savage, Napier College, who read the first drafts of all chapters and gave technical and stylistic suggestions on virtually every paragraph. He also provided many useful insights on programming practice and methodology.

My gratitude goes also to the Napier College Computer Studies Department. The students of this Department have been compelled to be the subjects of many experiments in my teaching of the C programming language. The thoughtful criticisms, suggestions and encouragement of colleagues is much appreciated.

Finally, I thank my wife, Irene, and children Dawn, Ria and Kim, for their love and patience while this book was in preparation.

Without the explicit newline symbol appearing in the first character string, the output from this program is:

My first program.It is wonderful.

In these first examples, the printf function was used to display a character string. The printf function is also capable of displaying the value of *expressions* and *variables*. Consider the following program employing these two new concepts.

Program 2.3

```
#include <stdio.h>

main()
  {
    int sum;

    sum = 10 + 20;
    printf("The sum of 10 and 20 is %d\n", sum);
  }
```

The first line of the function body is known as a *declaration*. In common with many other programming languages, C requires that all variables be declared before they are used. A variable is a name for a region of memory in which values may be stored. The variable *sum* is declared to be of type *int* (integer), that is, a variable which represents numbers without fractional parts.

The second line causes the integer constants 10 and 20 to be added and the resulting value placed in the memory location known as sum. This is an example of the C *assignment*. The expression 10 + 20 to the right of the equal symbol (=) is evaluated and the result assigned to the variable on the left. The integer constants are separated by a plus symbol (+). This is an example of a C *operator* which informs the computer that the two values are to be added together.

Finally, the printf function call has two arguments: a character string and the variable sum. The second argument is an example of an expression, the value of which is to be printed. In this case, the expression value is that of the variable sum, namely 30, which is printed together with the character string. The percent character within the string is a special character recognized by the printf function. It and the immediately following single character d determines that the value 30 is to be displayed at that point in the string as a decimal integer number. The program output is thus:

The sum of 10 and 20 is 30

Punctuation is used in C to define program and part program structures, and to separate constituent parts. In Program 2.3 a number of common punctuation symbols are present. We have already noted that blank space is used to form indentation. To heighten readability a blank line has been is known as a *function call* statement. It calls or invokes the library function printf. The actual objects to be printed by printf are supplied as *arguments* to the function. One or more arguments are given as a comma-separated list enclosed in parentheses (and). The single argument in the above example is the *character string* that is to be displayed. The sequence of characters enclosed between the double quotes is produced as the program output.

Finally, the braces { and } enclose the statements that constitute the function. The braces are analogous to the begin–end pair of Algol and Pascal. The statement or statements enclosed within the braces is the *function body*. In C, the semicolon is the statement terminator, rather like the full stop in natural language. Every C statement must have a terminating semicolon. Program 2.2 extends our first program by including two printf function call statements both with associated semicolons.

Program 2.2(a)

```
#include <stdio.h>

main()
  {
    printf("My first program.\n");
    printf("It is wonderful.\n");
  }
```

In this program two stylistic guidelines are being followed. First, each statement appears on separate lines. This is not essential but it does improve program readability. Second, the two statements are indented a number of character places from the left margin using blank or space characters. This helps to identify the program structure under consideration, particularly when dealing with large multifunction programs.

The sequence \n in the two character strings is the C notation for a newline symbol. When a newline is printed, all subsequent output starts from the left margin of the next line. Thus, the output from the last program is:

My first program.
It is wonderful.

Note that two printf function calls does not imply two separate lines of output. Consider now a second version of this program.

Program 2.2(b)

```
#include <stdio.h>

main()
  {
    printf("My first program.");
    printf("It is wonderful.\n");
  }
```

## CHAPTER 2

The essentials of a C program

This chapter provides an introduction to the elements of a C program. The aim is achieved by exploring the features of a number of 'actual' programs. In no sense are the programs of any real value or use. They are technically complete, however, and will compile and execute on a computer supporting a standard C compiler.

The features of C introduced are covered in greater depth later in this book. Details, formal specifications, exceptions and so on, are deliberately avoided. This way we concentrate on the structure of a C program without being overwhelmed by the volume of technical detail. Armed with these essentials, we may progress to later chapters and explore the fine detail.

2.1 A first program

We start by considering a very modest program to display the message "My first program." on the computer terminal. In C, the program to print this message is:

Program 2.1(a)

```
#include <stdio.h>

main()
    {
      printf("My first program.");
    }
```

In the C programming language, use is made of both upper-case and lower-case letters to name program objects, whch are considered distinct. In many other programming languages, notably FORTRAN and COBOL, upper-case letters are used exclusively. The names 'main' and 'printf' in the above program must appear as shown. The names 'MAIN' and 'Printf', for example, would be interpreted as different from their lower-case forms.

C programs are described as free-format. This means that there are few restrictions on the appearance of the program, and that it is the programmer's responsibility to choose the layout of the program. Languages such as

FORTRAN dictate the program form. This programmer freedom may be used or abused. The following two versions of the original program are equally acceptable to the C compiler. They all achieve the same result. They are, however, very difficult to read and are of doubtful quality. Certain stylistic conventions have been adopted by the C programming community and they are noted below and in subsequent programming examples.

Program 2.1(b)

```
#include <stdio.h>

main() { printf("My first program."); }
```

and:

Program 2.1(c)

```
#include <stdio.h>

main
(
)
{
printf
(
"My first program."
)
;
}
```

A C program, no matter its size and complexity, is composed of one or more *functions*. Each function specifies the actual computation to be performed by that piece of code. In this respect C functions are similar to FORTRAN subroutines or Pascal procedures/functions. Each function in C is identified by its name. The name of the function is chosen by the programmer. The exception to this rule is that there must exist one and only one function called *main* in any given program. A program starts executing from the first instruction in the function main.

The function main usually executes instructions and invokes other functions to perform their operations. The instructions are given as program *statements.* These other functions may be part of the same program or be members of *libraries* of previously developed functions. Function *printf* is an example of the latter, being a member of the standard library. The standard library is a collection of C functions designed to provide, amongst other things, standard input/output facilities. The functions are meant to exist in compatible form on any computer system which supports the C language (see Appendix F), and programs which confine themselves to the facilities of the standard library will be portable and can be moved among computer systems with minimum change.

Function printf delivers output to the user's terminal. The program line:

```
printf("My first program.");
```

## CHAPTER 1

The C programming language

C is a general-purpose programming language. It was designed by Dennis Ritchie of Bell Laboratories and implemented there in 1972 on a PDP-11. It was designed as the systems programming language for the UNIX* operating system. It is not, however, tied to any one operating system, and has proved very adaptable. In addition to being used to implement operating systems, language compilers and software tools, it has been used to write major numerical, text-processing and database management systems.

C evolved from the programming languages B and BCPL. BCPL is a typeless systems programming language developed by Martin Richards at Cambridge in 1967. B was written by Ken Thompson in 1970 for the first UNIX system on a PDP-7 and borrowed many features from BCPL. B is also a typeless programming language. The only data type supported by these languages is the machine word. In C, a richer set of data objects are supported, including characters, integers of several sizes, and two precisions of floating point numbers. Additionally, a hierarchy of derived data types may be created using arrays, structures, unions and pointers.

C is a 'middle-level' language, occupying a position between the low-level or machine-oriented languages and the high-level or problem-oriented languages. C is sufficiently close to the underlying hardware allowing detailed program control, yet supports advanced program and data structuring capabilities. C removes the need to program in CPU-specific assembly languages, removing retraining costs, reducing programming time, increasing reliability and improving portability.

C is also a small, lean language. Its modest size means that it is relatively easy to learn. Further, C compilers are simple, compact and straightforward to implement. This is evident by the availability of compilers for a wide range of hardware.

C provides the fundamental flow control primitives: statement grouping, selection (*if* and *switch*), and iteration (*while*, *for* and *do*). Subroutines are

---

*UNIX is a registered trademark of Bell Laboratories.

provided by recursive external functions with parameters. Modular programming is supported by the use of storage classes within program files. C has a rich and powerful set of operators giving considerable expressive powers to the programmer.

C is not a strongly typed language in the sense of Pascal or Ada. This makes it relatively permissive about data conversion. Existing compilers provide no automatic array-bound checking. C is terse, offering the opportunity to write very 'dense' code that is difficult to read.

These criticisms can all be overcome. Type checking can be imposed by using a separate version of the compiler, called *lint*. It detects type mismatches, inconsistent argument usage, uninitialized variables, etc. By providing the correct control structures and data types, and allowing almost unrestricted meaningful usage, C offers an uncommonly productive programming environment.

placed between the declarations and the statements of function main. Blank spaces, line separators and tab characters are classes of *whitespace* characters used extensively in C programs to improve their readability.

Besides whitespace characters, Program 2.3 uses a variety of punctuation symbols. Braces { and } have been noted as function body delimiters. Parentheses (and) are used to group related items, for example, the arguments of the function printf. Character strings are delimited by double quote (") characters. The semicolon is the statement terminator. The comma separates related items, such as the arguments of printf.

The final program we look at introduces the *comment*. A comment is used by the programmer to annotate the program code. Comments enhance a program's readability and provide a useful documentation tool. Proper documentation is an essential programming habit. Comments serve to inform the reader of the program — the original program author or the programmer responsible for its maintenance — of the intended logic. Comments can be applied to the overall program, to individual functions, or to a particular sequence of statements.

A comment is any sequence of characters enclosed between /* and */. In both cases, there should be no embedded spaces in /* and */. A comment may appear anywhere that whitespace is permitted in a program. A comment is ignored by the C compiler. An example of a comment is:

/* This is a comment */

A comment can extend over several program lines. Such a block of commenting is frequently used to describe the behavior of a piece of code. An example is:

```
/*
**    This comment extends over seven lines in total.
**    The first and last lines are simply the opening
**    and closing comment symbols. All other lines
**    are marked with a leading pair of asterisks. They
**    are used to emphasize a unit of commenting.
*/
```

The one restriction which applies to comments is that they may not be nested. Thus, it is impossible to, say, take the comment:

/* Program 1 version 3 */

and comment it out with:

/* /* Program 1 version 3 */ developed 28 October */

Program 2.4 repeats the last problem but includes embedded comments. The two programs are otherwise identical. The comments clarify the program's operation and improve its readability.

Program 2.4

```
/*
**      This program assigns the sum of two integer
**      constants to an integer variable, then displays
**      the result along with some annotation.
*/

#include <stdio.h>

main ()
  {
    int sum;                /* declare variable, ... */

    sum = 10 + 20;          /* ... then assign value, and ... */
                            /* ... display the result. */
    printf ("The sum of 10 and 20 is %d\n", sum);
  }
```

It is a good habit to insert comments into a program as it is being prepared. There are a number of reasons for this. First, it is easier to document the program when the logic is established. This saves having to return to the coding to insert appropriate commenting. Second, it is frequently the case that comments are not included once the program is operational. Given that a program is written once but read many times, comments can aid the programmer in reading the text and facilitate debugging erroneous programs.

2.2 Compiling and running

Before a program can be compiled and run, the source text must first be placed in a file. Generally, this is achieved with a text editor. The file containing the program text is identified by its filename. Most C compilers require that a source filename has a suffix or extension '.c', as in the filename 'example.c'.

The source program may then be compiled to create an executable image of the program. Compilation procedures differ considerably between compilers. Under UNIX, the C compiler is called cc. To compile the program in the file 'example.c', the command is:

    cc example.c

If there are no program errors in the source code, the executable program file 'a.out' is automatically created, and the program is ready for execution.

The compilation process consists of translating a program in the high-level language C into the equivalent sequence of machine code instructions. During the translation process, the compiler may detect errors in the programming language usage, for example, a missing comma or semicolon. The compiler reports these errors in a printout identifying the source and nature of the error. These are known as *compile time* errors.

If the program compiles correctly, it can be executed by entering the command:

    a.out

When running this executable program produced by the compiler, further situations, known as *run time* errors may occur. These cause programs to terminate abnormally during execution, and arise from executing perfectly plausible instructions but with erroneous data. For example, division of one number by another is perfectly acceptable providing the second number is not zero, otherwise the answer is infinity. Protection against run time errors to improve program robustness is discussed in later chapters.

A program that is free of both compile time and run time errors may still not produce the correct results. These errors, known as *logical* errors, arise from an incorrect specification of the language solution. A methodical approach to programming, as emphasized in the text, can significantly reduce this type of problem.

Appendix G gives a full exposition of the compilation process and the command cc under UNIX. On other systems the commands will be different and the reader is referred to the appropriate documentation and/or a local expert.

2.3 Summary

1. A simple program consists of the function main. The body of the function consists of declarations and statements enclosed within the braces { and }.
2. Every C statement and declaration concludes with a terminating semicolon.
3. C programs are free-format. Certain stylistic guidelines have, however, been adopted. Generally, have no more than one program statement per line. Indent to highlight the program structure and use whitespace characters to separate the program tokens.
4. Comments are written between /* and */. They are vital to good program documentation. Comments should assist the reader to understand the program logic.
5. The compiler translates a C program into its equivalent machine instructions. The input to the compiler is the source C program and the output is the executable program image.
6. Programs can exhibit compile time, run time and logic errors, all of which must be corrected to produce an operational program.

2.4 Exercises

1. Explain the meaning of the following terms:

   (a) function   (g) expression
   (b) standard library (h) constant
   (c) argument   (i) assignment
   (d) declaration   (j) compile time error
   (e) statement   (k) run time error
   (f) variable   (l) logic error

2. Carefully enter Program 2.1(a) into a file with an editor or word-processor then compile it and run it to ensure it produces the required output.

3. What output would you expect from the following program?

```
#include <stdio.h>
main()
    {
    printf("One.....");
    printf("Two.....");
    printf("Three\n");
    }
```

4. Write a program which divides the value 47 by the value 12 and displays the result with an appropriate message. The division operator is denoted by the slash symbol (/).

5. The following program contains a run time error. Carefully enter it into a file, and check that it compiles without any errors. What happens when you run the program? What messages, if any, are produced? Consult a local expert or compiler documentation to obtain an explanation.

```
#include <stdio.h>

main()
    {
    int first, second;

    first = 0;
    second = 27 / first;
    printf("second is %d\n", second);
    }
```

## CHAPTER 3

Types, operators and expressions

A C program describes the computational processes to be carried out on items of data. It is necessary in a C program to classify each and every item of data according to their type. In C, an infinite number of distinct types is possible. They are, however, all derived from four basic types: *integer, character, float* and *double*. For these simple types there are *denotations* or constants, i.e. a sequence of symbols possessing a specific value of a particular type. Constants are the subject of sections 3.1–3.4.

The data items manipulated by a program may be divided into two classes – those whose values remain fixed during execution of a program and those whose values change. The former are the constants in a program. The latter are known as variables, since the values possessed by such objects are allowed to vary during the program run. Items of both classes share the properties of the type as described above. Variables are considered in sections 3.5–3.7.

An *expression* is a rule by which a value may be computed. It consists of one or more *operands* (or values) combined by *operators*. C has an unusually rich set of operators which provide access to most of the operations implemented by the underlying computer hardware. The full complement of available operators naturally divides into a number of groups. The arithmetic operators, such as addition, are discussed fully in this chapter. The other operators are introduced in the chapters in which they are applied.

3.1 Integer constants

An integer constant is a whole number which may be positive, zero or negative (strictly, a negative integer is obtained by applying the unary negative operator to a positive integer; see section 3.8). Integer constants may be specified in decimal, octal or hexadecimal notation.

A decimal integer constant is written as a sequence of decimal digits (0 through 9), the first of which is not 0 (zero). The values:

1234   255   10   9999

are all valid examples of decimal integer constants. No embedded spaces or commas are permitted between the digits. The value 10,000, for example, is not a decimal integer constant because of the comma; it must be expressed as 10000.

A computer can only represent a finite subset of all possible integers. The precision of an integer depends on the particular hardware. For instance, on the IBM PC* an integer is usually held using a 16-bit 2s complement notation. An integer can, therefore, assume values from -32768 through 32767 inclusive.

An octal integer constant is written as a sequence of octal digits (0 through 7) starting with a zero (0). The values:

0377   0177   00000   01

are all valid examples of octal integer constants.

A hexadecimal integer constant is a sequence of hexadecimal digits starting with 0x or 0X. The hexadecimal digits include 0 through 9, and the letters A through F (or a through f). The letters represent the values 10 through 15 respectively. Examples of valid hexadecimal integer constants include:

0XFF   0x4B   0x1f   0XfF

Octal and hexadecimal constants frequently find their way into system programming applications. Examples of their use will appear later in this book.

The precision of an integer constant can also be *qualified*. A decimal, octal or hexadecimal integer constant immediately followed by the letter L (or letter l) is an explicit *long* integer constant. On the DEC VAX,† long integers employ 32-bits, and can thus express values in the range -2147483648 to 2147483647 inclusive. Valid explicit long integer constants are:

123L   04774771   0XFFL

Integer constants which exceed the single precision range are also implicitly long integers:

32768   0100000   0X4FFF

If the value of an integer constant exceeds the largest representable value, the result is unpredictable. Most C compilers generally warn the programmer of the problem.

To illustrate some C integer constants, consider an IBM PC implementation. In Table 3.1, some integer constants, their true mathematical value and their type and value are presented.

---

*IBM is a registered trademark of International Business Machines Corporation.
†DEC is a registered trademark of Digital Equipment Corporation.

Table 3.1

C constant	True value	C type	C value
0	0	int	0
32767	$2^{15} - 1$	int	32767
077777	$2^{15} - 1$	int	32767
32768	2^{16}	long	32768
0x10000	2^{16}	long	65536
2147483647	$2^{31} - 1$	long	2147483647
2147483648	2^{32}		undefined

3.2 Floating point constants

Numbers with fractional parts may be represented as floating point constants. If there is a preceding minus sign attached to the number, it is taken to be the unary negation operator applied to the constant, and not part of the constant itself (see section 3.8). Floating point constants may be written in two forms. The first, and simplest, is a sequence of decimal digits including the decimal point. Valid examples include:

3.1415926   12.0   0.1   0.00001

Note that the decimal point need not necessarily be embedded, allowing both leading and trailing decimal point forms. The second and third examples above might also be shown as:

12.   .1

It is suggested, however, that the readability is improved if the former notation is used.

In the second form, a floating point constant is expressed as an integer or as a floating point constant as defined above, multiplied by some integer power of ten. This power is shown as the letter E (or letter e) followed by an optionally signed integer constant. Examples of this form include:

1.0E2 (= 100.0)   12.34e − 3 (= 0.01234)
1E − 2(= 0.01)   1E + 3   (= 1000.0)

This latter representation is frequently referred to as scientific notation.

The range of floating point constants permitted by implementations is restricted like integers. Further, whereas integers are held exactly, floating point constants are held as a (close) approximation. The type of a floating point constant is always *double*. On the DEC VAX a double precision floating point constant has a 64-bit representation, with a magnitude between about 10E − 38 and 10E + 38, and an accuracy of approximately 17 decimal digits. A single precision representation for floating point values is also available with the same range as doubles but with only some seven significant decimal digits. These values are of type *float*.

If the magnitude of a floating point constant is too great to be represented, the result is unpredictable. Most compilers generate an appropriate error message in this case. If the magnitude of a floating point constant is below 10E − 38, zero is substituted.

For some further details on number representation for a range of computer hardware, see Appendix A.

3.3 Character constants

A character constant is a single character written within single quotes (apostrophe) as in 'X'. The value of a character constant is the integer numeric value of the character in the machine's character set. Character constants have type *int*. C programmers must be aware of the character set of the target computer. The two most commonly used character sets are EBCDIC (Extended Binary Coded Decimal Interchange Code) and ASCII (American Standard Code for Information Interchange). The two sets are not the same. In the ASCII character set, the character 'X' has decimal encoding 88, whilst the EBCDIC encoding is 231. The full ASCII character set is given in Appendix B.

Escape sequences can be used to represent characters that would be awkward or impossible to enter in a source program directly. An escape sequence consists of the backslash symbol (\) followed by a single character. The two symbols taken together represent the single required character. The characters which may follow the backslash, and their meanings are as follows:

```
newline            \n
horizontal tab     \t
backspace          \b
carriage return    \r
formfeed           \f
single quote       \'
double quote       \"
backslash          \\
```

Thus the character constant to represent the formfeed symbol in a program is '\f', and the character constant for a backslash is '\\'.

The escape sequence may also appear as a backslash symbol followed by one, two or three octal digits. The resulting octal value is taken as the octal number of the character from the machine's character set. The character constant 'X' (with ASCII encoding decimal 88, octal 130) may be represented as '\130'. More generally, this representation is used for non-printing characters. The ASCII character ACK (acknowledge) would be represented by '\006'. The first of the ASCII collating sequence is the character NUL and is shown as '\0'. This symbol is reserved for a particular role in C and is discussed fully later.

If the character following the backslash is neither an octal digit nor one of the character escape codes listed above, the result is considered unpredictable. Commonly, the effect is simply to ignore the backslash.

3.4 String constants

A string constant is a possibly empty sequence of characters enclosed in double quotes. The same escape mechanism provided for character constants can also be used in string constants. Examples of string constants include:

```
"Hello world"
"The C Programming Language"
""
"She said \"Good morning\""
"This string terminates with a newline\n"
```

A string is allowed to extend over one or more lines provided each line terminates with a backslash character followed immediately by a newline symbol. In this case, the backslash and the newline symbols are ignored.

```
"This string extends \
over two lines."
```

and is textually equivalent to:

```
"This string extends over two lines."
```

For each string constant of N characters, there is a block of $N + 1$ consecutive characters whose first N are initialized with the characters from the string, and whose last character is the ASCII NUL character '\0'. Thus, the string:

```
"hello"
```

is stored as shown in Fig. 3.1. As we shall discover later, the null character is used to delimit the end of all strings.

Care must be taken to recognize that the character 'X' and the string "X" are not the same. On the majority of computers the character 'X' is a single character 8-bit byte (see Fig. 3.2), whilst the string "X" is two character

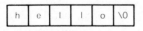

Fig. 3.1

Fig. 3.2

Fig. 3.3

bytes (see Fig. 3.3). Strings and characters are thus distinct, and must on no account be operated upon as if they were the same.

3.5 Identifiers

The C programming language requires that various quantities used in a program be given names by which they can then be referenced. These names are known as *identifiers* and are created by the programmer.

An identifier is created according to the following rule (see also Appendix D):

> An identifier is a combination of letters and digits the first of which must be a letter. The underscore symbol (_) is permitted in an identifier and is considered to be a letter.

From this, the following are valid examples of identifiers:

time	day_of_the_week	BUFFER
x	unit_cost	program_name
_MAX	h2o	AVeryLongIdentifier

Two identifiers are the same when they have the same spelling, including the case of all letters. The identifiers *abcd* and *abcD* are thus considered distinct.

Strictly, an identifier may be any length. However, many C compilers consider only the first eight characters as significant. The ninth and subsequent characters in identifiers are ignored by such compilers. The identifiers *convention* and *conventionally* would be considered identical in this case.

A C program may reference objects defined elsewhere. These are known as *external objects*. For example, the function *printf* is a member of the standard C library and is defined external to the program containing its use. Identifiers in a C program which refer to external objects are often subject to additional restrictions. These identifiers have to be processed by software other than compilers. Linkers and librarian managers may have their own limitations on the length of identifiers. These software tools may further not distinguish between the case of letters. Frequently, external identifiers are restricted to six characters and are not case sensitive.

Notwithstanding all these restrictions, the programmer is encouraged to use meaningful identifiers. The name of the identifier should reflect the purpose of the object in a C program. If a program operates on, say, a time of day, then the identifiers *hours*, *minutes* and *seconds* are superior to the shorter, but less obvious *h*, *m* and *s*.

Certain identifiers are reserved for use as *keywords* in a C program. A complete list of the C keywords is given below (and repeated in Appendix C). They may not be used as programmer-defined identifiers.

auto	else	long	typedef
break	enum	register	union
case	extern	return	unsigned
char	float	short	void
continue	for	sizeof	while
default	goto	static	
do	if	struct	
double	int	switch	

Some implementations have defined additional reserved keywords, including asm, entry and fortran used to reference non-C facilities. They too should be avoided as program identifiers. Finally, the emerging ANSII C standard includes the keywords const, signed and volatile.

3.6 Variable declarations

Variables are data items whose values vary during execution of a program. Variables in a C program are made to possess one of the four fundamental types – integers, characters, single precision floating point and double precision floating point. Variables must have their type indicated so that the compiler can record all the necessary information about them, and generate the appropriate code during translation. This is done by means of a *variable* declaration. A variable declaration has the form:

type-specifier list-of-variables

The list-of-variables is a comma-separated list of identifiers representing the program variables. Each named variable possesses a fundamental type as given by the type-specifier. The type-specifiers for the four fundamental types are introduced by the reserved keywords:

    int   (integer)
    char   (character)
    float   (single precision floating point)
    double   (double precision floating point)

A complete variable declaration is then:

    int hours, minutes, seconds

Thereafter, the variables hours, minutes and seconds may assume any legal integer value. Integer values may be assigned to these variables, and the integer value associated with a variable may be called upon in a program statement.

A sequence of variable declarations may appear using the semicolon symbol as the terminator. For improved readability, each declaration appears on separate lines:

    int day, month, year;
    float centigrade, fahrenheit;
    char initial;
    double epsilon;

Separate variable declarations may employ the same type specifier as in:

    int day, month, year;
    int hours, minutes, seconds;

This facility is often employed to bracket together related variables. In the first declaration, the variables are concerned with a calendar date. In the second, the variables are used to represent a time. Because C is free-format, we are, of course, free to extend a declaration over one or more lines. It is perfectly acceptable to write:

    int day, month, year,
        hours, minutes, seconds;

where the six variables are declared in the single declaration.

A variable may not be redeclared in a second declaration. Such declarations would cause the C compiler to issue an appropriate error message.

    int time, interval, period;
    float time;

The compiler would be unable to determine the correct type for the variable time. The compiler message would report that in the second declaration, variable time has been redeclared.

3.7 Integer qualifiers

In the same way that the accuracy of a variable containing a floating point number may be extended by declaring it to be of type double, so it is possible to control the range of an integer variable.

If the qualifier *long* is placed before the type-specifier int in a declaration, then the declared integer variables will have extended range. Long integer variables provide the largest range of signed integer values. An example of a long declaration is:

    long int memory_address, factorial;

On the IBM PC the range of values that may be stored in a long integer variable is that for long integer constants (see section 3.1). Operations on objects of type long are sometimes slower than the same operations on objects of type int, depending upon the implementation.

The qualifier *short* placed ahead of the type-specifier int in a variable declaration specifies that the named variables are used to represent a limited range of signed integer values. The motivation for using short integer variables is primarily one of conservation of memory space. An appropriate declaration is:

    short int day_of_week, week_of_year;

In both the examples above, the specifier int is optional, and the declarations may be alternatively presented as:

    long memory_address, factorial;
    short day_of_week, week_of_year;

Strictly, C does not specify the exact number of bits used to represent int, long and short variables. These quantities are implementation dependent, usually determined by the underlying hardware. The only relation guaranteed by C is that a short is shorter than a long. It is permissible for an int to be the same size as either a short or a long. On the DEC VAX both int and long are 32-bit quantities, whilst a short is 16-bits.

Finally, the qualifier *unsigned* may also precede int in a variable declaration. This restricts the integer variables to be positive values. On the IBM PC an unsigned integer variable is represented in 16-bits and can assume values from 0 through 65535 inclusive. Examples of these declarations are:

    unsigned int   natural;
    unsigned   record_number;

In the last example, the optional int is omitted.

All arithmetic operations on unsigned integers behave according to the values of modulo arithmetic. If the number of bits in an unsigned integer is N, the arithmetic is modulo 2^N. This amounts to computing the N low-order bits of the true 2s complement result.

Suppose unsigned int are represented using 16 bits. The range of possible values is 0 to 65535 inclusive. The arithmetic is then modulo 65536 (2^{16}). Adding 1 to the largest unsigned value is guaranteed to produce 0. Subtracting the unsigned value 9 from the unsigned value 6 produces the unsigned value 65533, that is $65536 - 3$ since this is modulus 65536 to the true arithmetical value -3.

3.8 Arithmetic expressions

The C programming language supports the normal arithmetic operators: addition (+), subtraction (−), multiplication (*) and division (/). Also provided is the modulus operator, denoted by the percent symbol (%), used to compute the remainder on dividing two integer values. These are the binary arithmetic operators which apply to two operands. The unary negation operator (−) is also available and is applied to a single operand to produce the arithmetic negative of its operand.

Examples of expressions involving such operators are:

```
12 * feet
− 1023
3.1415926 * radius * radius
60 * hours + minutes
distance / time
cents % 100
```

In the first example, the integer constant 12 is multiplied by the current value of the variable feet. In the second example, the integer constant 1023 is made negative using the unary negation operator.

As with normal arithmetic expressions, a C expression is evaluated according to the *precedence* of its operators. The precedence or priority of an operator dictates the order of evaluation in an arithmetic expression. An extract of the full table of precedences for all C operators is given in Table 3.2 below. The full table is given in Appendix E.

From Table 3.2, unary minus is shown to have the highest precedence, whilst addition and subtraction have the lowest equal precedence. The multiplication, division and modulus operators have intermediate precedence. From this, an expression involving a mixture of these operators will first perform all unary minus operations, then any multiplication, division and modulus operations, and then finally, addition and subtraction. Thus:

```
2 + 3 * 4
```

yields 14, since 3 is first multiplied by 4 giving 12, and then 2 is added producing 14.

An expression involving operators of equal precedence is resolved by reference to the column labeled *associativity* in Table 3.2. Associativity refers to the order (or direction) in which operators possessing the same precedences are executed. The expression 2 + 3 * 4 + 5 is evaluated in the following way. Multiplication has the highest precedence of the three operators and is evaluated first. The expression now reduces to 2 + 12 + 5. The two addition operators have equal precedence, and associate left to right. Thus, the 2 and 12 are first added to give 14, before finally the 14 and 5 are summed producing 19 as the final result.

If, in the expression 2 + 3 * 4 + 5, it is required to perform both the additions before executing the multiplication, then this is indicated by employing the parentheses (and) around the subexpressions. The expression would then be written as (2 + 3) * (4 + 5), and evaluate to 5 * 9, or 45.

The division operator functions normally, except in situations where both operands are of type integer. For two integer operands, the division operator determines the quotient with any fractional remainder truncated.

Table 3.2 Precedence and associativity of the arithmetic operators

Operator	Description	Associativity
−	Unary minus	Right to left
*	Multiplication	Left to right
/	Division	
%	Modulus	
+	Addition	Left to right
−	Subtraction	

Table 3.3

a	b	a/b	(a/b)*b	a%b	(a/b)*b + a%b
13	5	2	10	3	13
− 13	5	− 2	− 10	− 3	− 13
13	− 5	− 2	10	3	13
− 13	− 5	2	− 10	− 3	− 13

Thus:

13.0 / 5	evaluates to 2.6
13 / 5.0	evaluates to 2.6
13 / 5	evaluates to 2

When two positive integers are divided, truncation is always toward zero. If either operand is negative, however, the truncation is machine dependent. Normally, the quotient is positive if the signs of both operands are the same. Thus:

− 13 / 5	evaluates to − 2
13 / − 5	evaluates to − 2
− 13 / − 5	evaluates to 2

The modulus operator (%) yields the integer remainder from the division of two integer operands. Therefore:

13 % 5	evaluates to 3
15 % 5	evaluates to 0

Again, if either operand is negative, the remainder usually has the same sign as the dividend. Thus:

− 13 % 5	evaluates to − 3
13 % − 5	evaluates to 3

Irrespective of the particular implementation, it is always true that:

a % b   evaluates to a − (a/b) * b

where a and b are integer values and b is not zero. This is shown in Table 3.3.

3.9 Type conversions

The arithmetic operators may apply to operands of different types. When operands of different types appear in expressions, they are converted to a common type according to a few simple rules. The purpose of these conversions is to reduce the large number of arithmetic types to a small number that can be readily handled by the C operators.

There are certain preferred types. Any data value not already one of these preferred types is automatically converted. This process is known as *promotion* in which a data value of a lower type is promoted to one of a higher type. Table 3.4 shows this automatic promotion. These promotions are sometimes also known as *unary conversions*.

The representation of a data object of some type is the particular bit pattern that distinguishes the value of the object from all other possible values of that type. A conversion of a value from one type to another may or may not cause a *representation* change. For instance, when the two types have different sizes, a representation change has to be made, e.g. from a float to a double.

Some representation changes are very simple. This is the case with the examples in Table 3.4. If in a particular implementation a short is represented with fewer bits than an int, then the short is promoted to an integer and is achieved by padding with extra zero bits. If a short is of the same size as an int, then no change is necessary. Operands of type float are automatically promoted to type double. Again, a representation change is required, but the final result has the same value as the original.

With the following declarations:

```
char      c;
short     s;
int       i;
unsigned  u;
float     f;
double    d;
```

we can list some expressions and show how the operands are first promoted (see Table 3.5). In particular, note how the decimal constant 3.0 is, as indicated in section 3.2, of type double.

The promotion of operands of type char to type int means that it is sensible to perform arithmetic operations on data objects of type char. From the ASCII character set 'D' is represented by decimal 68; 'A' by 65; 'z'

Table 3.4 Promotions or unary conversions

Original type	Converted type
char, short	int
float	double

Table 3.5

C expression	Original types	Promoted types
c − i * s	char − int * short	int − int * int
3 * u − i	int * unsigned − int	int * unsigned − int
3 * f − i	int * float − int	int * double − int
3.0 * f + d	double * float + double	double * double + double

by 122 and 'a' by 97. Thus:

'D' − 'A'   evaluates to: 68 − 65 = 3
'z' − 'a' + 1   evaluates to: 122 − 97 + 1 = 26

If ch is a variable of type char and currently represents any upper-case letter in the ASCII character set, then the expression:

ch − 'A' + 'a'

evaluates to the integer value with the ASCII code that represents the equivalent lower-case letter. For example, if variable ch represents the character 'D', then using decimal representation of the ASCII encodings of the characters, the expression evaluates to:

68 − 65 + 97 = 100

and the corresponding ASCII character is 'd'.

The C language is ambiguous about whether the type char is signed or unsigned. This feature is fully implementation dependent. The only guarantee conceded to the C programmer is that characters from the standard character set are non-negative. The reader is advised to refer to the appropriate compiler documentation on character representation.

An arithmetic expression such as a + b computes a value of some type. For example, if both a and b are of type int, then the value of a + b is also of type int. However, if a and b are of different types, then a + b is a *mixed expression,* and we require rules to establish the type of the result itself.

In a mixed expression *binary conversions* determine whether and how operands are converted before a binary operation is performed. When two values are to be operated upon in combination, they are first converted to a

Table 3.6

Lower type			Higher type
int	unsigned	long	double

single common type. The result after applying the operation is also of that same common type.

The conversion is performed according to a hierarchy of types. Operands of lower type are promoted to that of the higher type. The hierarchy is shown in Table 3.6.

The ordered sequence of conversions that apply is as follows:

If either operand is a *double,* the other is converted to a *double* and that is the type of the result.

If either operand is a *long,* the other is converted to a *long* and that is the type of the result.

If either operand is an *unsigned,* the other is converted to an *unsigned* and that is the type of the result.

Otherwise, both operands must be *int*, and that is the type of the result.

In the context of the following declarations:

```
int    i;
short  s;
```

consider the evaluation of the mixed expression:

```
3.0 * i + s
```

Assume that the current values for the variables i and s are, respectively, 32 and 10. Firstly, the unary conversions cause the short to be promoted to type int. The resulting representation change will leave the value unaltered as 10. The expression is then viewed as:

double * int + int

operating on the values:

3.0 * 32 + 10

Since multiplication has higher precedence than addition, it is evaluated first. The left operand to the multiplier operation is a double. Therefore, the right operand is also promoted to type double if it is not already one. The expression is now:

double * double + int

The integer value 32 undergoes a representation change to the equivalent double precision floating point value:

3.0 * 32.0 + 10

Following execution of the multiplying operator, we have:

96.0 + 10

and the types involved in the expression are now:

double + int

Following the same argument, the int (10) is promoted to type double (10.0) before performing the addition. The final result is of type double and has the value:

106.0

These implicit arithmetic conversions operate much as expected. The programmer is cautioned, however, to be fully aware of the conversions. Without a full understanding, some unexpected results are possible.

For certain operations in C, it may be that the true mathematical result of the operation cannot be represented as a value of the expected result type (as determined by the usual conversion rules). This condition is referred to as *overflow*. For example, multiplication of two int results in an int. But if int are held as 2s complement 16-bit values, with largest integer representation of 32767, then multiplying 700 by 800 produces the true mathematical value 560000 which is not representable as an int. Another example is attempted division by zero, where the result is infinity.

Generally, C does not specify the consequences of overflow. A number of possibilities may arise. One is that an incorrect value of the correct type is generated. Another possibility is that the program is prematurely terminated with or without some appropriate error message. A third possibility is to trap the exception within the program and take the appropriate action. In all cases, the programmer must guard against these occurrences and, where possible, handle them within the program. A program that terminates prematurely is not a good program.

3.10 The assignment operator

The assignment operator allows the assignment of some new value to a program variable. The simplest form of the assignment operator is:

variable = expression

The effect of the operator is to evaluate the expression to the right of the assignment operator (=), and the resulting value is then assigned to the variable on the left. If both operands to the assignment operator are arithmetic, the type of the expression is converted to the type of the variable on the left before executing the assignment. Examples of assignments are:

(a) interest   = principal * rate * time / 100
(b) speed   = distance / time

(c) total_min = 60 * hours + minutes
(d) count   = count + 1

Since the assignment mechanism in C is implemented as a (binary) operator, like all other operators it has a precedence, an associativity, and indulges in automatic type conversions. The precedence and associativity is given in Appendix E. The low priority of the assignment operator guarantees that the right-hand expression is first evaluated before the assignment is performed.

In the same way that operand1 + operand2 evaluates to the arithmetic addition of the two operands, the assignment:

variable = expression

also evaluates to a value. That is, after evaluation of the expression and assigning it to the variable on the left, a value is delivered. The type and value is that of the variable, and may be discarded or used in multiple assignment expressions:

variable1 = variable2 = ... variablek = expression

The right-to-left associativity of the assignment operator means that the expression is evaluated, assigned to variable k; the value of this variable is then the delivered value, which in turn is assigned to variable k − 1, and so on. Thus, the expression:

x = y = z = p + q

is interpreted as:

x = (y = (z = p + q))

Implicit type conversions also occur across the assignment operator. For example, in an expression in which the left operand is a double and the right operand is an int as in:

double = integer

the value of the integer expression will be converted to a double before performing the assignment. The integer is automatically promoted to type double. A promotion or *widening* is normally well behaved, but *narrowing* or *demotion* such as in:

integer = double

can result in the loss of information. Precisely what happens in each case is implementation dependent. In this example, if the double were to evaluate to, say, 12.345 then we should reasonably expect the integer value 12 to be assigned after discarding the fractional part. The behavior of the conversion is undefined if the double value cannot be represented as an integer. For example, the magnitude of the double may be too large to be represented as an integer, or if a negative double is assigned to an unsigned integer. Questions of rounding versus truncation are also left to the discretion of the implementor. Again, the reader is advised to seek out the appropriate local documentation.

Some possible assignments and the likely effects are as follows:

Assignment	Effect
int = int	no conversion
float = double	truncate (possibly round) the double
int = long	normally implemented by truncation
char = int	normally implemented by truncation

Care must be taken when employing the multiple assignment. If iii is a variable of type integer, then in the assignment:

iii = 12.34

the floating point constant 12.34 will normally be truncated to integer 12 before assigning to the integer variable. The value of this integer variable is then the value delivered by this operation. Then in the multiple assignment:

fff = iii = 12.34

with variable fff of type float, the expression to the right of:

fff = ...

is of type integer, with value 12. The integer is converted back to a floating point representation (12.0) before assignment. One must not therefore read that the value 12.34 is assigned to *both* iii (after truncation) and fff.

3.11 The compound assignment operators

Assignments of the form:

count = count + 2

occur repeatedly in programming problems. The effect is to take the current value of the variable count and to it add the literal value 2. The resulting value is then assigned back to the variable count. Overall, the value of the variable count is increased by two. Such an assignment may also be represented in C by:

count + = 2

In fact, this compound assignment operator is applicable to all five binary arithmetic operators. Thus, we may have:

count + = 2
stock − = 1
power * = 2.71828
divisor / = 10.0
remainder % = 10

In all cases, except the modulus operator assignment (% =), the two operands may be of any arithmetic type. For the operator % = the two operands must be integral types.

All these new operators have the same precedence level as the simple assignment and associate right to left (see Appendix E).

If op = is a generalized denotation for the compound assignment operators, then the semantics of the expression:

variable op = expression

is specified by:

variable = variable op (expression)

Note the parenthesized subexpression is evaluated *before* applying the operator op. Thus, the expression:

sum / = 3 + 7

is equivalent to:

sum = sum / (3 + 7)

Multiple assignments employing both the simple assignment and the compound assignment are possible. Again, some care is required in their interpretation. If variable iii is of type integer and value 12, and variable fff is of type float and value 1.234, then the assignment:

fff = iii * = fff

operates as:

fff = (iii = iii * fff)

with iii assigned the value 14 (12 * 1.234 = 14.808, truncated) and fff assigned the value 14.0.

3.12 The increment and decrement operators

In the previous section, the compound assignment operators were introduced. With these operators, simple assignments of the form:

x = x + 1

may be represented by:

x + = 1

In fact, incrementing by one is such a commonly occurring operation in a program, that C supports two forms of unary increment operator. They are known as the *pre-increment operator* and the *post-increment operator*. The pre-increment expression has the form:

+ + variable

whilst the post-increment expression appears as:

variable + +

In both cases the constant 1 is added to the arithmetic operand. The usual binary conversions are performed on the operand and the constant 1 before addition is performed, and the usual assignment conversions are performed when storing the arithmetic sum back into the variable.

Both increment operators produce a side effect. In addition to increment- ing the value of the variable operand, a value is delivered. In the case of the pre-increment operator, the delivered value is the new (incremented) value of the variable. The type of value delivered is the same as the type of the operand. Given two integer variables called sum and count, then the effect of the assignment:

sum + = + + count

is two-fold. First, the value of the variable count is increased by 1. Second, this new value of count is added to the current value of the variable sum.

The post-increment operator also delivers a value, but this time it is the old value of the variable *before* it was incremented. The assignment:

sum + = count + +

again increments the value of the variable count by 1, and then adds the original value of count (before the incrementing took place) to the variable sum. Thus, if the initial values of sum and count are 10 and 20, respectively, then evaluation of the expression is two-fold:

(a) Variable *count* is post-incremented to produce 21.
(b) Variable *sum* is incremented by the original value of variable *count* and evaluates to 30.

Instead of incrementing a variable value by 1 we can also decrement its value by 1. This is achieved by the *pre-decrement* and *post-decrement* operators. The former appears as:

− − variable

whilst the latter has the form:

variable − −

In both cases the constant 1 is subtracted from the operand. Again, the usual binary conversions apply. The same side effect also applies with a value delivered after decrementing. The value delivered by the pre- decrement operator is the new variable value after decrementing. The value delivered by the post-decrement operator is the original value of the variable before decrementing.

The precedence and associativity of the increment and decrement operators are shown in the first table in Appendix E.

In certain constructions the side effects caused by these operators can produce unintended results. Consider the expression:

    a = + + c + c

Here + + is prefixed to variable c, meaning that c is to be incremented before it is used. But variable c occurs twice in the expression, and when c is incremented it changes both the values of c. The computation is unclear about whether the original or the new value of c is used in the part ... + c. Such expressions are considered bad programming practice and should be avoided by writing code that isolates the effect of the + + operator, as in:

    + + c;
    a = c + c;

or by:

    a = 2 * (+ + c);

3.13 The type cast operator

In addition to implicit type conversions which can occur across the assignment operator and in mixed expressions, there is an explicit type conversion called a *cast*. If variable date is an int, then:

    (double) date

will cast or coerce the value of date so that the expression has type double.

A cast expression consists of a left parenthesis, a type specifier, a right parenthesis and an operand expression:

    (type-specifier) expression

A cast is implemented as an operator. It possesses both a precedence and an associativity. Its relation to other operators is shown in Appendix E.

Some examples of the use of the cast operator are:

    (char) x
    (int) d1 + d2

Note how in the last example, the type cast int applies only to the operand d1. This is because the type cast operator has higher precedence than binary addition. To apply the cast to the result obtained by adding d1 and d2, parentheses are required:

    (int)(d1 + d2)

The cast operator is a specialized explicit type conversion operator. We shall discuss its use and application in later chapters.

3.14 The comma operator

The comma operator finds applications in a number of specialized areas. For completeness we discuss it here since it is an operator. Use of this operator will appear in later chapters.

The comma operator consists of a number of expressions separated by commas:

expression, expression, ..., expression

Of all the C operators, the comma operator has lowest precedence, and associates left to right (see Appendix E).

In the comma expression:

expression1, expression2

expression1 is fully evaluated first. It need not produce a value but if it does that value is discarded. The second expression is then evaluated. The type and value of the comma operator is that of the final expression.

An example of the comma operator is:

sum = 0, k = 1

If variable k has been declared an int, then this comma expression has value 1 and type int. In the comma expression:

s = (t = 2, t + 3)

variable t is assigned the value 2, and the value of the comma expression is 5 (the result of t + 3). The value 5 is then assigned to the variable s. This effect is achieved only through use of the parentheses, since the comma operator has lower precedence than the assignment operator. Without the parentheses:

s = t = 2, t + 3

both s and t would be assigned the value 2 and the result of the expression is 5. Depending upon the context of this expression, the result value may or may not be discarded.

3.15 Summary

1. The four fundamental types are *char, int, float* and *double*. Float and double provide two precisions for decimal numbers. The qualifiers *short, long* and *unsigned* offer several sizes for integral types.
2. *Denotations* or *constants* represent specific instances of a particular type. Integer constants preceded with 0 and 0X (or 0x) designate *octal* and *hexadecimal* integer constants respectively. Integer constants of type *long* are prepended with an L (or l). A constant with a decimal fraction is implicitly of type *double*.

3. A character value is delimited by single quotes ('). A string value is delimited by double quotes ("). Both may involve *escape sequences*.

4. *Identifiers* are used to name objects in a program. An identifier is a letter/digit sequence starting with a letter. The underscore symbol (_) is considered to be a letter. Good mnemonic names should always be chosen to improve program clarity.

5. The three types of identifier are reserved words, standard identifiers and user-defined identifiers. Reserved identifiers (keywords) have a special predefined meaning to the C compiler and cannot be redefined by the programmer. Standard identifiers (e.g. printf) may be redefined but it is not recommended.

6. A *declaration* contains the names and types of the variables used in a program.

7. An *expression* is a combination of operators and operands. The *operators* determine the computation to be performed. The *precedence* and *associativity* of operators determine the order of evaluation in an expression. *Assignment* is an operator and can occur as part of an expression.

8. When evaluating mixed mode expressions, automatic *type conversions* apply. *Unary* conversions promote data values of a lower type to one of a higher type. *Binary* conversions apply to operands before performing a binary operation.

9. The *comma operator* is used for sequential evaluation of a sequence of expressions. The value of the final expression is the value of the entire expression.

3.16 Exercises

1. Which of the following are valid C constants? For those which are valid, identify their type. If invalid, state why.

   (a) − 123   (d) OXFG   (g) '\z'
   (b) .123   (e) '4'   (h) 106
   (c) 10E − 4   (f) 'four'

2. Which of the following are invalid identifiers in C; give explanations.

   (a) June   (d) b   (g) _Z
   (b) int   (e) a$ (h) _12_
   (c) BBC_1   (f) X-RAY

3. Given the following declarations and initial assignments:

   int i, j, m, n;
   float f, g;
   char c;

   i = j = 2;
   m = n = 5;

```
f = 1.2;
g = 3.4;
c = 'X';
```

use the rules of precedence and associativity of the operators to evaluate the following expressions, showing any conversions which take place and the type of the result.

(a)   12 * m
(b)   m / j
(c)   n % j
(d)   m / j * j
(e)   (f + 10) * 20
(f)   (i+ +) * n
(g)   i+ + * n
(h)   − 12L * (g − f)

(i)   2 + c
(j)   (m+ +) − (m+ +)
(k)   (n+ +), (n+ +)
(l)   m = n = j− −
(m) (int) f
(n)   (double) m
(o)   (double) m + 10
(p)   (double)(m + 10)

4. Find the errors in the following series of declarations:

```
int        kilometers, meters;
float      meters;
integer    weeks;
int        fm, medium, long;
short      char, tiny;
```

Input and output

Strictly, input and output facilities are not part of the C language, unlike FORTRAN, for example, where the READ and WRITE statements are defined as part of the language. Nonetheless, real programs do communicate with their environment. In this chapter we will describe a subset of the standard I/O (input/output) library, consisting of a set of functions designed to provide a standard facility for performing input and output.

Since these library functions are not part of the definition of the C language, they sometimes differ in operation and name between implementations. The reader is advised to consult the local system documentation about individual functions.

We will not attempt to describe the entire I/O library here. We restrict our discussion to four functions which communicate with the user's terminal. This will be sufficient to permit us to write complete operational programs. In Chapter 14 we will revisit input/output and consider programs which operate on data held in computer files. Appendix F4 provides a reference section for those I/O functions normally members of the standard library.

4.1 Access to the standard library

Whenever a C program executes three 'files' are automatically opened by the operating system environment for use by that program. These files are known as the *standard input*, the *standard output* and the *standard error*. It is intended that normal input by the program will be read from the standard input. In an interactive environment the standard input normally associates with the user's terminal (keyboard). Similarly, normal output is written to the standard output and, again, is the user terminal (screen). Finally, an additional output file is opened. It is intended that any error messages produced by the program be written to this standard error file. In an interactive environment, this is also the user's terminal.

In this chapter we are concerned only with programs that operate with the standard input and standard output. In Chapter 14 where input/output through files are discussed, we consider more fully the standard input, standard output and the standard error.

All source program files which refer to a standard I/O library function must contain the line:

#include ⟨stdio.h⟩

near the beginning of the file. Strictly this is not entirely true, since only certain functions from this library need the information contained in the standard I/O header file, *stdio.h*. By always including it we then do not need to worry whether it is required or not. A detailed description of this #include statement is reserved until the next chapter. Suffice it to say that a file called stdio.h defines certain items required by the standard I/O library. For example, the standard input, standard output and standard error files are defined here. These details are incorporated or 'included' into the application program from this header file.

4.2 Formatted output

Formatted lines of output are achieved with the standard I/O library function *printf*. We used printf informally throughout Chapter 2. The complete and generalized description of printf is:

printf(format, argument1, argument2, ...)

The function printf formats and prints its arguments on the standard output. The arguments are any expressions delivering the values to be printed. The display of these arguments is under the control of the formatting string *format*. This string (see section 3.4) contains two types of information: ordinary characters, which are simply copied to the output; and *conversion specifications* which cause conversion and printing of the arguments to printf.

The simplest example of printf is one with a format string containing no conversion specifications and with no arguments. In this case, the string is copied verbatim to the standard output.

printf("A simple message.\n")

The result of executing this statement is to produce on the standard output the content of the format string. As the string contains a newline symbol as the last printed character, any subsequent output appears at the left margin on the line immediately following this output. Equally, this output follows any previous output to the standard output.

For each argument to printf, a corresponding conversion specification should appear in the format string. There should be exactly the right number of arguments of the right type to satisfy the conversions, otherwise the result of executing printf is unpredictable. If any conversion specification appearing in the format string is malformed, then the effect is also unpredictable.

A conversion specification in the format string is introduced by the percent (%) character. There then follows a sequence of none or more options to the conversion. The specification terminates with a *conversion operation* expressed as a single character. A full definition for a conversion specification is then:

$$
\text{percent symbol} \begin{Bmatrix} \text{flag} \\ \text{character} \end{Bmatrix}_{\text{opt}} \begin{Bmatrix} \text{minimum} \\ \text{field} \\ \text{width} \end{Bmatrix}_{\text{opt}} \begin{Bmatrix} \text{precision} \\ \text{specification} \end{Bmatrix}_{\text{opt}} \begin{Bmatrix} \text{long} \\ \text{size} \\ \text{specification} \end{Bmatrix}_{\text{opt}} \text{conversion operation}
$$

Note that only the percent symbol and the single character conversion operation need be present. All the other fields are optional (opt). Further, not all combinations of the fields are meaningful. For example, the precision specification controls the number of decimal places printed in a decimal number. This is meaningless if an integer value is being formatted and printed.

Not all the possible combinations are explored in this section. There are simply too many. We provide here an explanation of a range of examples of the fundamentals of formatted output. A full explanation of the functions in the standard I/O library and, in particular, the conversion specifications of printf is given in Appendix F4.

A minimum conversion specification is the percent symbol and a conversion operation. The latter is expressed as any one of the single characters:

c   d   e   E   f   g   G   o   s   u   x   X   %

The last conversion character shown is used to represent the percent symbol itself, since otherwise it is reserved to introduce conversion specifications in format strings. The output from:

    printf("Tax is 10%%\n")

is:

    Tax is 10%

Detailed explanations of how each conversion operation performs are given in Appendix F4. A brief description of each operation is given in Table 4.1, and provides a convenient reference. Some common examples then follow.

An argument expression evaluating to an integer value is formatted with the d conversion operator. In the context of the declarations and assignations:

    int a, b;
    a = 10;
    b = 15;

the function call:

    printf("The sum of %d and %d is %d\n", a, b, a + b)

Table 4.1 Conversion operations for use with printf

Conversion operation	Application
d	Signed decimal conversion of *int*
u	Unsigned decimal conversion of *unsigned*
o	Unsigned octal conversion of *unsigned*
x, X	Unsigned hexadecimal conversion of *unsigned*
c	Single character conversion
s	String conversion
f	Signed decimal floating point conversion
e, E	Signed decimal floating point conversion
g, G	Signed decimal floating point conversion

produces the following output:

The sum of 10 and 15 is 25

The conversion operation d causes signed decimal conversion of the argument value to be performed. For each %d, one argument is consumed. The argument value should be of type int. The converted value consists of a sequence of decimal digits. The sequence is as short as possible, necessary to print the value. Thus, the value of the variable a (10) requires two character positions in the output stream.

A minimum field width may also be present in the conversion specification. In its simplest form this consists of an unsigned decimal integer constant. If the argument value results in fewer characters than the specified field width, then the characters are right-justified in the field and padded on the left with space characters. The function call:

printf("The sum of %d and %d is %4d\n", a, b, a + b)

produces the output:

The sum of 10 and 15 is   25

with the value of the expression a + b displayed in a field width of four characters. If, however, the converted argument value results in more characters than the specified field width, the field is expanded sufficiently to accommodate the printed value. The value is not truncated but the formatted output is now different from expected. The example:

printf("The sum of %d and %1d is %3d\n", a, b, a + b)

produces the output:

The sum of 10 and 15 is 25

The conversion specification corresponding to the argument b is %1d. This directs the value to be printed in a field width of one, but since the converted argument value requires a field of two, the latter takes precedence.

Floating point values are displayed using the conversion specification f. The converted value consists of a sequence of decimal digits with an embedded decimal point, but no more than is necessary to represent the value. When no precision is specified, a precision of six decimal places is assumed. In the context of the declarations and assignments:

float x, y;
x = 1.234;   y = 56.78;

then:

printf(″%f from %f gives %f\n″, y, x, x − y)

produces the output:

56.780000 from 1.234000 gives − 55.546000

The minimum field width and the precision can be expressed as two unsigned integer constants separated by a period symbol. Both these elements are optional. If the precision is not present, then the period symbol is omitted and the default precision is 6. If necessary, rounding of the converted value may be performed. The example:

printf(″%5.2f from %4.2f gives %7.2f\n″, y, x, x − y)

produces:

56.78 from 1.23 gives − 55.55

Finally, we demonstrate how to control the formatting of a string. The required conversion operation is s. When no field width is given, the characters of the string are printed in the minimum field necessary. The example:

printf(″[%s]\n″, ″Hello there″)

produces:

[Hello there]

A field width is represented as an unsigned decimal integer constant preceding the conversion operation. The string is right-justified in the field and padded on the left with spaces. Thus:

printf(″[%20s]\n″, ″Hello there″)

produces:

[Hello there]

None of the examples we have introduced used a *flag* character. Flag characters modify the meaning of the main conversion operation. In all the examples where the converted value required fewer characters than the explicit field width, then the value is displayed right-justified in the field and padded on the left with spaces. Left justification in the field and padding on the right with spaces is achieved by prefixing the conversion specification with a hyphen symbol flag character. For example:

printf("[% − 20s]\n", "Hello there")

produces:

[Hello there   ]

A number of other flag characters are available. They are fully detailed in the Appendix F4. We may choose to employ any of these other flags in the programs which follow. It is therefore assumed that the reader has reviewed Appendix F4.

4.3 Formatted input

The function *scanf* is the counterpart of printf. The stream of input characters from the standard input are parsed according to a control string and input values assigned to program variables. The form of the function call is:

scanf(format, argument1, argument2, ...)

Note: Each argument is the address of the memory location to receive the input value. Each argument *must* therefore be the address of the receiving variable. This is expressed in C by preceding the variable name with the *address operator*, denoted by the ampersand (&) symbol. Further details of this operator are given in Chapter 5.

To input two data values and to store them in locations referred to by the identifiers *month* and *year*, we use:

scanf("....", &month, &year)

The *format string* is a *picture* of the expected form of the input. One may think of scanf as performing a simple parse of the stream of input characters according to the format string. The format string uses conversion specifications similar to those found with printf. There should be exactly the correct number of arguments of the correct type to satisfy the conversion specifications in the format string; otherwise the results are unpredictable. If any conversion specification is malformed the effect is also unpredictable.

In addition to conversion specifications, a format string may also include whitespace characters. A whitespace character in the format string causes one or more whitespace characters to be read from the standard input and discarded. The first non-whitespace character encountered in the input remains as the next character to be read.

Finally, a format string may include characters other than whitespace characters and the sequence of characters representing a conversion speci-' fication. These characters must match exactly the next characters of the

Table 4.2 Conversion operations for use with scanf

Conversion operation	Application
d	Signed decimal conversion to *int*
u	Unsigned decimal conversion to *unsigned*
o	Unsigned octal conversion to *unsigned*
x, X	Unsigned hexadecimal conversion to *unsigned*
c	Single character conversion
s	String conversion
f	Signed decimal floating point conversion
e, E	Signed decimal floating point conversion
g, G	Signed decimal floating point conversion
[	String conversion (special)

input stream. If there is no match, scanf terminates and the conflicting character remains in the input as the next available character.

A conversion specification commences with a percent symbol. The form of a conversion specification for use with scanf is:

$$
\text{percent symbol} \quad
\begin{Bmatrix} \text{assignment} \\ \text{suppression} \\ \text{flag} \end{Bmatrix}_{\text{opt}}
\begin{Bmatrix} \text{maximum} \\ \text{field} \\ \text{width} \end{Bmatrix}_{\text{opt}}
\begin{Bmatrix} \text{size} \\ \text{specification} \end{Bmatrix}_{\text{opt}}
\begin{matrix} \text{conversion} \\ \text{operation} \end{matrix}
$$

The conversion operations supported by scanf are similar to those of printf and are summarized in Table 4.2. Full details are given in Appendix F4.

The number of characters read from the input stream depends on the conversion operation. Generally, a conversion operation processes a sequence of one or more characters until either (a) a whitespace or other inappropriate character is read, or (b) the number of characters read equals the specified maximum field width.

Given the declarations:

```
int day, month, year;
char ch1, ch2;
```

then the scanf invocation:

```
scanf("%d %d %d", &day, &month, &year)
```

expects three integer values to be supplied. The first integer value read is assigned to the variable day. Any amount of leading whitespace characters before the digits of the number are ignored. The second integer value is separated from the first by one or more whitespace characters and is assigned to the variable month. Similarly for the final variable year. The input:

```
31    12
1985
```

causes the value 31 to be assigned to the variable day, 12 to the variable month and 1985 to the variable year. The input values are separated by a series of whitespace characters. The values 31 and 12 are separated by spaces and/or tabs whilst 12 and 1985 are separated by newline symbols. The value 1985 is also terminated by a newline character. This final character remains in the input buffer to be processed by any subsequent scanf call.

In the example:

scanf("%d/%d/%d", &day, &month, &year)

each integer value is expected to be separated by the slash (/) character. A valid input stream to the above is then:

12/4/1985

A conversion specification may also include a maximum field width. This is presented as an unsigned decimal integer constant not equal to zero. The conversion terminates when either the required number of characters are read or the input value terminates with whitespace or some invalid character. The last scanf example might also have been written as:

scanf("%2d/%2d/%4d", &day, &month, &year)

allowing for a two-digit day and month, and a four-digit year.

When maximum field widths are employed, it is no longer necessary to use whitespace characters. The input:

12051985

can be parsed so that the variable day is assigned the value 12, month the value 5, and year the value 1985. The scanf call to achieve this is:

scanf("%2d%2d%4d", &day, &month, &year)

Care is required when using the c conversion specification. This operation does not skip over any initial whitespace characters. The example:

scanf("%d%c%d%c%d", &day, &ch1, &month, &ch2, &year)

with input:

5-9/1985

assigns the value 5 to the integer variable day, 9 to the integer variable month and 1985 to the integer variable year. The character variables ch1 and ch2 are assigned respectively the hyphen (-) symbol and the slash (/) symbol.

4.4 The functions getchar and putchar

From the previous two sections we know how to perform single character transfers using formatted I/O routines. Given the declaration:

    char ch;

we may read a single character from the standard input and print it to the standard output with:

    scanf(" %c", &ch);
    printf(" %c", ch);

An unnecessary overhead is incurred by doing it this way. This is attributable to both scanf and printf having to process their respective format strings.

Two simpler facilities are provided for single character input and output: *getchar* and *putchar*. Strictly, we should not refer to them as functions, for as we shall show later in the book they are not library functions at all. Precisely what they are is given in Chapter 14. For the present, however, they can be considered as functions.

The function putchar takes a single argument and prints the character which it represents on the standard output. To output the value of the character variable ch, we use:

    putchar(ch)

To output a single newline character we could use:

    putchar('\n')

The function getchar reads the next character from the standard input stream. No arguments are given to getchar, but the parentheses are obligatory. The value of the character read is returned as an int as the function value. This can be captured by a suitable assignment:

    ch = getchar( )

If variable ch is type char then appropriate conversions take place across the assignment operator.

The original problem to input and then echo a single character can then be expressed by:

    ch = getchar( );
    putchar(ch);

Mixing the input/output operations scanf, printf, getchar and putchar is freely supported. For example, the input date:

    12-10/1985

could be read with the functions:

    scanf(" %d", &day);
    ch1 = getchar( );

```
scanf("%d", &month);
ch2 = getchar( );
scanf("%d", &year);
```

with the character variables ch1 and ch2 holding the delimiters between the three numbers.

When using formatted input with scanf, we must be aware that the input of, say, a number continues until the first occurrence of whitespace or a character that is not part of a number. From our earlier discussions, the above input could have been read by:

```
scanf("%d%c%d%c%d", &day, &ch1, &month, &ch2, &year)
```

The value for variable day is read as the character sequence up to but not including the hyphen symbol. This remains in the input stream for the next assignation. The next conversion specification is %c and hence a single character is entered and assigned to variable ch1. This single character is the hyphen symbol.

When a number is read and is terminated by whitespace, then the whitespace character remains as the first character in any subsequent input operation. Consider, then, a program which prompts the user for a number, reads the newline terminated value, asks the user if the value is correct, and reads the reply expected as the single character Y or N (respectively, yes or no). A first attempt at this programming might suggest the solution:

```
printf("Please enter the number: ");
scanf("%d", &number);
printf("Correct?");
reply = getchar( );
```

After the number has been read, the terminating newline symbol remains in the input buffer. When the prompt "Correct?" is displayed, the program does not await user input, but takes the newline symbol in the buffer as the reply. Processing continues without any user input. Clearly this is not the desired effect.

One simple solution to this problem is to discard the newline symbol before the reply is required. Provided that the number is terminated by an immediate newline character, we can insert an additional single character read. This can be done either in the first scanf itself, or as a separate getchar. We show the latter solution:

```
printf("Please enter the number: ");
scanf("%d", &number);
discard = getchar( );    /*remove newline from input */
printf("Correct? ");
reply = getchar( );
```

4.5 Summary

1. Input/output facilities in C are provided by a suite of functions from the standard library.
2. When using input/output constructs, the system header file *stdio.h* should be included in a program by means of the control line #include ⟨stdio.h⟩.
3. Formatted output is provided by the library function *printf*. Formatted input is provided by the library function *scanf*. Formatting is the process of controlling the layout of the printed output and the program input.
4. Format strings include a mixture of whitespace characters, plain characters and conversion specifications.
5. Single character transfers are accomplished with the library functions *getchar* and *putchar*.

4.6 Exercises

1. Produce the following two lines of output:

   PROGRAMMING IN C
   IS FUN

   using (a) two printf function calls; (b) one printf function call.

2. Given the integer variable *staffno* and the floating variable *salary*, write output statement(s) to produce:

   STAFF   PAY
    ddd   ddd.dd

   where each d represents a decimal digit.

3. Write statements for a program which reads a sum of money in the form ddd.dd, increases it by 10%, and prints out the increased sum. If the input was of the form ddd:dd, how would the program have to be modified?

4. In the context of the variable declarations:

   ```
   int    j, k;
   float  x, y, z;
   char   c;
   ```

   and the three lines of program input data:

   ```
   12.34              56.7
          - 89E10
   0.012
   ```

   what is the effect of executing each of the following input statements:

   (a) scanf("%f %f %f", &x, &y, &z);
   (b) scanf("%f", &x);
       scanf("%f %f", &y, &z);
   (c) scanf("%f %f %f", &x, &y, &z);
       scanf("%d", &j);
   (d) scanf("%d%c%d %f", &j, &c, &k, &x);

## CHAPTER 5

Program structure

In Chapter 2 we explored the fundamental features of a C program. In particular, a number of complete programs were presented. No attempt was made to specify the exact construction of a program. We merely explored the essentials of a C program. In this chapter we will define the exact composition of a basic program. In later chapters, where we introduce additional language features, extensions to this basic form are given.

5.1 The structure of a function

A C program consists of one or more functions. Functions within C facilitate partitioning large programs into smaller, manageable units, thus simplifying the programming task. In addition, functions developed in one program may be incorporated into others, saving the need to re-program them. The value of functions to the C programmer will be fully appreciated, when, in this and later chapters, we construct major items of software.

A C function describes the computational processes to be carried out on its data. The function must thus describe both its data objects (declarations) and its processing actions (statements). The simplest form of function definition reflects this minimum requirement:

```
function-name( )
    {
       optional-declaration-list
       optional-statement-list
    }
```

The *function-name* is the programmer-defined name (identifier) for that function. Function names must be unique otherwise the compiler is unable to distinguish between two distinct functions bearing the same name. A function name is constructed according to the rule for identifiers. A unit of text surrounded by and including the braces { and }, is called a *compound statement* – also called a *block*. A block consists of a (possibly empty) sequence of declarations, followed by a (possibly empty) sequence of statements. Individual declarations and statements are terminated by semicolons (;). The declarations identify the data items and the statements specify the processing actions.

All the programs introduced in Chapter 2 conform to this structure. Program 2.1(a), repeated below as Program 5.1(a), consists of the single function main. As noted in Chapter 2, all complete C programs must have a function called main. A program starts executing from the first executable statement in function main.

Program 5.1(a)

```
/*
**      A program to display a simple message to
**      the operator's console.
*/

#include <stdio.h>

main()
  {
    printf("My first program.");
  }
```

The function main has no variable declarations but does have a single statement. The statement is a function call to the standard C library function printf. This single statement is terminated with a semicolon.

When a function is called (such as printf, above), the actual objects to be manipulated by that function are supplied as arguments. In the case of printf, the item to be printed is the string:

"My first program."

This single argument is enclosed in the parentheses (and). Equally, main is a function. It has, for the present, no arguments and is shown:

main() . . . .

It is not permissible to omit the parentheses in a function with no arguments. The parentheses are obligatory.

A program which uses input/output functions from the standard C library must also have a #include statement as shown. This statement supplies the C compiler with details relating to some of the standard input/output functions. Strictly, not all input/output functions from the library require the presence of this particular #include. Rather than try to remember which functions need the #include and which do not, it is easier to put it into all programs. This redundancy is harmless.

Program 5.1(a) might alternatively have been written as Program 5.1(b).

Program 5.1(b)

```
/*
**      This program displays a simple message through
**      three separate calls to the printf function.
**      The output is the same as that of Program 5.1(a).
*/
```

```
#include <stdio.h>

main()
  {
    printf("My ");
    printf("first ");
    printf("program.");
  }
```

This time the function main employs three statements. Each is a separate invocation of the printf function. Again, no variable declarations are present. To assist with program readability, each function call appears on separate lines. This does not, however, imply that the outputs appear on separate lines. Output on to separate lines is governed by the arguments to printf and not by the program layout. Indentation and alignment are used to emphasize the structure of this program. The program output is:

My first program.

A function need not have any declarations, as in the examples above, or any statements, or both. For example, Program 5.2 is a perfectly valid C program. The function main, and hence the program, does absolutely nothing, except, perhaps, consume some processor time. Such a program has no real practical value.

Program 5.2

```
/*
**        A program to do nothing !
*/

#include <stdio.h>

main()
  {
  }
```

Consider now a program which includes variable declarations. The program is required to read two integer data values and to print them in reverse order. To achieve this the function main must include a declaration for two integer variables. These variables will be the repositories for the two data values.

Program 5.3

```
/*
**        This program accepts two integer data values
**        and displays them in reverse order.
*/

#include <stdio.h>

main()
  {
    int first, second;                    /* data stores */

    printf("Enter two integer values: ");
    scanf("%d %d", &first, &second);
    printf("Reversed data: %d and %d\n", second, first);
  }
```

Program 5.4, below, is similar to the last example. It reads some data, processes it, then displays the result of its computations. The processing this time involves some arithmetic operations. The program reads three integer data values representing a time expressed as hours, minutes and seconds. The time is converted into a total number of seconds, then printed.

Program 5.4

```
/*
**      This program accepts as input a time measured
**      in hours, minutes and seconds. The time is then
**      converted to the equivalent number of seconds.
*/

#include <stdio.h>

main()
  {
    int hours, minutes, seconds;        /* original data values */
    int time;                           /* converted value */

    printf("Enter the time to be converted: ");
    scanf("%d %d %d", &hours, &minutes, &seconds);

    time = (60 * hours + minutes) * 60 + seconds;

    printf("The original time of:\n");
    printf("%d hours, %d minutes and %d seconds\n",
        hours, minutes, seconds);
    printf("converts to %d seconds\n", time);
  }
```

The last two programs incorporated a prompt to the user before reading the data values. For interactive programs this is good practice since the user then knows when data should be entered. Without a prompt, the program hangs awaiting input from the user, which might be misconstrued that the program has, in some way, failed.

How did we arrive at the solution for Program 5.4? It is sufficiently complex to warrant applying some design process before its implementation. The technique of designing a system or program in steps that gradually define more and more detail is called *functional decomposition*.

Functional decomposition is a step-by-step process that begins with the most general functional view of what is to be done, breaks the view down into subfunctions, and then repeats the process until all subfunction units are simple enough to be easily understood and small enough to be easily coded. This method of systematically applying *stepwise refinements* is a powerful tool for dealing with the complexity of many related elements.

We express our functional decomposition through a *program design language* or PDL. The PDL is a design description language specifically intended for documenting software designs. It is not a compiled language in the sense of C. The language has no formal syntax, but is an extensible language which provides constructs to express the necessary program logic.

PDL descriptions may include informally stated actions, intended to be a self-explanatory description of the program. In our PDL we shall reserve upper-case for formalizations in terms of the programming language. We shall see examples of this in later chapters. Material in lower-case is an informal description of some action to be performed. The context of this description should be sufficient to make the action clear.

A first-level PDL description of Program 5.4 might then be:

```
prompt the user for the data
accept the data
perform the calculations upon the data
print the results
```

Each of these actions is at a level where no further decomposition is required. Each action is directly expressible as C code. The second action, for example, is encoded as:

```
scand("%d %d %d", &hours, &minutes, &seconds)
```

Applying the same to all other actions we can synthesize a complete program including all the necessary declarations. The result is Program 5.4.

Had any actions required further analysis, then the process of functional decomposition would have been repeated on these. Each action would be further refined and again expressed in our PDL.

As we progress through the remainder of the book introducing new program features, we shall also introduce an appropriate statement in our PDL.

5.2 Multifunction programs

As noted in the previous section, a C program may consist of one or more functions. One of the functions must, of course, be called main. Functions offer a means of controlling the complexity of large programs. A function provides a convenient way to encapsulate some discrete programming task. When the function is *called* or *invoked*, the task is executed. Consider a function as a named black box. The name given to the box is the means by which we select the box or function to execute. The box has one entry point and one exit point. During execution of the function some action is performed as described by the executable statements in the function body. Pictorially we represent this by Fig. 5.1.

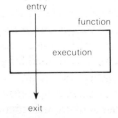

Fig. 5.1

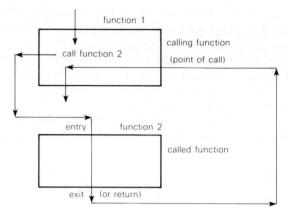

Fig. 5.2

Where one function calls a second function, the effect is to temporarily suspend execution of the first function at the *point of call* of the second. The second function is entered (at its entry point), executed and then exited. Upon completion control returns to the calling function and execution continues with the statement immediately following the point of call. We can express this diagrammatically by showing function 1 calling function 2 (see Fig. 5.2).

Functions can call other functions, building a hierarchical layer of interconnected functions, reflecting the functional decomposition performed during program design. The design can then map directly on to the programming language. For example, a first-level PDL description of a program might give rise to three actions: input the data, process the data, and output the results. If all three actions required further refinement, the same PDL analysis may be applied. Since the first-level refinement is also a top-level description of the problem, it is implemented in function main. Each action in main then becomes a call to a subsidiary function containing the details of the corresponding second-level refinement.

So far, all our programs have consisted of the single function main. Each main function specified the totality of actual operations to be performed. In Program 5.4, for example, the six operations are:

```
printf(. . . .);
scanf(. . . .);
time = . . . .;
printf(. . . .);
printf(. . . .);
printf(. . . .);
```

Consider now extending this program to operate upon, say, four sets of data. Each data set consists of a time measured in hours, minutes and seconds, and for each set the time is to be converted to its equivalent number of seconds. One possible solution would be to repeat the above six statements for a total of four times. This leads to a much larger main function but is, nevertheless, a viable solution.

Further analysis of this programming problem identifies that two sub-tasks are present. The first subtask is that there are four data sets to be operated upon and that the operations are identical. The second is that for a given data set a distinct series of operations is to be performed. These operations are captured by the six statements outlined above.

Expressed in our PDL, the subtask to control the processing of four data sets might appear as:

process the first data set
process the second data set
process the third data set
process the fourth data set

Informally, each statement is a description of the required action. They cannot, however, be directly expressed in our chosen programming language. We must further refine the actions. A second-level refinement of the operation 'process one data set' is the PDL description we arrived at for Program 5.4, namely:

prompt the user for the data
accept the data
perform the calculations upon the data
print the results

Given that the second-level refinements to process the second, third and fourth data sets are the same, the implementation is then realized by relegating the second subtask to a separate function. This function is fully responsible for the operations on a single data set. The function is subordinate to function main, which calls or invokes this subsidiary function four times and, in so doing, implements the first subtask.

Program 5.5

```
/*
**        This program operates on four data sets. Each set
**        consists of a time measured in hours, minutes and
**        seconds. For each set, the time is converted into
**        the equivalent number of seconds and printed.
*/

#include <stdio.h>

main()
   {
      convert();             /* Four function .... */
      convert();             /* .... calls to .... */
      convert();             /* .... convert */
      convert();
   }
```

```
/*
**          Function convert operates on a single data set,
**          reading, processing and printing.
*/

convert()
  {
    int hours, minutes, seconds;    /* data values */
    int time;                       /* computed result */

    printf("Enter the time to be converted: ");
    scanf("%d %d %d", &hours, &minutes, &seconds);

    time = (60 * hours + minutes) * 60 + seconds;

    printf("The original time of:\n");
    printf("%d hours, %d minutes and %d seconds\n",
        hours, minutes, seconds);
    printf("converts to %d seconds\n\n", time);
    return;
  }
```

The program shown above consists of two functions. The function main is, of course, always present. In addition, a function called *convert* is defined. This function contains all the variable declarations and statements required to operate on a single data set. Since it is this function which requires the variable space to hold the data and the computed values, then we declare the variables in this function. It would illegal to, say, declare the variables in function main and then use them in function convert. We shall have more to say on this matter shortly.

Function main now no longer possesses any variable declarations. They are, in this example, unnecessary since no values are processed by this function. Were this the case, then appropriate variable declarations would also be present in the function body of main. The actual body of function main consists of the statements to control processing the four data sets. This is achieved with four *function calls* to convert:

    convert( );

Each such statement causes the named function (convert) to be executed. Each invocation of this subsidiary function processes a single data set. When the function convert is complete, control reverts back to the calling function main. The called function (convert) is said to return control to the calling function (main). This return of control is explicitly specified by the *return* statement, the last executable statement in convert. Function main then arranges for three further calls to function convert.

The return statement is new. The effect of this statement is described above. The general form of this command is:

    return

or

    return expression

where return is a reserved keyword. We shall discuss the second form of the return statement in a section later in this chapter. If no return statement is present in a called function, then processing continues until the end of the function body, as indicated by the closing brace symbol, }. Upon encountering the function end, control returns to the calling function as if an explicit return had been present. The use of the implicit return is so common that we shall adopt it in all further examples.

The order in which the functions appear in a C program text file is unimportant. We might equally well have placed the function convert first. Since normally function main will describe the overall processing, with detail reserved for the subordinate functions, reflecting our functional decomposition of the problem, we will always choose to place function main first.

The invocation of a programmer-defined function is no different from that of calling a function from the standard library. A call to printf, for example, has the form:

printf(. . . .)

Equally, a call to function convert from function main is:

convert(. . . .)

The items to be printed by function printf are supplied to it through function arguments. These appear as a comma-separated list enclosed with the parentheses. For example:

printf("converts to %d seconds\n\n", time)

No communication of data takes place between function main and function convert. Neither function sends nor receives any information to or from the other function. The function declaration for convert indicates this by showing no arguments with the empty parentheses:

```
convert( )
   {
    . . . .
    . . . .
   }
```

Similarly, when this function is called in main, the empty argument list is shown by the parentheses:

convert( )

In both cases the parentheses are obligatory and may not be omitted.

A principle, present in Program 5.5, is that the program text is an expression of the idea of how the program operates (its *algorithm*). Functional decomposition facilitates expressing this algorithm. The question we must answer is where did this algorithm come from?

Programs are composed of two related elements: data items and the process to which the data are subject. These elements are also present in a C function which includes both data declarations and executable statements. A program then specifies what to do and what to do it to. The program structure is thus derived from the structure of its data. The justification for this approach is that the problem data represent a model of the real world. During its lifetime, a program may undergo many functional changes. We might, as shown in Program 5.8, operate on the same data set as above, yet produce a total of the number of seconds for the four supplied times. The structure of the data has, however, remained the same. Only the processing is different.

If the structure of the problem data is:

    data item 1
    data item 2
    data item 3

which means data items 1, 2 and 3 in that order, then the program will consist of a *sequence* of processing actions, such as:

    process data item 1
    process data item 2
    process data item 3

Since Program 5.5 operates upon four data sets, four sequential processing actions appeared in the PDL:

    process the first data set
    process the second data set
    process the third data set
    process the fourth data set

Since the actions for each data set are identical, we relegate this task to a subsidiary function convert, and code function main as four sequential calls to convert. Had each data set been different and had each process also been different the same sequential structure would still have been appropriate. This is a consequence of the problem data.

Thus, we shall deliberately set out our programs so that they reflect the structure of the problem data. Later problems introduce data structures other than sequential structures, and to maintain this one-to-one mapping new program control structures are presented.

5.3 Automatic variables

In the last section we developed a program with two functions — main and convert. It was noted that the variables in the program were declared in function convert since it is here that data space is required. Also, since no data items are required by function main, then no variable declarations are necessary.

It is known from Chapter 3 that the declaration:

int time;

appearing in function convert, introduces a data object called time and is of type int. Strictly, all variables have an attribute in addition to their type and name, and this is referred to as a *storage class*. The term refers to the manner in which memory is allocated by the compiler for variables.

The term *scope* refers to the extent of the meaning of a particular variable in a program. Variables defined in a function are said to be *local* to that function and their scope is the compound statement in which they are declared. This means that they have no meaning outside that function. The storage class for such variables is known as automatic. All variables declared within a function have storage class *auto*. This association is implicit. It is quite legal to state this explicitly by the declaration:

auto int time;

where auto is a reserved keyword. Since the storage class automatic is implicit because the declaration appears in the body of a function, most C programmers choose to omit this keyword.

To illustrate the concept of the scope of a variable, the program below is presented. The variable *two* declared in the function *func* is only referenced by this function. However, the variable *one* is defined in function *main*, but is illegally referenced by function func. The C compiler meeting such an illegal reference would generate a compilation error indicating that variable one is not declared in function func.

Program 5.6

```
/*
**        WRONG !
**        The automatic variable "one" is defined in function
**        main. Its scope is the body of function main. It is
**        illegal to reference it outside of main.
*/

#include <stdio.h>

main()
  {
    int one;          /* scope = main */

    one = 1;          /* valid reference, within scope */

    func();           /* call subordinate function */
  }


func()
  {
    int two;          /* has scope of func */

    two = one;        /* variable one undefined here !! */
  }
```

Automatic variables are only *visible* within the function in which they are declared. Each automatic variable is said to be *local* or *private* to its corresponding function. Because of this, variables with the same name appearing in declarations in separate functions are unrelated, except that they have been chosen with the same identifier. Operations performed on one automatic variable in one function have no effect whatsover on an automatic variable with the same name in another function. This is illustrated by the following program. The variables *local* declared in both program functions are quite distinct. This is shown by the program's output.

Program 5.7

```
/*
**        A program to illustrate local variables, with the
**        same identifier appearing in two subroutines.
*/

#include <stdio.h>

main()
   {
      int local;           /* this "local" belongs to main */

      local = 1;           /* "local" in main set to 1 */

      printf("Function main: local = %d\n", local);
                           /* confirm */

      subroutine();        /* call subordinate */

      printf("Function main check: local = %d\n", local);
                           /* unchanged */
   }


subroutine()
   {
      int local;           /* this "local" belongs to subroutine */

      local = 2;           /* set subroutine's "local" */
      printf("Function subroutine: local = %d\n", local);
   }
```

The output produced by this program is:

Function main: local = 1
Function subroutine: local = 2
Function main check: local = 1

The final line of output demonstrates that the two variables called local are unrelated and are unaffected by the operations performed upon them in separate functions.

This feature means that the C programmer is free to use the same variable name in any number of functions without fear of confusion. It also implies that where functions are written independently by a number of programmers, each has unrestricted use of automatic variable names.

In addition to declaring an automatic variable in a function, it is also permissible to assign an initial value. This process is called *initialization*. A variable is initialized with a value by following its name in the declaration with an equal symbol (=) and an expression. For example:

int time = 10, period = 20 + time;

Semantically, the declaration is equivalent to:

int time, period;

time = 10;
period = 20 + time;

Note how the variable period is initialized with a value that is dependent upon the (initialized) value of variable time. If a variable has no initializer, then its value at the point of declaration is *undefined*. Thus, the declaration:

int time, period = 20 + time;

is invalid since variable time has, as yet, no assigned value. This is a consequence of the C compiler elaborating declarations in their order of appearance. Most C compilers would not detect this as a compile time error. Strictly, we have a logic error, and the effect upon program execution is unpredictable. Most likely, a spurious value is assigned to variable period.

Since semantically an initialized declaration is equivalent to a declaration and an assignment, then the usual conversions apply. Thus, for example:

float sum = 0;

converts the integer constant 0 to the floating point constant 0.0 before performing the assignment. In this situation, the programmer might avoid the unnecessary run time conversion with the declaration:

float sum = 0.0;

5.4 Function values

Program 5.5 in section 5.2 employed a subordinate function convert, responsible for processing a single data set. The main function called convert the correct number of times. No data were actually communicated between these functions. The C language provides a mechanism whereby the result of a calculation performed by a called function may be transmitted back to the calling function. This is achieved with the return statement. The syntax of this construct is:

return expression

To ensure that the returned expression is adequately highlighted from the surrounding program text, it is often presented as a bracketed subexpression. Thus, commonly the statement form is:

return (expression)

The statement indicates that control is to return immediately from the called function, and that the value of the expression is to be made available to the calling function. The value returned may be 'captured' by the calling function with an appropriate assignment. For example, if convert is a function returning an integer value, and period is a variable of type int, then we may use:

    period = convert( );

to record the returned value.

Where a function returns a value, then the type of this returned value must precede the function name in the function declaration. Strictly, a function definition has the extended form:

    type-specifier function-name( )
      {
        optional-declaration-list
        optional-statement-list
      }

The type-specifier is any of the fundamental types supported by C. If, for example, function func delivers a floating point value through a return statement, then the definition should include:

    float func( )
      {
        _ _ _ _ _ _ _ _ _ _
        _ _ _ _ _ _ _ _ _ _
        return (some-floating-point-expression);
      }

The calling sequence for such a function is now different. Since the function makes available a returned value, a mechanism must allow the calling function to capture this value. The assignment operator, or one of its variants, is normally used. Assuming a floating point variable called *result*, then function func might be called by:

    result = func( );

The statement calls function func and picks up the returned value in the variable result.

In the preceding sections no functions have returned any values. If a function declaration now includes a type specifier, then what is the type for a function with no returned value? A function declaration with no type specifier is implicitly of type int. Thus, the function declaration:

    convert( )
      {
        _ _ _ _ _ _ _ _ _ _
        _ _ _ _ _ _ _ _ _ _
      }

is interpreted by the compiler as:

```
int convert( )
    {
        _ _ _ _ _ _ _ _ _ _
        _ _ _ _ _ _ _ _ _ _
    }
```

The call for such a function is also different. The function call is expected to return an integer value, yet no assignment is performed:

```
convert( );
```

The compiler arranges that the expected value is simply discarded. Many of the standard I/O library functions, including printf, also return function values. For the present we choose to ignore the value by having the compiler dispose of it by:

```
printf( .... );
```

Recent implementations of C introduce a new type specifically for a function with no return value. This new type is called *void*. Not all compilers support this type and we shall show in section 5.8 how this may be overcome. Function convert should then have the declaration:

```
void convert( )
    {
        _ _ _ _ _ _ _ _ _ _
        _ _ _ _ _ _ _ _ _ _
    }
```

This is the form we shall use throughout the remainder of the book.

In C, a data object is declared before it is used. This is necessary so that the C compiler can collect details of the attributes of the object, and then use this information when the object is referenced. A function, however, may be referenced (called) before it is declared. Unless otherwise told, the C compiler will assume that the return value of the function is of type int. Thus any function, such as main below, calling function func will erroneously interpret the returned value as an integer when the function is actually declared as one returning type float.

```
main( )
    {
        float result:
        _ _ _ _ _ _ _ _ _ _
        _ _ _ _ _ _ _ _ _ _
        result = func( );     /* erroneously interpreted */
        _ _ _ _ _ _ _ _ _ _
        _ _ _ _ _ _ _ _ _ _
    }
```

```
float func( )
  {
     _ _ _ _ _ _ _ _ _ _
     _ _ _ _ _ _ _ _ _ _
     return (expression);
  }
```

In function main the compiler will generate code for an integer returning function func. When function func is ultimately compiled, code is generated to return a floating point value since the function type is now known to be float. Strictly, a compilation error is generated at the start of the definition of function func:

```
float func( )
```

This is because the compiler has already assumed the existence of the integer function func:

```
int func( )
```

The error would report that the function func has already been declared.

From section 5.2 we know that function order is unimportant in a C program. If function main and function func are interchanged, then the compiler will meet the declaration for func first, and will record the fact that the function returns a float. Then when function func is subsequently called in function main, the correct code will be generated.

This approach is very much dependent upon the textual ordering of the functions and is best not relied upon. When a function is called before it is declared, then the calling function must indicate to the compiler the type of value returned by a called function. A declaration, called a *referencing declaration*, is present in the calling function, and indicates the value delivered by a called function. The general form for a referencing declaration is:

```
type-specifier function-name( ), function-name( ), . . . .
```

The program fragment above would now appear as:

```
main( )
  {
     float result;
     float func( );              /*referencing declaration */
     _ _ _ _ _ _ _ _ _ _
     _ _ _ _ _ _ _ _ _ _
     result = func( );           /* correctly interpreted */
     _ _ _ _ _ _ _ _ _ _
     _ _ _ _ _ _ _ _ _ _
  }
```

```
float func()
    {
    _ _ _ _ _ _ _ _ _ _
    _ _ _ _ _ _ _ _ _ _

    return (expression);
    }
```

These ideas are encapsulated in the following program. This program is a variant of Program 5.5. Again we have two functions main and convert. This time convert does not print the result of its computations, but returns with the value computed from processing one data set. Function main calls function convert four times, then computes and prints a running total of the returned values.

Program 5.8

```
/*
**      A program to operate on four data sets each representing
**      a time measured in hours, minutes and seconds. Each set
**      is converted to its equivalent number of seconds.
**      Additionally, a running total of the number of seconds
**      is maintained.
*/

#include <stdio.h>

main()
    {
    int total_time = 0;                /* accumulated total */
    int convert();                     /* forward reference */

    total_time += convert();
    total_time += convert();
    total_time += convert();
    total_time += convert();

    printf("The total time is %d seconds\n\n", total_time);
    }

int convert()
    {
    int hours, minutes, seconds;       /* data values */
    int time;                          /* computed result */

    printf("Enter the time to be converted: ");
    scanf("%d %d %d", &hours, &minutes, &seconds);

    time = (60 * hours + minutes) * 60 + seconds;

    return (time);
    }
```

5.5 Function arguments

The multifunction programs which we have developed either had no data transferred between individual functions, or had a single value returned from the called function by the return statement. Many programming problems exist in which functions are required to return more than one item to the calling function. Further, the calling function may wish to transmit values to the called function. We introduce *function arguments* by which values may be conveyed between functions. In this section we restrict the discussion to arguments passed from the calling function to the called function. Passing arguments in the opposite direction is considered in a later section of this chapter.

The concept of a called function receiving arguments passed from the calling function has already been alluded to. Most of the programs which we have developed use the standard library function printf. When calling this function a number of arguments are supplied. The arguments are a comma-separated list enclosed in parentheses. The call:

printf("My first program.")

invokes the function printf and passes it the single-string argument "My first program.". This represents the actual string to be printed by printf. For this reason, the string is referred to as the first *actual* argument. In the call:

printf("The sum is %d\n", first + second)

two actual arguments are supplied. Once again the first actual argument is a string. It represents the string to be printed and includes a conversion specification for the second actual argument. The second argument is the expression:

first + second

The value of this expression is computed and is delivered to printf as the second actual argument.

The means by which a function is invoked is known as the *calling sequence*. The calling sequence in C consists of the function name followed by a comma-separated list of actual arguments enclosed in parentheses. If any actual argument is an expression, that expression is first evaluated and the value is passed as the argument. For this reason, argument passing in C is implemented by the method known as *call by value*.

A function declaration including arguments has the form:

```
type-specifier function-name(argument-list)
   argument-declarations
      {
         optional-declaration-list
         optional-statement-list
      }
```

The new features are the argument list appearing within the parentheses and the argument declarations preceding the compound statement of the function body. The argument list in a function call is a list of actual arguments. The argument list in a function definition is referred to as the list of *formal* arguments. The formal and actual arguments should agree in number and type. For every formal argument, there should be a corresponding actual argument of the same type in the function call. The type of each formal argument is given in the argument declaration part of the function declaration. These argument declarations have the same basic form as declarations for automatic (local) variables.

To illustrate, consider a function called *sum* which receives two floating point values as arguments and which delivers their sum through the return statement. One complete definition is:

```
float sum(first, second)
   float first, second;          /* formal arguments */
   {
      float temp                 /* local variable */

      temp = first + second;
      return (temp);
   }
```

The formal argument list is a comma-separated list of identifiers. These identifiers represent the arguments to be received when the function is called. The behavior of the function is described fully in terms of these formal arguments and any local variables. The names of arguments and of any local variables must be distinct since they both have the same scope – namely, the function body.

The argument declaration part specifies the type of each and every formal argument. The argument declaration section is reserved solely to declare the types of the formal arguments. It would be incorrect, for example, to declare function sum by:

```
float sum(first, second)
   float first, second, temp;
   {
      temp = first + second;
      return (temp);
   }
```

The variable temp is local to this function and should be declared accordingly. Compilers would report a compilation error on the line:

```
float first, second, temp;
```

indicating that temp is not a member of the argument list. Equally, it would be illegal to declare this function as:

```
float sum(first, second)
   {
      float temp, first, second;

      temp = first + second;
      return (temp);
   }
```

The local data items first and second have the same names as the formal arguments. Again, a compilation error would be reported.

To call function sum we use the assignment mechanism introduced earlier. In addition, we provide two actual arguments. They may be any expression delivering floating point values. Possible uses are:

```
main ()
  {
      float result, total, second;    /* local data */
      float sum();                     /* forward ref. */
      _ _ _ _ _ _ _ _ _ _
      _ _ _ _ _ _ _ _ _ _
      result = sum(12.3, 17.21);      /* = 29.51 */
      _ _ _ _ _ _ _ _ _ _
      _ _ _ _ _ _ _ _ _ _
      total = sum(result, second);
      _ _ _ _ _ _ _ _ _ _
      _ _ _ _ _ _ _ _ _ _
      result = sum(total * 3, result − 17.111);
      _ _ _ _ _ _ _ _ _ _
      _ _ _ _ _ _ _ _ _ _

  }
```

Functions such as these have all been shown with the returned value captured by an assignment. The delivered values may equally appear in larger arithmetic expressions. To multiply the returned value from function sum before assigning we may write:

result = 3 * sum(total, 10.0)

Additionally, we might call the function sum and use its return value as the actual argument to another call on sum:

quadratic = sum(x*x, sum(x, 1.04))

The first or outer function call to sum has the square of the value for x as its first actual argument. Its second actual argument is the value delivered by the inner call to sum which has arguments x and 1.04. This inner call is executed first. The value delivered then becomes the second actual argument value to the outer call on sum.

Program 5.9 illustrates these features. The integer function *hms_time* translates its integer arguments representing a time measured in hours, minutes and seconds into a total number of seconds. The actual data values are collected by main and passed as actual arguments to this function. The returned value is then printed.

Program 5.9

```
/*
**        Read a time measured in hours, minutes and seconds
**        and convert it to the equivalent number of seconds.
*/

#include <stdio.h>

main ()
    {
        int hours, minutes, seconds;    /* data values */
        int time;                       /* computed value */
        int hms_time();                 /* referencing declaration */

        printf("Enter the time: ");
        scanf("%d %d %d", &hours, &minutes, &seconds);
        time = hms_time(hours, minutes, seconds);
        printf("Converted time is %d seconds\n", time);
    }


int hms_time(h, m, s)
    int h, m, s;                        /* hours, minutes, seconds */
    {
        int t;                          /* computed time */

        t = (60 * h + m) * 60 + s;
        return (t);
    }
```

Note how function hms_time is now responsible for a single task — namely, converting a time in hours, minutes and seconds to the equivalent number of seconds. In an earlier version of this function, it was responsible for three tasks — input, processing and output. In this new form we now have a primitive function that may find uses in other applications. We shall strive for this independence in other functions which we shall develop.

When a function with arguments is called, the value of each actual expression is calculated. The computed values are then matched with the corresponding formal argument. The formal argument within the function body behaves as an initialized local variable (initialized to the value of the actual argument). Thereafter, they may be treated as local variables and have their local copies modified. Only the local copy is changed. The changes do not alter the actual argument. This is demonstrated in the following program.

Program 5.10

```
/*
**        A program to demonstrate that a function argument
**        behaves as an initialized (by the actual argument)
**        local variable, having no effect whatsoever on the
**        actual argument.
*/

#include <stdio.h>
```

```
main()
  {
     int  actualarg = 20;
     void subroutine();              /* referencing declaration */

     printf("Main: actual argument is %d\n", actualarg);

     subroutine(actualarg);

     printf("Main check: actual argument is %d\n", actualarg);
  }


void subroutine(formalarg)
  int formalarg;                     /* dummy argument */
  {
     formalarg += 10;                /* change (local) value */
     printf("Subroutine: formal argument is %d\n", formalarg);
  }
```

The output from this program is:

Main: actual argument is 20
Subroutine: formal argument is 30
Main check: actual argument is 20

The value of the actual argument (actualarg) is unchanged even when the local copy in function subroutine is modified.

5.6 Function argument agreement and conversion

When employing a function with arguments, we have stated that the actual and formal arguments must agree in number and type. Modern programming languages such as Pascal and Ada strictly enforce this requirement. Compilers for these languages perform all the necessary checks. As in FORTRAN, this checking is not done in C. The responsibility lies with the programmer.

If the type of the actual and corresponding formal argument differs, erroneous data will be passed and no error issued. If too few actual arguments are supplied, then garbage is passed for the remainder. If too many actual arguments are given, the excess is discarded.

The UNIX operating system provides a program called *lint* that can be used to uncover problems such as these. The program can check for consistency between the number of formal and actual arguments, and between their types. Some details on lint are given in Appendix G1.

Because comma symbols are used to separate argument expressions, the comma operator may not be used in argument expressions unless enclosed by parentheses to prevent mistaking it for an argument separator. Conceivably, we might have the example:

```
main( )
  {
     int s, t, ...;
     void subroutine( );      /* referencing declaration */
     ..........
     ..........
     subroutine(s, (t = s + 1, t)); /* legal!! */
     ..........
     ..........
  }
void subroutine(a, b)
  int a, b;
  {
     ..........
     ..........
  }
```

The actual arguments passed to function *subroutine* are the values of variables s and t (the latter from the second expression of the comma operator t = s + 1, t). The first expression of the comma operator caused the value of s + 1 to be assigned to variable t. More naturally we might expect to find the call to subroutine to consist of:

```
t = s + 1;
subroutine(s, t);
```

The C programmer is particularly vulnerable to unmatched types between actual and formal arguments. C specifies certain adjustments in the types of the function arguments to simplify and regularize them. The adjustments are made in two places: on the actual argument types at the point of the function call, and on the formal argument types in the function definition.

If a formal argument is declared to be of type char, short or float, the compiler will expect an actual argument of type int, int or double (respectively) to be passed to the function. For this reason, formal arguments declared to be of type char, short and float are implicitly promoted to be of type int, int or double, respectively (see section 3.9).

When an expression appears as an argument in a function call, the result of the expression is adjusted using the usual conversions before being passed as an actual argument and should match the type of the corresponding formal argument following implicit promotion.

Failure to understand these conversions can lead to very obscure programming problems. Consider Program 5.11: it is an attempt to compute and print the square of the value 2 using the function *square*.

Program 5.11

```
/*
**        A program to illustrate that the type of actual
**        argument supplied to a called function must
**        match the type of the formal argument appearing
**        in the function declaration.
*/

#include <stdio.h>

main()
   {
     float sq;                          /* result variable */
     float square();                    /* referencing declaration */

     sq = square(2);                    /* argument type mismatch ! */
     printf("The square of 2 is %f\n", sq);
   }

float square(x)
   float x;                             /* note formal argument type */
   {
     return (x * x);
   }
```

The definition for function square employs a formal argument of type float. This is implicitly promoted to a double. The actual argument is of type int. The machine representation for the integer value 2 is passed to function square then misinterpreted as a double. An erroneous result would be produced.

One correct solution would be to use the floating point constant 2.0 instead of 2. Such a representation is of type double and is consistent with the promoted formal argument:

sq = square(2.0)

If the actual argument was, say, an integer variable called sum, then we would coerce it to the required type using an expression such as:

sq = square(sum + 0.0)

or by:

sq = square(1.0 * sum)

or with an explicit cast operator:

sq = square((double) sum)

The first two illustrations use the arithmetical operators to cause type conversion. Though this is perfectly legal, it is much less obvious to the reader why this is used. An explicit cast coercion is the preferred method, expressing clearly the necessary conversion, and avoiding any unnecessary computations.

5.7 Pointers and function arguments

The parameter passing which we have developed is asymmetric insofar as the calling function can supply values to the called function, but there is no equivalent in the opposite direction. We know from section 5.5 (Program 5.10) that changes to the values of formal arguments within a function do not alter the original actual argument values. This is attributable to the method of parameter passing in C known as call by value.

To allow a called function access to a value in the calling function, the latter must supply the *address* of one of its automatic (local) variables. If the called function then has the address of a variable in the calling function, it can arrange to assign a new value at that address. This is not a new concept, it has already been presented. Recall, that to use the function scanf, the address of variables is passed as arguments. The address of a variable is obtained by applying the unary *address operator* &:

scanf("%d, %d", &first, &second)

To write functions that operate with addresses we must first introduce the idea of a *pointer*. Pointers are one of the most sophisticated features of the C programming language. They are also one of the most dangerous. The power and flexibility that C provides in dealing with pointers is one of the language's most distinguishing qualities. In this section we will introduce sufficient features to allow us to use pointers with function arguments. In later chapters we shall look at further applications of pointers.

Let us, for a moment, revisit declarations. Consider the declaration and initialization:

int x = 27;

Our understanding of such a declaration is that an area of memory is set aside sufficient to accommodate an integer value. This area of memory is referenced in the program by the identifier x. At the machine level, this memory area has an address (say 5678). The area of memory is initialized with the binary pattern representing decimal 27 (see Fig. 5.3). The result of the expression x is 27, since this is the value of the variable. The result of the expression &x is 5678, since the & operator delivers the address of its variable operand x.

Our normal understanding of a variable (such as x) is that it represents a location in memory which has a unique address (5678 in the example), the

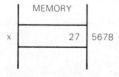

Fig. 5.3

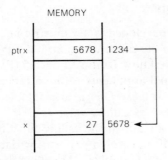

Fig. 5.4

content of which is a representation of some value currently assigned to the variable.

A pointer, however, is a variable which contains the address of some other object. If a pointer is a variable itself, then like all other variables it must occupy an area of memory which will have an address. The content of that area of memory is the address of some other variable. If ptrx is a variable capable of addressing the integer variable x, and if ptrx resides at memory location 1234, then the arrangement is as shown in Fig. 5.4.

The unary operator & gives the address of an object, so the statement:

ptrx = &x;

assigns the address of x to the variable ptrx; ptrx is said to point to the variable x. This is shown in Fig. 5.4.

If the variable x were to appear in an expression, we understand that the value of x is required. For example, in the assignment:

y = x;

for some integer variable y, the value of the integer variable x, namely 27, is assigned to y. Equally, if the variable ptrx were to appear on the right of an assignment operator, the value of ptrx is required (5678 in this example):

.... = ptrx;

On the other hand, the unary indirection operator * treats its operand as the address of the ultimate target, and accesses that address to fetch its content. Thus:

y = *ptrx;

assigns to y the content of to whatever ptrx points. Now ptrx points to x and so y is assigned the value of x (that is 27). The expression to the right of the assignment operator is evaluated in two stages. First, the value of ptrx is obtained (namely 5678). This is interpreted as the address of an integer object. The unary indirection operator then delivers the value of the integer at this address (namely 27). The sequence:

```
ptrx = &x;
y    = *ptrx;
```

assigns the same value to y as does:

```
y = x;
```

The value of x is, however, obtained indirectly, through the variable ptrx. This concept is known as *indirect addressing*, or simply *indirection*, and is implemented with the *indirection operator* (*). The precedence and associativity of this operator and the address operator are shown in Appendix E.

To declare all the variables which participate we arrive at:

```
int x, y;
int *ptrx;
```

The declaration for x and y is normal. The declaration for the pointer variable ptrx is new. The declaration:

```
int *ptrx;
```

is intended as a mnemonic; it states that the combination *ptrx is an int. It is no different then from saying that:

```
int x;
```

declares x as an int. If ptrx occurs in the context *ptrx it is equivalent to a variable of type int. It indirectly references the actual variable.

Pointers can appear in generalized expressions. If ptrx points to the integer variable x, then *ptrx can occur in any context where an integer could be found:

```
y = *ptrx + 1;
```

sets y to be one more than x. Equally:

```
printf("The value of x is %d\n", *ptrx);
```

prints the current value of x. Since integer variables can occur on the left side of an assignment operator, then so too can *ptrx. Then:

```
*ptrx = 0;
```

initializes x to zero.

Care must be taken when using the indirection operator with the increment and decrement operators. To increment the value of the variable to which ptrx points, we use:

```
(*ptrx) + + ;
```

The parentheses are necessary as both operators are of equal precedence and associate right to left. Without the parentheses:

```
*ptrx + + ;
```

would increment ptrx then access the value indirectly referenced by the original value of ptrx. In Chapter 11 we will discover what an incremented pointer value actually means.

Lastly, since pointers are variables, they can be manipulated like other variables. Given:

```
int x;
int *ptrx, *ptry;

ptrx = &x;
```

then:

```
ptry = ptrx;
```

copies the content of ptrx into ptry, making both ptrx and ptry point to x.

Strictly, when we declare ptrx as, say, a pointer to an integer variable, as in:

```
int *ptrx;
```

then we are constraining that pointer to point to a particular kind of object (int in this case). Given the declaration:

```
double x;
```

it is illegal to execute the assignment:

```
ptrx = &x;
```

We are now in a position to proceed and to discuss how pointers are used in function arguments. Consider a main function wishing to convert a time measured in hours, minutes and seconds to a total number of seconds. The function main will employ a subsidiary function hms_time to perform this processing. The function has four arguments: the final three represent the original time, whilst the first argument is the converted time computed by the function. The first argument needs to be an address so that function hms_time can place the computed value at that location. The function main might then appear:

```
main( )
    {
        int hours, minutes, seconds;
        int time;
        void hms_time( );

        scanf("%d %d %d", &hours, &minutes, &seconds);
        hms_time(&time, hours, minutes, seconds);
        printf("Converted time is %d\n", time);
    }
```

Note how the address of the local variable time is given as the actual argument to function hms_time. Operationally this is the same as giving the address of variable hours to function scanf.

In the declaration for the function hms_time we must indicate that the first formal argument is the address of an integer. In the function body we need also to assign a value to the integer pointed to by the argument. The coding is:

```
void hms_time(t, h, m, s)
  int *t, h, m, s;
  {
    *t = (60 * h + m) * 60 + s;
  }
```

The formal argument t is a pointer to an integer. This is shown by:

```
int *t, .... ;
```

The integer to which t refers is assigned a value by:

```
*t = .... ;
```

As a complete example, a program is required to input a time measured as a number of seconds and to convert that value to its equivalent form expressed in hours, minutes and seconds. The program is organized so that function main performs all the input and output, and the subordinate function time_hms performs the necessary conversions.

Program 5.12

```
/*
**      The program inputs a time measured in seconds
**      and converts it to its equivalent in hours,
**      minutes and seconds.
*/
#include <stdio.h>
main ()
  {
    int  time;                            /* original data value */
    int  hours, minutes, seconds;         /* computed values */
    void time_hms ();                     /* forward reference */

    printf("Enter the time in seconds: ");
    scanf("%d", &time);

    time_hms(time, &hours, &minutes, &seconds);

    printf("The time %d seconds\n", time);
    printf("converts to %d hours, %d minutes and %d seconds\n",
        hours, minutes, seconds);
  }

  void time_hms(t, h, m, s)
    int t;                                /* time */
    int *h, *m, *s;                       /* computed hours, .... */
    {
      int temp;

      *s   = t % 60;                      /* number of seconds */
      temp = t / 60;                      /* total minutes */
      *m   = temp % 60;                   /* number of minutes */
      *h   = temp / 60;                   /* number of hours */
    }
```

In any function, if a data value is to be read and recorded in a local variable, then the address of that variable is given to the scanf function:

```
void subroutine( arg, .... )
  int *arg, .... ;
  {
    int local;
    .....
    .....
    scanf("%d", &local);
    .....
  }
```

If the formal argument arg is to be used in the call to scanf instead of local, then the call is:

```
scanf("%d", arg);
```

No address operator is applied to arg since in the formal argument declaration part, arg is already a pointer to an int.

Program 5.13 illustrates this feature in the function *input*. The program is a repeat of Program 5.12. The program is structured into three subordinate functions: one to read the data, one to process it and one to display the results. The main function coordinates each, passing and receiving the necessary values.

Program 5.13

```
/*
**        Input a time expressed in seconds and convert to
**        the equivalent time in hours, minutes and seconds.
*/

#include <stdio.h>

main()
  {
    int   time;                       /* original data */
    int   hours, minutes, seconds;    /* computed results */
    void input(), process(), output();  /* forward declarations */

    input(&time);
    process(time, &hours, &minutes, &seconds);
    output(time, hours, minutes, seconds);
  }


void input(t)
  int *t;                            /* address of input value */
  {
    printf("Enter the time in seconds: ");
    scanf("%d", t);                   /* note: no address operator */
  }
```

```
void process(t, h, m, s)
  int t;                        /* input time */
  int *h, *m, *s;               /* output hours, .... */
  {
    int mins;

    *s   = t % 60;
    mins = t / 60;
    *m   = mins % 60;
    *h   = mins / 60;
  }


void output(t, h, m, s)
  int t, h, m, s;               /* time, hours, .... */
  {
    printf("The time %d seconds\n", t);
    printf("converts to %d hours, %d minutes and %d seconds\n",
        h, m, s);
  }
```

Decomposing the program in this manner allocates separate tasks to separate functions. The generalization of the functions permit their possible use in other programs. Further, the tasks are localized so that changes are readily implemented. If, for example, a new layout of the results is required, only function output need be modified, and this can be done without consideration for the other program elements. This is a consequence of the completeness of the function. The function is independent of its environment, described completely in terms of its arguments and any local variables.

This type of function exhibits *functional abstraction*. During program decomposition, we are concerned with what the function does, not how it does it. Abstractly we are only interested in the *what*. Pictorially, a function at this level of refinement is a black box. For example, function *process* might be as shown in Fig. 5.5, receiving a time (t) in seconds as input and delivering the equivalent time expressed in hours (h), minutes (m) and seconds (s). Later during development, the *how* is established by further refinement.

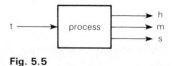

Fig. 5.5

5.8 The C preprocessor

The power and notation of the C programming language is extended by the use of a preprocessor. This preprocessor is associated with the C compiler and is used to process the source text of a C program before the compilation process proper. The features offered by the preprocessor are used to develop programs which are easier to read, easier to modify and easier to transfer to different computer systems.

As implied by the name, the preprocessor actually analyzes the pre-processor statements before full compilation takes place. Preprocessor statements are identified by the character #, which must be the first character on the line. The syntax of these preprocessor statements is independent of the C language. We will begin by examining the two most widely used preprocessor statements, the #define and the #include statements. A detailed study of all the facilities of the preprocessor is delayed until Chapter 8.

A *macro* is an identifier which represents and is replaced by a string composed of one or more *tokens*. The preprocessor statement #define accomplishes this function. The simplest form of this statement is:

    # define identifier   token-string

The end of the identifier is taken as the first whitespace character. The token-string (or replacement text as it is sometimes known) is the remainder of the line. After a directive of this form is encountered in a program, all subsequent occurrences of the specified identifier are replaced with the specified token-string.

The following example illustrates the use of this directive:

    # define PI   3.14159

Conventionally, the identifier is in upper-case. This is not, of course, obligatory. Reserving only upper-case letters in the identifier indicates to the reader that this is a #define'd item. From the point of definition, throughout the rest of the program text file, all occurrences of PI will be replaced by the preprocessor with the token-string 3.14159. This replace-ment is only valid outwith string constants. Any occurrence of PI inside a string is ignored. The statements:

    circumference = PI * diameter;
    print("PI is %f\n", PI);

would be transformed by the preprocessor into:

    circumference = 3.14159 * diameter;
    printf("PI is %f\n", 3.14159);

There are many important uses for simple #define statements. If a large C program contains many literal occurrences of the value 3.14159, say, then the #define above would allow us to use PI in its place. The program is now more readable since the *symbolic constant* PI reflects the actual processing being performed. Further, if we wished to use 3.1415926 instead, for this geometric value, then we merely have to change the single #define instead of all the appearances of 3.14159:

    # define PI   3.1415926

The preprocessor will now replace all occurrences of PI with the new token-string during the next program compilation.

The token-string can be any valid section of C code. The token string is taken as the string immediately following the first whitespace character after the identifier. Normally this replacement text is the remainder of the line. Where a long replacement string is required, it may be extended over several lines, provided each line (except the last) terminates with a backslash symbol (\) followed immediately by a newline character. For example:

```
#define LONG_MESSAGE      "A very long message extending \
over two lines"
```

Functions not returning values appear in all our programs with type specifier void. Not all C compilers support this feature. In these compilers, functions usually return the default type int. We might usefully employ the #define to conceal this by defining void to be the string int:

```
#define void     int
```

The scope of a named identifier in a #define statement is from its point of definition to the end of the source program text file. It is perfectly valid to put the #define statements anywhere in a file provided they precede their use. It is common, however, to find all the #define statements grouped together at the head of the program file. Generally, we will adopt this convention in all our programs.

The #include preprocessor statement causes the entire content of a specified source text file to be processed as if those contents had appeared in place of the #include command. The name of the file to be included is given as the command argument. The two forms of this statement are:

```
#include "filename"
```

and:

```
#include ⟨filename⟩
```

In the first example, the named file is searched for in the same directory in which the file containing the #include was found. In the second case, the named file is searched for in *standard places*. In UNIX and UNIX-like systems this is usually the directory /usr/include. We have already met and used this last form. We incorporate into all our programs details of the standard I/O library functions with the file stdio.h.

Generally, the #include mechanism is reserved to collect related groups of #define statements and other items. This way, if we are writing a series of programs, they can all share the same definitions. Consistency can then be better guaranteed by having all these definitions in one place. Such files are referred to as *header* files. Under UNIX the filenames normally have a .h suffix, for example, stdio.h.

Consider, for example, that a header file to package together a collection of symbolic constants defining characteristics of the Zilog Z80 microprocessor is:

```
/*
**     File :     z80.h
*/
```

```
# define WORD_SIZE        16
# define BYTE_SIZE        8
# define REGISTERS        6
# define ACCUMULATORS     1

# define LDAB             0x78     /* hex opcodes */
# define ADDB             0x80
# define JMP              0xC3
   etc.
```

5.9 Mathematical functions

There are no mathematical functions as part of the C language. Functions such as:

sqrt( )	square root
exp( )	exponential
sin( )	trigonometric

occur in a special library. If a programmer wishes to use these functions, the library must be available to the linker as shown in Appendix G. Many of these functions take an argument of type double and return a value of type double. Any program including any of these functions must, therefore, include appropriate referencing declarations, for example:

```
double exp( );
```

The library header file math.h is normally provided and contains all the necessary declarations. They may be incorporated into a program with the statement:

```
#include <math.h>
```

Program 5.14 computes the area of a triangle given by the formula:

$$sqrt(s(s - x)(s - y)(s - z))$$

where:

$$s = (x + y + z)/2$$

and x, y, z are the lengths of the sides of the triangle.

Program 5.14

```
/*
**        Determine the area of a triangle given
**        the lengths of its sides.
*/

#include <stdio.h>
#include <math.h>

main()
   {
   float a, b, c;                 /* triangle sides */
   float triangle();              /* forward reference */

   printf("Enter lengths of sides: ");
   scanf("%f %f %f", &a, &b, &c);
   printf("Area of triangle is %6.2f\n", triangle(a, b, c));
   }

float triangle(x, y, z)
   float x, y, z;                 /* sides */
   {
   float s;                       /* semi-perimeter */

   s = (x + y + z)/2.0;
   return (sqrt(s * (s-x) * (s-y) * (s-z)));
   }
```

5.10 Summary

1. A C program consists of one more *functions*. A complete C program has one function called *main*, and processing commences with the first statement in main. A function is a named *compound statement* or *block*.
2. A function compound statement may include the declaration for *local* or *automatic* variables. Automatic variables are *private* to a function and only exist when the function is called, and are deallocated when the function terminates.
3. When a function is called in a *function statement*, program control is passed to the called function. When a *return statement* is executed explicitly, or implicitly at the function end, control is passed back to the calling function. If the return statement contains an expression, the value of the expression is made available to the calling function.
4. Functions implicitly return a value of type *int*. Where a function returns a value other than an integer, a *forward reference* declaration is generally required and best provided. A function with no associated value is of type *void*.
5. *Arguments* are used to communicate data between the calling and the called functions. When a function is called, the *actual* arguments listed replace the *formal* arguments. Argument passing in C is implemented as *call by value*. The values passed as arguments may be data items or variable addresses (pointers).
6. *Stepwise refinement* consists of repeatedly decomposing a problem into smaller subproblems. A large program should be written as a collection of functions, each responsible for some identifiable task from the overall problem.

7. The structure of the problem data is reflected in the structure of the program. Sequential data items give rise to sequential program structures.

5.11 Exercises

1. Write a program that will convert a length measured in centimeters to its equivalent number of inches. Modify the program to process five data sets.

2. Write a program that reads a data set containing an invoice number, quantity of an item ordered and the unit price of the item. The total price should then be calculated, and the output should appear as follows:

INVOICE	QUANTITY	UNIT PRICE	TOTAL
xxx	xxxx	xxxx.xx	xxxxx.xx

3. Write a program to read four decimal values representing the coordinates of two points on a plane. Calculate the distance between the points and output the result. Use the formula:

   $$\text{distance}^2 = (x2 - x1)^2 + (y2 - y1)^2$$

4. Write a program to determine the number of gallons of paint required to paint a rectangular room. The windows and doors are to be ignored in the calculation. The width and length of the room and the height of the walls will be entered in feet. A gallon of paint is assumed to cover about 250 square feet.

5. Write a program that will convert a given number of minutes and seconds to the correct fraction of an hour. For example, 37 minutes and 30 seconds is 0.625 of an hour.

6. Assuming that the population of a city is 650,000 and that its rate of growth is 4.5 per cent a year, write a program to calculate the population each year over the next five years.

7. Write a program consisting of the single function main which reads two integer values representing the length and breadth of a rectangular figure, and which computes and prints the perimeter length.

   Repeat the same problem, but this time employ a second function called perimeter which performs the necessary calculation, given, as arguments, the dimensions of the rectangle. The function header is:

   ```
   int perimeter(length, breadth)
      int length, breadth;
   ```

8. Prepare a function called denominations which, when supplied with a positive integer argument representing a sum of money expressed in pence less than one pound in value, will print a list of each coin and the quantity required. The function header is to be:

   ```
   void denominations(money)
      int money;
   ```

The sample call:

    denominations(34);

would produce the output:

    34 pence is: 0 fifty pence
                   3 ten pence
                   0 five pence
                   2 two pence
                   0 one pence

Test this function in a program.

9. Predict the output from the following five programs and explain your reasoning.
   (a) #include ⟨stdio.h⟩
        main( )
          {
              int   x;
              void change( );
              x = 0;
              change( );
              printf("%d\n", x);
          }
        void change( )
          {
              int x;
              x = 1;
          }
   (b) #include ⟨stdio.h⟩
        main( )
          {
              int x;
              void change( );
              x = 0;
              change(&x);
              printf("%d\n", x);
          }
        void change(y)
          int *y;
          {
              *y = 1;
          }
   (c) #include ⟨stdio.h⟩
        main( )
          {
              int x;
              void change( );
              x = 0;
              change(x);
              printf("%d\n", x);
          }
        void change(y)
          int y;
          {
              y = 1;
          }

(d) #include ⟨stdio.h⟩
```
main( )
    {
        int thing;
        void cheat( );
        thing = 1;
        cheat(&thing, &thing);
        printf("%d\n", thing);
    }
void cheat(hee, haw)
    int *hee, *haw;
    {
        *hee = - 1;
        *haw = - (*hee);
    }
```

(e) #include ⟨stdio.h⟩
```
main( )
    {
        int thing;
        void untrue( );
        thing = 10;
        untrue(&thing, &thing);
        printf("%d\n", thing);
    }
void untrue(hee, haw)
    int *hee, *haw;
    {
        *hee = 20 + *haw;
    }
```

10. Prepare a function called swap which interchanges the values of its two integer arguments. The function header is:

```
void swap(x, y)
    int *x, *y;
```

Test this function in a program.

11. The function min, defined below, determines the least of its two integer arguments.

```
int min(a, b)
    int a, b;
    {
        return (a < b ? a : b);
    }
```

Design and write the corresponding function called max which finds the larger of its two integer arguments. Function max should make a call to function min in determining the correct value.

Similarly, write a function called min3 which returns the least of its three integer arguments. Use function min to determine the result.

12. A time, expressed in terms of the 24-hour clock, is provided by three integer

values: hours (0 $\leq$ hours $\leq$ 23), minutes and seconds (0 $\leq$ minutes, seconds $\leq$ 59). Write a function called hms_time which converts such a time to a total number of seconds. The function header is:

    long int hms_time(hours, minutes, seconds)
        int hours, minutes, seconds;

Why is it reasonable to declare the function returning a long int rather than an int?

Write also the converse function time_hms which converts a time in seconds back into its equivalent 24-hour clock value. The function header is:

    void time_hms(time, hours, minutes, seconds)
        long int time;
        int *hours, *minutes, *seconds;

in which the long int argument time represents the number of seconds, and the three pointer arguments are the recipient addresses of the converted value.

Prepare a program that checks the execution of both these functions.

Write a function called add_time_hms which adds a time in seconds on to a 24-hour clock time. The final answer is also expressed as a 24-hour clock time, updates the original input values, and ignores any advance of one or more days. This function should be written in terms of the previous two functions. The function header is:

    void add_time_hms(time, hours, minutes, seconds)
        long int time;
        int *hours, *minutes, *seconds;

Prepare a program to show that:

    add_time_hms(0L, ...)

produces no change of values.

Write a further function called difference which finds the number of seconds between two 24-hour clock times. It can be assumed that the first time (hr1, min1, sec1) is later in the day than the second time (hr2, min2, sec2). The function header is:

    long int difference(hr1, min1, sec1, hr2, min2, sec2)
        int hr1, min1, sec1;
        int hr2, min2, sec2;

Prepare a program to show that:

(a) difference(hr, min, sec, hr, min, sec) is 0L for some 24-hour clock time (hr, min, sec);
(b) add_time_hms(difference(h1,m1,s1,h2,m2,s2), &h2,&m2,&s2) sets the 24-hour clock time (h2, m2, s2) to the value of (h1, m1, s1).

## CHAPTER 6

Flow of control

The execution of C programming statements causes actions to be performed. The programs that we have developed execute one statement after another in a linear fashion. We can create abstract actions with function declarations and then treat these as if they likewise were primitive statements of the language. The simple statements which we have explored can be considered sequential, and include the assignment and the function call.

In addition, statements are available to alter the flow of control in a program. The full repertoire of C language statements is then classified into one of three control structures:

(a) sequence
(b) selection
(c) iteration

The new program control structures of *selection* and *iteration* permit us to process data with structures other than sequential. Repetitive data items are processed by iteration statements. Alternative data items are processed by selection statements. Through these statements we retain the correspondence between the structure of the problem's data and the program structure which we introduced in the previous chapter.

We shall now examine further C statements as instances of the two control structures iteration and selection. A feature of these new statements is the *condition*. A condition determines the *truth* or *falsity* of some expression. We commence this chapter by considering expressions yielding values which are either true or false.

6.1 Relational operators and expressions

The relational operators are:

$$\text{less than} : <$$
$$\text{greater than} : >$$
$$\text{less than or equal} : <=$$
$$\text{greater than or equal} : >=$$

All four operators are binary. They each take two expressions as operands and yield one of two possible values. Just as with arithmetic operators, the relational operators have rules of precedence and associativity that determine how expressions involving these operators are evaluated. All four operators have the same precedence levels and associate left to right. Their relationship with the other operators is shown in Appendix E.

Some examples of relational expressions are:

```
x < 0.0
ch2 > = 'A'
y *y <= 2 * y + 1
pointer > end_of_list
```

From Appendix E we observe that the relational operators have lower precedence than the arithmetic operators. Expressions like:

```
index < = limit − 1
```

are, therefore, interpreted as:

```
index < = (limit − 1)
```

The greater-than-or-equal and less-than-or-equal operators are described with two symbols. No embedded spaces are allowed, nor can the operators be expressed as equal-or-greater-than or equal-or-less-than. The following are illegal expressions:

```
p < = q     / * embedded space disallowed */
r = > s      /* no such operator */
```

Consider the relational expression a < b. Intuitively, if the value of a is less than the value of b, then the expression is true. If the value of a is not less than the value of b, then the expression is false. In C, the logical value false is represented by the integer value zero (0), and the logical value true by any non-zero integer value. In particular, the relational operators generate either the integer value 0 (for false) or the integer value 1 (for true).

In the context of the following declarations:

```
char c = 'x';
int i = 1, j = 3, k = − 4;
```

Table 6.1 gives a number of expressions involving the relational operators, together with the derived value. For each expression, the parenthesized equivalent is also shown. The logical value upon evaluation of the expression is indicated.

In C, the following relational expression may be derived:

```
2 < index < 6
```

For the reasons given below, it is inadvisable to use such a construct. The expression is frequently used in mathematics to indicate that the variable

Table 6.1

Expression	Equivalent expression	Logical value	Derived value
'b' + 1 < c	('b' + 1) < c	true	1
5 * j > = 12 − k	(5 * j) > = (12 − k)	false	0
i + j < = − k	(i + j) < = (− k)	true	1

index has the property of being greater than 2 and less than 6. It can also be considered as a C expression which, depending on the value of index, may or may not be true. For example, if index is 5, then the mathematical statement:

   2 < index < 6

is true, but if the index is 0, then the statement is false. Now consider:

   2 < index < 6

as a C relational expression. Since the relational operators associate left to right, the expression is equivalent to:

   (2 < index) < 6

For index = 5, the subexpression:

   2 < index

evaluates to the logical value true, represented as the integer value 1. The expression then reduces to the subexpression:

   1 < 6

and also evaluates to logical true or integer 1. In this case the C relational expression delivers the same as the mathematical statement.

However, when index = 0, the subexpression:

   2 < index

evaluates to the logical value false, integer value 0, and:

   0 < 6

evaluates to the logical value true, integer value 1. This time the C relational expression delivers a different interpretation from the mathematical statement. The correct way to express a relationship of this form is described in section 6.3.

6.2 Equality operators and expressions

The equality operators are:

   equal : = =
   not equal : ! =

These binary operators act on two expressions and yield either of the two logical values true or false. Appendix E shows these two new operators alongside the other operators.

Some valid examples of expressions using these operators are:

ch = = LTRZ
j + k ! = t

No embedded spaces are permitted between the two characters which represent these operators. Equally, the operator *not equal* may not be written = !.

The operator equal works perfectly correctly with integer operands. When used with operands of type floating point (float or double), some surprising results can arise. This is entirely attributable to the limited precision of the floating point representation. If we were to divide 1.0 by 3.0 and then multiply the result by 3.0, we might reasonably expect the answer to be 1.0. If the variable x is declared as:

float x = 1.0;

then we might assume the expression:

x = = x/3.0 * 3.0

to evaluate to the logical value true. The mathematical result of the division is 0.33333333 .... . If on some hypothetical computer, floating point values were held with six decimal digits of accuracy, then the result is 0.333333. When we multiply by 3.0 the result is 0.999999. The expression now reduces to:

1.0 = = 0.999999

which is clearly false.

The equality operator should be avoided when comparing two floating point expressions. The solution is normally not to ask if the two expressions are equal but if the two expressions are approximately equal. This is expressed by asking if the difference between each expression is small enough to be considered negligible. We will show in a later section how to formulate this.

Care is required not to confuse the equality operator (= =) and the assignment operator (=). This is a common programming mistake which can lead to unexpected results. For example, if we wish to determine if the integer variable a is equal to 2, the expression is:

a = = 2

and yields either true or false, according to the value of a. However, if the expression is mistakenly written as:

a = 2

then the expression is valid, has the effect of assigning the value 2 to the variable a, and delivers the value 2 interpreted as logical true. The expression is always true, irrespective of the original value of a.

6.3 Logical operators and expressions

The logical operators are:

$$\begin{aligned}
\text{logical and:} & \quad \&\& \\
\text{logical or:} & \quad \mid\mid \\
\text{(unary) negation:} & \quad !
\end{aligned}$$

The logical-and and logical-or operators are binary, both acting on two expressions and yielding either the logical value true or logical false. Both operators treat their operands as logical values. The logical negation operator is a unary operator. The single operand is taken to represent either logical true or logical false. The effect of applying these operators is shown in Table 6.2. The precedence and associativity of these logical operators is given in Appendix E.

Some expressions involving the negation operator are:

! 5	evaluates to 0
! 0	evaluates to 1
! 't'	evaluates to 0
3 + !x	evaluates to 3 if x is non-zero, and
	to 4 if x is zero
! ! 5	evaluates to 1
! ! 0	evaluates to 0

The expression !5 evaluates to false since 5 is interpreted by the unary negation operator as the representation for true. The expression !'t' is somewhat unusual but also yields false since the ASCII encoding for character 't' is decimal 116, namely true. The expression !!5 has the equivalent form !(!5). With the integer value 5 interpreted as true, then, as above, !5 is false. Negating this value again delivers true.

In the context of the following declarations:

```
char c = 'x'
int i = 1, j = 3, k = 4;
```

Table 6.3 shows some expressions involving the logical-and and the logical-or operators.

There is one subtlety about the logical-and and the logical-or operators. In the evaluation of subexpressions that are the operands of the operators && and ¦¦, the evaluation process stops as soon as the outcome is determinable. Suppose that *expression1* and *expression2* are the expression operands. If expression1 has value zero (false), then in:

```
expression1 && expression2
```

Table 6.2

P	Q	P && Q	P ¦¦ Q	P	! P,
false	false	false	false	false	true
false	true	false	true	true	false
true	false	false	true		
true	true	true	true		

Table 6.3

Expression	Equivalent expression	Logical value	Derived value
i && j &&k	(i && j) && k	true	1
i && j ¦¦ !c	(i && j) ¦¦ (!c)	true	1
k < i && i < j	(k < i) && (i < j)	false	0
i = = 2 ¦¦ j = = 1	(i = = 2) ¦¦ (j = = 1)	false	0
i > 2 && !j	(i > 2) && (!j)	false	0

expression2 will not be evaluated because the value of the logical expression is already determined to be false. Similarly, if expression1 has a non-zero value (true), then in:

expression1 ¦¦ expression2

expression2 will not be evaluated since the value of the expression is already determined to be true.

In both instances the second expression may never be evaluated. If the second expression includes a *side effect* of its evaluation, then this will not be obtained if the expression is not evaluated. For example, using the above declarations, the expression:

j < i && k + = 2

is interpreted as:

(j < i) && (k + = 2)

and since the subexpression (j < i) is false, then variable k is not incremented. Statements or expressions that employ this kind of side effect can make programs very difficult to correct or to maintain and are actively discouraged.

6.4 The conditional operator

For completeness we discuss here the conditional operator. Strictly, this is not an operator that delivers a logical value. It does, however, include a logical expression and so we consider it here. The conditional operator consists of three expressions, with the first and second expressions separated by the query symbol (?) and the second and third expressions separated by the colon symbol (:). The form is:

expression1 ? expression2 : expression3

The first operand is used to determine which of the other two operands should be evaluated. If the first expression delivers logical true (non-zero) then the result of the expression is expression2; if the first expression delivers logical false (zero) then the result of the expression is expression3.

To determine the least of two values we might use this operator. The minimum of the two values a and b can be obtained by:

min = a < b ? a : b

Like all operators, this operator has a precedence and an associativity. This is shown in Appendix E.

In section 6.2 we noted that equality comparisons on two floating point values are best performed by determining if the two values are approximately equal. Thus, instead of testing if:

a = = b

we should test if the absolute difference between a and b is negligible. Mathematically, we express this as:

$| a - b | <$ epsilon

where epsilon represents some small value and the notation $| x |$ means the positive value of x. To achieve this, we require a function to obtain the absolute value of some quantity. This function could be written using the conditional operator:

```
double absolute (x)
  double x;
  {
    return (x < 0 ? -x : x);
  }
```

With this function, the original expression may be written using:

```
#define EPSILON    1.0E - 4
absolute (a - b) < EPSILON
```

Note that the functions *abs* and *fabs* are normally members of the standard library and, respectively, obtain the absolute value of an integer and a floating point argument. For details, see Appendix F5.

6.5 The while statement

The fundamental means of constructing iterative clauses in C is the *while* statement. The syntax of the while statement is:

while (expression)
    statement

where while is a reserved keyword.

The while statement is executed by first evaluating the *control expression* within the parentheses. If the result is non-zero, that is logical value true, then the statement is executed. The entire process is then repeated starting once again with evaluation of the expression. This looping continues until either because of the effect on the expression by execution of the statement or by a side effect of the expression itself, the expression now evaluates to zero. The value zero is the C representation for logical false. When the expression is zero, the loop terminates and the program continues execution with the next statement. A flow diagram for the while statement is given in Fig. 6.1.

The principal feature of the while statement is that the control expression is first tested before deciding whether or not to execute the associated statement. This means that if the expression on first evaluation produces zero (logical false) then the loop is never obeyed. Because of this, a while statement is often described as causing the statement under its control to be obeyed *none or more times*.

Where the logic of a problem requires more than a single statement to be executed under control of the while, a compound statement may be used:

while (expression)
    {
    statement 1;
    statement 2;
    _ _ _ _ _ _ _ _ _ _ ;
    _ _ _ _ _ _ _ _ _ _ ;
    }

We are now ready to explore programs containing loops. As we shall note, problems with loops give rise to solutions with similar structures. By being able to recognize this, such programs are relatively straightforward to implement. We can then apply the same type of solution to most programs exhibiting this feature.

Program 6.1, which follows, reads single characters from the standard input, copying each character as it is read, to the standard output. The copying continues until the first occurrence of a period (.) symbol is encountered in the data. The period is not copied and the program terminates. The use of a distinguishing data item to mark the end of the data set is a common programming device. This sentinel guards the end of the data. It is often referred to as the *end of file record*.

The use of an iterative statement in the solution to this program is suggested by the form of the data. The program data are a list or series of

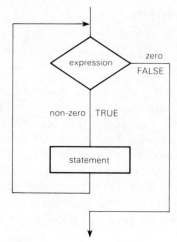

Fig. 6.1

single-character data items. Where the structure of the program's data has this form, the equivalent program structure is:

    while (more data items)
      process data item

To generate the program design, we first extend our PDL with an iterative clause based on the while statement. The structure is:

    WHILE some condition
    DO
      some statement(s)
    ENDWHILE

As before, both the condition and the statement(s) are expressed as concise informal descriptions of the actions to be performed. Applying this to our programming problem, we arrive at the first-level solution:

    read first character
    WHILE this character is not the period symbol
    DO
      print this character
      read next character
    ENDWHILE

Each action and expression is directly expressible in C. No further analysis is therefore necessary. We can immediately encode the solution as shown in Program 6.1.

Program 6.1

```
/*
**      Read a sequence of characters from the standard input
**      and echo them to the standard output. Terminate the
**      program upon the first occurrence of a period (.)
**      symbol in the data set.
*/

#include <stdio.h>

#define PERIOD              '.'

main()
  {
    char c;                     /* data item */

    c = getchar();              /* get first character */
    while (c != PERIOD)         /* test for end of data */
      {
        putchar(c);             /* copy to standard output */
        c = getchar();          /* get next character */
      }
  }
```

The program operates by first reading the initial data character. The character just read is then compared in the while control expression against the period symbol. Providing it is not the period, the character is copied to the output and the next data character is read. The looping continues until the period terminator appears in the data, at which point the loop and the program terminate. Notice that if the first data character is a period, the loop is never entered. An initial period means that there are no characters to be copied, corresponding to non-execution of the while loop.

This and many other programs involving loops have the same solution pattern. First some initialization is performed before entering the loop. This includes, among other things, any initialization associated with the first iteration of the loop. In Program 6.1 the first character is read so that the loop condition can be evaluated. This is known as the *read ahead* mechanism. We must read the first data item otherwise we cannot determine whether or not to obey the loop for the first time. Equally, the read ahead mechanism applies to all subsequent data items.

Second, the condition controlling repetition of the loop is expressed. This determines how the loop will be terminated. In the example program, the required condition is that the current character is not the period symbol.

Thirdly, some processing associated with the loop is executed. One or more statements will make up this processing logic. This often consists of processing one or more items of input data or of processing internally generated data. In the example, the processing is trivial. The data character previously read from the standard input is copied to the standard output.

Finally, the necessary actions are taken before determining whether the loop is to continue. This is the side effect which influences continuation of the loop. For our problem, the next data character is read from the input.

The shape of this solution in our PDL is:

initialize before entering loop
WHILE condition controlling execution of the loop
DO
    processing logic
    set up for next iteration
ENDWHILE

We observe the same solution structure in Program 6.2. This program reads a series of positive floating point values. The data set terminates with a negative value sentinel. The program forms the sum of the positive values. The initialization consists of zeroing the summation and reading the first data item. The condition for loop continuation is that the current data value is positive. The processing logic consists of forming a running total and setting up for another iteration by reading the next data value. Expressed in our PDL we arrive at:

initialize the sum to zero`
read first number
WHILE this number is positive
DO
    add the number to the sum
    read next number
ENDWHILE
print the sum

Program 6.2

```
/*
**      Read a series of positive floating point numbers
**      and form their sum. The data are terminated with
**      a unique negative value.
*/

#include <stdio.h>

#define ZERO                    0.0

main()
{
    float data, sum = ZERO;              /* data and running total */

    scanf("%f", &data);             /* get first data item */
    while (data >= ZERO)            /* data terminator? */
    {
        sum += data;                    /* form the sum */
        scanf("%f", &data);             /* get the next data item */
    }
    printf("The sum is %f\n", sum);
}
```

This same shape is also readily recognizable in the next program. The program operates on no input data. All the data are generated by the program itself. The program computes the sum of the first 20 integers:

$1 + 2 + 3 + ... + 20$. Once again the program's data are an iteration of values. This time, they happen to be generated by the program and not provided as input data. The same analysis still applies – the program structure mirrors the data structure.

Program 6.3(a)

```
/*
**        Compute the total of the first 20 positive integers.
**        The program requires no data. All data values in the
**        program are self-generated.
*/

#include <stdio.h>

#define INITIAL              1
#define MAX                 20
#define ZERO                 0

main()
   {
      int data, sum = ZERO;               /* data and running total */

      data = INITIAL;                     /* initial integer */
      while (data <= MAX)                 /* terminate loop? */
         {
            sum += data;                  /* form running total */
            data++;                       /* set up next integer */
         }
      printf("The sum of the first 20 integers is %d\n", sum);
   }
```

The same result can be achieved by counting downward from 20 to 1. The major difference between the two program versions is the condition to terminate the loop.

Program 6.3(b)

```
/*
**        Form the sum of the first 20 positive integers.
**        Self-generate the integer sequence 20, 19, ...,2, 1
**        and simultaneously sum.
*/

#include <stdio.h>

#define MAX                 20
#define ZERO                 0

main()
   {
      int data, sum = ZERO;               /* data and running total */

      data = MAX;                         /* first integer value */
      while (data > ZERO)                 /* loop control */
         {
            sum += data;                  /* form running total */
            data--;                       /* next integer value */
         }
      printf("The sum of the first 20 integers is %d\n", sum);
   }
```

It is common practice when writing such fragments of a C program to incorporate all or part of the loop control into one place in the program.

This unifies these related activities. The program is generally then more readable since control of the loop is no longer scattered amongst other processing statements.

Program 6.1 can be rewritten by incorporating the reading and testing of the single data character into the control expression. The solution is shown in Program 6.4.

Program 6.4

```
/*
**        Copy a character sequence from the standard input
**        to the standard output. The data are terminated by
**        the first occurrence of a period (.) symbol.
*/

#include <stdio.h>

#define PERIOD                  '.'

main()
  {
    char c;                                 /* data character */

    while ((c = getchar()) != PERIOD)   /* read and test data */
      putchar(c);
  }
```

Since the inequality operator has higher precedence than the assignment operator, it is necessary to ensure that the assignment is performed first. This we achieve with the additional parentheses. If we were to omit the extra parentheses, then the expression:

c = getchar( )! = PERIOD

would evaluate to:

c = (getchar( )! = PERIOD)

First a character is read and compared with the symbolic constant PERIOD. This evaluates to logical true (integer 1) or logical false (integer 0). The value 0 or 1 is then assigned to the character variable c.

In the program above, the strategy is to perform a combined assignment and conditional test in a single expression. The assignment is performed first, then the test. A similar approach can be taken when rewriting Program 6.2. The assignment is performed through a scanf function call. The condition is then tested. The sequencing of these two actions is achieved with the comma operator. The comma operator guarantees sequential execution of each expression. The returned value is that of the last executed expression – the required condition.

Program 6.5

```
/*
**        Sum a sequence of positive floating point values.
**        The series is of indeterminate length, but is
**        terminated with a negative number.
*/
```

```
#include <stdio.h>

#define ZERO                     0.0

main()
  {
    float data, sum = ZERO;
                                /* data and running total */

    while (scanf("%f", &data), data >= ZERO)    /* read and test */
      sum += data;                              /* processing */
    printf("The sum is %f\n", sum);
  }
```

A final example illustrates how the unary decrement operator combines with the loop condition testing. We remember that the logical value false is represented by the value zero, whilst any non-zero value represents logical true. We can therefore establish a loop which counts downward from some initial positive value, terminating when the count reaches zero. Whilst the count is not zero, the loop continues. In Program 6.6, the data consist of a single positive integer value followed by a series of floating point values. The integer specifies the number of supplied floating point values. The program calculates the mean (average) of the floating point numbers.

Program 6.6

```
/*
**        Compute the mean of a number of floating point values.
**        The program data consist of an integer N, followed
**        by N floats.
*/

#include <stdio.h>

#define ZERO                     0.0

main()
  {
    int    count, number;
                                /* loop control, number of values */
    float data, sum = ZERO;            /* data and running total */

    scanf("%d", &number);              /* read how many floats */
    count = number;                    /* initialize loop control */
    while (count--)                    /* cycle number of times */
      {
        scanf("%f", &data);            /* read data value */
        sum += data;                   /* process it */
      }
    printf("Mean is %f\n", sum/number);
  }
```

When developing software, we must endeavor to ensure its *robustness*. A robust program should, under all conditions, terminate in a controlled manner. If this last program was presented with the single data value 0, then no floating point numbers are to be averaged. The loop is therefore never executed, and the expression printed, i.e. sum/number, is evaluated as 0.0/0. Upon evaluation, the expression generates an overflow condition and the program abruptly terminates. To ensure that the program is more secure, this condition should be tested. Similarly, if the integer input value

is negative, the program loops forever. A negative-valued count is interpreted as logical true. The value remains negative through decrementing.
Ultimately, negative overflow occurs and the program dies. We introduce
the statement to achieve this level of security later in this chapter.

There is no restriction on the statement or statements under control of a
while statement. It is permissible to have while statements controlling other
while statements. This gives rise to a construct known as nested while loops
or simply *nested loops*. The operation of nested while statements is
analogous to the hour and minute hands of a clock. The minute hand moves
with rapidity from minute to minute. When the minute hand completes a
cycle of 60 minutes, the hour hand advances by one hour. The minute hand
then repeats the same rapid cycle. Similarly with nested while statements.
The outer while statement progresses more slowly than the inner while
statement. When the inner while statement completes one cycle, the outer
while advances to the next iteration and the inner while restarts with a new
inner loop.

Nested loops in a program arise from data sets which exhibit the same
nested structure. A bank account program may process the accounts for a
number of customers. The initial data analysis reveals that we have a series
or iteration on customers. The resulting program outline is then:

> WHILE more customers
> DO
>   process one customer
> ENDWHILE

Each customer, in turn, may hold a number of accounts. Again, an
iteration on accounts for a given customer. We refine 'process one
customer', replacing it with a loop over the customer's accounts:

> WHILE more customers
> DO
>   WHILE more accounts for this customer
>   DO
>   process customer's account
>   ENDWHILE
> ENDWHILE

These ideas are present in the next program, the output from which has a
nested iterative structure.

Program 6.7 plots a solid isosceles triangle composed of asterisk (*)
symbols. The first line contains a single asterisk. The second line contains
three asterisks centered below the first, and so on. The full triangle spans
five lines. The outer loop controls the number of lines to be displayed. Each
line consists of a number of leading blanks and a number of asterisks. The
number of blanks and the number of asterisks on any one line is dependent
upon which line is being printed. Both the leading blanks and the asterisks
are printed by two successive loops contained within the outer loop.

Program 6.7

```
/*
**      Form an isosceles triangle composed of asterisk
**      symbols. The first line contains a single * symbol.
**      The second line contains three asterisks centered
**      below the first, and so on. In all, the figure
**      spans five lines.
*/

#include <stdio.h>

#define NUMLINES            5
#define BLANK              ' '
#define ASTERISK           '*'
#define NEWLINE            '\n'

main()
   {
    int line;                           /* five line counter */
    int leading_blanks;                 /* left margin counter */
    int stars;                          /* number of asterisks */

    line = 1;
    while (line <= NUMLINES)             /* for each line */
       {
        leading_blanks = 1;
        while (leading_blanks++ <= NUMLINES - line)      /* margin */
          putchar(BLANK);

        stars = 1;
        while (stars++ <= 2 * line - 1)          /* asterisks */
          putchar(ASTERISK);

        putchar(NEWLINE);
        line++;
       }
   }
```

The control expression in a while statement governs whether the loop is to be obeyed or to be terminated. Any non-zero expression value represents logical true and causes the loop to be obeyed one further time. A non-zero integer constant for this expression gives rise to what is known as an infinite loop. An infinite loop cycles indefinitely, never terminating.

```
#define TRUE              1
_ _ _ _ _ _ _ _ _ _
_ _ _ _ _ _ _ _ _ _

while (TRUE)
{
   _ _ _ _ _ _ _ _ _ _
   _ _ _ _ _ _ _ _ _ _
}
```

A program containing such a construct will run forever unless some action is taken to stop it or some statement embedded within the body of the loop is able to break the cycle. Section 6.9 introduces the appropriate statement. An infinite loop containing a statement to break the cycle at some prescribed junction can provide a natural way of expressing certain constructs.

6.6 The for statement

The for statement is closely related to the while statement. The syntax of the for statement is given by:

```
for (expression1; expression2; expression3)
    statement
```

with for a reserved keyword. Like the while statement, the statement under control of the for may be a single statement or a compound statement. Any of the statements controlled by the for may be another for statement giving rise to nested for loops.

The for statement is semantically equivalent to:

```
expression1;
while (expression2)
    {
    statement;
    expression3;
    }
```

The first expression is used to initialize the loop. Then expression2 is evaluated and if it is non-zero (logical true) then the statement is executed. Expression3 is evaluated, and control passes back to the loop beginning, to re-evaluate expression2. Normally, expression2 is a logical expression used to control the iteration. Note that if this expression initially evaluates to zero (logical false), the loop is never entered. The third expression is frequently used to update some loop control variable before repeating the loop.

Two examples of the for statement are:

```
for (k = 1; k <= 10; k++)
    printf("The square of %d is %d\n", k, k * k);
```

and:

```
sum = 0;
for (i = 1; i <= m; i++)
    sum += i;
```

The first example generates and prints a table of the squares of the first ten integers. In the second example, the sum of the first m integers is computed. By employing the comma operator, the initialization of variable sum and the control variable i may both be accomplished in expression1. The second example may then be written as:

```
for (sum = 0, i = 1; i <= m; i++)
    sum += i;
```

The use of the comma operator is equally applicable to all three expressions in the for statement.

Any or all of the three expressions in a for statement may be omitted, but the two semicolon separators and the parentheses are mandatory. If expression1 is missing, no initialization step is performed as part of the for loop. The last example might have been coded:

```
sum = 0;
i = 1;
for (; i < = m; i + + )
    sum + = i;
```

Equally, we might have absorbed the increment to variable i into the assignment forming the running total for sum. In this case, the third expression can also be removed:

```
sum = 0;
i = 1;
for (; i < = m;)
    sum + = i + + ;
```

When expression2 is missing, the condition always evaluates to logical true. Thus, the loop in the code:

```
for (; ; )
    {
    _ _ _ _ _ _ _ _ _ _
    _ _ _ _ _ _ _ _ _ _
    }
```

is the infinite loop. It parallels the infinite while loop shown in the previous section. One frequently finds the following #define used to establish an infinite loop:

```
# define FOREVER        for (; ; )
FOREVER
    {
    _ _ _ _ _ _ _ _ _ _
    _ _ _ _ _ _ _ _ _ _
    }
```

The FOREVER explicitly indicates the nature of this specialized loop.

Since the for statement is semantically equivalent to the while statement, it can equally well be used with iterative data structures. In certain instances, the for statement more naturally expresses the iterative processing logic than the while statement. For example, the loop in Program 6.3(a) is better represented by:

```
for (data = INITIAL; data < = MAX; data + + ) ....
```

when a known number of iterations is required.

We illustrate a simple example of the use of a for statement by repeating

Program 6.1. The first and last expressions of the for are unused. The second expression controls the iteration.

Program 6.8

```
/*
**      Read a series of characters from the standard
**      input and echo them to the standard output. The
**      program finishes when the period symbol is
**      encountered in the data.
*/

#include <stdio.h>

#define PERIOD                  '.'

main()
   {
   char c;

   for (; (c = getchar()) != PERIOD; )
      putchar(c);
   }
```

Working with the same data as Programs 6.1 and 6.8, we can develop a modified version which counts the number of data characters. The terminating period is omitted from the count. The first expression is used to initialize the count. The final expression is empty as nothing is to be done before advancing to the next iteration. The second expression again controls program looping. The statement under control of the loop increments the counter for each character read.

Program 6.9(a)

```
/*
**      Count the number of characters read from the standard
**      input. The character stream is terminated with the
**      first occurrence of the period symbol.
*/

#include <stdio.h>

#define PERIOD                  '.'

main()
   {
   char c;                              /* data character */
   int  count;                          /* character counter */

   for (count = 0; (c = getchar()) != PERIOD; )
      count++;
   printf("Number of characters is %d\n", count);
   }
```

The third expression could also be the place to perform the increment to the counter. In that case, there is now no statement to be controlled by the for statement. The program logic is completely encapsulated by the three for statement expressions. The statement consisting solely of the semicolon symbol is called the *null* statement. As the semicolon is easily 'lost' when reading the code, we annotate it with a comment.

Program 6.9(b)

```
/*
**        Count the number of characters read from the standard
**        input. The character stream is terminated with the
**        first occurrence of the period symbol.
*/

#include <stdio.h>

#define PERIOD                      '.'

main()
   {
   char c;                              /* data character */
   int  count;                          /* character counter */

   for (count = 0; (c = getchar()) != PERIOD; count++)
      /* do nothing */  ;
   printf("Number of characters is %d\n", count);
   }
```

By using the comma operator in the three for statement expressions, very dense and cryptic C code can be produced. The code is both difficult to read and maintain if modification or correction is required. Because of this, the reader is not encouraged to indulge in this type of coding. This coding, however, may be experienced in others' programs. We illustrate with the following example.

A series of positive floating point values are given as data. The data set is terminated with a negative floating point number. Program 6.10 computes the mean of the positive data values. Note how all the processing and loop control logic is compacted into the three for statement expressions.

Program 6.10

```
/*
**        Compute the mean of a number of positive floating
**        point values. The data consist of a series of
**        positive values, terminated with a negative number.
*/

#include <stdio.h>

main()
   {
   int    count;                    /* count the positives */
   float data, sum;                 /* data item, running total */

   for (count = 0, sum = 0.0;
        scanf("%f", &data), data >= 0.0;
        sum += data, count++)
      /* do nothing */  ;
   printf("The mean is %f\n", sum/count);
   }
```

6.7 The do statement

As previously noted, the while statement tests the condition (expression) before obeying the loop. Since the for statement is semantically equivalent to the while, it too tests before entering the loop. In both cases if the condition is initially zero (logical false), then the loop is never obeyed at all.

Normally, iterative constructs are more logically coded using loops with initial condition checking (while and for). In a small number of cases, checking is required at the conclusion of the loop body. In these cases the do statement is the appropriate construct.

The do statement has the form:

```
do
    statement
while (expression)
```

The distinction between this statement and the while and for statements is that the conditional test is performed *after* executing the loop. The loop body is then guaranteed to be obeyed at least once. After first executing the statement, the expression is evaluated. If it is non-zero (logical true) then control passes back to the beginning of the do statement and the processing repeats. When the expression evaluates to zero (logical false), control passes to the next program statement.

The statement under control of the do may be a single statement or a compound statement. In the latter case, the form of the do statement is:

```
do
{
    statement 1;
    statement 2;
    _ _ _ _ _ _ _ _ _
    _ _ _ _ _ _ _ _ _
} while (expression)
```

Consider a program to read a single positive integer value and to output the digits of that number in reverse sequence. For example, if the input value is 1234, then the output is 4321. The logic consists of repeatedly extracting the rightmost digit of the number and printing it. The digit is then removed from the number before continuing. The iteration stops when the number is reduced to zero. The solution, expressed in our extended PDL, is:

```
read the number
REPEAT
    obtain the rightmost digit
    print the digit
    remove the digit from the number
WHILE number is non-zero
```

and the program is as follows.

Program 6.11

```
/*
**      Read a single positive integer value and output
**      the digits of that number in reverse sequence. For
**      example, if the input value is 1234, then the output
**      is 4321.
*/
```

```
#include <stdio.h>

main()
{
    int number, digit;          /* data value, rightmost digit */

    scanf("%d", &number);       /* input data item */
    do
        {
        digit = number % 10;    /* obtain rightmost digit .... */
        printf("%1d", digit);   /* .... and print it */
        number /= 10;           /* reduce the number */
        } while (number != 0);  /* repeat until nothing left */
    printf("\n");
}
```

We might have considered coding the problem with a while statement:

```
scanf("%d", &number);
while (number ! = 0)
    {
    digit = number % 10;
    printf("%1d", digit);
    number /= 10;
    }
```

The same input number 1234 produces the same output 4321. However, note what happens if the input value is 0 (zero). Since the do statement is obeyed once, the output is 0. However, when the solution is in terms of the while statement, which is obeyed none or more times, no output is produced as the loop is never entered. The do statement solution guarantees the display of at least one digit in all cases. This is the better solution since no output from a program can mislead the user into thinking that the program has somehow failed.

Case study 6.1: Reports

A student class is partitioned into a number of project groups. The number of students in each group is not necessarily always the same. Each student in the class is given an assessment and assigned a raw mark measured out of 80. A report is required showing the assessment for each student, for each group and for the entire class. The report format is shown below.

PROJECT REPORT

PROJECT GROUP 1

	IDENTIFICATION NUMBER	RAW MARK (/80)	PERCENTAGE MARK
	1234	40	50
	5678	55	68
	9012	30	37
GROUP 1 TOTAL			155

PROJECT GROUP 2

	IDENTIFICATION NUMBER	RAW MARK (/80)	PERCENTAGE MARK
	3456	10	12
	7890	20	25
	9876	30	37
	5432	40	50
	1098	50	62
	7654	60	75
	3210	70	87
GROUP 2 TOTAL			348
GRAND TOTAL			503

No account is to be taken of page breaks in the report.

The program input consists of a series of records presented one per line. Each record gives the student's identification number and the raw assessment mark. The records are batched into project groupings with the group number prepended to each record. A trailer record containing all zeros terminates the groups, whilst another trailer record containing all nines terminates the data. The sample data set for the illustrated report above is:

```
1    1234    40
1    5678    55
1    9012    30
0    0000    00
2    3456    10
2    7890    20
2    9876    30
2    5432    40
2    1098    50
2    7654    60
2    3210    70
0    0000    00
9    9999    99
```

Analysis of the data indicates that nested iteration is required. Two repeating groups are present in the data – a repetition over the project groups and a repetition over the students in each group. The outer iteration cycles through each project group, with the inner iteration processing each student in that group. The outline logic for this processing is:

```
initialize grand total
produce class report heading
read first record
WHILE not the end of data record
DO
        initialize project group total
        produce project group headings
```

REPEAT
>   process the current record
>   read the next record
> WHILE not the end of group record
> produce project group summary
> add project group total to grand total
> read the next record

ENDWHILE
produce class report summary

The coding for the program is now relatively straightforward. The PDL is
sufficiently close to the final version that we can convert to code directly.

```
/*
**      A student class is partitioned into a number of project
**      groups, not necessarily of equal sizes. Each student
**      in the class is assigned an assessment mark measured
**      out of 80. Produce a report showing the assessment for
**      each student, for each project group and for the whole
**      class.
*/

#include <stdio.h>

#define GROUP_TRAILER           0
#define FILE_TRAILER            9

main()
    {
    int grand_total;                        /* percent mark */
    int group_total;                        /* percent mark */
    int group_no, current_group_no;         /* project groups */
    int identification;                     /* student number */
    int raw, percent;                       /* student assessment mark */

    grand_total = 0;
    printf("\t\t\tPROJECT REPORT\n\n");

    while (scanf("%d %d %d", &group_no, &identification, &raw),
            group_no != FILE_TRAILER)
        {
        printf("PROJECT GROUP %2d\n", group_no);
        printf("\t\tIDENTIFICATION\tRAW\t\tPERCENTAGE\n");
        printf("\t\tNUMBER\t\tMARK (/80)\tMARK\n");
        current_group_no = group_no;

        group_total = 0;
        do
            {
            percent = raw * 100 / 80;
            printf("\t\t%4d\t\t%2d\t\t%3d\n", identification,
                    raw, percent);
            group_total += percent;
            scanf("%d %d %d", &group_no, &identification, &raw);
            } while (group_no != GROUP_TRAILER);
        printf("\tGROUP %2d TOTAL\t\t\t    %6d\n\n",
                current_group_no, group_total);

        grand_total += group_total;
        }
    printf("GRAND TOTAL\t\t\t\t    %6d\n\n", grand_total);
    }
```

6.8 The if statement

The general form of the if statement is:

```
if (expression)
    statement 1;
else
    statement 2;
```

where if and else are reserved keywords. If the expression evaluates to non-zero (logical value true), statement 1 is executed and control then passes to the next program statement following the if statement. If the value of the expression is zero (logical false), statement 2 is executed. Pictorially, the if statement can be described by the flow diagram in Fig. 6.2.

Both statement 1 and statement 2 may be single statements or compound statements. Any statement may be used, including another if statement, forming a nested if statement. Some examples of valid if statements are:

```
if (count = = 0)
    printf("The count is zero\n");
else
    printf("The count is not zero\n");

if (a < b)
    printf("Originally, a less than b\n");
else
    {
    temp = a;
    a = b;
    b = a;
    printf("Interchange a and b\n");
    }
```

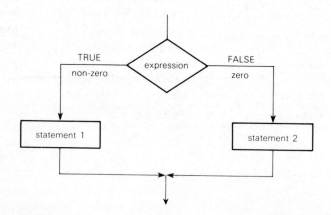

Fig. 6.2

```
if (ch = = ' ' || ch = = '\t' || ch = = '\n')
  {
  whitespace + + ;
  printf("More whitespace characters\n");
  }
else
  others + + ;
```

We may also include another if statement as either or both of the statement parts. This gives rise to what is known as a nested if statement. Examples include:

```
if (expression 1)
  if (expression 2)
    statement 1;
  else
    statement 2;
else
  statement 3;
```

Semantically this is equivalent to:

```
if (expression 1)
  {
  if (expression 2)
    statement 1;
  else
    statement 2;
  }
else
  statement 3;
```

In many instances it is better to incorporate the braces. Their presence highlights the structure of an otherwise complex statement. An actual example with explicit braces is:

```
if (number > 20)
  {
  if (number < 30)
    printf("Number between 21 and 29 inclusive\n");
  else
    printf("Number exceeds 29\n");
  }
else
  printf("Number does not exceed 20\n");
```

Similarly, an if statement may be used in the else clause of another if statement:

```
if (expression 1)
    statement 1;
else
    if (expression 2)
        statement 2;
    else
        statement 3;
```

Semantically, this is equivalent to:

```
if (expression 1)
    statement 1;
else
    {
    if (expression 2)
        statement 2;
    else
        statement 3;
    }
```

Again, the braces are often best included where it is felt the structure needs to be emphasized. An example of this form is:

```
if (ch > = 'a' && ch < = 'z')
    printf("Lowercase letter\n");
else
    {
    if (ch > = '0' && ch < = '9')
        printf("Digit symbol\n");
    else
        printf("Other symbol\n");
    }
```

In the present form the if statement provides a means of selecting one of two distinct logic paths. Sometimes we wish to select whether or not to obey some statement or statements. This is achieved through a shortened version of the if statement:

```
if (expression)
    statement;
```

If the expression evaluates to logical true (non-zero) the statement is obeyed. Having obeyed the statement the program continues with the next instruction following this if statement. If the expression evaluates to logical false (zero) the statement is ignored and the program continues with the next statement. The statement part under control of this if statement may, as before, be a single statement or a compound statement.

When using this last form of if statement, an ambiguous construct can arise where the statement part is itself an if statement:

```
if (expression 1)
   if (expression 2)
      statement 1;
   else
      statement 2;
```

The ambiguity arises from the fact that we are unable to say whether the else part belongs with 'if (expression 1)' or with 'if (expression 2)'. Two possible interpretations are:

```
(a) if (expression 1)              (b) if (expression 1)
       {                                  {
         if (expression 2)                  if (expression 2)
            statement 1;                       statement 1;
         else                               }
            statement 2;                  else
       }                                     statement 2;
```

In version (a) the else part associates with 'if (expression 2)'. In version (b) the else part associates with 'if (expression 1)'. This ambiguity, known as the 'dangling else problem', is resolved by the compiler always associating an else part with the nearest unmatched preceding if. Version (a) is therefore the correct interpretation. Explicit braces as shown in version (a) can often improve the readability of the code.

Various combinations of if statements can occur. The statement associated with the else clause may be another if-else statement. Equally, the next else clause may be yet another if-else statement, and so on. To illustrate, consider a program fragment to read an examination score and to assign a letter grade based on the score. The grading scheme that applies is:

```
Score: 80–100       Grade: A
       70–79              B
       60–69              C
       50–59              D
       40–49              E
        0–39              F
```

A single nested if statement can describe the necessary processing:

```
if (score > = 80)
   grade = 'A';
else
   if (score > = 70)
      grade = 'B';
```

```
    else
      if (score > = 60)
        grade = 'C';
      else
        if (score > = 50)
          grade = 'D';
        else
          if (score > = 40)
            grade = 'E';
          else
            grade = 'F';
```

The whole construct is a single statement forming a cascading chain of if statements. Suppose, for example, that the score is 65. The first two expressions evaluate to logical false and the corresponding two statements, grade = 'A' and grade = 'B', are skipped. The third expression evaluates to logical true and the statement grade = 'C' is executed. Control then passes to the end of this statement.

The proper indentation for such a construct is shown as above. As can be seen, the structure rapidly tracks to the right. To avoid this situation, these statements are generally presented as:

```
if (score > = 80)
  grade = 'A';
else if (score > = 70)
  grade = 'B';
else if (score > = 60)
  grade = 'C';
else if (score > = 50)
  grade = 'D';
else if (score > = 40)
  grade = 'E';
else
  grade = 'F';
```

The if statement is used in programs in which the data offer a selection. If the program data offer a choice between, say, data item 1 and data item 2, then the corresponding program structure (expressed in our PDL) is a conditional:

```
IF data item 1
THEN
  process data item 1
ELSE
  process data item 2
ENDIF
```

Program 6.12 illustrates a simple use of an if statement. The program inputs two floating point numbers and outputs them in ascending order. The program data can be either already ordered or in descending order. These alternatives are reflected in the solution structure:

read the two data values
IF first value less than second
THEN
    print first and second
ELSE
    print second and first
ENDIF

Program 6.12

```
/*
**        Read two floating point values and display them in
**        ascending order.
*/

#include <stdio.h>

main()
    {
    float first, second;                  /* data items */

    scanf("%f %f", &first, &second);
    if (first < second)
      printf("%f %f\n", first, second);
    else
      printf("%f %f\n", second, first);
    }
```

The second program in this series operates on a sequence of characters of unknown length. The data set is terminated with a period symbol. The character sequence spans a number of lines and the program determines the number of text lines by enumerating the number of newline symbols. The program employs an if statement with no else part, used to detect the newline characters. The program data are an iteration of single characters. The corresponding program structure is then a loop. The PDL is:

WHILE read next character; character is not terminator
DO
    process the character
ENDWHILE

The character processing is a selection. If the character is a newline symbol, the line counter is incremented. If the character is not a newline symbol it is ignored. The final PDL is:

initialize line counter
WHILE read next character; character is not terminator
DO

IF a newline symbol
THEN
    increment line counter
ENDIF
ENDWHILE
print final line counter value

Program 6.13

```
/*
**      Read a sequence of characters of indeterminate length
**      and count the number of lines of text by enumerating
**      the number of newline symbols. The data are terminated
**      by a period symbol.
*/

#include <stdio.h>

#define PERIOD                  '.'
#define NEWLINE                 '\n'

main()
   {
    char c;                              /* data character */
    int  lines = 0;                      /* line counter */

    while ((c = getchar()) != PERIOD)
      if (c == NEWLINE)
        lines++;
    printf("Number of lines is %d\n", lines);
   }
```

Operating with the same data as in the program above, we develop a program to count the number of 'words' in the input character sequence. A word is defined to be any character sequence separated by whitespace characters (blanks, tabs and newlines).

Once again the data are a repetition of characters, giving rise to the same initial program structure:

WHILE read next character; character not the terminator
DO
    process the character
ENDWHILE

The character processing must select from a whitespace character or a non-whitespace character. The former indicates that the input is no longer part of a word and a flag is set accordingly. For a non-whitespace character two possibilities exist. If the previous data item was also a non-whitespace character, then we continue to be part of the same word. If the preceding symbol was a whitespace character then we are processing the first character of a new word and the word counter is incremented. The overall PDL is:

initialize word count and in-word flag
WHILE read next character; character not the terminator
DO
   IF a whitespace character
   THEN
     unset the in-word flag
   ELSE
     IF start of new word
     THEN
       increment word count
       set the in-word flag
     ENDIF
   ENDIF
ENDWHILE
print final word count

Program 6.14

```
/*
**      A piece of text consists of a character sequence
**      spanning a number of lines and terminated by a period
**      symbol. Count the number of 'words' in the text.
**      A word is defined as any character string delimited
**      by whitespace (blank, tab and newline) symbols.
*/

#include <stdio.h>

#define PERIOD          '.'
#define BLANK           ' '
#define TAB             '\t'
#define NEWLINE         '\n'

#define FALSE           0
#define TRUE            1

main()
  {
    char c;                             /* data character */
    int  words = 0;                     /* word counter */
    int  inword = FALSE;                /* word indicator */

    while ((c = getchar()) != PERIOD)
      if (c == BLANK || c == TAB || c == NEWLINE)
        inword = FALSE;
      else if (! inword)
        {
          inword = TRUE;
          words++;
        }
    printf("Number of words is %d\n", words);
  }
```

Once more with the same data, we count the number of occurrences of lower-case letters, upper-case letters, digits and other symbols. A nested if statement provides the necessary logic.

Program 6.15

```
/*
**       Enumerate the number of occurrences of lower-case
**       letters, upper-case letters, digits and other symbols
**       in a data set consisting of a character sequence
**       terminated with a period symbol.
*/

#include <stdio.h>

#define PERIOD               '.'

#define LCASEA               'a'
#define LCASEZ               'z'
#define UCASEA               'A'
#define UCASEZ               'Z'
#define DIGIT0               '0'
#define DIGIT9               '9'

main()
    {
    char c;                                  /* data character */
    int  lowercase, uppercase, digits, others; /* counters */

    lowercase = uppercase = digits = others = 0;
    while ((c = getchar()) != PERIOD)
      if (c >= LCASEA && c <= LCASEZ)
        lowercase++;
      else if (c >= UCASEA && c <= UCASEZ)
        uppercase++;
      else if (c >= DIGIT0 && c <= DIGIT9)
        digits++;
      else
        others++;

    printf("Number of lower-case letters %d\n", lowercase);
    printf("Number of upper-case letters %d\n", uppercase);
    printf("Number of decimal digits %d\n", digits);
    printf("Number of other symbols %d\n", others);
    }
```

The final program in this section is a multifunction program making extensive use of the conditional if statement. The program accepts as input a date expressed in numerical form and verbalizes it. The input date appears in the form:

DD/MM/YYYY

for example:

10/12/1985

The input date is assumed to be valid. The output from the program (for the above) is:

Tuesday 10 December 1985

To calculate the day of the week for a given date, Zeller's congruence can be employed. The algorithm computes for any valid date an integer in the range 0 to 6 inclusive, with 0 representing Sunday, 1 Monday, and so on. The congruence is:

$$z = \left\{ \frac{26m - 2}{10} + k + D + \left[\frac{D}{4} \right] + \left[\frac{C}{4} \right] - 2C \right\} \bmod 7$$

The braces denote 'the greatest integer in', and mod 7 is the remainder (modulus) on dividing by 7. In the formula:

D = the year in the century
C = the century
k = the day of the month
m = month number, with January and February taken as months 11 and 12, respectively, of the preceding year. March is then month 1, April is 2, ..., December is 10

Thus, for 10/12/1985, D = 85, C = 19, k = 10 and m = 10. For January 1, 1800, k = 1, m = 11, C = 17 and D = 99.

The congruence for 10/12/1985 is:

$$z = \left\{ \frac{26 * 10 - 2}{10} + 10 + 85 + \left[\frac{85}{4} \right] + \left[\frac{19}{4} \right] - 2 * 19 \right\} \bmod 7$$

$$= \{25 + 10 + 85 + 21 + 4 - 38\} \bmod 7$$

$$= 107 \bmod 7$$

$$= 2$$

which, of course, is Tuesday. The program is as follows.

Program 6.16

```
/*
**        The program accepts as input a single date expressed
**        in the form DD/MM/YYYY and verbalizes it. For example,
**        the date 10/12/1985 produces the output:
**
**                Tuesday 10 December 1985
**
**        The input date is assumed to be valid and no checking
**        is performed.
*/

#include <stdio.h>

main()
   {
   int  day, month, year;                   /* input date */
   int  zell;                               /* congruence value */
   int  zeller();                           /* forward .... */
   void day_name(), month_name();           /* .... references */

   printf("Enter the date as DD/MM/YYYY: "); /* get the date */
   scanf("%2d/%2d/%4d", &day, &month, &year);
   zell = zeller(day, month, year);         /* apply congruence */
   day_name(zell);                          /* verbalize the day */
   printf("%2d", day);
   month_name(month);                       /* verbalize the month */
   printf("%4d\n", year);
   }

/*
**        Apply Zeller's congruence to a date expressed in
**        the form 21/11/1985. The date given is assumed to
**        be valid.
*/
```

```
int zeller(day, month, year)
  int day, month, year;                   /* input date */
  {
    int k, y, m, d, c;                    /* formula variables */
    int z;                                /* computed value */

    k = day;                              /* initialize */
    y = year;

    if (month < 3)                        /* formula month */
      {
        m = month + 10;
        y = year - 1;
      }
    else
      m = month - 2;

    d = y % 100;                          /* year and .... */
    c = y / 100;                          /* .... century */

    z = (26 * m - 2)/10 + k + d + (d/4) + (c/4) - 2 * c;
    return (z % 7);
  }

/*
**      Verbalize a day number, encoded according to Zeller's
**      congruence, into a variable length character string
**      surrounded by single blank characters.
*/

void day_name(d)
  int d;
  {
    if (d == 0)
      printf(" Sunday ");
    else if (d == 1)
      printf(" Monday ");
    else if (d == 2)
      printf(" Tuesday ");
    else if (d == 3)
      printf(" Wednesday ");
    else if (d == 4)
      printf(" Thursday ");
    else if (d == 5)
      printf(" Friday ");
    else
      printf(" Saturday ");
  }


/*
**      Verbalize a month number in the range 1 to 12 inclusive
**      into a variable length character string surrounded
**      by single blank characters.
*/

void month_name(m)
  int m;                                  /* month number, 1 .. 12 */
  {
    if (m == 1)
      printf(" January ");
    else if (m == 2)
      printf(" February ");
    else if (m == 3)
      printf(" March ");
    else if (m == 4)
      printf(" April ");
    else if (m == 5)
      printf(" May ");
    else if (m == 6)
      printf(" June ");
    else if (m == 7)
      printf(" July ");
```

```
    else if (m == 8)
      printf(" August ");
    else if (m == 9)
      printf(" September ");
    else if (m == 10)
      printf(" October ");
    else if (m == 11)
      printf(" November ");
    else
      printf(" December ");
}
```

Case study 6.2: Bank statement

A program is required to read details of transactions on a bank account and produce a statement summarizing these transactions. The program input consists of a sequence of integer values. The first value is a positive integer representing the bank account number. The second integer value is the initial balance of the account. The remaining integer values are either positive or negative and represent the transactions. The final transaction is the unique trailer value 0. A positive transaction represents a deposit (credit transaction) and a negative transaction represents a withdrawal (debit transaction).

For example, given the input data 1234, 847, − 150, − 35, + 30, − 249, − 172, + 55 and 0, the bank statement produced should appear as shown in Fig. 6.3.

The first-level design of the bank statement program is relatively straightforward. After the first two data values have been read, the statement headers and the initial balance line may be printed. Successive transactions are read and processed until the end of data trailer record is processed. Finally, the statement summary is generated. In outline, the program is:

    read account number and initial balance
    print statement headers and initial balance
    initialize credit and debit totals
    read the first transaction
    initialize the transaction counter
    WHILE not end of data value
    DO
        process and print this transaction
        read the next transaction
        increment the transaction counter
    ENDWHILE
    print the statement summary

Given this outline it is possible to be satisfied about its correctness. Using sample test data, such as that above, we can trace the program's behavior. Only when this implementation has been fully tested do we progress to the next phase and continue with the refinement.

| Bank Statement | | | |
Account number: 1234 Transaction	Credit	Debit	Balance
			847
1		150	697
2		35	662
3	30		692
4		249	443
5		172	271
6	55		326
Totals	85	606	326

Fig. 6.3

Printing the statement headers and producing the initial balance line is a self-contained task that should be isolated to a separate function. For it to operate correctly, the main function will need to provide this subsidiary function with the bank account number and the value of the initial balance.

The same analysis applies when we consider the statement summary. It too is programmed as a separate function. The summary is produced from the credit total, the debit total and the final balance. These values are communicated as arguments to the function.

Finally, we consider processing a single transaction. The transaction value is added to the current balance to produce the updated balance value. A positive transaction will increase the value of the balance when added to it. A negative transaction will reduce the value of the balance when added to it. Thus, no special processing is required to update the balance other than by adding the transaction value.

If the transaction is positive, the total credit value is changed. If the transaction is negative, the total debit is changed. When all the computations are complete, the transaction print line can be presented. The processing and printing of one transaction is assigned to a secondary function.

From this analysis we can complete the coding of function main. Note how even the detailed coding still reflects the original program design. Details concerned with printing headers, processing transactions and printing summaries are not allowed to clutter the simple logic of the main function.

```
main()
    {
    int account_number;               /* identification */
    int number_of_transaction;        /* transaction counter */
    int credit_total, debit_total;    /* total credits/debits */
    int transaction_value;            /* value of transaction */
    int balance;                      /* balance of the account */
    void print_headers(),
         process_transaction(), print_summary();

    credit_total = debit_total = 0;   /* initialize totals */
```

```
scanf("%d %d", &account_number, &balance);   /* initial data */
print_headers(account_number, balance);      /* initial headers */

scanf("%d", &transaction_value);     /* get first transaction */
number_of_transaction = 1;           /* initialize count */
while (transaction_value != 0)       /* end of data? */
    {
    process_transaction(number_of_transaction, transaction_value,
        &credit_total, &debit_total, &balance);

    scanf("%d", &transaction_value);   /* next transaction */
    number_of_transaction++;           /* update count */
    }

    print_summary(credit_total, debit_total, balance);
}
```

Processing and printing one transaction is covered by the function process_transaction. This function receives the transaction number and the value of the transaction. The function is also supplied with the addresses of the credit and debit totals and the current balance. Through these addresses the current values can be obtained and new updated values assigned. The new assignations are returned to main for transmission to the next processing task.

Coding the functions print_headers and print_summary is trivial. We leave these for the final program listing. The major subproblem we must solve is the coding for function process_transaction. Like main, we start with an outline:

add value of transaction to current balance
IF a credit transaction
THEN
    update current credit total
    print a credit statement line
ELSE
    update current debit total
    print a debit statement line
ENDIF

A positive transaction (credit) is added to the current credit total. The credit total is initially set to zero and increases positively when a transaction is accumulated. A negative transaction (debit) is subtracted from the debit total. Subtracting a negative value equates to adding a positive value. The debit total, therefore, also increases positively when a transaction is accumulated. Thus, both the credit and debit totals remain positive throughout the program execution, as required.

The format of a transaction statement line is determined by whether the transaction is a credit or a debit. Two prints using different formats selected by the if statement simplify this problem. The function coding is:

```
void process_transaction(number, transaction, credit, debit, balance)
   int    number;                          /* transaction number */
   int    transaction;                     /* transaction value */
   int    *credit;                         /* credit total */
   int    *debit;                          /* debit total */
   int    *balance;                        /* current balance */
   {
      *balance = *balance + transaction;
      if (transaction > 0)
         {                                  /* credit transaction */
            *credit = *credit + transaction;
            printf("%8d\t%8d\t\t\t%8d\n", number, transaction, *balance);
         }
      else
         {                                  /* debit transaction */
            *debit = *debit - transaction;
            printf("%8d\t\t\t%8d\t%8d\n",
                        number, -transaction, *balance);
         }
   }
```

The complete program listing follows.

```
/*
**      Read a series of transactions on a bank account and
**      produce a bank statement summarizing these transactions.
**      The program input consists of a sequence of integers.
**      The first value is a positive integer representing
**      the bank account number. The second integer is the
**      initial balance of the account. The remaining data
**      values are either positive or negative. A positive
**      value represents a deposit and a negative value
**      represents a withdrawal. The end-of-data trailer
**      record is the value zero.
*/

#include <stdio.h>

#define LINE           "------------------------------------\
----------------------"

main()
   {
      .....
   }

/*
**      Process a single transaction and produce a statement
**      line resulting from this. As a side effect, update
**      the balance and either the credit or debit totals.
*/

void process_transaction(number, transaction, credit, debit, balance)
   int    number;                          /* transaction number */
   int    transaction;                     /* transaction value */
   int    *credit;                         /* credit total */
   int    *debit;                          /* debit total */
   int    *balance;                        /* current balance */
   {
      .....
   }


void print_headers(number, balance)
   int    number;                          /* account number */
   int    balance;                         /* initial balance */
```

```
{
    printf("\t\t\tBank Statement\n\n");
    printf("Account number: %6d\n\n", number);
    printf("Transaction            Credit");
    printf("      Debit         Balance\n");
    printf("%s\n", LINE);
    printf("\t\t\t\t\t\t%8d\n", balance);
}


void print_summary(credit, debit, balance)
    int    credit;                        /* final credit total */
    int    debit;                         /* final debit total */
    int    balance;                       /* final balance total */
    {
    printf("%s\n", LINE);
    printf("Totals\t\t%8d\t%8d\t%8d\n", credit, debit, balance);
    }
```

6.9 The switch statement

The if-else statement chain that we encountered in the last section (Program 6.16), where the value of a variable is successively compared with different values, occurs so frequently that a special statement exists for this purpose. This is called the *switch* statement. Its format is:

switch (expression)
   {
   case constant-expression-1:
        statement 1a;
        statement 1b;
        _ _ _ _ _ _ _ _ _ _
        _ _ _ _ _ _ _ _ _ _

   case constant-expression-2:
        statement 2a;
        statement 2b;
        _ _ _ _ _ _ _ _ _ _
        _ _ _ _ _ _ _ _ _ _

   _ _ _ _
   _ _ _ _
   case constant-expression-N:
        statement Na;
        statement Nb;
        _ _ _ _ _ _ _ _ _ _
        _ _ _ _ _ _ _ _ _ _

   default:
        statement Da;
        statement Db;
        _ _ _ _ _ _ _ _ _ _
        _ _ _ _ _ _ _ _ _ _

   }

where switch, case and default are reserved keywords.

The control expression enclosed within parentheses is evaluated. The result must be of an integral type including char. The constant expressions associated with each case keyword must also resolve to an integer. These expressions, called *case labels*, may be an integer constant, a character constant or an integer constant expression. When evaluated, each constant expression must deliver a unique integer value. Duplicates are not permitted.

During execution of the switch statement, the control expression is first evaluated. The resulting value is then compared with each case label in turn. If a case label value equals the value of the expression, control is passed to the first statement associated with that case label. All statements through to the end of the switch are then executed. For example:

```
n = 2;
switch (n)
  {
  case   1 : printf("One\n");
  case   2 : printf("Two\n");
  case   3 : printf("Three\n");
  case   4 : printf("Four\n");
  default  : printf("Default\n");
  }
printf("End of switch\n");
```

The control expression is simply the value of the variable n. When evaluated it is compared with the integer literals 1, 2, 3 and 4. If a match is found, the corresponding statement and all subsequent statements in the switch are obeyed. If no match is found, the default statement(s) are obeyed. The output from the above example is:

```
Two
Three
Four
Default
End of switch
```

The statement or statements associated with a case label may also include the *null* statement. The case label then associates with the statements on the next occurring case label. The following fragment illustrates:

```
n = 2;
switch (n)
  {
  case   1 : printf("One\n");
  case   2 :
  case   3 : printf("Two or three\n");
  case   4 : printf("Four\n");
  default  : printf("Default\n");
  }
printf("End of switch\n");
```

and produces the output:

    Two or three
    Four
    Default
    End of switch

If no case constant expression evaluates to the same value as the control expression, then the statements associated with the *default* keyword are executed. Using the last program fragment above, but setting:

    n = 7;

before entering the switch statement, produces the output:

    Default
    End of switch

The default keyword and its associated group of statements is an optional component of the switch statement. If the value of the control expression does not equal any of the constant expressions, and no default is present, no statement in the body of the switch is executed. This is demonstrated by the example:

```
n = 7;
switch (n)
  {
  case 1 : printf("One\n");
  case 2 :
  case 3 : printf("Two or three\n");
  case 4 : printf("Four\n");
  }
printf("End of switch\n");
```

The output from this piece of code is:

    End of switch

We have noted that after control is transferred to a case label or to the default label, execution continues through successive statements ignoring any additional case or default labels that are encountered until the end of the switch statement is reached. Generally, however, the switch statement is used as a multiway selector. After transfer to a case label or to the default label, the group of associated statements is executed, then control is transferred to the end of the switch ignoring all other statement groups. This is achieved by making the last statement in each group the *break* statement. The break statement is fully discussed in the next section. In the context of a switch statement, the break statement is used to immediately terminate it. Consider now:

```
n = 3;
switch (n)
  {
  case 1 : printf("One\n");              break;
  case 2 :
  case 3 : printf("Two or three\n");  break;
  case 4 : printf("Four\n");             break;
  }
printf("End of switch\n");
```

which generates the output:

```
Two or three
End of switch
```

While the last break is logically unnecessary, it is a good thing to include it as a matter of style. It will help to prevent errors in the event that a fifth case label is later added to the switch during program maintenance.

The following program illustrates the use of the switch statement. The program operates on a character sequence of indeterminate length, terminated with the period symbol. The program counts the number of blanks, the number of tabs, the number of newline symbols and the number of all other symbols (cf. Program 6.15). The outline processing logic of this program is expressed by the PDL:

```
initialize all counters
read the first character
WHILE not the end of data character
DO
    SWITCH this character
    TO
        WHEN (a blank)     increment blank counter
        WHEN (a tab)       increment tab counter
        WHEN (a newline)   increment newline counter
        OTHERWISE increment all other counter
    END
    read the next character
ENDWHILE
```

Program 6.17

```
/*
**      A program to separately count the number of blank,
**      tab, newline and other characters. The input data
**      consist of a stream of characters terminated
**      by a period symbol.
*/
```

```
#include <stdio.h>

#define BLANK           ' '
#define TAB             '\t'
#define NEWLINE         '\n'
#define PERIOD          '.'

main()
  {
    int nblank = 0, ntab = 0, nnewline = 0, nother = 0;
    char c;

    while ((c = getchar()) != PERIOD)
      switch (c)
        {
          case BLANK    : nblank++;     break;
          case TAB      : ntab++;       break;
          case NEWLINE  : nnewline++;   break;
          default       : nother++;     break;
        }
    printf("%d %d %d %d\n", nblank, ntab, nnewline, nother);
  }
```

Note the additional PDL construction used in the last example representing a multiway switch. The structure used is:

SWITCH on-some-expression
TO
  WHEN (this-value) these-statements
  WHEN (........)   ....
  ....
  ....
  OTHERWISE   ....
END

If the expression evaluates to a value which matches any of the WHEN clauses, the associated statements, and only these, are executed. The switch then terminates and the program logic continues with the following statement. If no match occurs, the escape mechanism is to the statements of the OTHERWISE clause. Note that our PDL avoids the need to specifically incorporate break statements. Our concern at this level is solely with the overall program design. Equally, no restrictions are placed on the expressions or values. We are allowed to say, for example:

SWITCH day-of-week
TO
  WHEN (Mon, Tue, Wed, Thu, Fri)   working-days
  OTHERWISE   weekend
END

The program following also illustrates the use of the switch statement. The program is supplied with a date in the form of two integers representing the day and the month. The year is known not to be a leap year. The program calculates the date (day, month) of the day following the input date.

Program 6.18

```
/*
**      Determine tomorrow's date, given the date for
**      today. The year is known not to be a leap year,
**      and so only the day and month are provided as data.
*/

#include <stdio.h>

#define JAN       1
#define FEB       2
#define APR       4
#define JUN       6
#define SEP       9
#define NOV       11
#define DEC       12

main()
   {
       int day, month;                /* program data */
       void tomorrow();               /* referencing declaration */

       printf("Enter today's date: ");
       scanf("%d %d", &day, &month);
       tomorrow(&day, &month);
       printf("Tomorrow's date is %d %d\n", day, month);
   }

void tomorrow(d, m)           /* compute tomorrow's date */
   int *d, *m;                         /* date: d = day, m = month */
   {
       int days_in_month;

       switch (*m)                               /* which month? */
          {
          case APR :
          case JUN :
          case SEP :
          case NOV : days_in_month = 30;  break;
          case FEB : days_in_month = 28;  break;
          default  : days_in_month = 31;  break;
          }

       if (*d == days_in_month)                 /* end of month? */
          {
          *d = 1;                               /* yes, first day */
          if (*m == DEC)                        /* end of year? */
             *m = JAN;
          else
             (*m)++;
          }
       else
          (*d)++;
   }
```

Case study 6.3: Printing bank checks

Computerized banking systems issue checks to bank customers. The checks include, amongst other things, the value of the check expressed numerically and as words. For example, the numerical sum of money 123:45 is expressed as:

ONE HUNDRED AND TWENTY THREE DOLLARS AND FORTY FIVE CENTS

A program is required to accept an indeterminate number of numerical monetary values and to output each value both in its numerical form and in its word equivalent form. Each monetary data value appears on a separate line and is represented by two integers separated by a colon symbol. The first integer is the number of dollars. The second integer is always given as two digits and represents the number of cents. All input values are less than 1000 dollars. The data are terminated with the zero monetary value 0:00.

The overall program structure is relatively simple. Each data value is read and processed. This iteration continues until the terminator is read. The program then stops. The PDL is:

> read the first sum of money
> WHILE not the terminating monetary value
> DO
>   print the sum of money numerically
>   print the sum of money in words
>   read the next sum of money
> ENDWHILE

Only the step 'print the sum of money in words' causes us any difficulty. Further work is necessary to refine this stage. We can, in the meantime, relegate it to a subordinate function, passing the value of the dollars and cents as arguments. Armed with both these values the function can do its work. The main function is then immediately coded as:

```
main ()
  {
    int dollars, cents;                /* input data */
    void do_conversion ();

    scanf ("%d:%2d", &dollars, &cents);
    while ( !(dollars == 0 && cents == 0) )
       {
         printf ("%3d:%02d    ", dollars, cents);
         do_conversion (dollars, cents);
         scanf ("%d:%2d", &dollars, &cents);
       }
  }
```

The subordinate function, do_conversion, receives the monetary sum as two integer values − the number of dollars and the number of cents. The first value contributes to the first part of the alphabetical output as far as the word DOLLARS:

.... DOLLARS ....

The second value is responsible for the phrase starting AND:

.... AND ....

Care must be taken if either case is zero. If there are no dollars, the phrase up to and including the AND is omitted. Similarly, if there are no cents, the output stops at DOLLARS. The design for function do_conversion is:

```
IF non-zero dollars
THEN
   convert dollars into words
   print "DOLLARS"
ENDIF

IF non-zero cents
THEN
   IF non-zero dollars
   THEN
     print "AND"
   ENDIF
   convert cents into words
   print "CENTS"
ENDIF
```

and is programmed as:

```c
void do_conversion (dollars, cents)
   int     dollars, cents;
   {
     void convert_to_words ();

     if (dollars > 0)
        {
          convert_to_words (dollars);
          printf (" DOLLARS");
        }

     if (cents > 0)
        {
          if (dollars > 0)
            printf (" AND");
          convert_to_words (cents);
          printf (" CENTS");
        }
     printf ("\n\n");
   }
```

The interesting feature of this function is that converting both the
dollars and the cents into words is achieved with the same function
(convert_to_words). The suffix DOLLARS and CENTS is the responsibility
of the function do_conversion. Otherwise, the words produced are the
same for both the dollars and the cents. The PDL for function
convert_to_words is:

```
obtain the number of hundreds in the number
obtain the number of tens in the number
obtain the number of units in the number

IF non-zero hundreds
THEN
   convert to words the number of hundreds
   print "HUNDREDS"
ENDIF
```

IF some tens or some units in the number
THEN
  print "AND"
  IF the tens and units is expressible as teens
  THEN
    convert to words the tens and units
  ELSE
    convert to words the number of tens
    convert to words the number of units
  ENDIF
ENDIF

The function convert_to_words is then:

```
void convert_to_words (number)
   int    number;
   {
      int   hundreds, tens, units;
      void do_units (), do_teens (), do_tens ();

      hundreds = number / 100;
      tens     = (number % 100) / 10;
      units    = number % 10;

      if (hundreds > 0)
         {
            do_units (hundreds);
            printf (" HUNDRED");
         }

      if (tens + units > 0)
         {
            if (hundreds > 0)
              printf (" AND");
            if (tens == 1)
              do_teens (units);
            else
            {
              do_tens (tens);
              do_units (units);
            }
         }
   }
```

The completed program is listed below, together with some sample input data and the resulting output.

```
/*
**        Accept as input an indeterminate number of monetary
**        values each less than 1000 dollars and output the sum
**        both numerically and in words. Each value is expressed
**        in the form PPP.pp, where PPP represents the dollars
**        and pp represents the cents. The data are terminated
**        with the value 0.00.
*/

#include <stdio.h>

main ()
   {
      .....
   }
```

```
/*
**        Convert a sum of money into words by first expressing
**        the dollars and then expressing the cents.
*/


void do_conversion (dollars, cents)
  int    dollars, cents;
  {
      .....
  }




/*
**        Convert a numerical value into its equivalent expressed
**        in words.
*/


void convert_to_words (number)
  int    number;
  {
      .....
  }




/*
**        Routines to express selected values in words.
*/


void do_units (units)
  int    units;
  {
    switch (units)
      {
        case 0 : break;
        case 1 : printf (" ONE");      break;
        case 2 : printf (" TWO");      break;
        case 3 : printf (" THREE");    break;
        case 4 : printf (" FOUR");     break;
        case 5 : printf (" FIVE");     break;
        case 6 : printf (" SIX");      break;
        case 7 : printf (" SEVEN");    break;
        case 8 : printf (" EIGHT");    break;
        case 9 : printf (" NINE");     break;
      }
  }



void do_teens (units)
  int    units;
  {
    switch (units)
      {
        case 0 : printf (" TEN");        break;
        case 1 : printf (" ELEVEN");     break;
        case 2 : printf (" TWELVE");     break;
        case 3 : printf (" THIRTEEN");   break;
        case 4 : printf (" FOURTEEN");   break;
        case 5 : printf (" FIFTEEN");    break;
        case 6 : printf (" SIXTEEN");    break;
        case 7 : printf (" SEVENTEEN");  break;
        case 8 : printf (" EIGHTEEN");   break;
        case 9 : printf (" NINETEEN");   break;
      }
  }
```

```
void do_tens (tens)
  int    tens;
  {
    switch (tens)
      {
        case 0 : break;
        case 1 : break;
        case 2 : printf (" TWENTY");       break;
        case 3 : printf (" THIRTY");       break;
        case 4 : printf (" FORTY");        break;
        case 5 : printf (" FIFTY");        break;
        case 6 : printf (" SIXTY");        break;
        case 7 : printf (" SEVENTY");      break;
        case 8 : printf (" EIGHTY");       break;
        case 9 : printf (" NINETY");       break;
      }
  }
```

Sample data:

123:45
1:07
10:00
0:66
0:00

Program output:

123:45   ONE HUNDRED AND TWENTY THREE DOLLARS
          AND FORTY FIVE CENTS
  1:07   ONE DOLLARS AND SEVEN CENTS
 10:00   TEN DOLLARS
  0:66   SIXTY SIX CENTS

6.10 The break statement

The break statement is used to alter the flow of control inside loops and inside switch statements. We have already introduced the break statement in the previous section, where it was used to cause immediate exit from within the nearest enclosing switch statement. The break statement can also be used with while, for and do statements. Execution of a break statement causes immediate termination of the innermost enclosing loop.

A break statement in loops is normally used in conjunction with an if statement. Firstly, a loop is established to repeat some specified number of times or until some expected condition occurs. If, at any time, some abnormal situation occurs, the loop is terminated. The latter is achieved with a combination of if and break statements.

Program 6.19 illustrates this idea. Essentially, the program is a revised version of Program 6.13. An unknown number of single characters up to and including the period symbol are input. The number of lines in the text is enumerated by counting the number of occurrences of the newline symbol.

Instead of iterating until the terminator is discovered in the input, an infinite loop is established. The loop conveys the fact that an iteration is the major program construct. From within the loop we test for the end of data sentinel, and quit from the loop. The PDL is:

    initialize the line counter
    FOREVER
    DO
      read the next data character
      IF the terminator symbol
      THEN
        quit the loop
      ENDIF
      IF a newline symbol
      THEN
        increment the line counter
      ENDIF
    END
    print the result

resulting in Program 6.19.

Program 6.19

```
/*
**      Input a stream of characters from the standard
**      input and count the number of lines of text by
**      enumerating the number of newline symbols. The
**      text is terminated by a period symbol.
*/

#include <stdio.h>

#define PERIOD          '.'
#define NEWLINE         '\n'

#define FOREVER         for (;;)

main()
   {
      int  lines = 0;                        /* line count */
      char c;                                /* data character */

      FOREVER
        {
          c = getchar();
          if (c == PERIOD)
            break;
          if (c == NEWLINE)
            lines++;
        }

      printf("Number of lines is %d\n", lines);
   }
```

The break statement can also reduce the complexity of the expression governing repetition of a loop. A simple description of the normal termination of the loop is handled by the loop test itself. The abnormal termination of the loop is the responsibility of a break statement within the loop. Program 6.20(a) illustrates this use for the break statement. The program reads and forms the sum of 100 floating point data values. If at any time a negative floating point value is encountered in the data, the summation terminates. Firstly, the PDL:

initialize the running total
FOR 100 times
DO
   read the next data value
   IF a negative data item
   THEN
     quit the loop
   ENDIF
   add the data value to the running total
END
print the result

Program 6.20(a)

```
/*
**        Read and form the sum of at most 100 positive
**        floating point numbers. If at any time a
**        negative value is encountered in the input
**        terminate with the sum thus formed.
*/

#include <stdio.h>

#define MAX                      100

main()
   {
      float data, sum = 0.0;              /* data, running total */
      int   k;                            /* loop counter */

      for (k = 1; k <= MAX; k++)
         {
            scanf("%f", &data);
            if (data < 0.0)
               break;
            sum += data;
         }

      printf("Sum is %f\n", sum);
   }
```

Consider the above solution against the following version, Program 6.20(b). This second attempt is more complex and harder to understand since we have combined the tests for normal and abnormal loop termination. The increased complexity also lessens the likelihood that the program is correct.

Program 6.20(b)

```
/*
**        Read and form the sum of at most 100 positive
**        floating point numbers. If at any time a
**        negative value is encountered in the input
**        terminate with the sum thus formed.
*/
```

```
#include <stdio.h>

#define MAX                       100
#define FALSE                     0
#define TRUE                      1

main()
  {
    float data, sum = 0.0;              /* data, running total */
    int   k;                           /* loop counter */
    int   abort = FALSE;               /* abnormal termination */

    for (k = 1; k <= MAX && !abort; k++)
      {
        scanf("%f", &data);
        if (data < 0.0)
          abort = TRUE;
        else
          sum += data;
      }

    printf("Sum is %f\n", sum);
  }
```

6.11 The continue statement

The continue statement complements the break statement. Its use is restricted to while, for and do loops. When a continue statement is executed, control is immediately passed to the test condition of the nearest enclosing loop. All subsequent statements in the body of the loop are ignored for that particular loop iteration. The continue statement, like the break statement, is normally used in conjunction with an if statement. The syntax of the continue statement is simply:

continue;

The following short program demonstrates an application of the continue statement. The program reads 10 floating point numbers, summing only the positive values. Negative data values are ignored by skipping the processing actions of the loop. Firstly, the PDL:

initialize the running total
FOR 10 times
DO
    read the next data value
    IF a negative data item
    THEN
        skip the loop
    ENDIF
    add data value to running total
END

Then the program:

Program 6.21

```
/*
**        Input 10 floating point values, summing only
**        those values which are positive.
*/

#include <stdio.h>

#define MAX                    10

main()
  {
    float data, sum = 0.0;              /* data, running total */
    int   k;                            /* loop counter */

    for (k = 0; k < MAX; k++)
      {
        scanf("%f", &data);
        if (data < 0.0)
          continue;
        sum += data;
      }

    printf("Sum of positive values is %f\n", sum);
  }
```

6.12 Summary

1. The three principal program control structures are *sequence, selection* and *iteration*. The *while, do* and *for* statements provide the loop mechanism in C; selection is provided by the *if* and *switch* statements.

2. Logical expressions have an *int* value of 0 or 1, in which 0 represents logical *false* and 1 represents logical *true*. Further, any non-zero value is interpreted as logical *true* when evaluating a logical expression. Logical expressions are constructed from the relational operators ($<$, $<=$, etc.) and the logical operators (&&, ¦¦, !), as well as the usual arithmetic operators.

3. The *while* statement is the fundamental loop construct in C. Since the control expression is tested before execution of each iteration, the statement(s) under control of the while may be executed zero or more times.

4. The *for* statement is semantically equivalent to the while statement, providing an abbreviated version of the latter. A for loop, therefore, executes zero or more times.

5. The *do* statement's control expression is computed following execution of the statement body. A do loop is therefore guaranteed to be obeyed one or more times.

6. The *if* statement provides a means of choosing whether or not to execute a statement. The *if-else* statement decides which of two statements to execute. In nested if statements, the compiler always associates an *else* part with the nearest unmatched preceding if.

7. The *switch* statement is a multiple-alternative control statement. It compares an integer expression against many possible values selected from *case labels*.

8. The *break* statement is used to alter flow of control inside loops and switch statements. The break statement when used with a loop (while, for and do), causes immediate termination of the innermost enclosing loop. When used with a switch statement, the break causes immediate exit from the enclosing switch clause.

9. The *continue* statement is used solely with while, for and do statements, and an execution causes control to immediately pass to the nearest enclosing loop's conditional expression for re-evaluation.

6.13 Exercises

1. Give equivalent logical expressions without using the negation operator:

   !(a > b)   !(a <= b + 3)
   !(a + 1 = = b + 1)   !(a > 2 || b < 5)
   !(a < b && c < d)

2. In the context of the following initialized declarations:

   char c = 'X';
   int h = 2, i = − 3, j = 7, k = − 19;

   Complete Table 6.4.

   Table 6.4

Expression	Equivalent expression	Value
h && i && j	(h && i) && j	1 (true)
h && i || j		
h || i && j		
h || i && j || k		
!h && !j		
!h + !j		
h > j		
h <= j		
(j < k) || h		
j < (k || h)		

3. What is the difference between the two operators = and = = ?

4. Is the following statement correct? If not, why?

   if (q > = r)
       printf("q is greater than or equal to r");
       a = b;
   else
       printf("r is less than q");
       x = y;

5. We have already explained that:

   while(1)
       {
           ....
       }

is an infinite loop. What happens when the following program is executed? If you are unsure, try it.

```
#include ⟨stdio.h⟩
main( )
    {
    while(− 22.55)
        {
        printf("run forever, perhaps?");
        }
    }
```

6. What happens when you run the following program on your system? If it does not run as expected, change it so that it does.

```
#include ⟨stdio.h⟩
main( )
    {
    float x, total = 0.0;
    for (x = 0.0; x ! = 0.9; x + = 0.1)        /* bad test */
        {
        total + = x;
        printf("x = %f, running total = %f\n", x, total);
        }
    }
```

7. Input three positive integers representing the sides of a triangle, and determine whether they form a valid triangle. [Hint: In a triangle, the sum of any two sides must always be greater than the third side.]

8. Write a program which computes the sum of the first 10 integers. Modify the program to compute the sum of the first N integers, where N is given as a data value.

9. Prepare a function *quotient* which finds the quotient of two positive integers using only the operations of addition and subtraction:

    int quotient (numerator, denominator)
        int numerator, denominator;

    Employ this function in a program which inputs two integers and outputs their quotient.

10. Prepare a function called *power* which computes a to the power b for two non-negative integer values a and b, using repeated multiplication:

    long int power (a, b)
        int a, b;

    Then write a program to tabulate x, x^2 and x^3 for x = 1, 2, ..., 10.

11. Write a program that reads a single positive integer data value, extracts each digit from the integer and displays it as a word. For example, the input value 932 should display:

    932: nine three two

12. Write a program that reads a number, then reads a single digit and determines how many times the digit occurs in the number.

13. Data to a program consist of a sequence of characters of unknown length. The data set is terminated with a unique period symbol. Write a program which counts the number of lines, the number of words and the number of characters in the input. Each input line is terminated by the newline symbol. A word is any sequence of characters that does not contain a blank, tab or newline symbol. The terminating period is not included in any count.

14. Using the data of question 13, write a program which prints the words in the input one per line.

15. A prime number is one that is divisible only by one and by itself. Write a program to input a series of numbers and determine whether they are prime or not. Perhaps the simplest way to determine if a number is prime is to test whether the number is divisible by any value from two to one less than the number. The process can be shortened appreciably by performing the test from two to some lesser value than that given. How is this value obtained? Use it in your solution.

16. Write a program to display a multiplication table with the format shown in Table 6.5. The range of the table is given as program input.

Table 6.5

X	1	2	3	4
1	1	2	3	4
2	2	4	6	8
3	3	6	9	12
4	4	8	12	16

17. Write a program to remove all comments from a C program.

18. Write a program to operate on the data of question 13 and to compress repeated characters. The program copies its input to its output, replacing strings of repeating character sequences by [nX], where n is an integer count of the number of repetitions, and X is the character. For example, the input:

    ABCCCDEEFFFFG.

produces the output:

    AB[3C]D[2E][4F]G.

Prepare a second program to expand the compressed text. Using the output of the first program, this second program should recreate the original input.

19. Input to a program is the monthly sales figures for a sales team. For each salesman, show his identification number, total sales, value of sales, profit (total sales − value of sales), and commission (= 10% of profit). The output is to have the format shown in Table 6.6.

Table 6.6

Number	Total sales(A)	Value(B)	Profit (A − B)	Commission 10%(A − B)
1234	234.56	174.56	60.00	6.00
⋮	⋮	⋮	⋮	⋮
⋮	⋮	⋮	⋮	⋮
XXXX	XXX.XX	XXX.XX	XXX.XX	XX.XX
Totals	XXXX.XX	XXXX.XX	XXXX.XX	XXX.XX

20. Write a program which accepts a time expressed in hours, minutes and seconds and verbalizes that time as suggested by the following outputs:

09 : 10 : 00	ten past nine
10 : 45 : 00	quarter to eleven
11 : 15 : 00	quarter past eleven
17 : 30 : 00	half past five
19 : 50 : 00	ten to eight
06 : 12 : 29	just after ten past six
06 : 12 : 30	just before quarter past six
00 : 17 : 29	just after quarter past midnight

## CHAPTER 7

Programming in the large

Writing large programs in C, as in any language, poses difficult problems of organization. Many modern programming languages contain constructs designed to help structure large systems. These constructs, variously known as *modules* or *packages*, make it possible to partition large software systems into reasonable-sized components. Further, they usually support separate compilation of *program units* and make it possible to assemble libraries of shareable components. The use of such constructs to impose structure on large programs is often called 'programming in the large' in contrast to 'programming in the small', which is concerned with the detailed implementation of algorithms in terms of data items and program control structures.

When we design software we must endeavor to capture the structure of the design in a form that reflects our view of the real-world problem. We have alluded to these issues in earlier chapters by having our program structures reflect the problem's data structures. Effective modifications to the system must honor the original and existing structures, otherwise we apply fragmentary patches which destroy the original fabric of the software.

As we explore larger, even more complex problem domains, our difficulties increase and our software systems become unmanageably complex. Software engineering is concerned with building large software systems which are reliable, understandable, and easy to maintain and modify. These goals are achieved by applying a number of principles including abstraction, modularity, information hiding and localization.

Our inability to cope with complexity is at the root of all our programming problems. The basic tool we use to overcome complexity is *abstraction*. Abstraction is a conscious decision to ignore irrelevant details and to concentrate only on the relevant properties. Functional decomposition is a form of abstraction. At the highest problem and program levels we ignore details to concentrate on the original higher-level structures. Using a standard library routine such as printf is an application of functional abstraction. We are not concerned with the inner operations of this function, only how to use it. Equally, when we introduce our own functions at the design stage the actual implementation details are ignored. The only relevant features are its operation and its interface. The implementation is detail to be considered later.

Ultimately our abstractions must be realized as program parts. This may involve the definition of data types and variables to represent the abstract concept, and a set of functions to implement the applicable operations. For every abstraction in a program, a module is constructed. A module or program unit is a resource center − a collection of data types, variables and functions for the particular abstraction. This way we can look upon the module in terms of *what it does* rather than *how it does it*. The details of implementation need not concern us, only the interface to the facilities supported by the module.

The C programming language supports independent compilation of program units. A program unit is a collection of related resources − data and operations. Function (operations) and data items may be *private* or *public* elements of a program unit. Public resources are accessible from other program units. Private members are inaccessible beyond the program unit in which they are declared and provide support for *information hiding*.

The aim of information hiding is to make inaccessible those details which do not concern other parts of the programming system. Information hiding also makes programs more secure. Hidden information may not be corrupted by a program unit which is not supposed to have access to that information. In certain circumstances, information hiding can also facilitate data independence − the data representation may be changed without recourse to the program units which make use of that data. The C program unit is thus the cornerstone of abstraction.

In the next two sections we shall consider abstraction through data design and through those language features necessary to support such an approach. The remainder of the chapter details the relevant language constructs. In subsequent chapters, particularly with the larger case studies, we will use these additional facilities to control the construction of the software.

7.1 Systematic data design

Much of the early work in software engineering and structured programming concentrated on procedural decomposition and upon the use of control structures in programming languages. An equally important area is data decomposition and the selection of appropriate logical and physical data structures in programs. Program procedures, while well suited to the description of algorithmic abstractions (operations), are not particularly suited to the descriptions of abstract data objects. For a program to be comprehensible and easy to maintain, design of data structures is as important as the program's functional decomposition. This is why in the earlier part of the book we encouraged the construction of programs whose structure reflected that of the program's data.

The data decomposition is derived from our modeling of reality in terms of the objects and their operations present in the problem space. The result is that we structure our system around the objects that exist in our model. Further, we may also find that there are several similar objects in the problem and we would, therefore, establish a *class* of objects of which there are many instances, sharing common characteristics. From this we can derive general, reusable items of code.

As an example, suppose in our problem space we identify an object exhibiting the behavior of a queue. The queue, therefore, may be considered as an (abstract) data object. The meaningful operations that may be applied to queues might include:

create(q)	create a new empty queue named q
enterq(i, q)	data item i joins end of queue q
serveq(q)	remove the item at the front of queue q
emptyq(q)	test whether queue q is empty
lengthq(q)	determine the number of items in queue q

The description of the abstract data structure queue and the operations upon the structure have been developed jointly without recourse to low-level program representations. The queue now becomes an abstract data structure with supporting operations which can be referred to in other parts of the system without requiring any knowledge of their implementation. The data objects and associated operations are packaged into a C program unit.

Identifying those program modules that must operate directly upon the logical data structures is an important activity during this design phase. This way, the *scope of effect* of individual data design decisions can be constrained (information hiding). The scope of effect concept may be used to measure the impact of changes to the system by quantifying the number of program modules that are affected by changes in a given module. By this means we are able to *decouple* one object from another.

One should attempt to minimize the scope of effect of design decisions by minimizing the number of modules that are aware of the representation chosen for any data object. As a consequence, only the basic operations upon an object need to be aware of the representation. Other parts of the software system can be constrained to use only the operations provided and can be prevented from modifying or even inspecting the physical representation.

As a result, one could change the actual representation without affecting other parts of the system. For example, in our queue we may initially realize it with an *array* (Chapters 11 and 12). We may subsequently rework the implementation as a *linked list* (Chapter 16). This is a consequence of our program design where changes are much more localized. With functional decomposition, a program's data are frequently global to the entire system, so that any representation changes affect all subordinate modules.

It is common to have multiple levels of abstraction in data design. If one particular physical representation for queues had been chosen, and that concrete form is associated with another abstraction for which an implementation already exists, then the queue is built on this second abstraction. The queue operations use the subordinate operations as another instance of data abstraction without recourse to their representational detail.

7.2 Designing into C

In expressing our problem solution we require a language which provides sufficient tools so that our view of the problem space is directly expressible in that language. The language must provide facilities to express both the object and operations on these objects of the real-world problem. Only by having these capabilities will we be able to express our problem solution in terms of the structures of the problem space.

C is such a programming language. It provides a rich set of constructs for describing both data structures and operations upon these objects. Further, it offers a packaging facility by which we may build our abstractions of the problem into the program. The package or program unit is the cornerstone of abstraction, information hiding, visibility and locality.

We represent compilable program units as rectangular figures, annotated with the resources contained within the unit. The invisible features remain fully enclosed within the figure. The *exportable* resources are shown in windows, accessible beyond the module. For example, in Fig. 7.1, variable length and function middle are invisible outside the unit, while functions left and right are exportable, and hence may be used in other program units.

The provision of program units offers a number of advantages, which include:

1. Abstract data types, as described in the previous section. The representation of the abstract data type is visible only within the module in which it is specified. Another application program module may manipulate the abstract data type through the provision of exportable primitive operations (external functions, section 7.5). Furthermore, the representation

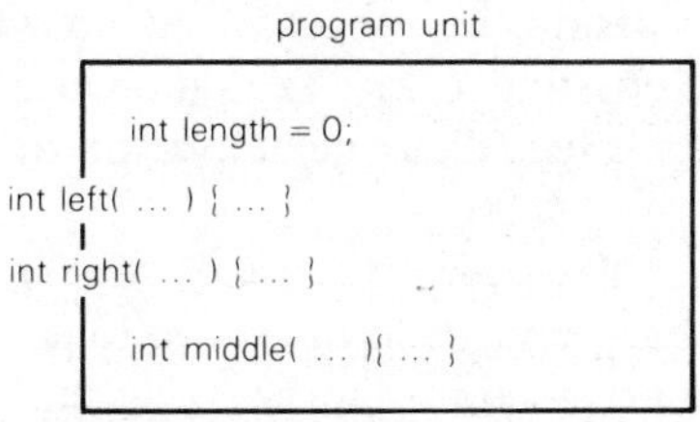

```
                    program unit

          ┌─────────────────────────────────────┐
          │  int length = 0;                     │
          │                                      │
   int left( ... ) { ... }                       │
          │                                      │
   int right( ... ) { ... }          ..          │
          │                                      │
          │     int middle( ... ){ ... }         │
          │                                      │
          └─────────────────────────────────────┘
```

Fig. 7.1

of the abstract data type may be changed without affecting the higher-level program modules that employ these primitives.

2. Related operations may be grouped together, sharing variables in a controlled way. Data structures may be made private to a program unit and not exportable to other program units.

3. The module is a convenient unit for separate compilation. A module is constructed as a self-contained program unit. No reference to its environment, other than external function calls, means that it can be compiled independently of other modules.

The C programming language is not the perfect vehicle on which to base our software engineering principles. It is incapable of enforcing strict rules upon the programmer. For example, it lacks the strong type checking required. Its packaging facility is only provided to support separate compilation. Nevertheless, the features of C should be fully exploited in the design of large-scale software systems. Further, the lint utility (Appendix G) available under UNIX can be used to supplement the compiler and provide the necessary type checking.

A programming principle is that the names of objects in a program should be introduced close to where they are used and only be accessible to those parts of the program where they are required. In C, this is achieved through the scope rules. The block structure of C permits the declaration of variables at any level.

The declaration of a variable within a block (automatic or local variables) restricts the scope of that variable to that block. Storage associated with the variable is allocated at run time when the block is entered and then released when the block is left. Blocks may be nested so that local variables can be introduced close to where they are required with access to variables in an outer block permitted from an inner block.

Multilevel locality contributes significantly to program readability. The characteristics of names are declared close to where they are used. The provision of local names also means that the temptation to use one variable for different tasks in different parts of a program can be avoided. This is normal practice in languages that do not support block structure and is a common source of error.

Block structure on its own is an inadequate mechanism for controlling the visibility of names. An additional mechanism is required to control which local names may be accessed from outside the program unit in which the names are declared. It should also be possible to specify that a variable local to a program unit should maintain its value from one activation of the unit to the next.

The constructs in C used to achieve these objectives are the storage classes *extern* and *static*. External variables and external functions may be exported from one program unit and accessed by another program unit. On the other hand external static variables and functions are visible only within the program unit in which they are declared. They are described as *private* to that program unit.

7.3 Storage classes

A C program is composed of one or more program units. Each unit is separately compiled then linked and loaded with other compiled units ready for execution. A program unit is a collection of logically related resources including data items and subprograms (functions). All or parts of the program unit may be visible to some other program unit, supporting a degree of logical abstraction and information hiding.

Program units permit a programmer to encapsulate related items. Another programmer need never see nor be concerned with the implementation of that program unit. Elements of the program unit may be totally invisible to him. Other parts, including both data items and operations (functions), may be exported to his application.

Complete abstraction is not fully enforceable in C. Some implementation details must be made available to the user of a program unit. The burden on the user is minimized, however, by making the exportable information available in header files. These details can then be included in the user's application program.

The block structure features of C provide some control over the visibility of objects. Objects declared in one block are not accessible outside of that block. Block structure on its own is not totally adequate for controlling the visibility of names. In C these additional features are provided by the storage class of objects.

Section 5.3 introduced the storage class auto. Automatic variables are local to the function body in which they are declared. Functions, unless otherwise stated, have storage class extern (external). Functions can, therefore, be referenced by functions in the same program unit or by functions in a separate unit. Data items may also be declared as external objects. They too can be accessed by functions in the same unit in which they are declared and by functions in other units.

Invisibility is achieved through the storage classes auto and static. Automatic variables are local to the block in which they are declared and neither exists at run time nor can be referenced outwith the block. Functions and data items declared in one program unit with storage class static are not exportable to other program units.

In the following sections we shall define and demonstrate the features of these storage classes.

7.4 Storage class auto

C is not a block structured programming language in the sense of Algol or Pascal. In these languages, functions may be declared nested within other functions. On the other hand, C does permit the declaration of variables in a block structured fashion. Variables declared in the body of a function have storage class auto (automatic). Automatic variables are internal to a function; they come into existence when a function is entered (called) and disappear when it is exited. Arguments to functions are processed in a similar manner.

The term *scope* is used to define the region of the C program text over which a declaration is active. An identifier declared at the beginning of a function block has a scope that extends from its declaration to the end of the block. Formal arguments to a function also have the function block as their scope. In the function shown below, the variable *temp* has the storage class auto (as do the formal arguments a and b). The scope of the variable temp is the body of the function. The identifier temp cannot be accessed outside of this function.

```
void order(a, b) /* arrange a, b into ascending order */
  int *a, *b;
  {
    int temp;
    if (*a > *b)
      {
        temp = *a;
        *a   = *b;
        *b   = temp;
      }
  }
```

The declaration for variable temp explicitly specifies the type int and implicitly specifies the storage class auto. It is permissible to include the storage class explicitly with the reserved keyword auto, as in:

```
auto int temp;
```

though in normal practice it is usually omitted.

A function body is a *compound statement* – also called a *block*. It consists of a possibly empty sequence of declarations followed by a possibly empty sequence of statements, all enclosed in braces:

```
{
  optional-declaration-sequence
  optional-statement-sequence
}
```

Additionally, a compound statement may appear as a replacement for any single statement. When the compound statement has no declarations, it simply represents a group of statements. In the function *order*, a statement group is used with the if statement:

```
if (*a > *b)
    {                           /* compound statement */
      temp = *a;
      *a   = *b
      *b   = temp;
    }
```

When the compound statement includes declarations, it brings into existence a new scope. Recognizing that the variable temp is only required within the if statement, the function may be rewritten:

```
void order(a, b)      /* arrange a, b into ascending order */
    int *a, *b;
    {
      if (*a > *b)
        {
          int temp = *a;
          *a = *b;
          *b = temp;
        }
    }
```

The scope of the variable temp is reduced to the inner compound statement which is part of the if statement. Any reference to the variable temp outwith this compound statement is illegal, even within the remainder of the function itself.

Compound statements that are nested may include declarations for identifiers with names the same as those in surrounding blocks. This introduces the concept of *visibility*. In the assignment:

```
*b = temp;
```

appearing in the function order, the use of the identifier temp is *bound* to the declaration:

```
int temp = *a;
```

in the compound statement in which they both appear. The declaration for this identifier is said to be visible since the use of the identifier is associated with that declaration.

A declaration for an identifier can become temporarily invisible when the declaration for an identifier with the same name appears in an enclosing inner compound statement. For example, in the following program the declaration for the integer variable sum is hidden by the declaration of sum as a floating point variable in the inner block. This loss of visibility is temporary. The integer variable sum reappears when the inner block terminates.

Program 7.1

```
/*
**      A program to demonstrate the concepts of scope
**      and visibility. Variables in an inner block with
**      the same name as those on an outer block
**      temporarily make invisible those outside the
**      block.
*/

#include <stdio.h>

main()
  {
    int sum = 10;                   /* sum at the top level */

    {                               /* inner block */
      float sum = 3.1416;           /* outer sum hidden */

      printf("Inner sum (float): %6.4f\n", sum);
    }

    printf("Outer sum (int): %2d\n", sum);
  }
```

The output from this program is:

Inner sum (float): 3.1416
Outer sum (int): 10

The declaration of an automatic variable may also be accompanied by an initializer. The initializer is any expression which specifies the initial value a variable may have at the beginning of its lifetime. An automatic variable comes into existence upon entry to the compound statement in which it is declared. The initial expression may employ any item having a valid run time value at the point of entry to the block. The following program illustrates these ideas.

Program 7.2

```
/*
**      Initialization of local variables by any known
**      run-time expression.
*/

#include <stdio.h>

main ()
  {
    int  k;                         /* loop control */
    void square ();                 /* referencing declaration */

    for (k = 1; k < 10; k++)
      square (k);
  }

void square (d)
  int d;
  {
    int dsquared = d * d;           /* initialized expression */

    printf ("%2d squared is %3d\n", d, dsquared);
  }
```

The automatic variable *dsquared* declared in the body of the function *square*, and local to it, has a perfectly valid initializer. The initializer is based on the formal argument *d*. When the function is executed an actual value for the argument will be available to initialize dsquared. The initialization takes place each time the automatic variable is established; that is, each time the function square is invoked. At each call a different actual argument value is provided and a different initial value computed. The program output is thus:

```
1 squared is    1
2 squared is    4
3 squared is    9
4 squared is   16
5 squared is   25
6 squared is   36
7 squared is   49
8 squared is   64
9 squared is   81
```

7.5 Storage class extern

A C program consists of a collection of *external* objects. The adjective external is used in contrast to *internal* which describes the arguments and automatic variables defined in functions. External items are defined outside of functions. Functions themselves are external since C does not permit functions to be declared inside other functions. These external objects have storage class *extern*.

In the programs that we have developed, it has been assumed that all the program source code resides in a single file. C actively supports the concept of modular programming in that it does not require that all of the code for a program be contained in a single source file. The separate modules equate to our idea of a program unit.

To allow one function in one program unit to call another function in a second program unit, an *external referencing declaration* is required. The declaration informs the compiler that a function is to be called before its definition, that the function has a particular return type, and that the function's definition is in another program unit. These declarations are similar to forward references but are preceded by the keyword extern.

Consider an application constructed from two program units main.c and time.c. The program determines the difference between two times both expressed as a 24-hour clock time.

The main function resides in the program unit main.c. The problem solution is expressed in terms of the subordinate functions hms_to_time and time_to_hms. Both these complementary functions are contained in the second program unit. Function hms_to_time converts a 24-hour clock time

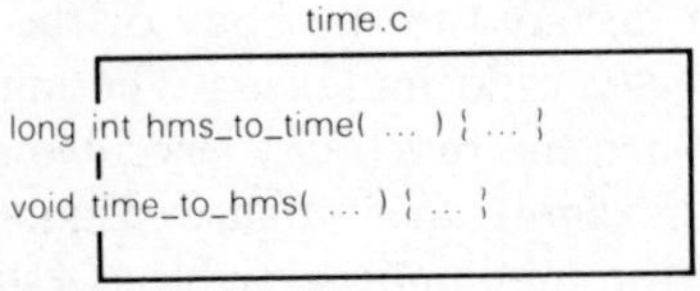

time.c

Fig. 7.2

into its equivalent number of seconds. Function time_to_hms performs the inverse operation. Using our notation, the second program unit is shown by Fig. 7.2.

Both these functions are *exported* from this module and *imported* into the client program unit main.c. The latter thus contains two external referencing declarations for these subordinate functions. The coding for these two program units is then as shown in Program 7.3.

Program 7.3

```
/*
**      File:           main.c
**
**      Determine the difference between two 24-hour
**      clock times. The input data and the result
**      are all expressed in the same 24-hour format.
*/

#include <stdio.h>

main()
   {
   int       hours1, minutes1, seconds1;        /* 1st time */
   int       hours2, minutes2, seconds2;        /* 2nd time */
   int       hours, minutes, seconds;           /* result */
   long int time1, time2;                       /* conversions */
   long int labs();                             /* forward ref. */

   extern long int hms_to_time();               /* external */
   extern void time_to_hms();                   /* ref. decl. */

   scanf("%d %d %d", &hours1, &minutes1, &seconds1);
   scanf("%d %d %d", &hours2, &minutes2, &seconds2);

   time1 = hms_to_time(hours1, minutes1, seconds1);
   time2 = hms_to_time(hours2, minutes2, seconds2);

   time_to_hms(labs(time1-time2), &hours, &minutes, &seconds);
   printf("The difference is %d %d %d\n", hours, minutes, seconds);
   }

long int labs(x)                      /* absolute value */
   long int x;
   {
   return(x < 0L ? -x : x);
   }

/*
**      File:    time.c
**
**      Two functions to convert between a time measured
**      in a total number of seconds and a time expressed
**      in hours, minutes and seconds. Each function is
**      the complement of the other.
*/

#include <stdio.h>
```

```
#define SECS_IN_MIN            60
#define MINS_IN_HOUR           60

void time_to_hms (t, h, m, s)
  long int t;                           /* original time */
  int *h, *m, *s;                       /* computed time */
  {
    int mins;

    mins = (int)(t / SECS_IN_MIN);
    *s   = (int)(t % SECS_IN_MIN);
    *m   = mins % MINS_IN_HOUR;
    *h   = mins / MINS_IN_HOUR;
  }

long int hms_to_time (h,m,s)
  int h, m, s;                          /* input time */
  {
    return(((long)h * MINS_IN_HOUR + m) * SECS_IN_MIN + s);
  }
```

As previously noted, the C compiler does not perform type checking of function arguments (but see Appendix H). However, there is some merit in documenting the formal argument declarations in the external referencing declaration. Thus, function hms_to_time might be shown as:

extern long int hms_to_time(/* int hours, minutes, seconds */);

or as:

extern long int hms_to_time(/* int, int, int */);

Further, the C programmer who is the author of the program unit time.c minimizes the burden on the client by providing a header file containing all the necessary external declarations. We extend our notation by showing both the program unit and its associated header file with Fig. 7.3.

The actual content of this header file might be:

```
/*
** File:    time.h
**
** Header file providing the specification of
** the two time conversion functions.
*/
```

extern long int hms_to_time(/* int, int, int */);
extern void time_to_hms(/* long int, int *, int *, int * */);

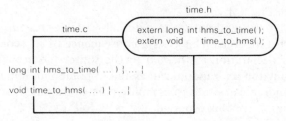

Fig. 7.3

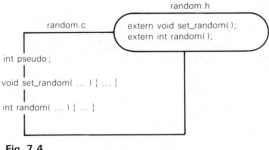

Fig. 7.4

The two external referencing declarations in the application program unit (main.c) can then be replaced by a preprocessor #include statement:

    #include "time.h"

The C programming language also supports external variables. An external variable is declared outside a function. Such variables are described as *global* since they may be referenced in the body of functions.

Because external variables are globally accessible, they provide an alternative to function arguments and return values as a means of communicating data between functions. An external variable has scope that extends from its declaration point to the end of the source program unit in which it appears. Any function declaration following this point may access the external variable by simply referring to its name.

We present these ideas by introducing a program unit for pseudo random number generation. The functions in the unit produce an apparently random sequence of integer values. The sequence begins with an initial value provided as an argument to the function set_random. Successive values of the sequence are produced by the integer function random. Each new value is computed from the previous value, which must, therefore, exist across successive calls of function random. Whereas automatic variables exist when a function is entered and disappear when it is left, external variables are *permanent*. Thus, if two functions share data or one function is repeatedly called and uses the previous value of some variable, then that variable has storage class extern. The program unit random.c has the signature shown in Fig. 7.4.

In the program unit random.c, the external variable *pseudo* can be referenced by both functions. This is as a consequence of its scope being from the point of declaration to the end of the source file in which it is declared. Thus, function set_random can assign to pseudo an initial value, whilst function random can use it to compute a new random value.

The implementation for this program unit is as follows:

```
/*
**      File:           random.c
**
**      Package of pseudo random number generating
**      code. Each random is generated from the
**      previous. The initial value is established
**      by the function set_random.
*/

#include "mystdio.h"

#define MULTIPLIER      97
#define MODULUS         256
#define INCREMENT       59

int pseudo;                     /* permanent */

void set_random(seed)
  int seed;
  {
    pseudo = seed;
  }

int random()
  {
    pseudo = (MULTIPLIER * pseudo + INCREMENT) % MODULUS;
    return (pseudo);
  }
```

The associated header file for this program unit is given below. It is incorporated into an application program using an #include preprocessor statement, and provides the necessary external referencing declarations.

```
/*
**      File:           random.h
**
**      Specification of the exportable items from
**      the random number package.
*/

extern void set_random( /* int seed */);
extern int  random();
```

We now complete our application program. A program simulates the throw of a six-sided die. The program tabulates the number of occurrences of each of the six sides of the die which is thrown 100 times.

Program 7.4

```
/*
**      File:           main.c
**
**      Tabulate the number of occurrences of each
**      of the six sides of a die which is thrown
**      100 times.
*/

#include <stdio.h>
#include "random.h"

#define SIDES           6
#define TIMES           100
#define SEED            17
```

```
main()
  {
    int throw, face;
    int one = 0, two = 0, three = 0,
        four = 0, five = 0, six = 0;

    set_random(SEED);
    for (throw = 1; throw <= TIMES; throw++)
      {
        face = random() % SIDES + 1;    /* 1 to 6 inclusive */
        switch (face)
          {
            case 1: one++;        break;
            case 2: two++;        break;
            case 3: three++;      break;
            case 4: four++;       break;
    case 5: five++;       break;
            case 6: six++;        break;
          }
      }
    printf("Face distribution %d %d %d %d %d %d\n",
        one, two, three, four, five, six);
  }
```

Note how the header file random.h is included at the topmost level. This means that these external references have global scope and can be referenced in any function in the program unit containing their declarations. Hence, a function subordinate to main appearing in the same file may also use any of the randomizing functions.

The desire to make every program variable an external object, because it seems to simplify communication, must be resisted. Firstly, it is difficult to modify such programs – there are too many functions using and modifying the values of these global variables. Secondly, the previous generality of functions programmed in terms of their arguments and local variables, is, in this new version, now inextricably wired to the names of the external variables. Functions written with arguments are self-contained entities that could usefully be employed in other programs.

In the absence of explicit initialization, external variables are guaranteed to be set to zero. It is generally considered good programming practice, however, to show all initializations explicitly. To avoid any errors caused by the application programmer failing to initialize the random sequence, variable pseudo is explicitly initialized to 1 (see Fig. 7.5).

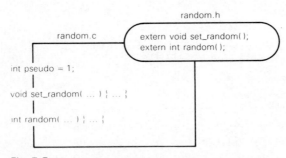

Fig. 7.5

The visibility of an external variable may be temporarily obscured by the declaration for an automatic variable within a function having the same name as the external variable. For example, consider Program 7.5.

Program 7.5

```
/*
**        The visibility of external variables may be
**        temporarily obscured by the declaration for an
**        automatic variable in a function. Variable
**        sum in the program exhibits this feature.
*/

#include <stdio.h>

int sum;                        /* defining declaration .... */
                                /* .... for external variable */

main()
    {
    void subroutine();                      /* forward reference */

    sum = 15;                               /* the external variable */
    subroutine();                           /* call the function */
    printf("External sum is %d\n", sum);
    }


void subroutine()
    {
    float sum = 1.234;          /* automatic, shields external */

    printf("Local sum is %f\n", sum);
    }
```

The variable sum assigned the value 15 in the main function binds to the declaration for the external variable of type integer. However, within the function subroutine the variable sum appearing in the printf function call associates with the declaration for the local of type float. Thus, the output from the program is:

Local sum is 1.234
External sum is 15

External variables are initialized conceptually at compile time. The initialization is performed once. The initial value may be any *constant expression*, that is, any expression not involving a program variable:

#define KILO   1024

int sum = 0;
long int memory = 64 * KILO;
char ampersand = '&';

An important issue with external names is ensuring consistency among declarations. It is possible for two or more referencing declarations of the same external variable to specify different initializations. The recommended course of action is two-fold. First, only the defining declaration should include an explicit initialization. All other referencing declarations use the storage class extern and do not include an initializer:

int errors = 0;   /* defining declaration, ... */
                     /* .... explicit initializer   */

extern int errors;   /* referencing declaration, .. */
                     /* .... no initializer   */

7.6 Storage class static

We know that variables may be declared either within a function body or outside the body of a function. We refer to the former as local variables and to the latter as global variables. *Static* variables offer a third class of storage management. Static variables may be either local or global.

Local static variables are internal to the particular function in which they are declared, that is, they have local scope. Unlike automatic variables, static variables remain in existence, they do not come and go each time a function is called and they retain their values between function calls. Internal static variables provide *private* and *permanent* variable storage to a function.

Static variables, like externals, may be initialized with a constant expression. A static local variable is initialized *once* at the start of program execution. Thereafter, the value of a static variable when leaving a function is the same when the function is next entered. This is demonstrated by Program 7.6.

Program 7.6

```
/*
**      Local static variables are initialized once
**      at compile time. Local variables, on the other
**      hand, are initialized each time the function
**      is entered.
*/

#include <stdio.h>

main()
    {
    int  i;                         /* loop counter */
    void subroutine();              /* forward reference */

    for (i = 0; i < 5; i++)
        subroutine();
    }


void subroutine()
    {
    static int static_var = 0;      /* performed once */
    int        auto_var   = 0;      /* for every function call */

    printf("automatic = %d, static = %d\n", auto_var, static_var);

    auto_var++;                     /* redundant operation */
    static_var++;                   /* carried forward */
    }
```

The function subroutine contains declarations for two local variables. The variable auto_var is an automatic of type int. The value is initialized to zero at each function invocation. The increment performed on this variable, following the printf call, is lost on function termination. On the other hand, the initialization of the local static variable static_var is performed once but the increment is executed on each function call. As a consequence, the output from the program is:

    automatic = 0, static = 0
    automatic = 0, static = 1
    automatic = 0, static = 2
    automatic = 0, static = 3
    automatic = 0, static = 4

External static variables are also supported by C. An external static variable is known within the remainder of the source file in which it is declared, following the point of declaration, but not in any other program file. External static variables cannot be exported from a program unit. In C, static connotes not only permanence but also a degree of *privacy*. Internal static variables are known only inside the function in which they are declared; external static variables are known only within the source file in which they are declared. Their names do not interfere with variables or functions of the same name appearing in other files.

In the program unit random.c introduced in the previous section, the external variable pseudo is used to hold successive values of the sequence of random numbers. The associated header file random.h provides the application program unit with the external references to the two exportable functions. There is nothing, however, to stop the application program from also including an external reference to the variable pseudo. If the application program contains the declaration:

    extern int pseudo;

then this variable may now be referenced in any application program statement. In particular, it is capable of being erroneously assigned. The effect would be, of course, to corrupt the sequence of pseudo random numbers.

By giving this variable storage class static (strictly, external static), it will be global to the functions in the program unit in which it is declared, but not exportable to other program units. Controlled access to this variable is then provided by the exportable functions. Figure 7.6 illustrates how the program unit now reads.

The application's programmer cannot now misuse the variable pseudo. Further, a link error would occur if the client program unit contained an explicit external referencing declaration to variable pseudo. The identifier pseudo may, however, be used in some other context, for example, as a local or global variable in program unit main.c. It is not confused with the private variable with the same name in program unit random.c.

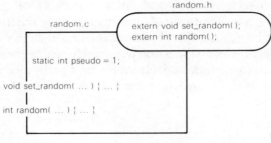

Fig. 7.6

The storage class static can also be applied to functions. External static functions are known only within the source file in which they are declared. The concept of privacy applies as well to functions as to static variables. External functions are exportable to other program units, whereas external static functions are not. This way the programmer of a module may select which functions in the module are to be accessible in other program units. External static functions can be considered as the building blocks of a module from which higher-level functions are constructed. These higher-level functions are exported to the application program, whilst the lower-level functions remain concealed. External static functions support the concept of information hiding.

7.7 Storage class register

The final storage class is called register. A register declaration informs the compiler that a variable will be referenced on numerous occasions and, where possible, such variables should use the CPU registers. The result may be a smaller and faster program.

The storage class register is only applicable to automatic variables and to function arguments. This storage class is indicated by prefixing a normal declaration with the reserved keyword register. A function to swap two integer values written in terms of register variables is:

```
void swap (a, b)
   register int *a, *b;
   {
      register int temp = *a;

      *a = *b;
      *b = temp;
   }
```

Register variables are restricted in a number of ways. First, most CPUs have a small number of registers available. Therefore, only a few variables in each function may be kept in registers. Where a C programmer names too many register class variables for the number of available CPU registers, the C compiler simply ignores the storage class register on the remaining declarations.

Storage class register is also restricted to certain types. This is very much machine dependent. Often, the only supported types are int, char and pointer. The local system documentation needs to be consulted on this matter.

Normally, one is not allowed to take the address of a register variable. The address operator (&) is used to obtain the memory address of a variable. Where that variable resides in a CPU register, such an operation is meaningless.

None of the remaining examples in this book uses register variables. Where some piece of logic is identified as time-critical, register storage class should be used. Unless specifically mentioned, we shall choose to ignore this storage class.

7.8 Summary

1. Identifiers associate with some C object, such as a variable or a function, in a *declaration*. Declarations include both *type* and *storage class*. Storage classes may be given *implicitly* or *explicitly* in a declaration.
2. Declarations also have *scope* which determines the region of the C program over which that declaration is active. An identifier declared in a top-level declaration has a scope that extends from the declaration point to the end of the source program unit. Such objects have storage class *extern* and are described as *global*. Parameter declarations and declarations at the head of blocks have storage class *auto*, described as *local*.
3. A declaration is *visible* in some context if the use of the identifier in that context is bound to the declaration. A declaration might be visible throughout its scope, but may also be temporarily *hidden* by other overlapping declarations (see Program 7.5).
4. To permit the use of an identifier before its *defining* declaration, a *forward referencing* declaration is used. These declarations were introduced in Chapter 5 to permit a function to be called before its declaration.
5. Top-level declarations are assumed to have storage class *extern*. However, extern that is assumed and extern that is stated are usually reserved for two different meanings. Generally, the storage class extern is explicitly included on all referencing declarations to objects defined in another program unit. The storage class extern is omitted for the (one) defining declaration for each external object.
6. Variables and functions have an existence at run time. The *extent* of these objects is the period of time for which storage is allocated to them. An object has *static extent* when it is allocated storage at the commencement of the program and remains allocated until program termination.

Automatic variables and function arguments have *local extent* and are created upon entry to the block or function and are destroyed upon exit.

7. Static variables have static extent. Internal static variables have local scope. External static variables have scope which is limited to the program unit in which they are declared. External static functions are also restricted to the unit in which they are declared. External static storage class provides privacy not inherent to extern storage class.

8. The *register* storage class specifier is only applicable to local variables and function arguments. The register storage class is a strong recommendation to the compiler that the associated variable be kept in a CPU register to improve program execution. Many restrictions, including type and maximum number of objects, usually apply to this class.

9. The declaration of variables may be accompanied by an initializer. Initializers for automatic variables may be arbitrary expressions which are evaluated at run time upon block entry. Variables with static extent can only be initialized with compile time (constant) expressions. Variables with static extent and no explicit initializers are guaranteed to be initialized to zero.

7.9 Exercises

1. Explain what is meant by the following terms:

   (a) abstraction   (f) scope rules
   (b) program unit   (g) private
   (c) information hiding   (h) storage class
   (d) localization   (i) abstract data type
   (e) exportable

2. Distinguish between defining declarations and referencing declarations.

3. Why would an error occur at link time when the following two files are compiled and linked? Why is there no error at compile time?

file1	file2
. . . . .	. . . . .
extern int time;	static int time = 0;
. . . . .	. . . . .

4. What output is produced when the following three files ae separately compiled then linked and run?

file1	file2
#include ⟨stdio.h⟩	static int date = 10;
extern int date;	
main( )	
{	
printf("%d\n", date);	
}	

file3
int date = 20;

5. Why is the following considered bad programming? Is it acceptable to the compiler?

file1	file2
int day = 7;	extern int day = 14;

6. A programmer has designed a screen-handling program unit, an outline of which is provided below. In the package, a screen is identified as an abstract data type for which a representation and a number of operations are provided.

```
#include <stdio.h>
static int nrows, ncols;        /* screen dimensions */
static int row, col;            /* cursor coordinates */

static void loadcursor(ro, co)  /* position ... */
  int ro, co;                   /* ... cursor */
  {
    . . . . .
    row = ro;
    col = co;
  }

void home()                     /* cursor at top left */
  {
    loadcursor(0, 0);
  }

void atsay(ro, co, ch)          /* print ch at ... */
  int ro, co;                   /* ... screen pos ... */
  char ch;                      /* ... ro, co */
  {
    loadcursor(ro, co);
    putchar(ch);
  }
```

etc.

(a) What are the resources in this program unit?

(b) What are the resources that represent the operations on the screen abstraction?

(c) Why do the integer variables nrows, ncols, row and col have storage class external static?
    What was the programmer's reasoning behind this decision?

(d) What are the exportable resources from this unit?
    What resources are hidden?
    Provide a suitable interface header file for this package.

(e) Suggest why the function loadcursor has storage class static.

## CHAPTER 8

The C preprocessor

The C preprocessor is a simple *macro* processor that conceptually processes the source text of a C program immediately before the compilation process. In some implementations, the preprocessor is actually a separate program which reads the program source file and produces a new intermediate file that is then used as input to the compiler proper. In other implementations a single program supports both the preprocessing and compiling phases, with no intermediate file produced.

The preprocessor is controlled by preprocessor *command lines* or *directives*, which are lines in the source program text beginning with the character '#'. The preprocessor removes all directives from the source file, and makes any necessary transformations to the source, as directed by these commands. The resultant text is then processed by the compiler.

A line whose first character is '#' is treated as a preprocessor command. The name of the command immediately follows the '#' character. Most implementations require the '#' character to be in column 1 of the line. Others permit whitespace (blanks or tabs) to precede it. Some implementations permit whitespace to appear between the '#' character and the preprocessor command name. The use of these whitespace separators can improve program layout and readability but will render it less portable. Generally, it is best to avoid these features.

8.1 Simple macro definitions

A macro definition (or simply a macro) is an identifier that symbolizes a defined string composed of one or more tokens. The preprocessor statement that establishes this association is the *# define* statement. The preprocessor then guarantees to textually replace occurrences of that identifier appearing in the remainder of the program file with the *token string*. The token string is frequently referred to as the *body* of the macro.

The string of tokens is not a string as defined in section 3.4, but rather a character sequence terminated by a newline symbol. This character sequence without the newline symbol is the macro body.

There are two different forms for the # define statement. One is for use in simple string replacement and the second is used to perform string replacement with argument passing. We shall consider the simple string replacement first.

A token string is associated with an identifier by the #define statement. The form of this statement is:

#define identifier   token-string

The end of the identifier is taken as the first whitespace character to occur following the start of the identifier. The identifier is as defined in section 3.5. The token string is the remainder of the line. This simple form is frequently used to introduce named symbolic constants into a program. This way program constants such as the number of bits in a word or the number of days in a month, may be defined once in a program and then referred to elsewhere by name. This facilitates changing the value later if the need arises, providing a mechanism to isolate implementation-dependent values and assist program portability.

The following example illustrates the use of this preprocessor statement:

#define DAYS_IN_WEEK   7

From the point of definition throughout the remainder of the program source file, the preprocessor will replace all occurrences of DAYS_IN_WEEK with the token string 7. The replacement does not operate within strings. The program statements:

days = DAYS_IN_WEEK * weeks;
printf("%d weeks * DAYS_IN_WEEK is %d days\n", weeks, days);

would, after preprocessing, be compiled as:

days = > * weeks;
printf("%d weeks * DAYS_IN_WEEK is %d days\n", weeks, days);

The following program illustrates a rather novel way of applying the #define statement. A criticism often made against C is that it is terse and cryptic. A C program may be made more verbose and its structure highlighted, by flavoring it to resemble languages like Pascal. The flavoring is achieved by defining Pascal-like constructs using the #define statement. Program 8.1 repeats Program 6.2.

Program 8.1

```
/*
**      Read a series of positive floating point values
**      terminated with a negative value and compute the
**      sum of the non-negative values.
*/

#include <stdio.h>

#define PROGRAM             main()
#define FLOAT               float
#define FORMATIN            "%f"
#define WHILE               while (
#define DO                  )
#define BEGIN               {
#define END                 }
#define FORMATOUT           "The sum is %8.2f\n"
```

```
PROGRAM
  BEGIN
    FLOAT data, sum = 0.0;                    /* data and running total */

    scanf(FORMATIN, &data);
    WHILE data >= 0.0 DO
    BEGIN
      sum += data;
      scanf(FORMATIN, &data);
    END
    printf(FORMATOUT, sum);
  END
```

8.2 Macro arguments

A #define preprocessor statement of the form:

> #define identifier(identifier, identifier, ...)   token-string

is a macro definition with arguments. The macro name is the identifier
following the #define. The left parenthesis must immediately follow the
macro name with no intervening whitespace. If whitespace were to separate
the identifier and the left parenthesis then the definition is considered a
simple definition with no arguments. The macro body is then taken to
commence with the left parenthesis.

The comma-separated list of identifiers appearing between the parentheses gives the formal macro arguments. The identifiers must be unique.
Normally, the macro body is defined in terms of these formal arguments.
The formal arguments appearing in the macro body act as templates for the
actual arguments supplied when the macro is invoked.

Such a macro is invoked in a program by stating its name. The name
must, again, be immediately followed by the left parenthesis. After the left
parenthesis is a comma-separated list of actual arguments terminated by a
right parenthesis. The macro invocation is textually replaced with the body
of the macro. Each formal argument appearing in the macro body is
substituted by the corresponding actual argument.

For example:

> #define READINT(I)   scanf("%d", &I)

Unlike a function, the type of argument I is not defined, since we are merely
performing a textual substitution and not invoking a C function. With such
a definition we can write the statement:

> READINT(distance);

The preprocessor replaces this with:

> scanf("%d", &distance);

Another example, this time with two arguments, is:

> #define SWAPINT(X, Y)   {int temp = X; X = Y; Y = temp;}

By using block structure we introduce a local integer variable *temp* enabling us to provide a macro definition to interchange the values of the integer variables. A call is:

SWAPINT(low,high);

In all our examples, the token string extends to the end of the line. If the token string extends over multiple lines, then each line, except the last, must terminate in a backslash symbol (\) followed immediately by a newline symbol. For example, a macro to determine whether a year is a leap year or not is:

#define IS_LEAP(Y) Y % 4 = = 0 && Y % 100 ! = 0 ¦ ¦ \
    Y % 400 = = 0

With this definition we can write statements such as:

if (IS_LEAP(year)). . . .

evaluated as:

if (year % 4 = = 0 && year % 100 ! = 0 ¦ ¦ year % 400 = = 0) . . . .

When using macros with arguments one must be careful to avoid a subtle pitfall. Consider the apparently innocent definition:

#define SQUARE(X)   X * X

The assignment:

bsquared = SQUARE(b);

behaves quite normally, being textually processed into:

bsquared = b * b;

However, the expression:

y = SQUARE(x + 1);

expands to:

y = x + 1 * x + 1;

Because of the precedence rules for arithmetic operators, the expression is interpreted as:

y = x + (1*x) + 1;

which does not produce the same as the intended result:

y = (x + 1) * (x + 1);

This last example is generally the required result. Its form gives us a clue for preparing the macro definition: all formal parameters appearing in a macro body should always be parenthesized. To avoid another obscure side effect of macro expansion, it is generally safer to enclose the whole macro body in parentheses if it is an expression. The definition for SQUARE is now:

#define SQUARE(X)   ((X) * (X))

The statement:

y = SQUARE(x + 1);

now expands into:

y = ((x + 1) * (x + 1));

To avoid confusion between formal macro arguments and simple macro definitions, some identifiable labeling is encouraged. It is common programming practice to restrict formal arguments in macros to be identifiers commencing with an underscore symbol. Reserving the underscore in this way informs the reader of the particular use of the identifier. The final form for macro SQUARE is then:

#define SQUARE(_X)   ((_X) * (_X))

In section 6.6 an infinite loop was symbolically defined by:

define FOREVER   for (;;)

A variant is one of the most common for constructs. Frequently, a for statement is required in which a control variable is set to some initial value, then increments by one to some upper limit. We might define this with a macro employing arguments as shown in the following program.

Program 8.2

```
/*
**      Form the sum of the first 20 integers. The data to
**      this program are self-generated by the sequence
**      1, 2, 3, ..., 20.
*/

#include <stdio.h>

#define FOR(_CONTROL, _INIT, _FINAL)    for ((_CONTROL) = (_INIT);\
                                             (_CONTROL) <= (_FINAL);\
                                             (_CONTROL)++)

main()
    {
        int number, sum = 0;            /* number and running total */

    FOR(number, 1, 20)
        sum += number;
    printf("Sum of the first 20 integers is: %d\n", sum);
    }
```

8.3 Macro expansion

The preprocessor operates by replacing the macro name (and any actual arguments if present) with the body of the macro. If the macro definition involves formal arguments, then each occurrence of a formal argument is replaced with the corresponding actual argument. The process is know as macro expansion.

Once a macro call has been expanded, the scanning for further macro calls resumes at the *beginning* of the expansion. This permits one macro to be defined in terms of another. Thus, when a macro is expanded and its body contains a call to another macro this too is expanded upon rescanning. For example:

```
# define PI          3.1415926
# define TWOPI      2 * PI
```

Given those two definitions, the statements:

```
area = PI * radius * radius;
circumference = TWOPI * radius;
```

expand into:

```
area = 3.1415926 * radius * radius;
circumference = 2 * 3.1415926 * radius;
```

The second statement is produced as a consequence of TWOPI being first expanded into 2 * PI then a rescanning produces 2 * 3.1415926.

This feature of rescanning is also used when symbolic names are used to define the size of a table (see Chapter 11). Frequently, a second related table is also declared whose size is a function of the size of the first table, for example, twice the first or one more than the first. We can then define:

```
# define SIZE            128
# define SIZEPLUS1     (SIZE + 1)
```

8.4 Redefining and undefining macros

It is generally permissible in C to define a name with #define which has already been defined. The result of such a redefinition is very much compiler dependent. Some implementations simply discard the old definition and replace it with the new one. Others consider it to be an error. To avoid any such problems, it is best to remove a definition first before assigning a new one. A definition is removed (undefined) with the *#undef* preprocessor command. The command form is:

```
# undef identifier
```

This command causes the preprocessor to forget the macro definition with the given name. A completely new definition may then be given to the identifier using a #define command. If the identifier is currently not defined, then normally the #undef command is ignored.

```
#define TAX      10
#undef TAX
#define TAX      15
```

would define TAX as 15

8.5 File inclusion

The #include preprocessor statement causes the content of a named text file to be processed as if it had appeared in place of the #include command. There are two forms of the command:

#include "filename"

and

#include ⟨filename⟩

The two forms differ in how the specified file is located in the computer's file store. If the filename is surrounded by double quotes then the file is expected in the same 'directory' as the file containing the #include command. Generally, this form is used to refer to other files written by the user. If the filename is delimited by diamond brackets ⟨ and ⟩, the search for the file takes place in certain standard places. On UNIX systems, the files are expected in the directory /usr/include. This form is generally used to reference standard system files. In all our programs which perform input/output we have included the standard header ⟨stdio.h⟩.

An included file may itself contain other #include commands. Nested #include is therefore supported. The depth of nesting is implementation dependent. Nesting to at least five or six levels is common.

8.6 Conditional compilation

The C preprocessor supports a facility known as conditional compilation. Conditional compilation features in a number of common programming problems. It is used to enhance program portability by establishing definitions which are themselves the subject of other definitions. Conditional compilation can also be used to selectively incorporate or omit a series of statements in a program. Commonly this is used to activate or deactivate debugging statements.

In this and in previous chapters we have shown how to use the #define statement to give symbolic names to constants as in:

#define INTSIZE   16

The latter might be used to specify the number of bits in an integer for a particular machine. Thereafter, the symbolic constant INTSIZE may be used throughout the program source text in place of 16. If the program had to be moved to a machine with a different number of bits in an integer then this, and possibly other machine-dependent definitions, would have to be changed.

The problem of changing all the #defines when moving the program from one machine to another can be reduced by anticipating this likelihood and programming it by making use of the conditional compilation capabilities of the preprocessor. The statements we use are:

```
# ifdef identifier      # ifndef identifier
     lines-1                 lines-1
# else                  # else
     lines-2                 lines-2
# endif                 # endif
```

and:

```
# if constant-expression
     lines-1
# else
     lines-2
# end
```

The series of lines, denoted lines-1 and lines-2, is any number of lines of program text. The lines may be program declarations, program statements or even other preprocessor statements. The *# else* directive and its associated group of lines is optional and may be omitted. Either series of lines may also contain one or more sets of nested conditional compilation commands.

In the first form, the identifier is taken as a name defined in a #define preprocessor macro. If such an identifier has been previously defined, then the first group of lines is compiled whilst the second group is discarded. The definition of the identifier can be in a form as previously discussed. It is even sufficient to define an identifier with:

```
# define VAX
```

Every occurrence of VAX in our program is replaced with the null token string, that is, with nothing. However, as far as the preprocessor is concerned, the identifier VAX is now defined.

Addressing the original problem, we can now establish a definition for INTSIZE which can be conditionally compiled for the target computer. If we write:

```
# define INTEL8086

# ifdef INTEL8086
#       define INTSIZE    16
# endif
```

```
#ifdef VAX
#      define INTSIZE     32
#endif

#ifdef IBM370
#      define INTSIZE     32
#endif
```

then INTSIZE is defined as 16 bits for an Intel 8086 microprocessor. To move to a different machine we can either replace #define INTEL8086 with, say:

```
#define VAX
```

or use the more convenient -D argument in the C compiler command line (see Appendix G). In this case we would not include definitions for the INTEL8086, VAX or IBM370 in the program source file. A single definition is established when the compiler is invoked.

The preprocessor statement *#ifndef* (if not defined) is the converse of *#ifdef*. The #ifndef determines if the identifier is not the subject of a #define statement or has been undefined by an #undef statement. As an alternative to the example above, we might once again select INTEL8086 architecture with:

```
#define VAX
#define IBM370

#ifndef INTEL8086
#      define INTSIZE     16
#endif

#ifndef VAX
#      define INTSIZE     32
#endif

#ifndef IBM370
#      define INTSIZE     32
#endif
```

The final form of the conditional compilation facility is:

```
#if constant-expression
    lines-1
#else
    lines-2
#endif
```

The preprocessor operates by first evaluating at compile time the constant-expression. If the expression evaluates to 0 (logical false), the first group of lines, lines-1, is discarded and the second group is passed on for compilation. If the expression evaluates to other than zero (logical true), lines-1 is passed on and lines-2 is discarded. The expression must be capable of being determined at compile time. That is it may involve C operators but only with constants (literal or symbolic). No run time values such as a program variable may be used in these expressions.

This last facility (or the others for that matter) may be used to turn on and off debugging statements. When developing a program we might incorporate statements to trace a program's behavior, for example statements to print messages or the values of program variables. During program development these statements are invaluable for detecting program errors. When the program is fully operational they are no longer required or even desirable and are compiled out of the code. Consider a function to convert a distance in yards, feet and inches to its equivalent distance in inches. The function behavior is traced by including an additional printf function call. This is conditionally compiled into the code:

```
#define DEBUG            1

#define YARDS_TO_FEET    3
#define FEET_TO_INCHES   12


int distance (yards, feet, inches)
   int yards, feet, inches;


   {
#if DEBUG
     printf("function distance\n");
     printf("arguments: %d yards, %d feet, %d inches\n",
        yards, feet, inches);
#endif
        return((YARDS_TO_FEET*yards + feet)
          *FEET_TO_INCHES + inches);
   }
```

To turn off the tracing we merely have to redefine DEBUG to logical false:

```
#define DEBUG    0
```

As before, the whole operation may be controlled at compile time with the -D option in the C compiler.

Since the preprocessor supports nested include files, experience has shown that sequential dependencies lead to interminable conflicts during program integration. Each include file should be included only once during compilation, and if the includes are nested unconditionally, this property

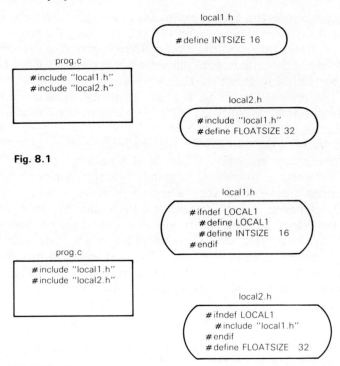

Fig. 8.1

Fig. 8.2

becomes hard to control. For example, consider the erroneous duplicate definition of INTSIZE during compilation of the program unit *prog* caused by the inclusion of local1.h and local2.h, the latter containing a nested inclusion of local1.h (see Fig. 8.1).

To avoid multiple inclusions of the same include file, each include file should begin with a #ifndef that tests whether some #define symbol has already been defined (see Fig. 8.2).

8.7 Line numbering

Certain C tools that generate C source text as output use the # *line* preprocessor command so that compiler errors can reference the input file to the tool and not to the actual source text produced. The command:

#line constant "filename"

causes the compiler to treat subsequent lines in the program as if the program source file is named *filename*, and as if the line number begins at *constant*. The filename is optional, and if omitted, then the last file name in the last #line is adopted or the name of the source file containing this #line is adopted if no name was previously specified.

This statement is not considered further in this book.

Case study 8.1: Pseudo random numbers

This case study revisits Program 7.4 which determines the distribution of the throw of a die using a pseudo random number generator. The enhancements made to this version illustrate the use of the C preprocessor.

The problem naturally divides into two parts. The first is the application itself, enumerating the number of times each face of the die is obtained. A sequence of 100 throws of the die is simulated. The second part is responsible for generating the series of pseudo random numbers. We choose, therefore, to package these as two program units called, respectively, *main.c* and *random.c*. The functions necessary to support the application are exported from the second module.

In any program unit, resources (functions and data) are either private, exportable to other program units or imported from program units. These three attributes are emphasized by the storage classes PRIVATE, IMPORT and EXPORT, equivalenced by #define in the header file visible.h:

```
/*
**      File:   visible.h
**
**      Symbolic names are defined for the terms EXPORT,
**      IMPORT and PRIVATE. A data item or function that
**      is labeled PRIVATE is synonymous with the storage
**      class static. An object that is IMPORTed from another
**      program unit is an extern object. Objects that are
**      EXPORTed from a module are implicitly global.
*/

#define EXPORT
#define IMPORT                  extern
#define PRIVATE                 static
```

The header file random.h operates as the specification part for the program unit random.c. The specification contains definitions for the resources imported from that program unit into an application program. Pictorially we have Fig. 8.3.

We introduce a further header file called pdl.h. Throughout the text we have applied stepwise refinement in the analysis of our software. The problem pseudo code is expressed using a program design language or PDL. The header file pdl.h contains preprocessor constructs for this PDL so that

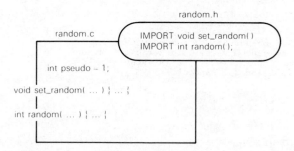

Fig. 8.3

we may actually use them directly in our program coding:

```
/*
**        File:    pdl.h
**
**        Provide all the necessary definitions to support
**        the program design language introduced in the text.
*/

#define BEGIN             {
#define END               }
#define PROGRAM           main()

#define WHILE             while (
#define DO                ){
#define ENDWHILE          }

#define IF                if (
#define THEN              ){
#define ELSE              } else {
#define ENDIF             }

#define SWITCH            switch (
#define TO                ){
#define WHEN(LABEL)       case LABEL :
#define OTHERWISE         default :
#define ENDSWITCH         }

#define AND               &&
#define OR                ||
#define NOT               !
```

The program units random.c and main.c may now be programmed using these header files. Essentially, the logic is unchanged from Program 7.4. The principal difference is organizational, with the sequential dependencies amongst header files controlled by conditional compilation switches.

```
/*
**        File:        random.h
**
**        Specification of the exportable items from
**        the random number package.
*/

#ifndef EXPORT
#        include "visible.h"
#endif

IMPORT void set_random( /* int seed */);
IMPORT int  random();


/*
**        File:        random.c
**
**        Package of pseudo random number generating
**        code. Each random value is generated from the
**        previous. The initial value is established
**        by the function set_random.
*/

#include "visible.h"
#include "random.h"
#include "pdl.h"

#define MULTIPLIER        97
#define MODULUS           256
#define INCREMENT         59
```

```
PRIVATE int pseudo = 1;

EXPORT void set_random(seed)
   int seed;
   BEGIN
     pseudo = seed;
   END

EXPORT int random()
   BEGIN
     pseudo = (MULTIPLIER * pseudo + INCREMENT) % MODULUS;
     return (pseudo);
   END


/*
**      File:          main.c
**
**      Tabulate the number of occurrences of each
**      of the six sides of a die which is thrown
**      100 times.
*/

#include <stdio.h>
#include "random.h"
#include "pdl.h"

#define SIDES          6
#define TIMES          100
#define SEED           17

PROGRAM
  BEGIN
    int throw, face;
    int one = 0, two = 0, three = 0,
        four = 0, five = 0, six = 0;

    set_random(SEED);
    for (throw = 1; throw <= TIMES; throw++)
      BEGIN
        face = random() % SIDES + 1;      /* 1 to 6 inclusive */
        SWITCH face TO
            WHEN(1) one++;        break;
            WHEN(2) two++;        break;
            WHEN(3) three++;      break;
            WHEN(4) four++;       break;
            WHEN(5) five++;       break;
            WHEN(6) six++;        break;
        ENDSWITCH
      END

    printf("Face distribution %d %d %d %d %d %d\n",
        one, two, three, four, five, six);
  END
```

8.8 Summary

1. The C preprocessor is a simple macro processor which conceptually processes the source text of a C program before compiling. The preprocessor is controlled by command lines, which are lines of the source program beginning with the character '#'. The standard preprocessor commands are #define, #undef, #include, #if, #ifdef, #ifndef, #else, #end and #line.

2. The #define command introduces a macro definition. A macro is an identifier which symbolizes a token string. The preprocessor replaces

occurrences of that identifier with the token string, possibly replacing any formal arguments appearing in the macro body with the actual arguments supplied when the macro is invoked. The #undef command removes a previous macro definition.

3. The #include preprocessor command line causes the content of a named file to be processed as if it appeared in place of the command. Two forms of file naming are provided; they differ in how the specified file is located in the computer's file store.

4. Conditional compilation is used to selectively incorporate or omit a series of program statements. The commands used are #if, #ifdef and #ifndef, as well as the associated #else and #end. Conditional compilation is used to enhance program portability and to embed debugging statements.

8.9 Exercises

1. Define a macro MIN that gives the minimum of two values, then write a program to test the definition.

2. Define a macro MAX3 that gives the maximum of three values. Test the definition in a program.

3. Write the macros IS_UPPER_CASE and IS_LOWER_CASE which respectively, return a non-zero value if a single character argument is an upper-case (lower-case) alphabetic letter.

4. Write a macro IS_ALPHABETIC that gives non-zero if its argument is an alphabetic character. Let this macro use the two macros defined in the previous example.

CHAPTER 9

More on data types

We have already seen that the use of symbolic constants can improve program readability. By providing a suitable name (identifier) for a constant, as in the definition:

#define AUGUST   8

we can concentrate on the significance of the 'constant' AUGUST rather than on its specific 'value'. Should it be necessary to change this constant's value, only the definition need be changed, rather than scanning the whole program source file to locate and replace every occurrence of the literal 8.

For similar reasons, C provides the *type definition* whereby a programmer-defined name is given to a type. This facility is explored in the next section.

So far, we have met the fundamental data types provided by C. Sometimes we require a wider choice than this. For example, we might need a data type whose values are the days of the week. In this way we could naturally express the assignment:

day = MONDAY;

where MONDAY is a constant for this particular data type and day is a variable of the same type. C provides a means for us to specify our own data types. These features greatly enhance the ability to express programs in the abstract terms of the problem domain. We discuss these concepts in section 9.2.

9.1 The typedef statement

The C programming language supports a number of fundamental data types such as char and int. A variable declaration for the fundamental types employs the *type specifiers* char, int, etc. The declaration:

int hours, minutes;

specifies that the variables hours and minutes are of type int. The C language also provides the *typedef* declaration, which allows a type to be explicitly associated with an identifier. The statement:

typedef int   Time;

defines the type name Time to be equivalent to the C data type int. The named identifier can be used later to declare a variable or function in the usual way. The declaration:

Time hours, minutes;

declares the variables hours and minutes to be of type Time, equivalent to the typé int.

The principal advantage of the use of the typedef in the above example is in the added readability that it lends to the definition of the variables. The declaration additionally incorporates the intended purpose of these variables in the program. Declaring them to be of type int in the normal way would not have made the intended use of these variables clear. A second advantage is that it allows abbreviations for long declarations. This will be made apparent when arrays and structure declarations are introduced.

To define a new type name, the following procedure is applied. Firstly, write a declaration as if a variable of the desired type were being declared. For example, to declare a variable *var* of type int, the declaration is:

int   var;

Secondly, substitute the variable name with the new type name:

int   Time;

Finally, prepend with the reserve keyword typedef:

typedef int   Time;

We illustrate the use of the *typedef* statement in Program 9.1. The program is supplied with a date represented as three positive integers, respectively, the day, month and year. The program calculates the day number of the date for the given year. The 1 January for all years is day number 1. The 31 December is day number 365 for a non-leap year and day number 366 for a leap year.

Program 9.1

```
/*
**      Read a valid date in the form DD/MM/YYYY and determine
**      from it the day of the year. The 1 January for all years
**      is day number 1. The 31 December is day number 365 for
**      a non-leap year and 366 for a leap year.
*/

#include <stdio.h>

#define FALSE        0
#define TRUE         1
#define ISLEAP(Y)        ((Y) % 4 == 0 &&\
  (Y) % 100 != 100 || (Y) % 400 == 0)
```

```
typedef int               Day;
typedef int               Month;
typedef int               Year;
typedef int               Daynumber;
typedef int               Daysinmonth;
typedef int               Boolean;

main ()
  {
    Day          day;              /* supplied data value */
    Month        month, m;         /* m is month counter */
    Year         year;
    Daynumber    daynumber;        /* computed value */
    Daysinmonth daysinmonth (); /* forward reference */

    scanf ("%2d/%2d/%4d", &day, &month, &year);

    daynumber = 0;
    for (m = 1; m < month; m++)
      daynumber += daysinmonth (m, year);
    daynumber += day;

    printf ("%2d/%2d/%4d is daynumber %d\n",
                    day, month, year, daynumber);
  }

Daysinmonth daysinmonth (month, year)
  Month month;                     /* month within .... */
  Year year;                       /* .... year */
  {
    switch (month)
      {
        case 4: case 6:        /* April, June, .... */
        case 9: case 11:       /* .... September, November */
          return (30);

        case 2:                /* February -- special */
          if (ISLEAP(year))
            return (29);
          else
            return (28);

        default:
          return (31);
      }
  }
```

A type name introduced by a typedef statement may clash with the names of other program variables and functions. This is known as *name overloading*. In the example above, we have used *Day* to represent a type name and *day* to represent a variable of that type. Since C is case-sensitive, they are, of course, considered distinct by the C compiler. Name overloading, however, permits us to use the same identifier for both type names and variables or function names. Thus, it would be perfectly acceptable to declare:

    typedef int   day;

and:

    day   holidays;
    long int   day;

The compiler resolves the ambiguity by employing contextual information.

It does, of course, make the program more difficult to read and, perhaps, more difficult to debug if there are problems. It is better to use a different case for programmer-defined type names, as above. If lower-case type names are to be used then they should be distinct from other program names.

9.2 Enumeration types

The keyword *enum* is used to declare enumerated types. The enumeration type provides a means of naming (or enumerating) the elements of a finite set, and of declaring variables that take values which are elements of that set. The set of values is represented by identifiers called *enumeration constants*. For example, the declaration:

enum day { SUN, MON, TUE, WED, THU, FRI, SAT} d1, d2, d3;

creates a new enumeration type 'enum day', whose values are SUN, MON, ..., SAT. It also declares three variables d1, d2 and d3 of the enumeration type enum day. These variables may be assigned values which are elements of the set:

d1 = MON;

We may also test the values of enumerated variables:

if (d1 = = d2) . . . .

or

if (!(d2 = = SUN ¦ ¦ d2 = = SAT)) . . . .

The 'enumeration tag' day appearing in the declaration above is optional. The declaration is then equivalent to:

enum {SUN, MON, TUE, WED, THU, FRI, SAT} d1, d2, d3;

The enumeration tag day, however, allows an enumeration type to be referenced after its definition. The single declaration:

enum day {SUN, MON, TUE, WED, THU, FRI, SAT} d1, d2, d3;

is exactly equivalent to the declarations:

enum day {SUN, MON, TUE, WED, THU, FRI, SAT};
enum day d1, d2, d3;

The first declaration does not allocate any storage, but a *template* is set up for the type enum day. This type may be used, as shown, in any subsequent declaration (including function argument declarations and function type specifiers).

From the previous section, we may use a typedef statement to associate the type name Day with the enumerated type enum day as in:

enum day {SUN, MON, TUE, WED, THU, FRI, SAT};
typedef enum day   Day;

On the basis of these declarations we might imagine a program processing the days of the week. For a given day we may wish to compute what day is tomorrow. MON is the day after SUN, TUE is the day after MON, ..., SUN is the day after SAT. The declaration for the function is:

```
Day tomorrow(d)
  Day d;
    {
       Day nextd;

       switch (d)
         {
            case SUN:  nextd = MON;  break;
            case MON:  nextd = TUE;  break;
            case TUE:  nextd = WED;  break;
            case WED:  nextd = THU;  break;
            case THU:  nextd = FRI;  break;
            case FRI:  nextd = SAT;  break;
            case SAT:  nextd = SUN;  break;
         }
       return(nextd);
    }
```

By employing an enumerated type, the program meaning is enhanced as demonstrated in Program 9.2. This program computes an employee's weekly pay, determined from the number of hours worked in each day of the week. Payment for Saturday is one-and-a-half times the basic rate and Sunday is twice the basic rate.

Program 9.2

```
/*
**    Compute the week's pay for an hourly paid employee.
**    Overtime is applied for weekend working.
*/

#include <stdio.h>

#define SATADJUSTMENT       1.5
#define SUNADJUSTMENT       2.0

enum weekday {SUN, MON, TUE, WED, THU, FRI, SAT};
typedef enum weekday        Weekday;
```

```
main()
  {
    int     hours;                        /* hours worked per day */
    float   baserate, rate, wages;
    Weekday day;
    Weekday tomorrow();                   /* forward reference */

    printf("Enter the basic hourly rate: ");
    scanf("%f", &baserate);

    wages = 0.0;
    printf("Enter the hours worked\n");
    printf("for Monday through Sunday: ");
    day = SUN;
    do {
      day = tomorrow(day);
      scanf("%d", &hours);

      switch (day)
        {
          case MON: case TUE:
          case WED: case THU: case FRI:
            rate = baserate;                          break;

          case SAT:
            rate = SATADJUSTMENT * baserate;          break;

          case SUN:
            rate = SUNADJUSTMENT * baserate;          break;
        }

      wages += rate * hours;

    } while (day != SUN);

    printf("Total wages for the week: %8.2f\n", wages);
  }


Weekday tomorrow(d)
  Weekday d;
    {
      Weekday nextd;

      switch (d)
        {
          case SUN: nextd = MON; break;
          case MON: nextd = TUE; break;
          case TUE: nextd = WED; break;
          case WED: nextd = THU; break;
          case THU: nextd = FRI; break;
          case FRI: nextd = SAT; break;
          case SAT: nextd = SUN; break;
        }
      return(nextd);
    }
```

Strictly, the C compiler assigns an int value starting with 0 to each enumeration constant in a set. In the example:

enum day {SUN, MON, TUE, WED, THU, FRI, SAT};

SUN has value 0, MON has value 1, ... and SAT has value 6. These default assignations may be altered by assigning an explicit constant to an enumeration constant in the list. Successive elements from the list are then assigned subsequent values. Consider:

enum navigate {NORTH, EAST = 4, SOUTH, WEST};

The enumeration constant NORTH has default value 0; EAST has explicit value 4; SOUTH and WEST are, respectively, 5 and 6, following the value for EAST.

When writing programs with enumerated type variables, one should not rely on the fact that the enumeration constants are treated as integer constants. Instead, these variables should be treated as distinct variable types. The motive behind this segregation deals with one of the main strengths of the enumerated type, namely, safety. It is more difficult to accidently assign a variable the wrong value if proper mnemonics are used.

If it does prove necessary to mix enumerated types and, say, integer values, casts may be employed. The function tomorrow, shown earlier, may be written more succinctly as:

```
Day tomorrow(d)
  Day d;
  {
    Day nextd;

    nextd = (Day) ((int) d + 1)%7;
    return (nextd);
  }
```

The assignment within function 'tomorrow' makes use of two casts. First the formal argument d of type enum day is coerced to type int. If d is SUN the coerced value is 0, if d is MON, the coerced value is 1, and so on. To this value we then add 1 (moving on to tomorrow), then find the remainder on dividing by 7. The derived value is the integer constant associated with tomorrow. This is coerced back to the type enum day before assigning to the variable nextd.

9.3 Summary

1. The *typedef* statement associates a programmer-defined identifier with an existing type or with a programmer-defined type. Programmer-defined type names are used as abbreviations for longer type specifiers and to incorporate the intended purpose of the variables or functions in declarations.

2. An *enumeration* data type is defined by listing the identifiers by which the values of the type are to be denoted. In most cases it is preferable to separate the type definition from the variable declaration, in which case the former does not allocate storage but simply acts as a template for the type. Unless assigned explicit integer values, the compiler assigns successive integer values to each enumeration constant, starting with zero.

9.4 Exercises

1. Repeat case studies 6.1, 6.2, 6.3 and 7.1 using typedef statements as appropriate.

2. Prepare a function which verbalizes its single argument of type Day (as defined in section 9.2).

3. Repeat case study 6.3 using an enumeration type for the decimal digits used in the functions do_units, do_teens and do_tens.

4. Prepare enumeration data type declarations for: (a) the suits in a pack of cards, (b) the colors of the rainbow, (c) monetary denominations, and (d) the integer binary operators supported by C.

## CHAPTER 10

Recursion

Any function may invoke any other function, as we have already seen (Chapter 5). Programmers exploit this facility to build programs constructed hierarchically, in which the main function invokes subfunctions F1, F2,... to perform subsidiary tasks; these subfunctions in turn invoke further subfunctions G1, G2,... to perform simpler tasks; and so on (Chapters 5 and 7). A functionally decomposed program design can then be directly implemented through this language feature.

This is not the only way of exploiting the use of functions. In particular, a function may call or invoke itself. Such a function is said to be *recursive*. Many programming problems have solutions which are expressible directly or indirectly through recursion. The ability to map these solutions on to recursive functions leads to elegant and natural implementations.

Recursion is commonly used in applications in which the solution can be expressed in terms of successively applying the same solution to subsets of the problem. Common applications involve the searching and sorting of recursively defined data structures (Chapters 11, 12, 14 and 15). A recursive solution is frequently an alternative to using iteration.

To illustrate, consider a function to evaluate the factorial of a number. The factorial of a positive integer n, written n!, is defined as the product of the successive integers 1 through n inclusive. The factorial of zero is treated as a special case and is defined as equal to 1. So:

$$n! = n*(n-1)*(n-2)*...*3*2*1 \qquad \text{for } n >= 1$$

and

$$0! = 1$$

It follows that:

$$5! = 5 \times 4 \times 3 \times 2 \times 1 = 120$$

The iterative solution is:

```
long int factorial(n)
  int n;
  {
     int k;
     long product = 1L;

     if (n = = 0)
        return (1L);
     else
        {
           for (k = n; k > 0; k - - )
              product * = k;
           return (product);
        }
  }
```

Customarily, the definition of factorial is given recursively. We observe that:

$$n! = n*(n - 1)*(n - 2)* \ldots 3*2*1$$

which we can group as:

$$n! = n*[(n - 1)*(n - 2)* \ldots *3*2*1]$$

The bracketed group is, of course, the definition for $(n - 1)!$. Thus, the recursive definition is:

$$n! = n*(n - 1)!$$

with the special case:

$$0! = 1$$

We can now develop a function to calculate the factorial of an integer n according to this recursive definition. Such a function is illustrated in Program 10.1.

Program 10.1

```
/*
**      Tables of factorials for 0, 1, 2, ... , 10. The
**      factorials are determined by a recursive function.
*/

#include <stdio.h>

main()
  {
     int      j;
     long int factorial();

     for (j = 0; j <= 10; j++)
        printf("%2d! is %ld\n", j, factorial(j));
  }
```

```
long int factorial(n)
  int n;
  {
    if (n == 0)
      return (1L);
    else
      return (n * factorial(n-1));
  }
```

The program's output is:

0! is 1
1! is 1
2! is 2
3! is 6
4! is 24
5! is 120
6! is 720
7! is 5040
8! is 40320
9! is 362880
10! is 3628800

The function *factorial* is recursive since it includes a call to itself. Let us see what happens in the case where the function is called to calculate the factorial of 5, for example. When the function is entered, the formal parameter n is set to 5. The conditional if statement determines that this n is not zero, and returns with the value obtained by evaluating n * factorial(n − 1), with n = 5, namely:

5 * factorial (4)

The expression specifies that the factorial function is to be called again, this time to obtain factorial (4). The multiplication of 5 by this value is left pending while factorial (4) is computed.

We call the factorial function again. This time, the actual argument is 4. Each time any C function is called it is allocated its own set of automatic variables and formal parameters with which to work. This applies equally to recursive or non-recursive functions. Therefore, the formal argument n that exists when the factorial function is called to calculate the factorial of 4 is distinct from the first call to calculate the factorial of 5.

With n = 4 this time, the function executes the return with the expression:

4 * factorial (3)

Once again, the multiplication by 4 is left pending while the factorial function is called to calculate the factorial of 3. The process continues in this manner until formal argument n has value 0. The situation is then as described by Table 10.1.

When the formal argument n is reduced to zero, the conditional if statement causes an immediate return with long value 1. The recursive

Table 10.1

factorial(n)	return (n * factorial(n − 1))
5	5 * factorial (4) = 5 * ?
4	4 * factorial (3) = 4 * ?
3	3 * factorial (2) = 3 * ?
2	2 * factorial (1) = 2 * ?
1	1 * factorial (0) = 1 * ?

Table 10.2

factorial(n)	return (n * factorial(n − 1))
1	1 * factorial (0) = 1 * 1 = 1
2	2 * factorial (1) = 2 * 1 = 2
3	3 * factorial (2) = 3 * 2 = 6
4	4 * factorial (3) = 4 * 6 = 24
5	5 * factorial (4) = 5 * 24 = 120

descent can now start to unwind and all the pending multiplications can be evaluated in reverse order. Repeating Table 10.1, but in reverse sequence, we obtain Table 10.2.

Lest it be argued that this last example is an artificial example, consider the Euclidean algorithm to determine the highest common factor of two positive integers n and m. The procedure can be written:

HCF(n, m) = if m > n then HCF (m, n)
            if m = 0 then n
            otherwise HCF (m, remainder when n is divided by m)

The recursive function can be written directly from the definition:

```
int hcf(n,m)
  int n,m;
    {
        if (m > n)
          return (hcf(m,n));
        else if (m == 0)
          return (n);
        else
          return (hcf(m, n % m));
    }
```

```
int hcf(n,m)
  int n,m;
  {
     if (m > n)
     {
        int temp = m;
        m = n;
        n = m;
     }

     while (n % m ! = 0)
        {
           int temp = m;
           m = n % m;
           n = temp;
        }

     return (m);
  }
```

It is also possible to write a function which calls a second function which in turn calls the the original function. This is known as *indirect recursion* and involves a circle of function calls. For example, function A calls function B, B calls C, and C calls A again. As usual, to permit a function call to precede the function declaration, a forward referencing declaration is employed. This is necessary with indirect recursion since it is impossible textually to rearrange the program so that every function declaration precedes its use. For example, consider the mutually recursive functions A and B. Since A calls B then we might consider placing the declaration for B before A, but since B also calls A this is clearly impossible.

Recursion is not always the most efficient solution to a problem. Many problems which can be solved recursively can also be solved using iteration, as shown above. The solution may be less elegant but can be more efficient in terms of program execution time and memory requirements. For each recursive function call a separate region of memory is established to hold the values of the arguments and local variables. Hence, recursive algorithms are expensive in terms of memory space utilization. Further, for each recursive call, processor time is used to pass function arguments, establish the new memory area for that call, and to return its result upon completion.

The most persuasive argument in support of recursive functions is that they reflect recursively defined data structures, and algorithms which are defined recursively. Further, some recursive algorithms are almost impossible to construct iteratively. Recursive functions which map recursive data structures are consistent with our philosophy of programs matching their data.

10.1 Summary

1. Recursion is a powerful tool for solving particular categories of problems. The result is elegant and natural program solutions.
2. A recursive function calls itself either directly or indirectly. Recursion usually consists of a general case and one or more base cases. It is vital in

the program implementation that the recursive function can terminate through its base conditions.
3. Recursive functions can be written in an equivalent iterative form. Owing to system overheads, a recursive function may be less efficient than its iterative one.

10.2 Exercises

1. Prepare a recursive function to form the sum of the first n positive integers using the recursive definition:

    sum(n) = n + sum(n − 1)

    What is the base case for this definition?

2. The following equations define the Fibonacci sequence of numbers:

    Fib(1) = 1
    Fib(2) = 1
    Fib(n) = Fib(n − 1) + Fib(n − 2)   for n > 2

    Produce a recursive C function directly from these definitions.

3. Write a recursive function to calculate values of Ackermann's function, Ack(m, n), defined for m > = 0 and n > = 0 by:

    Ack(0, n) = n + 1
    Ack(m, 0) = Ack(m − 1, 1)
    Ack(m, n) = Ack(m − 1, Ack(m, n − 1)),
                          for m > 0 and n > 0

    What is the value for Ack(3, 2)?

4. Write a function, digit(n, k), that returns the value of the kth digit from the right of the number n. For example:

    digit(234567, 2) = 6
    digit(1234, 7)   = 0

5. Write a function, count(n, k), that returns a count of the number of occurrences of the digit k in the number n. For example:

    count(4214, 4) = 2
    count(73, 5)   = 0

6. Write a function, reverse(n), that returns a number that is the digits of the number n reversed. For example:

    reverse(1234) = 4321
    reverse(222) = 222

7. A game called the 'Tower of Hanoi' consists of a platform carrying three posts and a number of discs of different size. The object of the game is to move a tower of discs, arranged as a pyramid, from the left-hand rod to the right-hand rod using the middle rod. The conditions of the game are that only one disc may be moved at a time, and at no stage may a larger disc rest on a smaller disc.

## CHAPTER 11

Arrays and pointers

In the programs written thus far, each variable was associated with a single data value. These variables are called simple variables. In this chapter we will begin the study of *aggregate types*. An aggregate type is a grouping of related data items. This class includes *arrays*, *structures* and *unions*.

The array is a data structure used to store a collection of data items that are all of the same type. By using an array, we can associate a single variable name with an entire collection of data. To process an individual item we need to specify the array name and indicate which array element is being referenced. Specific elements are distinguished by an *index* or *subscript*.

The motivation behind arrays is illustrated with the following problem. Suppose, for example, that we wish to construct a program which reads five integer values and prints them out in reverse order. To do so we might declare and use five integer variables as in:

```
main( )
    {
        int first, second, third, fourth, fifth;

        scanf("%d %d %d %d %d", &first, &second, &third,
            &fourth, &fifth);
        printf("%d %d %d %d %d\n", fifth, fourth, third,
            second, first);
    }
```

If, instead of five integer values to reverse we had, say, fifty, then manipulating the data by means of unique identifiers is an extraordinarily cumbersome approach.

11.1 Declaring and referencing arrays

In C, an array is declared just like any other variable. The syntax for an array declaration is:

type-specifier name[number-of-elements]

Type specifier is any of the fundamental types of C which we have already met, including the enumeration type. The type void is not included in this permissible set. The array size is specified as a constant expression representing the maximum number of elements. The array name is introduced as an identifier. An array called *table* with eight elements of type integer would be given by the declaration:

int table[8];

An array occupies a block of consecutive memory locations. Pictorially, the storage space reserved for the array table might appear as shown in Fig. 11.1.

To process the data stored in an array, we must be able to reference each individual element. The array subscript is used to differentiate between different elements of the same array. A *subscripted variable* consists of an array name followed by an integer expression enclosed in square brackets. The subscripted variable table [0] refers to the first element of the array table, table [1] references the second element, and table [7] references the last element. Observe how the array declaration specifies the number of elements (8), whilst the elements themselves are referenced by the subscripts 0, 1, 2, 3, 4, 5, 6 and 7.

A subscripted variable may be used in any expression in which a simple variable of the same type may be used. Examples of expressions involving subscripted variables are:

sum4 = table[0] + table[1] + table[2] + table[3];

table[7] = 7;

if (table[0] > table[7])
    printf("First is greater than last\n");

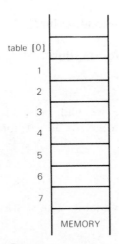

Fig. 11.1

The expression used in a subscript is any generalized expression which yields an integer value. Thus, we may write for the simple integer variables i, j and k:

```
table[i + j] = 0;
for (k = 0; k < 8; k + + ) printf("%d\n", table[k]);
table[7 − table[j]] = j;
```

Like FORTRAN, C does not support any array bounds checking. The programmer must be especially diligent to ensure that the code does not attempt to access an array element that is outwith the bounds of the array declaration. In the context of the declaration for array table, the following statements are syntactically and semantically correct:

```
table[10] = 0;
if (table[ − 4] < 0)
  printf("Negative\n");
```

It is anticipated, however, that the statements are not those required by the programmer. Nevertheless, the C compiler will accept both these statements. The effect of the first statement is that some area of memory is initialized to zero, possibly with disastrous effects if it is an area of memory assigned to another program variable. The second statement erroneously accesses the wrong area of memory.

We can now address and reprogram the original problem. Five integer values are read as input and printed in reverse order. An array is used in the solution, as shown in Program 11.1.

Program 11.1

```
/*
**      Read five integers from the standard input and
**      output them in reverse order.
*/

#include <stdio.h>

#define SIZE            5

main()
  {
    int k;                        /* loop control */
    int table[SIZE];              /* data values */

    for (k = 0; k < SIZE; k++)
      scanf("%d", &table[k]);     /* data input */

    for (k = SIZE - 1; k >= 0; k--)
      printf("%d\n", table[k]);
  }
```

It was stated earlier that array elements may be any of the fundamental or enumeration types. Further valid array declarations include:

```
#define TSIZE        10
#define NAMESIZE     20
#define ADDRSIZE     30

enum month {JAN, FEB, MAR, APR, MAY, JUN,
            JUL, AUG, SEP, OCT, NOV, DEC};
typedef enum month     months;

int        age[TSIZE];
float      size[TSIZE + 1];

months     date [8];
char       name[NAMESIZE], address[ADDRSIZE];
```

The array *size* has 11 elements of type float. The array *date* has 8 elements each of which is any of the enumeration constants JAN, FEB, ..., DEC. In the last declaration, both *name* and *address* are character arrays. As a systems programming language, C is used extensively to process character arrays. Character arrays or strings are reserved until the next chapter.

The following program performs a simple *bubble sort* on an array of integer values. The algorithm is one of many of the interchange sorts. The inner loop rearranges out-of-order adjacent pairs on each pass. By the end of the first pass, the largest element has been 'bubbled' to the end, that is, on the ith pass to the ith element in the array. The outer loop repeats the process, each time decreasing the array limit i by one.

Data to our program consist of a single integer value followed by a number of integer data values. The first integer specifies the number of data items to follow.

Program 11.2

```
/*
**      Input a series of integer values, sort them, and
**      print them out. The ordering of the data into
**      ascending sequence is performed by a simple
**      bubble sort. The data set is preceded with an
**      integer count of the number of data items.
*/

#include <stdio.h>

#define TABLESIZE       100
#define SWAP(_X,_Y)      { int temp;\
  temp = (_X); (_X)=(_Y); (_Y)=temp; }

main()
  {
    int size;                       /* number of data values */
    int i, j;                       /* loop counters */
    int table[TABLESIZE];           /* data set */

    printf("Enter the number of data values: ");
    scanf("%d", &size);
```

```
      if (size > TABLESIZE)
        printf("Too many elements, max is %d\n", TABLESIZE);
      else
        {
          for (i = 0; i < size; i++)        /* accept data */
            {
              printf("data item %3d: ", i);
              scanf("%d", &table[i]);
            }

          for (i = size - 1; i > 0; i--)   /* bubble sort algorithm */
            for (j = 0; j <= i - 1; j++)
              if (table[j] > table[j+1])
                SWAP(table[j], table[j+1]);

          for (i = 0; i < size; i++)        /* print sorted data */
            printf("data item %3d: %5d\n", i, table[i]);
        }
    }
```

11.2 Multidimensional arrays

C provides for rectangular multidimensional arrays. In practice they are
much less common than are one-dimensional arrays. Consider a table
containing the marks scored by a class of students in each of several
examination papers. The marks of one student could be stored in a
one-dimensional array:

#define NUMBER_OF_PAPERS   5

int student[NUMBER_OF_PAPERS];

The complete marks table for all the students could be stored in an array of
such arrays, that is, in a two-dimensional array:

#define NUMBER_OF_PAPERS   5
#define NUMBER_OF_STUDENTS   50

int marks [NUMBER_OF_STUDENTS] [NUMBER_OF_PAPERS];

We can visualize a two-dimensional array as having rows and columns. A
row in this example would represent the marks obtained by a single student.
A column would represent the marks gained by all students in an individual
examination paper. The intersection of a given row and column is the mark
obtained by a student in a particular examination.

As suggested by the declaration for a two-dimensional array, C treats a
two-dimensional array as really a one-dimensional array, each of whose
elements is themselves an array. Hence, a subscripted variable to reference
the mark of an individual student in a single paper is written:

marks[row] [column];

As an example of the use of multidimensional arrays, we present a
program that measures the frequencies of pairs of adjacent letters in words.
The program counts only within-word pairs, so that, given the input THE

DOG., it will count TH, HE, DO and OG, but not ED. The input stream is terminated by a period symbol as shown.

The counters are stored in a two-dimensional array whose declaration is:

```
#define ALPHABET      26
int counter[ALPHABET][ALPHABET];
```

The letter pair AA is recorded in counter[0][0], the pair AZ in counter[0][25], the pair ZZ in counter[25][25], and so on. Note how the letter A results in an index value 0, the letter B index value 1, etc. We must, therefore, translate each letter into the correct index value. If ch is the variable representing an input character, then the conversion is readily achieved with the expression:

ch – 'A'

To process the text we use a two-character 'window'. The window moves through the input stream one character at a time, and whenever both characters in the window are letters, the corresponding element of counter is incremented.

Program 11.3

```
#include <stdio.h>

#define ALPHABET        26

#define BLANK           ' '
#define PERIOD          '.'
#define NEWLINE         '\n'

#define ISLETTER(_X)    ((_X) >= 'A' && (_X) <= 'Z')

int counter[ALPHABET][ALPHABET];

main()
    {
    void initialize(), process(), display();

    initialize();
    process();
    display();
    }

void initialize()       /* counter array to zero */
    {
    int row, col;

    for (row = 0; row < ALPHABET; row++)
      for (col = 0; col < ALPHABET; col++)
        counter[row][col] = 0;
    }

void process()          /* input stream */
    {
    char thischar, prevchar;                /* input window */

    prevchar = BLANK;                       /* initialize */
    thischar = getchar();
    while (thischar != PERIOD)
```

```
        {
          if (ISLETTER(thischar) && ISLETTER(prevchar))
            counter[prevchar-'A'][thischar-'A']++;
          prevchar = thischar;
          thischar = getchar();
        }
  }

void display()
  {
     int row, col;

     for (row = 0; row < ALPHABET; row++)
       {
         for (col = 0; col < ALPHABET; col++)
           printf("%2d", counter[row][col]);
         putchar(NEWLINE);
       }
  }
```

11.3 Arrays as function arguments

When an array name is passed to a function, what is passed is the location of the beginning of the array. Within the called function, this argument is truly a pointer, that is, a variable containing an address. The called function may then use this address to access an individual item of the array by employing the usual subscripting notation.

An array formal argument to a function is declared as:

```
void f(t, .... )
  float t[ ];
  ....
```

which specifies that the argument t is an array of floats. The length of the array is not specified. The notation t[ ] indicates that t is an array. The actual array dimension will be established by the calling function.

If a two-dimensional array is to be passed to a function, the argument declaration in the function must include the column dimensions, that is, all but the first dimension. Thus, if array counter in the last exercise was to be passed as an argument to the subordinate functions, the declaration for initialize, for example, would be:

```
initialize(counter)
  int counter[] [ALPHABET];
```

All but the first dimension of a formal array argument are required so that the compiler can determine the correct *storage mapping function*. Effectively, a two-dimensional array such as:

```
int table[3] [4];
```

is stored in consecutive storage locations in row-order (Table 11.1). To access, for example, element table[1][3] the storage mapping function determines that it is seven locations relative to the base of the array (element table[0][0]). In general, element table[i][j] is $4*i + j$ locations relative to

Table 11.1

```
|            |
|  table[0][0]  |
|  table[0][1]  |
|  table[0][2]  |
|  table[0][3]  |
|  table[1][0]  |
|  table[1][1]  |
|  table[1][2]  |
|  table[1][3]  |
|  table[2][0]  |
|  table[2][1]  |
|  table[2][2]  |
|  table[2][3]  |
|            |
```

MEMORY

the array base. The storage mapping $4*i+j$ is dependent upon 4, the number of elements in the second dimension. Hence the need to include this value in a formal array argument.

Program 11.2 performed a sort on a series of integer values using the bubble sort algorithm. We repeat the same problem on the same data, this time separating the task of reading, sorting and writing the array into three separate functions, passing the array between functions as an argument.

Program 11.4

```
/*
**      Input a sequence of integer values and sort them
**      into ascending order using the bubble sort
**      algorithm. The data set is preceded with an
**      integer count of the number of items.
*/

#include <stdio.h>

#define TABLESIZE       100

#define SWAP(_X,_Y)     { int temp;\
 temp = (_X); (_X) = (_Y); (_Y) = temp; }

main()
  {
    int  size;                          /* number of data items */
    int  table[TABLESIZE];              /* data values */
    int  input();                       /* referencing .... */
    void sort(), output();              /* .... declarations */

    if ((size = input(table, TABLESIZE)) > TABLESIZE)
      printf("Too many elements, max is %d\n", TABLESIZE);
    else
      {
        sort(table, size);
        output(table, size);
      }
  }

/*
**      Read a stream of integers from the standard input
**      and record in an array. The user is first prompted
**      for the number of data items. If this value exceeds
**      the maximum permissible value, then the program
**      terminates.
*/
```

```
    int input(table, limit)
      int table[];                              /* data values */
      int limit;                                /* max size of array */
      {
        int size;                               /* expected number */
        int k;                                  /* loop control */

        printf("Enter number of data items: ");
        scanf("%d", &size);

        if (size > limit)                       /* sufficient room? */
          return (size);                        /* no, return error */

        for (k = 0; k < size; k++)
          scanf("%d", &table[k]);

        return (size);
      }

/*
**        Sort an array of integers into ascending order
**        by application of the bubble sort algorithm.
**        Out of order pairs are repeatedly exchanged
**        'bubbling' the largest item to the end of the
**        array. The process repeats, with the second
**        largest element displaced into the penultimate
**        entry in the array, and so on.
*/

void sort(table, size)
  int table[];
  int size;                                     /* number of items */
  {
    int i, j;

    for (i = size - 1; i > 0; i--)
      for (j = 0; j < i; j++)
        if (table[j] > table[j+1])
          SWAP(table[j], table[j+1]);
  }
/*
**        Print the sorted array.
*/

void output(table, size)
  int table[];
  int size;
  {
    int k;

    printf("Sorted list:\n");

    for (k = 0; k < size; k++)
      printf("%5d\n", table[k]);
  }
```

The main advantage of the bubble sort is its simplicity. Its drawback, a serious one, is that it gets very slow as the number of elements to be sorted rises. Having constructed the program in a modular manner, we can readily replace this sort routine with an improved version.

The Shell sort is much faster for large arrays. The basic idea is that in the early stages far-apart elements are compared and, if necessary, exchanged. This eliminates large amounts of disorder quickly, so later stages have less work to do. Gradually, the interval between compared elements is decreased, until it reaches one, at which point it effectively reduces to an adjacent interchange method. The replacement algorithm is then:

```
/*
**        Sort an array of integers into ascending order
**        by application of the Shell sort algorithm.
**        In the early stages distant elements are
**        compared and, if necessary, exchanged. Gradually
**        the interval between compared elements is
**        reduced until adjacent elements are involved
**        in the comparison.
*/

void sort(table, size)
  int table[];
  int size;                                 /* number of items */
  {
    int interval, i, j;

    for (interval = size/2; interval > 0; interval /= 2)
      for (i = interval; i < size; i++)
        for (j = i-interval;
               j >= 0 && table[j] > table[j+interval];
               j -= interval)
           SWAP(table[j], table[j+interval]);
  }
```

11.4 Array initialization

It is permissible within C to initialize external arrays and internal static arrays. Automatic arrays *cannot* be initialized. The array initializer consists of a brace-enclosed, comma-separated list of constant expressions. For example, a six-element integer array may be initialized by:

   int array [6] = { 0, 1, 2, 3, 4, 5};

Strictly, the bounds of the array need not be given explicitly. In this case, the C compiler counts the number of initializers and from it determines the array size. The above might also have been written:

   int array [ ] = { 0, 1, 2, 3, 4, 5};

Where the array size is given explicitly and the number of items in the initializer is fewer than the number of elements, then the remaining elements are initialized to zero. Therefore:

   int array [6] = {0, 1, 2, 3};

is equivalent to:

   int array [6] = {0, 1, 2, 3, 0, 0};

If the number of initializers exceeds the number of elements in the array declaration, then the initializer is in error.

Multidimensional arrays may also be initialized. The initialization follows the same pattern. A multidimensional array with, say, N elements in the first dimension is initialized with an initializer appearing as:

   int array [N] .... [...] = $\{I_0, I_1, \ldots I_{N-1} \}$;

The initializers I apply the definition of an initializer recursively for the remaining array dimensions. Thus, the two-dimensional integer array rectangle [3][4] has an initializer having the form:

int rectangle [3][4] = {I_0 , I_1 , I_2 };

Each initializer I is appropriate to an integer array now reduced to one dimension having four elements. Such an initializer would appear as:

{1, 2, 3, 4}

A complete initializer for rectangle is then:

int rectangle [3][4] = { {1,2,3,4},
                         {5,6,7,8},
                         {9,10,11,12} };

Again, where there are fewer than the required number of items, remaining elements are initialized to zero. The initialization:

int rectangle [3][4] = { {1,2,3},
                         {5}
                                    };

is equivalent to:

int rectangle [3][4] = { {1,2,3,0},
                         {5,0,0,0},
                         {0,0,0,0}   };

The following program unit supports two date conversion routines. Function day_of_year determines the day number within a year for a given date, taking account of possible leap years. Function day_and_month performs the inverse operation. Both functions employ the same (private) data, namely, a two-dimensional array in which the first row is the days in each month in a non-leap year, and the second row is the days in each month in a leap year. Note how the macro LEAP delivers the logical value TRUE (integer 1) or logical FALSE (integer 0), and how these provide the row index into the array.

```
/*
**    File:      date.c
**
**    Convert a date expressed as day, month and year into
**    the day number for that year; and the reverse
**    procedure.
*/

#define LEAP(_Y)      ((_Y)%4 == 0 && (_Y)%100 != 0 || (_Y)%400 == 0)

#define YEARS      2
#define MONTHS     13          /* Note extra month */

static int days_in[YEARS][MONTHS] =
      {      {0, 31, 28, 31, 30, 31, 30, 31, 31, 30, 31, 30, 31 },
             {0, 31, 29, 31, 30, 31, 30, 31, 31, 30, 31, 30, 31 }
      };
```

```
int day_of_year(day, month, year)
  int day, month, year;
  {
    int mon, leap;
    int days = 0;

    leap = LEAP(year);
    for (mon = 1; mon < months; mon++)
      days += days_in[leap][mon];
    return (day + days);
  }


void day_and_month(day, month, day_of_year, year)
  int *day, *month, day_of_year, year;
  {
    int mon, leap;

    leap = LEAP(year);
    for (mon = 1; day_of_year > days_in[leap][mon]; mon++)
      day_of_year -= days_in[leap][mon];
    *month = mon;
    *day = day_of_year;
  }
```

11.5 Pointers and arrays

Chapter 5 introduced the concept of a pointer. Specifically it has been used to pass the address of a variable to a called function enabling that function to obtain the variable's current value and, if necessary, to modify that value.

There is also a strong relationship between pointers and arrays in C. Pointers and arrays are used in almost the exact same way to access memory. However, there are subtle and important differences which, to the uninitiated, are somewhat hard to grasp. A pointer is a variable that takes addresses as values. An array name is also an address. The address associated with an array name is the initial location in memory in which the array is stored. Since an array name is an address, it is also a pointer, but one which is fixed at compile time. Suppose we have the declaration:

   #define SIZE   8

   int table[SIZE];

and that the compiler assigns the base address 400 to the array, then the memory image might appear as illustrated in Fig. 11.2. In the figure we are assuming that an integer occupies two storage locations (bytes).

If ptr is a pointer to an integer, declared as:

   int *ptr;

then the assignment:

   ptr = &table[0];

sets ptr to point to the zeroth element of table. That is, ptr contains the address of table[0], namely, address 400 (see Fig. 11.3).

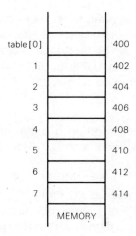

Fig. 11.2

Fig. 11.3

By the usual notation, the assignment:

t = *ptr;

will copy the content of table[0] into t. Equally, the assignment:

*ptr = 0;

sets the value of table[0] to zero.

Since an array name is treated by the compiler as the base address of the array in memory, the name of an array is synonymous for the location of the zeroth element. Instead of writing:

ptr = &table[0];

we may also express it as:

ptr = table;

Pointer arithmetic is one of the most powerful features of C, providing an alternative to array indexing. If ptr is a pointer to a particular element of array table, then ptr + 1 points to the next element. In general, for some integer i, ptr + i points i elements after ptr, and ptr − i points i elements before. Thus if ptr points to table[0] by:

ptr = table;

then *(ptr + 1) refers to the content of table[1]. Similarly, *(ptr + i) refers to the content of table[i]. Also, since ptr is the address of the base of the array, then ptr + i is the address of table[i].

When we define a pointer that will be used to point to the elements of an array, we designate the pointer as pointing to the type of the elements contained in the array. Hence, ptr is declared as a pointer to an integer since it is used to access the integer array table. Had table been an array of floating point values, the ptr would have had to be declared:

```
float *ptr;
```

This *base type* is used in all pointer arithmetic. In ptr + i, i is multiplied by the size of the objects of the base type to which ptr points, before being added to ptr.

An array with an index expression and a pointer with an offset can be used interchangeably. Since C treats an array name as a (fixed) pointer to the base address of the array, then all expressions involving table[i] are immediately converted to the equivalent form, namely, *(table + i). If ptr is a pointer to the zeroth element of the array table, *(ptr + i) references table[i]. Additionally, ptr may be subscripted: ptr[i] is identical to *(ptr + i). This is allowable since both table and ptr are treated as pointers; one is fixed and the other is variable.

Finally, pointer expressions such as ptr = table, ptr + i, ptr + + and ptr − = i, all make sense. If p and q are both pointing to elements of the one array, then p − q yields the integer value representing the number of array elements between p and q.

The one difference between an array name and a pointer is that the latter is a variable but the former is a constant. So ptr = table and + + ptr are valid operations, but constructs like table = ptr or table + + are illegal.

To set all the elements of the array table to zero we previously would have used:

```
for (i = 0; i < SIZE; i + + )
    table[i] = 0;
```

Knowing that table[i] and *(table + i) are equivalent, we could also have used:

```
for (i = 0; i < SIZE; i + + )
    *(table + i) = 0;
```

In fact, this conversion is automatically performed by the C compiler. Using a pointer variable, we express the same logic by:

```
for (ptr = table; ptr < &table[SIZE]; ptr + + )
    *ptr = 0;
```

In this loop, the pointer variable ptr is initialized to the base address of the array table. Successive values of ptr, obtained from the operation ptr + + , are equivalent to &table[0], &table[1], and so on. Processing the array continues until the pointer *ptr* no longer references an array element, and is determined when *ptr* has an address beyond the address of the final array item.

In a function definition, a formal argument that is declared as an array is actually a pointer. When an array is passed, its base address is passed call-by-value. Hence, the following two definitions are considered to be the same:

```
void f(t, ... )      void f(t, ... )
   float t[ ];          float *t;
```

Reprogramming Program 11.1 in terms of pointers, we have the alternative solution:

Program 11.5

```
/*
**       Read five integers and output them in reverse
**       order. Use an array to record the values, and
**       a pointer to reference the elements of the array.
*/

#include <stdio.h>

#define SIZE                 5

main()
  {
    int table[SIZE];                    /* data values */
    int *ptr;                           /* array access method */

    for (ptr = table; ptr < &table[SIZE]; ptr++)
      scanf("%d", ptr);

    for (ptr = &table[SIZE-1]; ptr >= table; ptr--)
      printf("%d\n", *ptr);
  }
```

We previously noted that an array formal argument is actually a pointer. When an array argument is passed in a function call, the base address of the array is passed call-by-value. The array elements themselves are not copied. The formal argument operates as an initialized local variable whose value may be altered during function execution. The formal argument can then be used as a pointer to reference the elements of the array.

In Program 11.4, the function *output* cycles through successive elements of the array argument table, printing each value. A revised version expressed in terms of pointers is:

```
/*
**       Print the sorted array.
*/
void output(table, size)
  int table[];
  int size;
  {
    int *base;

    printf("Sorted list:\n");

    for (base = table; table < base+size; table++)
      printf("%d\n", *table);
  }
```

Incrementing table is perfectly legal, since it is a pointer variable; table + + has no effect on the actual array used in the function call to output. It is the private copy of that array's address that is incremented.

11.6 Functions returning pointers

A function processing an array and returning a reference to an array element can do so by returning the integer value of the array element subscript. Here, it is appropriate to describe the processing logic with subscripts. For example, consider a function called *smallest* that returns the integer index of the smallest item in an array of floats:

```
int smallest(array, limit)
  float array[];
  int    limit;
  {
    int    index = 0, subscript;
    float least = array[index];

    for (subscript = 1; subscript < limit; subscript++)
      if (array[subscript] < least)
        least = array[index = subscript];

    return (index);
  }
```

This function might then be invoked in some calling function to find the smallest element in an array table with SIZE elements:

printf("Smallest is %f\n", table[smallest(table, SIZE)]);

In some applications it is often more appropriate to describe the processing in terms of pointers. To achieve this, C supports functions returning pointers to data items. Reprogramming the previous function with pointers:

```
float *smallest(array, limit)
  float *array;
  int    limit;
  {
    float *index, *final, *subscript;
    float least;

    index = array;
    final = array + limit;
    least = *index;

    for (subscript = array + 1; subscript < final; subscript++)
      if (*subscript < least)
        least = *(index = subscript);

    return (index);
  }
```

The declaration for function smallest now specifies that the returned value is a pointer to a float. This is indicated by the notation:

float *smallest(....) ....

The corresponding function call is now:

    printf("Smallest is %f\n", *smallest(table, SIZE));

11.7 External array referencing

We have followed the principle that all objects in a C program *must* be declared before they are used. Where the defining declaration follows a reference to the item, then an explicit referencing declaration appears. This has been used in a number of cases: functions called before they are defined, references to data items declared in other program units, and so on.

The same principle applies to arrays. If a defining declaration for an array appears in a separate file or appears after it is to be referenced, then a referencing declaration must be used. Defining declarations are responsible for having actual storage allocated. For an array, a defining declaration might appear as:

    int table[SIZE];

Referencing declarations act as compiler directives, informing the compiler of the attributes of the object. No space is allocated. An appropriate referencing declaration for array table is:

    int table[ ];

indicating that table is an array of integers. The number of array elements is given in the corresponding defining declaration. Similar to formal array arguments, multidimensional arrays are referenced using declarations containing all but the first dimension. The referencing declaration for a two-dimensional array having four elements in the second dimension is:

    float code[ ] [4];

If the referencing declaration is to an array declared in another program unit then, as usual, the declaration is preceded with the storage class keyword extern:

    extern float code[ ] [4];

11.8 Arrays and typedef declarations

The *typedef* statement can be used to introduce synonyms for arrays. The declaration:

    typedef char   String[80];

defines a type called String which is an array of 80 characters. Subsequently declaring variables to be of type String as in:

    String text, line;

has the effect of defining the variables to be character arrays of size 80. The declarations for the variables text and line are equivalent to the definitions:

    char text[80], line[80];

To define a type name involving arrays, the procedure introduced in section 9.1 is used. First, we establish the form for a normal array declaration:

    char   message[80];

Then replace the variable name, message, with the new type name, String:

    char   String[80];

and finally prepend with the keyword typedef:

    typedef char   String[80];

Case study 11.1: Quicksort

Of all the various sorting techniques, quicksort is perhaps the most widely used internal sort. An internal sort is one in which all the data to be sorted are held in primary memory.

Let us suppose that we want to sort an array of integers of size n into ascending order. The essential characteristic of the quicksort algorithm is to partition the original array by rearranging it into groups. The first group contains those elements less than some arbitrarily chosen value from the set, and the second group contains those elements greater than or equal to the value. The chosen value is known as the *pivot element*. Once the array has been rearranged with respect to the pivot, the same partitioning is then applied to each of the two subsets. When all subsets have been partitioned, the original array is sorted. Since the partitioning is applied in turn to the subsets, quicksort is best described recursively.

Suppose we wish to sort the elements a[lo], a[lo + 1], ..., a[hi] of the integer array a into ascending order. We denote this task by:

    rquick (a, lo, hi)

If, by some means, we are able to identify the pivotal element a[piv] and perform the rearrangement, then the problem divides into:

    IF lo < hi
    THEN
       partition the elements a[lo], ... a[hi] so that
       a[lo], a[lo + 1], ... a[piv − 1] < a[piv] < = a[piv + 1],
       ... a[hi], where lo < = piv < = hi

       rquick (a, lo, piv − 1)
       rquick (a, piv + 1, hi)
    ENDIF

Ideally, the pivot should be chosen so that at each step the array is partitioned into two sets with equal (or nearly equal) numbers of elements. This would then minimize the total amount of work performed by the quicksort algorithm. Since we do not know in advance what this value should be, we select for the pivot the first value that will provide a partition. Assuming that the array elements are randomly distributed, this is equivalent to choosing the pivot value randomly. We select as the pivot element the last in the set, a[hi]. The elements are rearranged entirely within the subset of a between a[lo] and a[hi]. A outline of the partitioning algorithm is:

```
low = lo
high = hi
pivot = a[hi]
REPEAT
    increase low until low  > =  high or a[low] > pivot
    decrease high until high  < =  low or a[high] < pivot
    IF low < high
    THEN
        exchange a[low] and a[high]
    ENDIF
UNTIL low > = high
exchange a[low] and a[hi]
```

Putting these elements together we arrive at a program to read a series of integer values, to sort them into ascending order using the quicksort algorithm, and then to print the sorted list. The data are preceded by an integer N representing the number of data items. The program is subdivided into three principal functions performing input, sorting and output respectively.

```c
/*
**      Sort a sequence of integer values using the quicksort
**      algorithm. The set of integer data values is preceded
**      by the integer N representing the number of items.
*/

#include <stdio.h>

#define MAXTABLE        1000
#define SWAP(_X,_Y)        { int Z; Z = (_X); (_X) = (_Y); (_Y) = Z; }
void    input(), output();              /* referencing declarations */
void    quicksort(), rquick();
main()
    {
    int table[MAXTABLE];                /* data items */
    int number;                         /* number of values */

    input(table, &number);              /* read the data */
    if (number <= MAXTABLE)             /* check sizes */
        {
        quicksort(table, number);       /* apply algorithm */
        output(table, number);          /* print results */
        }
    else
        printf("Too many data items\n");
    }
```

```
/*
**   -------------------------------oOo-------------------------------
**   -------------------------------oOo-------------------------------
*/
void input(table, number)
  int   table[];                        /* data destination */
  int   *number;                        /* count of data items */
  {
    int k;

    scanf("%d", number);
    if (*number > MAXTABLE)
      return;

    for (k = 0; k < *number; k++)
      scanf("%d", &table[k]);
  }

/*
**   -------------------------------oOo-------------------------------
**   -------------------------------oOo-------------------------------
*/
void output(table, number)
  int   table[];                        /* data values */
  int   number;                         /* count */
  {
    int k;

    for (k = 0; k < number; k++)
     printf("%d\n", table[k]);
  }

/*
**   -------------------------------oOo-------------------------------
**   -------------------------------oOo-------------------------------
*/

void quicksort(table, number)
  int   table[];                        /* items to be sorted */
  int   number;                         /* number of values */
  {
    rquick(table, 0, number-1); /* recursive quicksort */
  }

/*
**   -------------------------------oOo-------------------------------
**   -------------------------------oOo-------------------------------
*/

void rquick(table, lo, hi)
  int   table[];                 /* data values */
  int   lo, hi;                  /* subset of table (indices) */
  {
    int low, high, pivot;

    low = lo;
    high = hi;
    if (low < high)
      {
        pivot = table[high];
        do {
          while (low < high && table[low] <= pivot)
            low++;
          while (high > low && table[high] >= pivot)
            high--;
          if (low < high)                      /* out of order pair */
            SWAP(table[low], table[high]);
        } while (low < high);
        SWAP(table[low], table[hi]);    /* move pivot to low */
        rquick(table, lo, low-1);
        rquick(table, low+1, hi);
      }
  }
```

Case study 11.2: Integer sets

In Chapters 5 and 6 we introduced a systematic approach to program construction based upon abstraction. In particular, functional decomposition or stepwise refinement described the program in terms of intermediate abstract actions. These abstractions reduce the complexity and details that must be considered at any stage during program development. The abstract operations identify the *what* is to be done, rather than the *how* it is to be done.

In Chapter 7 we encouraged the application of the same abstraction principle to the description of data. All data types in a program consist of a set of values and a set of operations upon these values. *Abstract data types* free the programmer from knowing how the values are actually represented by providing operators to manipulate them.

Consider then a program which manipulates *sets* of integers. The actual program will be defined presently. Irrespective of how the sets are implemented, we will need to perform basic set operations such as clearing a set to the empty set, inserting and removing elements of a set, and a test for set membership. Other possible operators include set union, set intersection and set difference. For our particular application, the latter are not required and are ignored.

All of the operations are best expressed as functions whose specifications are independent of the final representation for the sets. The implementation for the operators will have knowledge of the actual implementation, but this will not be evident in the calling sequence. This we achieve in C by encapsulating both the set data type and the operators in a program unit. The latter are exportable to the application program, while details of the former remain invisible. For instance, Fig. 11.4 specifies the abstract data type integer set.

The implementation details of the abstract data type integer set are private to the program unit intset.c. Several implementations are possible.

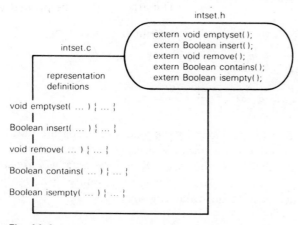

Fig. 11.4

The packaging permits one representation to be substituted by another, providing that the operator interface remains unchanged.

Our implementation maintains a list of the members of a set using an array to hold the values. The implementation choice is reasonable if an upper bound, say SETMAX, can be placed on the number of members contained by the set. The set is then implemented by an array of int, together with a size variable indicating the number of present members in the set. The declarations are:

```
#define SETMAX        64

typedef int             SET[SETMAX];
typedef unsigned int    MEMBERS;

static SET              set;
static MEMBERS          size = 0;
```

In this array version we choose the most convenient representation for set member insertion. Each new member is appended to the end of the existing set using the next available free array element without including duplicates. Set removal involves moving the later members toward array element 0 to fill the gap created by this operation. Both the *remove* and *contains* operators will use a linear search through the members to find the required value. By recording the members in ascending order in the array, a binary search algorithm might be employed. To do so, however, means the *insert* operator must now determine the correct position for insertion.

The header file for this package follows.

```
/*
**      File:         intset.h
**
**      Integer set abstract data type. The set abstraction
**      is defined by a representation-independent
**      specification. The specification consists of a
**      a set of operators for creating objects of the
**      type, retrieving certain information from the
**      objects, and updating the objects.
*/

#define FALSE         0
#define TRUE          1
typedef int           Boolean;

extern void emptyset();
extern Boolean insert( /* int member */ );
extern void remove( /* int member */ );
extern Boolean contains( /* int member */ );
extern Boolean isempty();
```

The implementation is provided by the associated program unit intset.c. To preserve the meaning of the variable size, we arrange that when the set contains, say, K members, variable size = K and the members are stored in array elements 1, 2, 3, ..., K. Array element 0 is unused (though it could have been the place to hold the value for size). The listing for file intset.c now follows:

```
/*
**       File:              intset.c
**
**       Integer set abstract data type. The set abstraction
**       is defined by a representation-independent
**       specification. The specification consists of a
**       a set of operators for creating objects of the
**       type, retrieving certain information from the
**       objects, and updating the objects.
*/

#include <stdio.h>
#include "intset.h"

#define SETMAX            64

typedef int              SET[SETMAX];     /* array representation */
typedef unsigned int     MEMBERS;         /* number of elements */

static SET               set;
static MEMBERS           size = 0;                    /* default size */

/*
**       Operator EMPTYSET disposes of the records
**       representing any existing members of the set.
*/

void emptyset()
   {
     size = 0;
   }


/*
**       Private function LOCATE finds the position of the
**       first set element = MEMBER in the array, if one
**       is present; otherwise position = size+1.
*/

static MEMBERS locate(member)
   int    member;
   {
     MEMBERS position = 1;

     while (position <= size)
       if (set[position] == member)
         break;
       else
         position++;

     return (position);
   }

/*
**       The REMOVE operator searches the set for an
**       occurrence of the value to be removed. If one
**       is found, it is deleted from the array
**       representation and all successive elements
**       are brought forward one position.
*/

void remove(member)
   int    member;
   {
     MEMBERS      position, next;

     if ((position = locate(member)) <= size)
        {
          size--;
          for (next = position; next <= size; next++)
            set[next] = set[next+1];
        }
   }
```

```
/*
**        Function CONTAINS searches the set members
**        and returns the appropriate logical value.
*/

Boolean contains(member)
  int    member;
  {
     return (locate(member) <= size ? TRUE : FALSE);
  }

/*
**        The order of the members of a set is unimportant.
**        The most convenient method to implement
**        the operation INSERT is to perform a simple
**        append. Duplicates are ignored.
*/

Boolean insert(member)
  int    member;
  {
     if (contains(member))
        return (TRUE);

     if (size < SETMAX - 1)
        {
           set[++size] = member;
           return (TRUE);
        }
     else
        return (FALSE);
  }

/*
**        Function ISEMPTY simply tests whether the set
**        contains no elements. If so, the logical value
**        TRUE is returned, otherwise FALSE.
*/

Boolean isempty()
  {
     return (size == 0 ? TRUE : FALSE);
  }
```

And now for the problem itself. The classical algorithm for enumerating prime numbers is the Sieve of Eratosthenes. Suppose that we want to find all the prime numbers less than 12. We start by putting all the numbers from 2 to 12 inclusive on to the sieve:

2 3 4 5 6 7 8 9 10 11 12

We then repeat the following actions until the sieve is empty:

(a) Select and remove the lowest number from the sieve, claiming that it is a prime.
(b) Remove all multiples of that number from the sieve.

After the first step, we have 2 as a prime. From step (b), the sieve now contains the odd numbers:

3 5 7 9 11

Repeating the process, we know that 3 is the next prime and only 5, 7 and 11

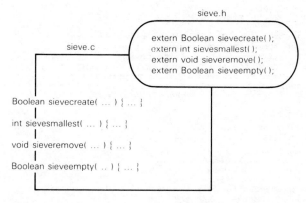

sieve.h

sieve.c

```
extern Boolean sievecreate( );
extern int sievesmallest( );
extern void sieveremove( );
extern Boolean sieveempty( );
```

```
Boolean sievecreate( ... ) { ... }

int sievesmallest( ... ) { ... }

void sieveremove( ... ) { ... }

Boolean sieveempty( .. ) { ... }
```

Fig. 11.5

remain on the sieve. The process continues until the sieve is empty. The identified primes not exceeding 12 are then 2, 3, 5, 7 and 11.

There are many ways to program this problem. One possibility is to employ the integer set abstraction. The sieve is represented by a set and is initially established to contain 2, 3, ..., N for some data value N. Members are entered on the sieve with the insert operation and deleted with the remove operation. Since the set abstraction does not guarantee any particular ordering of the members, a procedure must be found to determine the lowest member of the set and those elements which are multiples of this smallest value. In both cases this is done by cycling through all the possible sieve values 2, 3, ..., N seeking the desired condition. Because of this the method we are applying is not the most efficient.

The problem domain is expressed in terms of a sieve. The solution we arrive at will also be in terms of the sieve. In effect, the sieve is an abstract data object. Ignoring the implementation for such an object, what are the operations performed in association with it? Four operations that have been alluded to in the problem statement are as follows:

(a) Initially establish a sieve containing the values 2, 3, ..., N, for some N.
(b) Select and remove the smallest number in the sieve.
(c) Remove all multiples of the smallest from the sieve.
(d) Determine when the sieve is empty.

Using our usual notation, we develop the sieve package shown in Fig. 11.5.

A hierarchy of abstractions is now present. The application program is expressed in terms of the sieve abstract data type. For this, a package is established to define the specification and implementation attributes of a sieve. The sieve operators themselves are expressed in terms of the integer set abstraction. A suite of listings for the sieve abstraction and the program now follows.

```
/*
**        File :             sieve.h
**
**        Sieve abstraction. To obtain the prime numbers
**        less than some arbitrary value N, the classical
**        algorithm is the Sieve of Eratosthenes. The sieve
**        initially contains the numbers 2, 3, ... , N. The
**        lowest number is removed (the first prime) and
**        all numbers that are multiples of the lowest. The
**        process is repeated until the sieve is empty.
*/


#ifndef FALSE
#define FALSE             0
#define TRUE              1
typedef int               Boolean;
#endif

extern Boolean sievecreate( /* int n */ );
extern int sievesmallest( /* int n */ );
extern void sieveremove( /* int smallest, n */ );
extern Boolean sieveempty();



/*
**        File :             sieve.c
**
**        Sieve abstraction. To obtain the prime numbers
**        less than some arbitrary value N, the classical
**        algorithm is the Sieve of Eratosthenes. The sieve
**        initially contains the numbers 2, 3, ... , N. The
**        lowest number is removed (the first prime) and
**        all numbers that are multiples of the lowest. The
**        process is repeated until the sieve is empty.
*/


#include <stdio.h>
#include "intset.h"
#include "sieve.h"




/*
**        Operation SIEVECREATE establishes the initial
**        condition for the sieve. A set representation for
**        the sieve is employed, and contains the values
**        2, 3, ..., N.
*/

Boolean sievecreate(n)
  int    n;
  {
    int k;

    emptyset();                          /* an empty sieve */
    for (k = 2; k <= n; k++)             /* the initial values */
      if (!insert(k))                    /* set overflow? */
        return (FALSE);                  /* then abort */

    return (TRUE);                       /* all ok */
  }



/*
**        Determine the lowest value in the sieve with
**        operation SIEVESMALLEST. All possible sieve values
**        are generated, tested for set membership, and
**        the least value determined.
*/
```

```
int sievesmallest(n)
  int    n;
  {
    int k, least = 32767;

    for (k = 2; k <= n; k++)              /* all possible values */
      if (contains(k))                    /* a member of the sieve? */
        if (k < least)                    /* new smaller value? */
          least = k;

    return (least);
  }

/*
**       Remove the smallest member of the sieve and
**       all those values that are multiples of the
**       smallest.
*/

void sieveremove(smallest, n)
  int    smallest, n;
  {
    int k;

    remove(smallest);                     /* remove least value */
    for (k = smallest+1; k <= n; k++)     /* all sieve values */
      if (contains(k))                    /* sieve member? */
        if (k % smallest == 0)            /* multiple of smallest? */
          remove(k);
  }

/*
**       Determine when there are no more sieve elements.
*/

Boolean sieveempty()
  {
    return (isempty());
  }

/*
**       File :          case11.2.c
**
**       Generate all the prime numbers less than
**       some value N using the Sieve of Eratosthenes
**       algorithm. The positive integer N is given as
**       program input.
*/

#include <stdio.h>
#include "sieve.h"

main()
  {
    int size, lowest;

    printf("Enter the upper limit, N: ");
    scanf("%d", &size);

    if (!sievecreate(size))          /* initial sieve configuration */
      printf("Cannot create sieve of size %d\n", size);
    else
      {
        printf ("Prime numbers not exceeding %d:\n", size);
        while (!sieveempty())                 /* until no more elements */
          {
            lowest = sievesmallest(size);   /* smallest = prime */
            printf("%d\n", lowest);
            sieveremove(lowest, size);   /* remove least and
                                            all multiples */
          }
      }
  }
```

Observe how errors are dealt with in both packages. In the same way that integer division by zero generates the error condition overflow, the abstract data type operators should also detect error conditions. For example, in the integer set data type, it is an error to attempt to insert a new member into the set already containing the maximum permissible.

It is vital that the implementation of an abstract data type detects error situations. There are several ways to implement error handling. One strategy is to treat all errors as *fatal errors* which immediately terminate program execution. The other strategy is to treat these error situations such that the user program may detect and react to them. It is this method that is used in both the integer set and the sieve data types. In both cases, error situations are handled by implementing certain functions to return Boolean values such that FALSE represents an error and TRUE represents success.

11.9 Summary

1. An array is an example of an *aggregate type* in which a collection of data items that are all of the same type are associated with a single name. An array declaration includes the type of the elements and the number of elements. Elements of an array are accessed by a subscripted variable, where the subscript or index is an integer expression. It is the programmer's responsibility to ensure that an array index is within bounds.
2. When an array name is passed as a function argument, a copy of the base address of the array is actually passed. In the header to a function definition, the declaration:

    int table[ ];

   is equivalent to:

    int *table;

   Within the function body either form can be indexed or used as a pointer.

   The declaration for a multidimensional array in a function definition must have all the dimensions specified, except the first.
3. An external array or an internal static array can be initialized with a list of compile time values. Automatic arrays cannot be initialized. If an external or internal static array is not initialized, then all the elements are guaranteed to be set to zero.

11.10 Exercises

1. In the context of the declarations:

    float table[10]
    float *pt, *qt;

what is the effect of the following statements:

(a) pt = table;
     *pt = 0;
     *(pt + 2) = 3.14;
(b) pt = table + 2;
     qt = pt;
     *qt = 2.718;

(c) pt = table;
     qt = table + 10;
     printf("%d\n", qt – pt);
(d) pt = table
     qt = table + 10;
     for(; pt < qt; pt + +)
       *pt = 1.23;

2. What is the purpose of the following two functions:

(a) void fff(t, limit)
        float *t;
        int limit;
        {
          float *pt;

          for (pt = t; pt < t + limit; pt + +)
            printf("%f\n", *pt);
        }

(b) float ggg(t, limit)
        float *t;
        int limit;
        {
          float *pt, x;

          pt = t;
          x = *pt;
          for (pt = t + 1; pt < t + limit; pt + +)
            if (*pt < x)
              x = *pt;
          return (x);
        }

3. A firm employs a group of 20 salesmen (with reference numbers 1–20 inclusive) who are paid commission on that portion of their sales which exceeds two-thirds of the average sales of the group. A program is required to read the sales value of each salesman and to print out the reference numbers of those who qualify for commission, together with their sales.

4. Data to a program consist of a sequence of alphabetic characters terminated by a period symbol. Determine if the text is palindromic, i.e. reading the same both forwards and backwards.

5. Assume that the number of rooms in a hotel is given by a constant NMBROFROOMS. Write: (a) an array declaration suitable for keeping track of which rooms are free; and (b) a function to count how many rooms are free, given that appropriate values have been stored in the array.

6. A hospital patient's temperature is recorded four times a day for a week. Construct a program that will input the readings for each day, and:

(a) Output the data as shown in Table 11.2.

Table 11.2

		SUN	MON	TUE	WED	THU	FRI	SAT
TEMP	1	X	X	X	X	X	X	X
	2	X	X	X	X	X	X	X
	3	X	X	X	X	X	X	X
	4	X	X	X	X	X	X	X

(b) Output the highest and lowest recorded temperatures, together with the day and the number of the reading on which they occurred.

7. In case study 11.2, the number of members in a set is controlled by the integer size. To permit a client program to determine this value, why is it considered bad programming practice to redeclare size with storage class extern. How should it be done?

8. Reprogram program unit integer set (intset.c) in case study 11.2 such that the members of the set are recorded in ascending order. Rework the private function locate to use a binary search algorithm.

What are the effects of this change of representation on the sieve abstraction?

## CHAPTER 12

Character strings

Strings are one-dimensional character arrays. By convention, a string in C is terminated by an end-of-string sentinel consisting of the ASCII null character '\0'. It is useful to think of strings as having variable length but with a maximum allowable length determined by the size of the character array holding the string. The size of the array must be sufficient to include the end-of-string sentinel. As usual it is the programmer's responsibility to ensure that the array bounds are not exceeded.

String constants were defined in section 3.4 as a character sequence enclosed in a matching pair of double quotes. The string "abc" is implemented as a character array of size 4. The final element of the array is the ASCII null character (see Fig. 12.1).

From section 11.4, a character array may be initialized with these same values using the construct:

static char word [ ] = {'a', 'b', 'c', '\0'};

C additionally permits a character array to be initialized with a string constant rather than having to list the individual characters. The above can also be expressed by:

static char word [ ] = "abc";

The latter is preferred since it is that much more readable.

A string constant such as:

"hello"

is an array of characters. The C compiler associates a pointer to the first character of the array. A variable declared of type *pointer to char* may be assigned the pointer to a character string. If variable greeting is declared as:

char *greeting;

Fig. 12.1

then the statement:

char *greeting

greeting = "hello";

assigns to greeting a pointer to the actual character string. It must be emphasized that this is *not* a string copy; only pointers are involved. The declaration and assignation may be combined into:

char *greeting = "hello";

Care is required to distinguish between the declaration:

char word [ ] = "hello";

and:

char *greeting = "hello";

Superficially, both appear to achieve the same. The literal strings are treated as pointers to characters which then associate with the identifiers word and greeting. The difference is that the former is a *constant pointer* to a character, whilst the latter is a *variable* of type pointer to a char. All array names, such as word, are treated as constant pointers. On the other hand, greeting is a variable and may subsequently be assigned some new value, as in:

greeting = "Good morning";

As an illustration of how variable length character strings are used, let us develop a function to count the number of characters in a string. We shall call our function *length* and have it defined in terms of a single character array argument. The character array is terminated with the null character in the usual way. The null character is not included in the character count.

Program 12.1

```
/*
**      Implement a function to count the number of characters
**      in a character string. The count is enumerated by
**      searching through the string for the terminating
**      null character whilst maintaining the count. The null
**      character is not included in the count.
*/

#include <stdio.h>

main()
   {
   static char word[] = { "abc" };
   static char *greeting = "hello";

   int length();                        /* forward reference */

   printf("Lengths %d and %d\n", length(word), length(greeting));
   }

/*
** ----------------------------------oOo----------------------------------
** ----------------------------------oOo----------------------------------
*/
```

```
int length(string)
  char string[];
  {
    int count = 0;

    while (string[count] != NULL)
      count++;

    return (count);
  }
```

In function length, the local variable count is declared and initialized to zero. The while loop sequences through the character array until the null character is reached. NULL is defined in the file stdio.h as zero, the ASCII encoding for the null character. The null character signals the end of the string, the loop terminates and the value of the count returned as the function value. This value represents the number of characters in the string, excluding the null character. The program output is then:

Lengths 3 and 5

being the lengths of the two respective strings.

In practice, it is customary to express the control expression in the while statement in function length in another way. We observe that every non-null character in the string is counted. All non-null ASCII characters have a non-zero internal representation. Non-zero is interpreted in C as logical true. Only the ASCII null character has the internal value zero (logical false). The loop may therefore be written as:

```
while (string[count])
  count + + ;
```

A formal argument to a function that is an array is immediately converted by the C compiler into a pointer to the type of the array elements. The function length is treated as:

```
int length(string)
  char      *string;
```

This is still consistent with the function usage, since it is called with actual arguments word and greeting which are pointers to type char. Normally, the function would be coded in terms of pointers:

```
int length(string)
  char *string;
  {
    int count = 0;

    while (*string)
      {
        count++;
        string++;
      }

    return (count);
  }
```

Again, observe that the explicit comparison against ASCII null is redundant, and, accordingly, is omitted.

One further revision is possible. The control expression in the while statement determines if the character pointed at is the null character. If it is not, both the counter and the pointer are incremented. The test and increment to the pointer may be combined using:

*string + +

The value of *string + + is the character that the string pointed to before incrementing. The postfix operator + + does not change string until after the character has been fetched. The final version for function length is:

```
int length(string)
  char *string;
  {
    int count = 0;

    while (*string++)
      count++;

    return (count);
  }
```

12.1 String comparisons

It is not possible in C to perform direct comparison of two strings. Statements such as:

if (string1 < string2) . . . .

and:

while (string1 ! = string2) . . . .

are not permissible since the relational and equality operators can only be applied to simple data types such as int, char and float. To determine if two strings are equal, say, we must perform a character-by-character comparison of the two strings under discussion. If we simultaneously exhaust both strings, and all the characters to that point are identical, the strings are equal, otherwise they are unequal.

We develop a function called *equal* with two character string arguments. If the strings are identical, function equal returns the logical constant TRUE, otherwise it returns FALSE. This way, the function may be used in tests:

if (equal (string1, string2)) . . .

and:

while (! equal (string1, string2)) . . .

The function and driver program is shown in Program 12.2. The while loop in the body of function equal compares corresponding character elements of the two strings. Provided that the characters are the same, the scanning continues. When they differ, or when the end of one string is obtained, the loop terminates. One of three possible conditions now exists – the end of both strings has occurred, in which case the strings are identical; one or other string has terminated and they now differ from this point; or the two corresponding characters are not the same. From this, the correct return code is determined.

Program 12.2

```
/*
**         Determine if two strings are equal. Direct string
**         comparisons are not implemented in C. The function
**         'equal' compares two strings and if they are
**         identical, returns the value TRUE, otherwise
**         returns FALSE. The equality test is implemented by
**         a character by character comparison.
*/

#include <stdio.h>

#define FALSE              0
#define TRUE               1

typedef int               Boolean;
typedef char              *String;

Boolean equal ();                          /* referencing declaration */

main ()
   {
   static char str1 [] = { "Programming in C" };
   static char str2 [] = { "Programming is fun" };

   if (equal (str1, str2))
     printf ("Equal\n");
   else
     printf ("Unequal\n");

   if (equal (str2, "Programming is fun"))
     printf ("Equal\n");
   else
     printf ("Unequal\n");
   }

Boolean equal (stringa, stringb)
   String stringa, stringb;
   {
   while (*stringa == *stringb && *stringa != NULL)
     stringa++, stringb++;

   if (*stringa == NULL && *stringb == NULL)
     return (TRUE);
   else
     return (FALSE);
   }
```

12.2 Character string input

The standard I/O library function scanf can be used with the %s conversion to read a string of characters (see Appendix F4). The declaration and statement:

char message[80];

scanf ("%s", message);

have the effect of reading a character string from the standard input and storing it in the character array message. Note that unlike previous scanf calls, the address operator & is not required before an array of character variable name. The operator is not necessary since the C compiler has already equivalenced message into a pointer to type char. Variable message, therefore, is already treated as an address.

If the above scanf call were executed and the following characters entered at the terminal:

Hello

then the null-terminated string "Hello" is read by scanf and stored in the character array message. If instead, the following line of text were supplied:

Good morning

then only the string "Good" is stored in the array message, since any whitespace character terminates the %s conversion. If the same scanf call were executed a second time, then the string "morning" would be stored in the array.

Program 12.3 illustrates the use of scanf with the %s conversion to read three strings.

Program 12.3

```
/*
**      Program to illustrate character string input
**      through use of the standard function 'scanf'.
*/

#include <stdio.h>

#define SIZE            80

main()
   {
    char word1[SIZE], word2[SIZE], word3[SIZE];

    printf("Enter the text: ");
    scanf("%s %s %s", word1, word2, word3);
    printf("word1 = %s\nword2 = %s\nword3 = %s\n",
        word1, word2, word3);
   }
```

The program operates by first issuing the prompt "Enter the text: ". If, in response, the user were to enter two character strings separated by a space, then the first is assigned to variable word1 and the second to variable word2. The space acts as a separator between each string, terminating the first string and discarded as leading whitespace preceding the second string.

If the second string is terminated by a newline, it too is discarded when reading the third string.

The program was tested with the following dialogue. User input is in italic to distinguish from program output.

Enter the text: *Programming in*
C
word1 = Programming
word2 = in
word3 = C

Many text processing applications require that an entire line of text be read from the terminal before processing can commence. To use scanf and the %s conversion we would need to know in advance the number of individual strings appearing on a single line. Commonly this is not available. Lines of text often contain different numbers of words or strings.

To support line-at-a-time reading, we implement a function called read_line. This function reads a line of text up to and including the newline symbol. All the text characters, but excluding the newline character, are stored in the character array string. The string is null terminated. The integer argument *limit* denotes the length of the array. If more characters appear in the input line than can be successfully stored in the array, the input continues to the newline, but all excess characters are ignored.

```
void read_line(s, limit)
  string s;                              /* recipient line */
  int    limit;                          /* max permissible chars */
  {
    char c;                              /* input character */
    int  count = 0;                      /* character count */

    while ((c = getchar()) != NEWLINE)   /* read until end of line */
      {
        count++;
        if (count < limit)               /* room in string? */
          *s++ = c;                      /* then record */
      }
    *s = NULL;
  }
```

We are now in a position to develop a string handling program to read a series of lines of text from the standard input and to echo each line to the standard output with the characters of the line reversed. The input is terminated with a line consisting of the string "ZZZ". The text lines are input using the function read_line. Each input line is compared (using function equal) against the terminator. Upon discovering the unique terminator, the program stops. Otherwise, an in-place reversal of the character strings in the line is performed, and the line echoed to the standard output.

Program 12.4(a)

```
/*
**      Read a series of lines from the standard input
**      and write each line to the standard output with
**      the characters reversed. The input terminates
**      with the line ZZZ.
*/

#include <stdio.h>

#define FALSE           0
#define TRUE            1
typedef int             Boolean;

#define SIZE            132
#define TERMINATOR      "ZZZ"
#define NEWLINE         '\n'
#define NOT             !

typedef char            Text[SIZE];
typedef char            *String;

void    read_line ();                   /* referencing declarations */
void    reverse ();
Boolean equal ();
int     length ();

main ()
   {
     Text          line;

     read_line (line, SIZE);                    /* first data line */
     while (NOT equal (line, TERMINATOR))       /* end of data? */
        {
          reverse (line);                       /* reverse it .. */
          printf ("%s\n", line);                /* .. print it */
          read_line (line, SIZE);               /* next data line */
        }
   }

/*
** ---------------------------oOo---------------------------
** ---------------------------oOo---------------------------
*/

void read_line (s, limit)
  String s;                                     /* recipient line */
  int    limit;                                 /* max permissible chars */
  {
    char c;                                     /* input character */
    int  count = 0;                             /* character count */

    while ((c = getchar ()) != NEWLINE) /* read until end of line */
       {
         count++;
         if (count < limit)                     /* room in string? */
            *s++ = c;                           /* then record */
       }
    *s = NULL;
  }

/*
** ---------------------------oOo---------------------------
** ---------------------------oOo---------------------------
*/

Boolean equal (stra, strb)
  String stra, strb;
  {
    while (*stra == *strb && *stra != NULL)
      stra++, strb++;
```

```
        if (*stra == NULL && *strb == NULL)
          return (TRUE);
        else
          return (FALSE);
    }

/*
**     ---------------------------oOo---------------------------
**     ---------------------------oOo---------------------------
*/

void reverse (s)
  String s;                    /* in-place reversal */
    {
      char c, *t;

      t = s + length (s) - 1;    /* end of string */
      while (s < t)              /* two ends approaching center */
        {
          c = *s;                /* exchange */
          *s++ = *t;
          *t-- = c;
        }
    }

/*
**        ---------------------------oOo---------------------------
**        ---------------------------oOo---------------------------
*/

int length (s)
  String s;
    {
      int count = 0;

      while (*s++)
        count++;

      return (count);
    }
```

12.3 Standard library string handling functions

The standard C library contains many useful string handling functions.
They are fully documented in Appendix F4. A number of the more common
examples are illustrated below.

Two character strings s1 and s2 may be compared using the function
strcmp:

```
  int strcmp(s1, s2)
    char *s1, *s2;
```

An integer is returned which is less than, equal to, or greater than zero,
depending on whether s1 is lexicographically less than, equal to, or greater
than s2. The character-by-character comparison is performed in terms of
the implementation character set, for example, ASCII.

This function could have been used in place of function equal in the last
example. The test:

```
  while (NOT equal(line, TERMINATOR)) ...
```

would be replaced by the equivalent:

while (strcmp(line, TERMINATOR)! = 0)...

since a non-zero returned by function strcmp implies that the two string arguments line and TERMINATOR are unequal.

A count of the number of characters in a null-terminated string is performed by the function *strlen*. The header for this function is:

int strlen(s)
  char *s;

Again, in the last example, strlen could be used as a direct replacement for function length.

The function *strcpy* copies the content of the string s2 to the string s1, overwriting the old content of s1. The entire content of s2 is copied, including the terminating null character. A pointer to the first character of s1 is returned as the function value. The function header is:

char *strcpy(s1, s2)
  char *s1, *s2;

Thus, to copy the content of a string called oldname to a second string called newname, we use:

(void) strcpy(newname, oldname);

Note how we have void cast the return value from the function, explicitly declaring that the return value is irrelevant. The same effect can be achieved implicitly with the statement:

strcpy(newname, oldname);

This is the more common usage, but a precompiler such as lint would complain about this statement, observing that the return value is not used.

The function *strcat* appends the content of the string s2 to the end of string s1. The pointer to the first character string s1 is returned as the function value. The null character that terminates s1 initially and the characters that follow it are overwritten with the characters from s2, including a new terminating null character. The function header is:

char *strcat(s1, s2)
  char *s1, *s2;

Consider three strings called prefix, name and suffix which are to be concatenated to produce a string called filename. The effect is achieved by copying the prefix string into the destination, and then concatenating the other two strings to the destination. The coding is:

```
strcpy(filename, prefix);
strcat(filename, name);
strcat(filename, suffix);
```

Again, the function return values are simply discarded.

Using appropriate functions from the standard library, Program 12.4(a) is rewritten below. In particular, functions length and equal are replaced by strlen and strcmp, respectively. Also from the standard library, function *gets* (see Appendix F4) replicates the role of function read_line in the original program.

Program 12.4(b)

```
/*
**        Read a series of lines from the standard input
**        and write each line to the standard output with
**        the characters reversed. The input terminates
**        with the line ZZZ.
*/

#include <stdio.h>

#define SIZE         132
#define TERMINATOR   "ZZZ"

typedef char         Text[SIZE];
typedef char         *String;

void     reverse ();                     /* forward declarations */
char     *gets ();

main ()
  {
    Text         line;

    gets (line);                             /* first data line */
    while (strcmp (line, TERMINATOR) != 0)   /* end of data? */
      {
        reverse (line);                      /* reverse it */
        printf ("%s\n", line);               /* .. print it */
        gets (line);                         /* next data line */
      }
  }


/*
**  ---------------------------o0o---------------------------
**  ---------------------------o0o---------------------------
*/

void reverse (s)
  String s;                          /* in-place reversal */
  {
    char c, *t;

    t = s + strlen (s) - 1;      /* end of string */
    while (s < t)                /* two ends approaching centre */
      {
        c = *s;                  /* exchange */
        *s++ = *t;
        *t-- = c;
      }
  }
```

Case study 12.1: Word concordance

A program is required to examine a piece of text and produce a list, in alphabetical order, of all the distinct words which appear in the text. It may be assumed that no word is more than 20 characters long, that the words are separated by one or more whitespace characters, that the text contains no punctuation symbols (hyphens, commas, apostrophes, etc.) and that the text terminates with the unique word 'zzz'. The sample input:

    the quick brown fox jumped
    over the lazy dog
    zzz

would produce the corresponding output:

    brown
    dog
    fox
    jumped
    lazy
    over
    quick
    the

The overall form of the program to solve the problem can be as follows:

    initialize the list of words
    get the first word from the input text
    WHILE not the end of text
    DO
        record the word in the list
        get the next word from the input text
    ENDWHILE
    print the words in the list

At this stage we identify two abstractions involved:

(a) A stream of words extracted from the input text, one at a time.
(b) A list of the words.

For the present, we shall ignore the input stream abstraction and concentrate on the list of words. To implement the program, the word list abstraction must allow operations to:

(a) Record a word in the list.
(b) Print the entire list content in dictionary order.
(c) Initialize an empty list.

The number of words in the list is unpredictable. However, since we shall represent the list as an array of words of some fixed size, then we also require an operation to:

(d) determine when the capacity of the list is exhausted.

A representation independent version of the word list abstraction is achieved by packaging the data structures and operations in a program unit wordlist.c. The features of the word list abstraction required by the application program are the operations to initialize the list, insert a word into the list, print the list of words in alphabetical order, and determine if the list is full. Details of the list are otherwise hidden from the client program. Using our usual notation, the package outline is shown in Fig. 12.2. Note the that no explicit initialization function is provided since this operation is performed by an initializer within the package body.

The word list is implemented as an array of words. Defining the type Word as a character string of length 21 (maximum of 20 characters plus the null character), provides a suitable data representation for a word:

```
#define WORDSIZE      21
typedef char          Word[WORDSIZE];
```

Setting the word list table to length 256, say, then the implementation is an array of this size, each element of type Word:

```
#define LISTSIZE    256
typedef Word         List[LISTSIZE];
```

The program output is to be an alphabetically ordered list of the words occurring in the input text. We may approach this problem in two ways: construct an unsorted list as the text is input then perform a sort immediately before outputting the list; or, construct the list in such a way that its contents are always in alphabetical order. We shall choose the latter method since it is more efficient. To do so, each new entry inserted into the list must maintain the ordering of the list.

The complete word list is then represented as a variable of type List. In addition, an integer variable is maintained as the current length of the list,

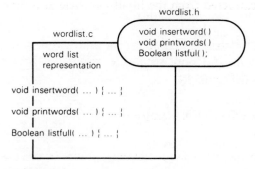

Fig. 12.2

i.e. the actual number of words presently in the list. This variable is called listlen. The variable declarations are then:

    static List   wordlist;
    static int   listlen;

Note that both have storage class static and are hence private to the program unit.

An empty list is trivially represented by initializing the variable listlen to zero, so we have:

    static int   listlen = 0;

Recording a new word read from the input text into the word list can be expressed as an operation described by the function header:

    void insertword(word)
        Word   word;   /* new word to be inserted */

The procedure takes a new word and searches the current list to determine whether or not that word has already occurred in the text. If it has, it already appears in the list and the duplicate is discarded. If not, the new word is inserted in its correct position in the list, maintaining the alphabetical ordering of the list.

We shall perform a linear search of the list in looking for duplicates. Beginning the search at the first element of the list, we inspect successive elements until one of three possibilities occurs:

(a) An entry in the list matches the new word – the duplicate is ignored and no further processing is performed on the list.
(b) The list is exhausted with no match found – the new word is introduced at the end of the list.
(c) A word alphabetically greater than the new word is found in the list – the located word and all successive words are displaced down the list by one place and the new word introduced into the vacated location.

This action may be expressed as:

    initialize index to the first word in the list
    WHILE the list is not exhausted
    DO
        IF the new word is alphabetically after
            the referenced word in the list
        THEN
            advance the index to the next word in the list
        ELSE
            terminate the search on a match
        ENDIF
    ENDWHILE

IF not a duplicate word
THEN
    displace all words in list from reference point
    insert new word into available location
ENDIF

The list is maintained by recording the number of words currently held. If there are listlen words in the list, they are indexed as 0, 1, 2, ..., listlen − 1. This value is used to control the search:

for (index = 0; index < listlen; index + +)
DO
    IF the new word is alphabetically after
        the referenced word in the list
    THEN
        advance the index to the next word in the list
    ELSE
        terminate the search on a match
    ENDIF
ENDFOR

Upon completion of the loop, the integer variable index refers to the entry in the list containing a word that either matches the new word or is alphabetically after the new word. For example, if the new word to be entered into the list is GOAT, and the list is of length 5 and contains the information shown in Fig. 12.3, then the index value is 2, as shown.

To add a new word to the list, we increase the word list length by one, and move all the words alphabetically greater than the new word down the list by one position, inserting the new word in the vacated slot. This repositioning must begin at the end of the list, otherwise the entries in the list will be

Fig. 12.3

Fig. 12.4

overwritten. The procedure in outline is:

listlen + + ;
for (shift = listlen; shift > index; shift − −)
    copy list element [shift − 1] into list element [shift]
copy new word into list element [index]

After increasing the length of the list and moving the entries from the index position the list now appears as shown in Fig. 12.4, with the new word to be entered into the vacated location in the list. The final configuration for the list after copying the new word into the correct position is shown in Fig. 12.5.

Printing the ordered list of words is straightforward. The operation is implemented by cycling through each word in the list in turn, and printing

Fig. 12.5

it:

FOR each word in the list
DO
   print the word
ENDFOR

The word list is exhausted if there is no more room in the table. This is determined if the variable listlen equals the table size (256). If the capacity of the word list is exhausted before all the input text is read, no more entries are made in the table. Reading the input continues until the terminator is input. The table is then displayed.

The second abstraction in this problem is the stream of input words. The single operation upon this abstraction delivers the next word from the input text. Recollect that the library function scanf with the conversion operator %s will read a string of non-whitespace characters into a character array. Further, any leading whitespace is discarded. Thus, reading the next word from the input is implemented with the built-in:

scanf("%s", word)

where word is an array of characters.

The completed program is as follows.

```
/*
**      Examine a piece if text and produce a list, in
**      alphabetical order, of all the distinct words
**      which appear in the text. The text is read from
**      the standard input, terminates with the unique
**      word 'zzz', contains no punctuation symbols, and
**      has no word with more than 20 characters.
**
**      The word list is maintained by an array. Each new
**      word is compared with those words presently in the
**      list. A duplicate word is discarded, and a new
**      word is correctly inserted into the list.
*/

#include <stdio.h>
#include "wordlist.h"

main ()
    {
    Word         word;                      /* next data word */

    scanf ("%s", word);                     /* read first word */
    while (strcmp (word, TERMINATOR) != 0)       /* end of data? */
        {
        if (! listfull ())                  /* room in table? */
            insertword (word);
        scanf ("%s", word);                 /* read next word */
        }

    printwords ();                          /* tabulate */
    }
```

```
/*
**      File:   wordlist.h
**
**      Header file for the word list abstraction. This file
**      defines a series of manifest constants, a word list
**      table, and a set of associated operators.
*/

#define FALSE           0
#define TRUE            1
typedef int             Boolean;

#define WORDSIZE        21
typedef char            Word[WORDSIZE];
#define TERMINATOR      "zzz"

/*
**      Specification interface to the word list operators.
**
**      void insertword (word)
**        Word          word;
**
**      Insert a new word into the existing word list.
**      It is assumed that the list length has been
**      determined to ensure that there is room. A
**      duplicate word is simply discarded, a new word
**      is correctly inserted.
**
**      void printwords ()
**
**      Produce a table of the words in the list. The list
**      is presented as per the table -- alphabetical order.
**
**      Boolean listfull ()
**
**      Return the logical value TRUE if there is no more
**      room in the word list, otherwise return FALSE.
*/

extern void insertword( /* Word word */ );
extern void printwords();
extern Boolean listfull();

/*
**      File:   wordlist.c
**
**      Word list abstraction implementation. The abstraction
**      is realized using an array of WORDs. The number of
**      words presently in the list is maintained by 'listlen'.
*/

#include <stdio.h>
#include "wordlist.h"

#define LISTSIZE        256
typedef Word            List[LISTSIZE];

static int      listlen = 0;            /* list initially empty */
static List     wordlist;               /* word list realization */


void printwords ()                      /* produce a table of .... */
  {
    int         index;                  /* list index */

    for (index = 0; index < listlen; index++)
      printf ("%s\n", wordlist[index]);
  }

/*
** ----------------------------------oOo----------------------------------
** ----------------------------------oOo----------------------------------
*/
```

```
void insertword (word)
  Word          word;                     /* new word */
  {
    int         index, shift;             /* table indices */
    int         comp;                     /* comparison flag */
    Boolean     found;                    /* search indicator */

    found = FALSE;                        /* look for word in list */
    for (index = 0; index < listlen; index++)
      if ((comp = strcmp (wordlist[index], word)) > 0)
                                          /* insert here? */
        {
          found = TRUE;                   /* new word position .... */
          break;                          /* .... is 'index' */
        }
      else if (comp == 0)                 /* if duplicate word .... */
        return;                           /* .... discard */

    if (! found)                          /* insert new word at .... */
      index = listlen;                    /* .... end of list */

    for (shift = listlen; shift > index; shift--)    /* move each */
      strcpy (wordlist[shift], wordlist[shift - 1]); /* word down */
    strcpy (wordlist[index], word);                  /* list and */
    listlen++;                   /* .. insert and update list length */
  }

/*
**  ---------------------------------oOo---------------------------------
**  ---------------------------------oOo---------------------------------
*/

Boolean listfull ()
  {
    return (listlen == LISTSIZE);
  }
```

12.4 Conversions between strings and numerics

Many string handling programs require conversions from both string to number and number to string. Programs are required to read a string of characters and to extract from that string a sequence of decimal digits and convert then to their equivalent numerical value.

As an example, here is a function called *atoi* (ASCII to integer conversion) for converting a string to its numerical equivalent. The function operates by first ignoring any leading whitespace characters in the string. An optional plus ($+$) or minus ($-$) symbol may then precede the digit sequence. The digits are terminated by any character that is not a decimal digit.

```
#define BLANK     ' '
#define TAB       '\t'
#define NEWLINE   '\n'

#define PLUS      '+'
#define MINUS     '-'

#define POSITIVE  +1
#define NEGATIVE  -1
```

```
#define DIGIT0        '0'
#define DIGIT9        '9'

int atoi(s)
    char *s;                    /* ascii character string */
{
    int sign, value;           /* sign of integer */
                               /* value of integer */
                               /* ignore all leading white */
    while (*s = = BLANK ¦¦ *s = = TAB ¦¦ *s = = NEWLINE)
        s + + ;
    sign = POSITIVE;           /* assume positive */
    if (*s = = PLUS)           /* if a plus symbol, then */
        s + + ;                /* .... skip it */
    else if (*s = = MINUS)     /* if a minus symbol, then */
    {
        s + + ;                /* skip it and .... */
        sign = NEGATIVE;       /* set sign indicator */
    }
                               /* cycle through successive */
                               /* constructing the integer */

    value = 0;
    while (*s > = DIGIT0 && *s < = DIGIT9)
        value = 10 * value + (*s + + ) - DIGIT0;

    return (sign * value); /* adjust for sign */
}
```

This function atoi and possibly its counterpart *itoa* (integer to ASCII string), may be members of the standard library. Other associated functions include *atol* (ASCII to long) and *atof* (ASCII to float). They too may be included in the standard library. The reader is referred to the appropriate local documentation to determine the exact membership of the standard library.

If no such functions exist, the same effect can be achieved by an alternative route. The standard library function scanf performs a parse of the stream of characters from the standard input, placing the converted characters into memory locations. For example, the function call:

scanf("%d", &number)

reads and converts a stream of input characters into a decimal integer value, storing the result at the address of the integer variable *number*. The form of this function call is:

scanf(format, argument1, argument2, ...)

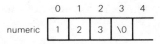

Fig. 12.6

A variant of this function is known as *sscanf*. Its function call is:

    sscanf(string, format, argument1, argument2, ...)

This function is like scanf in operation. The only difference is that sscanf takes input character from a string, while scanf always takes its input from the standard input. In the context of the declarations:

    int number;
    char *p = " 123 is an integer";

the statements:

    number = atoi(p)

and:

    sscanf(p, "%d", &number)

achieve the same effect – the decimal value 123 is assigned to the integer variable number.

Equally, a numerical value may be converted to a null-terminated character string by employing the function *sprintf*:

    sprintf(string, format, expression1, expression2, ...)

The function performs output formatting, writing the output characters to the string specified as the first actual argument. Operationally, the function behaves like printf. Given the declaration:

    char numeric[10];

then the statement:

    sprintf(numeric, "%d", number)

reconverts the value 123 in the integer variable number back into a null-terminated string called numeric (see Fig. 12.6).

12.5 Arrays of pointers

Since pointers are themselves variables, it is possible to construct arrays of pointers. That is, each array element is a pointer to some object. In the declaration:

    int *ptr[4];

variable ptr is an array of 4 elements of pointers to integers. If x and t are integer variables, then the assignment:

    ptr[3] = &x;

sets the last element of the array to the address of the variable x. By the usual notation, the assignment:

    t = *ptr[3];

copies the content of x into the variable t.

Equally, any element of the array ptr may address any element of an integer array. Given the declarations:

    int v4[4], v7[7], v2[2], v3[3];

we may set the zeroth element of ptr to address the first item in integer array v4 by the assignment:

    ptr[0] = &v4[0];

or, more commonly, by:

    ptr[0] = v4;

If we were to assign successive elements of the array ptr to the base address of arrays v4, v7, v2 and v3, then in effect we have constructed a two-dimensional *jagged* array. The rows of this array have varying numbers of elements. The array is no longer the conventional rectangular shape. Pictorially, the two-dimensional array may be viewed as shown in Fig. 12.7.

The necessary assignments are:

    ptr[0] = v4;
    ptr[1] = v7;
    ptr[2] = v2;
    ptr[3] = v3;

The array v7 may be printed with the function call:

    print_row(ptr[1], 7);

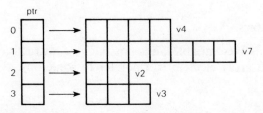

Fig. 12.7

where function print_row has been programmed as:

```
void print_row(pt, n)
    int     *pt;                /* pointer to array */
    int     n;                  /* number of elements */
    {

        int     k;              /* loop counter */

        for (k = 0; k < n; k + +)        /* for every element */
            printf("%d\n", *pt + +);     /* print and advance */
    }
```

More commonly, arrays of pointers are used with strings. We illustrate by designing a program that sorts a series of test lines into alphabetical order.

Program 11.3 sorted an array of integers by the Shell sort method. In this example we shall employ the same algorithm to sort lines of text. For this we need a suitable data representation that will operate efficiently and conveniently with lines of text of varying length.

One solution is to refer to the lines indirectly by pointers. Since there is likely to be more than one line of text, an array of pointers is required. A large array called *linebuffer* holds the lines that are to be sorted in an end-to-end fashion. A second array, *linepointer,* contains pointers to where in linebuffer the corresponding line begins. That is, linepointer[k] is the position in linebuffer for the beginning of the kth line, for k > = 0. Figure 12.8 illustrates this organization.

When the sort algorithm calls for an exchange of out-of-order line pairs, only the pointers are exchanged, not the text lines themselves. This eliminates the high overhead associated with moving larger quantities of data. Further, it simplifies the storage management where the lines being swapped are of different lengths.

The sort program reads lines of text into the data structure, sorts them (by rearranging the pointers) then prints them. Since the array linepointer will be of some fixed size, this dictates the maximum number of lines that can be stored. Another maximum is the total amount of space available in

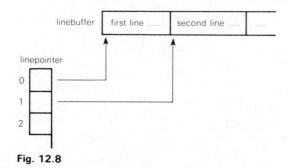

Fig. 12.8

linebuffer. If this space is exceeded when reading the data lines, this too is an error condition. The function responsible for performing the input returns an appropriate status code to indicate if the input was successful or whether either of the limits had been exceeded. The text lines of input are terminated with the end of data trailer "zzz".

The previous version of Shell sort must be modified to accommodate string and string pointers instead of integers. The only changes necessary to the sort function are where values are compared and values are exchanged. String comparisons are performed by the standard library function strcmp. The exchanging of two integer values is replaced with an exchange of two string pointers, implemented with a macro.

Program 12.5

```
/*
**          Input a series of lines of text and output them
**          in alphabetical order. The lines are first recorded
**          then sorted using the Shell sort algorithm. The
**          input is terminated with the unique line 'zzz'.
*/

#include <stdio.h>

#define MAXCHARS                10000
#define MAXLINES                200
#define MAXTEXT                 128

#define TERMINATOR              "zzz"

#define OFLOLINES               0
#define OFLOCHARS               1
#define SUCCESS                 2

typedef int                     Status;   /* after reading input */

Status  read_lines ();                    /* forward references */
void    shell_sort (), print_lines ();
char    *gets ();

#define SWAP(X, Y)                    { char *P;\
 P = (X); (X) = (Y); (Y) = P; }

main ()
    {
    char        linebuffer[MAXCHARS];     /* lines of text */
    char        *linepointer[MAXLINES];   /* indices to lines */
    Status      stat;                     /* success or failure */
    int         numlines;                 /* number of input lines */

    if ((stat = read_lines (linepointer, linebuffer, &numlines))
                        == SUCCESS )
        {
        shell_sort (linepointer, numlines);
        print_lines (linepointer, numlines);
        }
    else
        switch (stat)                          /* error type */
            {
            case OFLOLINES :
                    printf ("Too many lines\n");    break;
            case OFLOCHARS :
                    printf ("Too many chars\n");    break;
            }
    }
```

```
/*
**   -----------------------------oOo-----------------------------
**   -----------------------------oOo-----------------------------
*/
Status read_lines (linepointer, linebuffer, numlines)
  char  *linepointer [];          /* indices of text lines in */
  char  linebuffer [];            /* .... line storage */
  int   *numlines;                /* number of input lines */
  {
    char *buffer, *endbuffer;     /* next space, end of space */
    char line[MAXTEXT];           /* single line of text */

    buffer = linebuffer;                    /* init next space pointer */
    endbuffer = linebuffer + MAXCHARS;  /* char beyond avail space */

    *numlines = 0;
    while (gets (line), strcmp (line, TERMINATOR) != 0)
      if (*numlines == MAXLINES)          /* too many lines? */
        return (OFLOLINES);
      else if (buffer + strlen (line) + 1 >= endbuffer)
                                          /* enough store? */
        return (OFLOCHARS);
      else
        {
          linepointer[(*numlines)++] = buffer; /* establish index */
          strcpy (buffer, line);               /* copy into buffer */
          buffer += strlen (line) + 1;         /* update pointer */
        }

    return (SUCCESS);
  }

/*
**   -----------------------------oOo-----------------------------
**   -----------------------------oOo-----------------------------
*/
void shell_sort (linepointer, numlines)
  char  *linepointer [];                  /* indices to text */
  int   numlines;                         /* number of text lines */
  {
    int interval, i, j;                   /* interval and counters */

    for (interval = numlines/2; interval > 0; interval /= 2)
      for (i = interval; i < numlines; i++)
        for (j = i - interval; j >= 0; j -= interval)
          {
            if (strcmp (linepointer[j], linepointer[j+interval])
                        <= 0)
              break;
            SWAP(linepointer[j], linepointer[j+interval]);
          }
  }

/*
**   -----------------------------oOo-----------------------------
**   -----------------------------oOo-----------------------------
*/
void print_lines (linepointer, numlines)
  char  *linepointer [];                  /* pointers to text lines */
  int   numlines;                         /* number of lines */
  {
    int k;

    for (k = 0; k < numlines; k++)
      printf ("%s\n", linepointer[k]);
  }
```

12.6 Pointers to pointers

A formal argument of a function declared to be of type 'array of T' where T
is some arbitrary type, is treated as if it were declared to be of type 'pointer
to T'. Because of the equivalence of pointers and arrays (see section 11.5),
this change is invisible to the programmer and performed automatically by
the C compiler. For example, in the function:

```
int sumarray(a, n)
   int      a[];             /* array elements to be summed */
   int      n;               /* number of items */
   {
      int sum, k;            /* running total and counter */

      sum = 0;
      for (k = 0; k < n; k++)
        sum += a[k];

      return (sum);
   }
```

the arguments a and n could have been declared by the programmer as:

   int *a, n;

This, in fact, is what the C compiler does.

Where a function argument is declared to be of type 'array of T' and T is
of type 'pointer to S' for some arbitrary type S, it is equivalenced to type
'pointer to pointer to S'. For example, the function print_lines in Program
12.5 which has the declaration:

   void print_lines(linepointer, numlines)
      char   *linepointer[ ];
      int   numlines;
      {
         _ _ _ _ _ _ _ _ _
         _ _ _ _ _ _ _ _ _
      }

is converted to:

   void print_lines(linepointer, numlines)
      char   **linepointer;
      int   n;
      {
         _ _ _ _ _ _ _ _ _ _
         _ _ _ _ _ _ _ _ _ _
      }

That is, linepointer has as its value the base address for a series of memory
locations, each of which is the address of the first character of a null-
terminated array of characters (a string). Pictorially, the arrangement
appears as shown in Fig. 12.9.

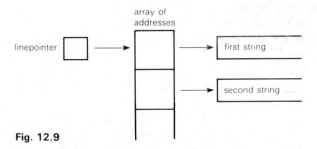

Fig. 12.9

The object referred to as linepointer possesses the value that is the address of the array of addresses. The object referred to as *linepointer is the first address contained in that array and is therefore the address of the first character in the first string. Finally, the object referred to as **linepointer is the first character in the first string.

The precedence and associativity of the indirection operator * and the other operators must be carefully noted. Particular attention should be paid to the operators * (indirection), + + (increment) and − − (decrement), all having equal precedence and all associating right to left. Thus *(*linepointer + 1) references the first character of the second string; **linepointer + + references the first character of the first string (and advances linepointer by one); whilst ** + + linepointer references the first character of the second string (having first advanced linepointer by one).

From this discussion, we could remodel function print_lines in terms of these multilevel indirections:

```
void print_lines(linepointer, numlines)
   char    **linepointer;              /* pointers to text lines */
   int     numlines;                   /* number of lines */
   {
      int    k;

      for (k = 0; k < numlines; k + +)
         printf("%s\n", *linepointer + +);
   }
```

12.7 Command line arguments

Normally a C program exists in an environment established by the resident operating system. The environment usually supports passing *command line* arguments to a program when it begins execution. For example, consider a program called sum which is invoked with two arguments on the command line. These arguments are an integer pair which are summed and printed by the program. The program might be activated by:

    sum 123 456

The output from the program is, of course, 579.

Function main of a program is often defined with two formal arguments conventionally called *argc* and *argv*. The first argument, argc, is the number of command line arguments. Since the program name is always included in the count, argc always exceeds 0. In the example call of program sum, argc is 3. The second argument, argv, is an array of pointers to char, pointers to the first character in the null-terminated array of characters that represent the argument strings. By convention, argv[0] is the program name. In the example, argv[0], argv[1] and argv[2]are respectively sum, 123 and 456. The first argument proper is argv[1]. The last argument is argv[argc − 1]. One possible version for this program follows.

Program 12.6

```
/*
**      Form the sum of two integers given as command
**      line arguments.
*/

#include <stdio.h>

main(argc, argv)
   int    argc;
   char   *argv[];
   {
     int first, second;

     if (argc != 3)                /* check number of arguments */
       printf("Usage: %s number number\n", argv[0]);
     else
       {
         sscanf(argv[1], "%d", &first);
         sscanf(argv[2], "%d", &second);
         printf("%d\n", first + second);
       }
   }
```

Another simple illustration of command line arguments is the program *echo,* which echoes its arguments to the standard output, with each string separated by a single blank character. That is, if the command is:

echo My first   program

the output is:

My first program

In this example, argc is 4, and argv[0], argv[1], argv[2] and argv[3] are echo, My, first and program, respectively. Note how all leading whitespace characters are not included in the arguments. Their appearance in the command line serves only to act as separators. The program is:

Program 12.7(a)

```
/*
**      Echo all command line arguments each separated
**      by a single blank character.
*/
```

```
#include <stdio.h>

#define NEWLINE          '\n'

main(argc, argv)
   int   argc;
   char  *argv[];
   {
     int k;

     for (k = 1; k < argc; k++)          /* for each argument */
       printf("%s ", argv[k]);
     putchar(NEWLINE);
   }
```

Note that the program has been coded such that an extra single blank character is printed after the last argument has been echoed. Generally, this is not visible to the user, and thus is harmless.

Since argv is a pointer to an array of pointers, there are several ways to implement this program, manipulating the pointer rather than indexing an array. One variation is given in Program 12.7(b).

Program 12.7(b)

```
/*
**      Echo all command line arguments each separated
**      by a single blank character.
*/

#include <stdio.h>

#define NEWLINE          '\n'

main(argc, argv)
   int   argc;
   char  **argv;
   {
     while (--argc > 0)
       printf("%s ", *++argv);
     putchar(NEWLINE);
   }
```

Since argv is a pointer to the beginning of the array of pointers (to the command line argument strings), incrementing it by 1 (+ +argv) makes it point to argv[1]. Each successive increment moves to the next argument address; *argv is then the pointer to that string. At the same time, argc is simultaneously decremented and when it becomes zero there are no more arguments to print.

Many C programs are supplied with arguments in this manner. Often, the arguments are the names of files to be processed by the program, permitting the program to be constructed such that these file names are run time arguments. In some instances, these arguments are supplemented with *options* used to further vary the effect of the program. Options are frequently introduced as single characters preceded by a leading hyphen (-) symbol.

One possible variation of the echo program might support the option '-r'. If the option is present as the first command line argument, then the remaining arguments are printed in reverse order. If the option is omitted, the echo program behaves as before. Any other option appearing with the leading hyphen is flagged as an error. For example:

echo -r my   first   program

would produce the output:

program first my

Program 12.8

```
/*
**        Echo all command line arguments to the standard
**        output. Each argument is separated by a space.
**        If the first argument is the option '-r' then
**        the arguments are echoed in reverse order. All
**        other options are illegal.
*/

#include <stdio.h>

#define NEWLINE            '\n'
#define HYPHEN             '-'
#define LETTERR            'r'

main(argc, argv)
   int    argc;
   char   *argv[];
   {
      int k;

      if (argv[1][0] == HYPHEN)               /* first argument option? */
        if (argv[1][1] == LETTERR)            /* permissible option? */
          for (k = argc - 1; k > 1; k--)      /* reverse printing */
            printf("%s ", argv[k]);
        else
          printf("%s: illegal option\n", argv[0]);
      else
        for (k = 1; k < argc; k++)            /* normal printing */
          printf("%s ", argv[k]);

      putchar(NEWLINE);
   }
```

Optional arguments should be permitted in any order if more than one is supported by the program. The program should also be insensitive to the actual number present. Where there is more than one option given, it is often convenient for the user if they can be concatenated. The final version of program echo which we shall develop supports the arguments '-r' and '-n'. As before, the -r option reverses the printed arguments. The -n option causes no newline symbol to be printed at the end of the output. In this way, the echoed arguments appear as a prompt, with the cursor immediately following the output. The command:

echo -n -r date: the Enter

produces the output:

Enter the date:

which is not terminated with a newline. Concatenating the two options so that they appear:

echo -nr date: the Enter

or:

echo -rn date: the Enter

produces the same results as in the first example. An option which is duplicated has the same effect as if it only appeared once. The same output is produced by:

echo -nr -r date: the Enter

where the additional option -r is redundant. All other options are illegal and are flagged accordingly. Here is the program:

Program 12.9

```
/*
**      Echo command line arguments to the standard
**      output. The two supported options are '-r' (reverse)
**      and '-n' (newline).
*/

#include <stdio.h>

#define NEWLINE         '\n'
#define HYPHEN          '-'
#define LETTERR         'R'
#define LETTERN         'N'

#define FALSE           0
#define TRUE            1
typedef int             Boolean;

main (argc, argv)
   int     argc;
   char    *argv[];
   {
     Boolean     reverse = FALSE, newline = TRUE;   /* option flags */
     char        *s;                                /* string pointer */
     int         k;

     while (--argc > 0 && **++argv == HYPHEN)       /* every option */
       for (s = *argv+1; *s != NULL; s++)
         switch (*s)
           {
             case LETTERR :      reverse = TRUE;         break;
             case LETTERN :      newline = FALSE;        break;
             default      :
               printf ("Echo: illegal option %c\n", *s);
               argc = 0;                        /* force termination */
               break;
           }

     if (reverse)                               /* order? */
       for (k = argc - 1; k >= 0; k--)
         printf ("%s ", argv[k]);
     else
       for (k = 0; k < argc; k++)
         printf ("%s ", argv[k]);

     if (newline)
       putchar (NEWLINE);
   }
```

12.8 Initializing pointer arrays

In Program 6.16 we encountered a function called day_name which printed the day of the week when given Zeller's congruence for that day. Consider the problem rewriting this function to return a pointer to a character string containing the name of the nth day of the week (n is 0–6 inclusive, representing Sunday, Monday, ..., Saturday). The function operates by having a private array of character strings containing the day names, and returns a pointer to the correct one when called. The function is:

```
char *day_name(n)
   int      n;                    /* day number, 0 - 6 */
   {
   static char *name[] =
      { "Sunday",    "Monday", "Tuesday", "Wednesday",
        "Thursday", "Friday", "Saturday" "Illegal day" };

   if (n < 0 || n > 6)
      return (name[7]);
   else
      return (name[n]);
   }
```

The declaration for name, which is an array of character pointers, is the same as for linepointer in Program 12.6. The initializer is a list of character strings, each assigned the correct position in the array. Note how a measure of robustness is maintained by filtering out the special case. The characters in the kth string are stored somewhere in memory and a pointer to them is stored in name[k].

Case study 12.2: Postfix expression evaluation

A *stack* is a data structure for which the principal operations are those of inserting a new item on to the stack and removing the last item inserted. The insertion and removal of items take place at one end, usually referred to as the *top* of the stack. The order of manipulation of items within a stack is thus last-in, first-out.

A stack is normally viewed as a sequence of data items drawn vertically, with the topmost item representing the most recent addition to the stack (see Fig. 12.10).

Four operations on a stack are immediately identifiable:

(a) push (item)   insert a new item on to the stack
(b) pop (item)   remove the topmost item
(c) empty?   determine whether the stack is empty
(d) full?   determine if the stack is full

The operation *empty* is necessary to ensure that we do not *pop* a value from a stack which contains no elements. Equally, a stack may have some finite size and hence the test *full* is required to determine this condition.

Stacks are of great importance in many computing applications. One

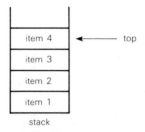

item 4 ←——— top

item 3

item 2

item 1

stack

Fig. 12.10

example is to implement a desk calculator using reverse Polish notation. In a normal arithmetic expression the operators are listed between their operands. This is referred to as *infix notation.* In reverse Polish notation, each operator follows its operands. Table 12.1 gives an example. Because the operators follow their operands, reverse Polish notation is also known as *postfix notation.* Note how in the last illustration, no parentheses are required in the equivalent postfix notation. For this reason, postfix notation is sometimes also described as *parentheses free notation.*

A postfix expression is evaluated by pushing each operand on to a stack until an operator is met. The top two items on the stack are popped and the operator applied to them. The result is then pushed back on to the stack. The left to right processing of the postfix expression then continues. The postfix expression:

1   2 + 3   4 + *

is evaluated through the stack sequences shown in Fig. 12.11.

The algorithm for a postfix expression calculator is readily expressed by the following program structure:

```
WHILE another postfix operand/operator
DO
  IF an operand
  THEN
    push the operand on to the stack
  ELSE IF an operator
      pop the operands from the stack
      apply the incoming operator to the operands
      push the result back on to the stack
    ELSE
      error – unknown postfix expression item
    ENDIF
ENDWHILE
print the top stack item as final expression value
```

The data items to the program will appear as command line arguments. The program name is *calc* (calculator). The infix expression (1 + 2) * (3 + 4)

Table 12.1

Infix notation	Equivalent reverse Polish
1 + 2	1 2 +
1 − 2 * 3	1 2 3 * −
(1 + 2) * (3 − 4)	1 2 + 3 4 − *

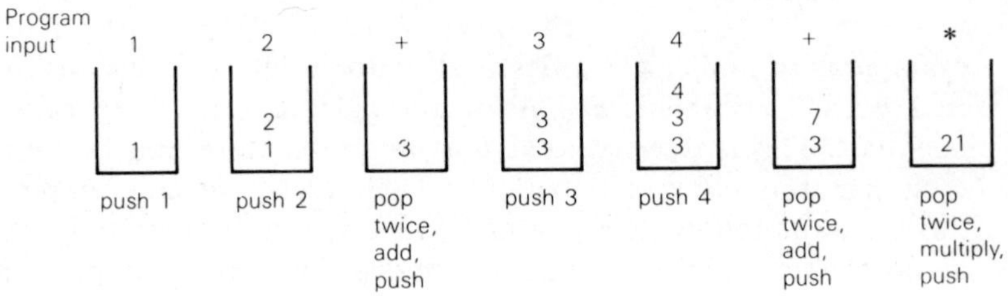

Program
input   1   2   +   3   4   +   *

push 1   push 2   pop   push 3   push 4   pop   pop
                  twice,   twice,   twice,
                  add,   add,   multiply,
                  push   push   push

Fig. 12.11

would be evaluated by the program invocation:

    calc 1 2 + 3 4 + *

The principal abstraction in this problem is the stack. The features of the stack required by this application program are the operations push and pop. Provided these operations perform the necessary error checks, the operators empty and full need not be visible to the application. If an attempt is made to push an item on to an already full stack, or remove an item from an empty stack, an appropriate error message is issued and the program terminates.

Stack handling is, therefore, encapsulated in a program unit. Those resources required by the application are exported to it, the other details remain invisible. The initial module outline is shown in Fig. 12.12.

Given an implementation for a stack of double precision floating point numbers (Stacktype), and given a corresponding header file for the exported functions, we may proceed to implement the program calc. Since the postfix expression is presented to the program through its command line arguments, we need to distinguish between operands and operators. An operator is any valid arithmetical operator from the set +, −, * and /. An operand is a valid floating point constant for which the first character is a decimal digit. The first character of a command argument can therefore be used to distinguish between operators and operands − if it is a digit it is a number, otherwise it is an operator, unless it is an error.

First, the header file by which we import the stack handling functions into the application program:

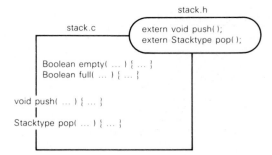

stack.h

stack.c

```
extern void push( );
extern Stacktype pop( );
```

```
Boolean empty( ... ) { ... }
Boolean full( ... ) { ... }
```

```
void push( ... ) { ... }
```

```
Stacktype pop( ... ) { ... }
```

Fig. 12.12

```
/*
**      File:   stack.h
**
**      A package of defined types and operators (functions)
**      supporting a stack of doubles.
*/

typedef double          Stacktype;

extern void push ();                    /* referencing declarations */
extern Stacktype pop ();
```

The program calc is essentially a multiway switch. For each command argument a decision is made about its type and the appropriate service called. The decision is based on the initial character of each argument.

```
/*
**      File:   calc.c
**
**      Reverse Polish calculator. The postfix expression
**      is presented as command line arguments, consisting
**      of a series of operands (numbers) and operators.
**      The supported operators are +, -, * and /.
*/

#include <stdio.h>
#include "stack.h"

#define EPSILON                 1.0E-4

main (argc, argv)
  int    argc;
  char   *argv[];
  {
    int        arg;                      /* argument counter */
    Stacktype operand;                   /* next operand value */

    for (arg = 1; arg < argc; arg++)     /* for every command arg. */
      switch (argv[arg][0])              /* first character of arg. */
        {
          case '+' : push (pop () + pop ());   break;
          case '-' : push (pop () - pop ());   break;
          case '*' : push (pop () * pop ());   break;
          case '/' : operand = pop ();         /* get divisor */
                     if (operand < EPSILON)    /* too small? */
                       {
                         printf ("Division by zero\n");
                         argc = 0;             /* force termination */
                       }
                     else
                       push (pop () / operand); break;
```

```
case '0' : case '1' : case '2' : case '3' : case '4' :
case '5' : case '6' : case '7' : case '8' : case '9' :
          sscanf (argv[arg], "%f", &operand);
          push (operand);
          break;

default :
          printf ("Argument not recognized %s\n",
                          argv[arg]);
          argc = 0;
          break;
}

if (argc != 0)                      /* calculator ok? */
  printf ("Expression value is %f\n", pop ());
}
```

Where it is convenient to operate with a stack with some specified bounds on the maximum number of items, then an array may be used to represent the stack. A stack with a capacity for STACKSIZE items, and having the topmost item referenced (indexed) by top, is shown in Fig. 12.13.

New items are pushed on to the stack at position top + 1. Items are removed (popped) from the stack from position top. Initially, the stack is empty and so top must firstly be set to − 1. If our stack items are of type Stacktype, then the data structure required to realize the stack is defined by:

Stacktype   stack[STACKSIZE];
int   top = − 1;

With this representation, we may now define our four operators push, pop, empty and full. The full and empty operators are implemented as functions which examine the current value of top and return a Boolean result:

```
static Boolean empty( )
  {
    return (top < 0);
  }
```

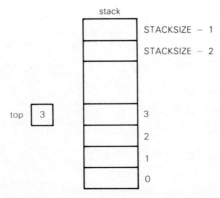

Fig. 12.13

```
static Boolean full( )
  {
    return (top = = STACKSIZE − 1);
  }
```

The push operator inserts a given item on top of the stack by incrementing top and assigning the value to the element of the array indexed by top, first checking that the stack is not already full:

```
void push(item)
  Stacktype item;
  {
    if (full( ))
        stackerror(OVERFLOW);
    else
        stack[ + + top] = item;
  }
```

The pop operator has a similar implementation. The topmost item is returned as the function value, whilst the index top is decremented. The stack is first checked to ensure it is not empty. The listing below shows a complete version of the stack program unit.

```
/*
**      File:   stack.c
**
**      An implementation of a set of stack handling
**      operators. The stack is implemented using an
**      array.
*/

#include <stdio.h>
#include "stack.h"

#define STACKSIZE              100

#define FALSE                  0
#define TRUE                   1
#define OVERFLOW               0
#define UNDERFLOW              1

typedef int                    Boolean;

static Stacktype stack[STACKSIZE];
static int       top = -1;

void    stackerror ();                    /* internal routine */

static Boolean empty ()
  {
    return (top < 0);
  }
/*
**      --------------------------------oOo--------------------------------
**      --------------------------------oOo--------------------------------
*/
```

```
static Boolean full ()
   {
   return (top == STACKSIZE - 1);
   }

/*
**  ---------------------------------oOo---------------------------------
**  ---------------------------------oOo---------------------------------
*/

void push (item)
  Stacktype item;
   {
   if (full ())
     stackerror (OVERFLOW);
   else
     stack[++top] = item;
   }

/*
**  ---------------------------------oOo---------------------------------
**  ---------------------------------oOo---------------------------------
*/

Stacktype pop ()

   {
   Stacktype item;

   if (empty ())
     stackerror (UNDERFLOW);
   else
     {
     item = stack[top--];
     return (item);
     }
   }

/*
**  ---------------------------------oOo---------------------------------
**  ---------------------------------oOo---------------------------------
*/

static void stackerror (code)
  int   code;                           /* error code */
   {
   switch (code)
      {
      case OVERFLOW  : printf ("stack overflow\n");    break;
      case UNDERFLOW : printf ("stack underflow\n");   break;
      }

   exit (1);                            /* STOP RUN */
   }
```

The principal limitation of the array implementation is that the implementor has to estimate an upper bound for the number of items in the stack.
If this is too low, the stack will overflow during program execution; and if it
is too high, then this may result in poor utilization of memory. A solution to
overcome this problem is discussed in Chapter 16 when non-contiguous
storage allocation is introduced.

12.9 Summary

1. Strings are one-dimensional arrays of type char. The null character \0 is
   used to delimit a string. System functions such as strcmp will only work
   on properly null-terminated strings.

2. The standard library I/O function scanf can be used to read a sequence of non-whitespace characters using the %s formater. On completion, the input string is automatically null-terminated.

3. Arrays of pointers to type char (i.e. pointer to pointers) are used to process lists of strings. The second argument to function main is of this type, allowing a program access to its command line arguments.

4. External and static strings may be initialized. Initializations of the form:

```
char s[ ] = {'a', 'b', 'c', '\0'};
char s[ ] = "abc";
```

are considered identical by the compiler. A list of strings can be used to initialize an array of character pointers:

```
char *list[ ] = {"Programming", "in", "C"};
```

12.10 Exercises

1. Prepare a function to capitalize every lower-case alphabetical character in the string argument s. All other characters remain untouched. The function header is:

```
void capitalize(s)
    char    *s;
```

2. Prepare a function to shift the characters of the string argument s one place to the left, overwriting the original initial character. Develop the complementary function to shift the characters of a string one place to the right, padding with a single blank (space) character on the left.

3. Write a function called left_rotate with the following header, to rotate cyclically the characters of the argument string s, n character places to the left.

```
void left_rotate(s, n)
    char    *s;
    int     n;
```

Write the corresponding function right_rotate.

4. With suitable definitions, write a Boolean function 'less' which returns TRUE if the string s is lexicographically less than the string t, and FALSE otherwise. The function header is:

```
Boolean less(s, t)
    char    *s, *t;
```

Design the corresponding functions 'less than or equal', 'equal', 'not equal', 'greater than' and 'greater than or equal'. Each function may employ any previously written function in this suite.

5. Write a function that accepts strings of any length and determines whether they are palindromes. Additionally, allow the function to accept a sentence string containing spaces which are to be ignored when determining if the sentence is palindromic.

6. Write a function which, given two strings s and t, returns the position of the first occurrence of s in t. For example, if s is "ram" and t is "programming", the value returned is 4. If s does not occur in t, the value − 1 is returned. If s is longer than t, then zero is also returned.

7. Write a function called substring to extract a portion of a character string. The function header is:

```
void substring(source, start, count, result)
    char    *source,  *result;
    int     start, count;
```

where *source* is the character string from which we are extracting the substring; *result* is the array of characters which receives the extracted string; *start* is an index into the source string and is the position of the first character in the source string (start > = 0); and *count* is the number of characters to be extracted (count > = 0). Ensure that the function performs all the necessary checks and operates correctly under all circumstances.

8. Write a function called remove_string to remove a specified number of characters from a character string. The function header is:

```
void remove_string(source, start, count)
    char    *source;
    int     start, count;
```

where *source* is the character string from which we are removing the substring; *start* is an index into the source string and is the position of the first character in the source string (start > = 0); and *count* is the number of characters to be removed (count > = 0). The resulting string is returned through source.

9. Write a function called 'insert_string' which inserts one character string into another. The function header is:

```
void insert_string(source, text, start)
    char    *source,  *text;
    int     start;
```

where *source* is the source string; *text* is the string to be inserted; and *start* is the position in the source string where the *text* string is to be inserted.

10. Input to a program represents the text of a telegram. The input consists of one or more lines containing a number of words each separated by a number of spaces. The unique word 'END' terminates the input. Produce a bill for this telegram with each word costing 10 cents and an additional charge of 5 cents for every word over eight letters long. The output is to appear as:

Number of words	: 23
Number of normal-sized words	: 19 at 10 is 1.90
Number of oversized words	: 4 at 15 is 0.60
TOTAL	: 2.50

11. The input to a program contains the text of a number of telegrams. Each record in the input appears on a single line and consists of a block of words each separated by one or more spaces. The block is terminated by the reserved word 'EOB' (end of block). Each telegram consists of a number of words followed by

the reserved word 'ZZZ'. A telegram may begin and end anywhere in a block, i.e. a telegram may span several blocks, or a single block may contain several telegrams. The end of input is signified by a block containing only the text 'EOF' (end of file).

A sample input is:

```
HAPPY BIRTHDAY JOE FROM EOB
FRED ZZZ THANK YOU AND GOODBYE ZZZ EOB
HI YA ZZZ SEE YOU TOMORROW ZZZ THE EOB
PRINCIPAL RESOURCE CENTER IS EOB
THE PROGRAM UNIT ZZZ EOB
EOF
```

The program is required to print each telegram one per line, for example:

```
LINE 1: HAPPY BIRTHDAY JOE FROM FRED
LINE 2: THANK YOU AND GOODBYE
LINE 3: HI YA
LINE 4: SEE YOU TOMORROW
LINE 5: THE PRINCIPAL RESOURCE CENTER IS THE
        PROGRAM UNIT
```

12. Modify the concordance program to optionally print the word list in reverse alphabetical order. The option is indicated by the command line argument '-r'.

13. Extend the last question to support the optional command line argument '-f', where the words are printed in order of increasing frequency.

## CHAPTER 13

Storage management

A *variable-sized* data structure is one in which the number of components may change *dynamically* during program execution. Some of the major types of variable-sized data structures include *lists*, *stacks*, *queues* and *trees*, and are the subject of Chapters 15 and 16.

Variable-sized data objects are used when the amount of data in a problem is not known in advance. Use of fixed-sized arrays requires that large amounts of storage are reserved in advance for the maximum size of data that might be encountered. Variable-sized data structures allow storage to be allocated incrementally during program execution.

There are two fundamentally different approaches to these dynamic data structures. In some languages they are provided directly. In others, a pointer data type and facilities for the dynamic allocation of storage are provided. This is the approach taken in C. Several language features are then necessary to make this possible:

1. An elementary data type *pointer*. A pointer data object contains the location of another data object, or it may contain the special null pointer, NULL. Pointers are ordinary objects that may be simple variables or components of arrays (or structures; see Chapter 16). Pointers were the subject of Chapters 5, 11 and 12.
2. A *creation operation* for data objects of fixed size, such as elementary types or arrays. The creation operation both allocates a block of storage for the data object and returns a pointer to its location, which may then be stored as the value of a pointer variable. The creation operator differs in two ways from the ordinary creation of variables caused by declarations:

   (a) The data objects created have no names, their values are accessed through pointers.
   (b) Data objects may be created in this way at any point during program execution, not just on entry to a function.
3. A *selection operation* for pointer values that allow the data object to which it points to be accessed.

13.1 Implementation

The creation operator both allocates storage for a fixed-sized data object and delivers a pointer to the new data object. In C this operation is provided by a number of standard library functions. Function *malloc* allocates a contiguous region of memory of *size* bytes, and returns a pointer to the beginning of the allocated block. The function header for malloc is:

```
char *malloc(size)
    unsigned size;
```

The region of memory is not specially initialized in any way; the caller must assume that it contains garbage. As shown, the value returned by malloc is a pointer to type char. If ptr and pt are variables declared as:

```
char *ptr, *pt;
```

then:

```
ptr = malloc(20);
```

establishes a region of memory of 20 bytes with ptr a pointer to the beginning of this area. The block of memory is anonymous. No variable name associates with it. The variable ptr provides a pointer to this unnamed area. Using ptr as shown in the previous two chapters, we can reference any of the allocated 20 bytes. For example, to fill the region with 20 letter B symbols, we might use:

```
for (pt = ptr, k = 0; k < 20; k + + )
    *pt + + = 'B'
```

If it is impossible for some reason to perform the requested allocation, malloc returns the null pointer, NULL, as defined in the standard I/O header, stdio.h. The last illustration may be shown incorporating the additional check:

```
if ((ptr = malloc(20)) = = NULL)
    printf("Cannot allocate\n");
else
    for (pt = ptr, k = 0; k < 20; k + + )
        *pt + + = 'B';
```

When a region of memory is allocated in response to a request, a pointer to the region is returned to the caller. This pointer will be of type pointer to char but is guaranteed to be properly aligned for *any* data type. The caller may then use a cast operator to convert this pointer to another pointer type. If it is known, for example, that for a particular implementation an integer occupies 2 bytes, then:

    int *px;

    px = (int *) malloc(2);
    *px = 15;

allocates an area of memory sufficient to store a single integer using malloc, then coerces with a cast the return address to be a pointer to an int assigned to px. This anonymous integer location is then assigned the value 15.

 In this last illustration, we needed to know the size of an int object. The number of bytes occupied by an int is machine-dependent and this reduces the portability of the code presented. This problem is removed by employing the *sizeof* operator.

The sizeof operator is used to obtain the size of a type or a data object. The sizeof expression has the form:

    sizeof(type-name)

or:

    sizeof expression

Applying this operator to a parenthesized type name yields the size of an object of the specified type; that is, the number of storage units (usually bytes) that would be occupied by an object of that type. The type name may be any of the fundamental types, the type void, a function type or an array type with no explicit length. The portability problem of the previous example is removed by using:

    px = (int *) malloc(sizeof(int));

Applying the sizeof operator to an expression yields the same result as if it had been applied to the name of the type of the expression. Although a generalized expression is permitted, more commonly this form is used with a variable name as the expression. Clarity is improved if the expression is parenthesized. Given the declaration:

    int x, *px;

an area sufficient to store an int may be established with:

    px = (int *) malloc(sizeof(x));

The operator sizeof is described as a compile time operator insofar as the result of applying this operator to an expression can always be deduced at compile time by examining the type of the objects in the expression. The result of sizeof is not dependent on the particular values of any run time objects. When sizeof is applied to an expression, the expression is analyzed at compile time to determine its type. This means that any side effect as a result of execution of the expression is not a matter for compile time determination. For example, compilation of the declaration:

int obj1 = 1, obj2 = sizeof(obj1 + +);

results in some initial value assigned to obj2 (the number of bytes for an int, since obj1 + + is an expression of type int), but will not increment obj1.

The following program demonstrates one use of the library function malloc. The program inputs two integer data values and outputs them in reverse order. Instead of declaring two integer variables to represent the data items, pointers are employed. Space for two integers is created dynamically (by malloc) and pointers assigned to the space. The program then operates in terms of the pointers, rather than in terms of integer variables. The example is intended merely to illustrate dynamic storage. It is not recommended as the solution to this problem. The conventional solution is given in Program 5.3.

Program 13.1

```
/*
**        This program reads two integer values from the
**        standard input, and outputs them in reverse order.
**        The locations for the two integers are created
**        dynamically using the library function "malloc".
*/

#include <stdio.h>

char      *malloc();

main()
   {
      int *first, *second;          /* pointers to the data values */

      if ((first = (int *) malloc(sizeof(int))) == NULL)
         printf("Cannot create first\n");
      else if ((second = (int *) malloc(sizeof(int))) == NULL)
         printf("Cannot create second\n");
      else
         {
            printf("Enter the data: ");
            scanf("%d %d", first, second);
            printf("Reversed data: %d %d\n", *second, *first);
         }
   }
```

Since memory is frequently a critical resource, available in limited quantities, it is desirable that the storage allocated by a call to malloc is returned to the system for later re-use. The function *free* allows the programmer to deallocate a region of memory previously allocated by malloc. The header for this function is:

void free(pointer)
    char   *pointer;

The argument to free is a pointer to a char value previously returned by malloc. If, as in Program 13.1, the returned pointer has had an explicit type cast, then this intermediate value must be restored for use with free. Once a region of memory has been freed, it should no longer be referenced by the program. The storage manager recycles the memory region for use with subsequent calls to malloc.

Program 13.2 repeats the previous example but, additionally, explicitly frees the region of memory dynamically established by malloc. Once again, the example is merely for illustrative purposes. Practical uses of free will be shown in later chapters.

Program 13.2

```
/*
**       This program reads two integer values from the
**       standard input, and outputs them in reverse order.
**       The locations for the two integers are created
**       dynamically using the library function "malloc".
*/

#include <stdio.h>

char    *malloc();
void    free();

main()
   {
     int *first, *second;          /* pointers to the data values */

     if ((first = (int *) malloc(sizeof(int))) == NULL)
       printf("Cannot create first\n");
     else if ((second = (int *) malloc(sizeof(int))) == NULL)
       printf("Cannot create second\n");
     else
        {
          printf("Enter the data: ");
          scanf("%d %d", first, second);
          printf("Reversed data: %d %d\n", *second, *first);
          free((char *) first);
          free((char *) second);
        }
   }
```

When the region of memory to be allocated represents an array of N elements each of type T, then the call to function malloc has the argument expression which represents the total number of bytes required by the storage structure, namely:

char *ptr;

ptr = malloc(N * sizeof(T));

Alternatively, we can employ the related library function *calloc*. The heading is:

char *calloc(count, size)
    unsigned count, size;

which allocates memory sufficient to hold an array with *count* elements each requiring *size* bytes of storage. A pointer to the first byte is returned, or NULL if the request is impossible. The example above can also be expressed by:

ptr = calloc(N, sizeof(T));

Data to a program consist of a single integer followed by a series of floating point values, the number of which is given by the leading integer. The floating point values are read and printed in reverse order by the program. The values are stored in an array during input. The array is dynamically created and the size is determined by the initial data item.

Program 13.3

```
/*
**        Read a series of floats from the standard input and
**        write them to the standard output in reverse order.
**        The values are preceded by an integer count of the
**        number of data items. This value is used to
**        dynamically create an array to store the data.
*/

#include <stdio.h>

char       *calloc();

main()
    {
    int    n, k;                        /* count and loop control */
    float *base, *ptr;                  /* array base and index */

    scanf("%d", &n);
    if ((base = (float *) calloc(n, sizeof(float))) == NULL)
      printf("Unable to create the array\n");
    else
       {
       for (ptr = base, k = 0; k < n; k++)
          scanf("%f", ptr++);
       for (ptr = base + n, k = 0; k < n; k++)
          printf("%f\n", *(--ptr));
       }
    }
```

Program 12.5 produced an alphabetical sort of a number of lines of text. To operate efficiently and conveniently with lines of text of varying lengths, a suitable data structure was devised. The implementation consisted of a large array called *linebuffer* holding the lines to be sorted in an end-to-end fashion; and a second array, *linepointer*, containing pointers to where (in linebuffer) the corresponding lines begin. Both these arrays must be reserved (declared) in advance for the maximum size of data that might be encountered. Robustness in the program is ensured by including array bounds checking in function read_lines where the input is read and stored in the arrays.

For many programs this form of static allocation is satisfactory. However, it is incompatible with data structures whose size is dependent on input data. In the application, the size of both linepointer and linebuffer is dependent upon the number of lines of text and the total number of characters in the text respectively.

In Chapter 16 we will introduce how to make both structures grow dynamically. For the present, dynamic storage allocation is applied to linebuffer only. Provided that storage can be created dynamically without restriction, no limit is imposed upon the total number of characters in the text.

Whereas in Program 12.5 storage is drawn from a fixed sized pool (linebuffer), Program 13.4 obtains space for each input line by a call on malloc (through function *strsave*). Function strsave copies the string argument into a safe place, obtained through a call on malloc. The function returns a pointer to the allocated storage area.

Program 13.4

```
/*
**        Input a series of lines of text and output them
**        in alphabetical order. The lines are first recorded
**        then sorted using the Shell sort algorithm. The
**        input is terminated with the unique line 'zzz'.
*/

#include <stdio.h>

#define MAXLINES           200
#define MAXTEXT            128

#define TERMINATOR         "zzz"

#define OFLOLINES          0                   /* status codes */
#define OFLOCHARS          1
#define SUCCESS            2

typedef int                Status;      /* after reading input */

Status  read_lines ();                         /* forward references */
void    shell_sort (), print_lines ();
char    *gets (), *malloc (), *strsave ();
int     strlen ();

#define SWAP(X, Y)              { char *P;\
 P = (X); (X) = (Y); (Y) = P; }

main ()
    {
    char        *linepointer[MAXLINES];     /* indices to lines */
    Status      stat;                       /* success or failure */
    int         numlines;                   /* number input lines */

    if ((stat = read_lines (linepointer, &numlines)) == SUCCESS )
        {
        shell_sort (linepointer, numlines);
        print_lines (linepointer, numlines);
        }
    else
      switch (stat)                         /* error type */
        {
        case OFLOLINES :
                printf ("Too many lines\n");    break;
        case OFLOCHARS :
                printf ("Too many chars\n");    break;
        }
    }
/*
**  ---------------------------------oOo---------------------------------
**  ---------------------------------oOo---------------------------------
*/
```

```
Status read_lines (linepointer, numlines)
  char  *linepointer [];           /* indices of text lines */
  int   *numlines;                 /* number of input lines */
  {
    char line[MAXTEXT], *ps;                /* single line of text */

    *numlines = 0;
    while (gets (line), strcmp (line, TERMINATOR) != 0)
      if (*numlines == MAXLINES)            /* too many lines? */
        return (OFLOLINES);
      else if ((ps = strsave (line)) == NULL)   /* enough store? */
        return (OFLOCHARS);
      else
        linepointer[(*numlines)++] = ps;           /* establish index */

    return (SUCCESS);
  }



/*
** ----------------------------oOo----------------------------
** ----------------------------oOo----------------------------
*/

void shell_sort (linepointer, numlines)
  char  *linepointer [];        /* indices (pointers) to text */
  int   numlines;               /* number of text lines */
  {
    int interval, i, j;                    /* interval and counters */

    for (interval = numlines/2; interval > 0; interval /= 2)
      for (i = interval; i < numlines; i++)
        for (j = i - interval; j >= 0; j -= interval)
          {
            if (strcmp (linepointer[j],
                        linepointer[j+interval]) <= 0)
              break;
            SWAP(linepointer[j], linepointer[j+interval]);
          }
  }



/*
** ----------------------------oOo----------------------------
** ----------------------------oOo----------------------------
*/

void print_lines (linepointer, numlines)
  char  *linepointer [];            /* pointers to text lines */
  int   numlines;                   /* number of lines */
  {
    int k;

    for (k = 0; k < numlines; k++)
      printf ("%s\n", linepointer[k]);
  }



/*
** ----------------------------oOo----------------------------
** ----------------------------oOo----------------------------
*/

char *strsave (s)                        /* save string s somewhere */
  char *s;
  {
    char *ps;

    if ((ps = malloc (strlen (s) + 1)) != NULL)
      strcpy (ps, s);
    return (ps);
  }
```

Case study 13.1: Queues

A city center car park has room for N vehicles. Cars enter the garage from the in gate and exit from the out gate. The cars are garaged in a queue-like discipline. New arrivals join the end of the garage queue. Departures, however, can be from anywhere in the queue. When a vehicle leaves the queue, the original ordering is maintained. If the garage is full, new arrivals join a waiting queue outside the garage facility. When a vacancy occurs in the car park, the vehicle at the front of the waiting queue (if any) enters the garage.

A *queue* is a data structure in which all insertions take place at one end, the *rear*, and all removals from the other end, the *front*. Conceptually, we visualize a queue as:

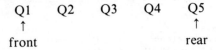

The vehicles waiting to enter the garage are ordered and maintained as a queue. When the garage is full, new arrivals join the end of this waiting queue. A car may leave this waiting queue without having entered the garage. A departure from this queue may also be from any position.

The two principal operations associated with a queue are the insertion and removal of items. The insertion operation adds a new item to the rear of the queue. A check must be performed to ensure that there is room in the queue. If the queue is not empty, the removal operation takes an item from the front of the queue. Operations are also available to obtain statistics about the queue, e.g. is the queue full?

We now formulate an abstract specification of a queue of items (of type int) as a package of queue operators and data structures. In addition to the operators mentioned above, we define a *createq* operation which establishes a new queue of some given maximum size. The abstraction is provided through the header file queue.h:

```
/*
**      File :          queue.h
**
**      Implementation of a queue of integers using an
**      array. The functions are parameterized to permit
**      a number of arrays to be processed. Arrays are
**      dynamically created by operation 'createq' for
**      some given queue length, N. The queue itself is
**      indexed by 1 to N inclusive. Array element 0
**      contains the queue size N, element N+1 is the
**      present queue length, element N+2 is the queue
**      front, and element N+3 is the queue rear. The
**      queue is organized cyclically around the array.
*/

#define FALSE       0
#define TRUE        1
typedef int         Boolean;
```

```
typedef int              *Queue;

extern Queue createq( /* int   size */ );
extern void appendq( /* Queue queue; int item */ );
extern void removeq( /* Queue queue; int item */ );
extern Boolean fullq( /* Queue queue */ );
extern Boolean emptyq( /* Queue queue */ );
extern int lengthq( /* Queue queue */ );
```

The data to the parking program consist of a series of records, one per line. Each record consists of a four-digit license plate number, and the character 'A' or 'D' representing, respectively, arrival and departure. The data set terminates with the unique sentinel 0000Z. Every departure is guaranteed to correspond to a previous arrival. For the sample data:

    1234A
    2345A
    3456A
    4567A
    3456D
    5678A
    6789A

and a garage queue of length N = 4, the garage and waiting queues appear as shown in Fig. 13.1. The further data items:

    4567D
    7890A
    8901A
    1234D

leave the two queues as shown in Fig. 13.2.

The program is required to produce a snapshot of both queues for every arrival and departure. We assume in the program that the garage has a capacity of 4, and that a safe upper bound for the waiting queue is 100. The program, expressed in terms of arrivals and departures, is as follows.

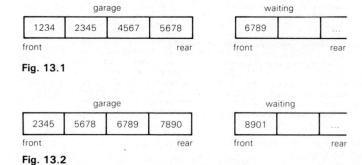

Fig. 13.1

Fig. 13.2

```
/*
**      File :              case13.1
**
**      Implement the city center car park. The two
**      queue abstractions in the problem are
**      provided by the Queue data type and the
**      associated operations.
*/

#include <stdio.h>
#include "queue.h"

void    arrival(), departure(), report();   /* forward references */

main()
  {
    int    plate;                           /* license number */
    char   code;                            /* arrival/departure */
    Queue garage, waiting;                  /* the two queues */

    if ((garage = createq(4)) == NULL)
                                            /* establish the garage */
      printf("Cannot create the garage\n");
    else if ((waiting = createq(100)) == NULL)
                                            /* establish waiting queue */
      printf("Cannot create the waiting queue\n");
    else
      {
        while (scanf("%4d%c", &plate, &code), plate != 0)
                                            /* more data? */
          {
            switch (code)
              {
                case 'A' :
                            arrival(garage, waiting, plate);      break;
                case 'D' :
                            departure(garage, waiting, plate);    break;
              }
            report(garage, waiting);
          }
      }
  }
```

If the garage is not already full, then a new arrival enters the garage queue. If the maximum number of vehicles is already in the garage, the new arrival joins the waiting queue which is assumed to have sufficient capacity to hold any number of cars. The procedure for function *arrival* then becomes:

```
/*
**      A new ARRIVAL enters the garage if it is not
**      already full; otherwise it joins the waiting
**      queue.
*/

void arrival(garage, waiting, plate)
  Queue         garage, waiting;
  int           plate;
  {
    if (! fullq(garage))                 /* room in garage? */
      appendq(garage, plate);            /* yes - no checks reqd. */
    else
      appendq(waiting, plate);           /* no - join waiting */
  }
```

A vehicle can leave from either of the two queues. If the departing vehicle is not in the garage, it can safely be assumed to be in the waiting queue. Whichever queue the car is deleted from, queue discipline is maintained.

The removal of an entry from a queue can be expressed in terms of the queue operators. A queue can be cyclically rotated by repeatedly removing an item from the front of the queue and reinserting it at the rear of the same queue. The reinsertion can be made conditional, so that if the removed item matches that to be deleted, then it is not reinserted.

First, we build the function *member* which determines if a given search key item is a member of a queue. The function is implemented using the cyclical rotate algorithm.

```
/*
**      Rotate cyclically all the items in the queue
**      such that the queue is undisturbed. The full
**      rotation is achieved by removing and then
**      reinserting. If any item matches the search key
**      TRUE is returned, otherwise FALSE is returned.
*/

Boolean member(queue, key)
   Queue          queue;
   int            key;
   {
      int      k, lngth, item;
      Boolean found = FALSE;

      lngth = lengthq(queue);
      for (k = 0; k < lngth; k++)
         {
            removeq(queue, &item);
            if (key == item)
               found = TRUE;
            appendq(queue, item);
         }

      return (found);
   }
```

A departure operation nominates a vehicle guaranteed to be in either the garage or the waiting queue. If the car is in the waiting queue, it is simply deleted. If the vehicle is in the garage queue, it is removed and the first car in the waiting queue (if any) joins the garage. Function *delete* implements the removal of a single item from the queue; a departure is implemented by a similarly named function.

```
/*
**      Rotate all the items in the queue by removing
**      and then reinserting. If any item removed
**      matches the item to be deleted, it is not
**      inserted back on to the queue.
*/

void delete(queue, key)
   Queue          queue;
   int            key;
   {
      int k, lngth, item;

      lngth = lengthq(queue);
      for (k = 0; k < lngth; k++)
         {
            removeq(queue, &item);
            if (item != key)
               appendq(queue, item);
         }
   }
```

```
/*
**      The vehicle next to depart is either in the
**      garage or in the waiting queue. If the car is
**      in the waiting queue it is simply removed.
**      If the car is not in the waiting queue, it is
**      guaranteed to be in the garage. The car is then
**      removed from the garage and the first of any
**      waiting vehicles now enters the garage.
*/

void departure(garage, waiting, plate)
  Queue           garage, waiting;
  int             plate;
  {
    int item;

    if (member(waiting, plate))       /* in waiting queue? */
      delete(waiting, plate);         /* yes - remove it */
    else
      {
        delete(garage, plate);        /* no - remove from garage */
        if (! emptyq(waiting))        /* any waiting? */
          {                           /* yes ... */
            removeq(waiting, &item);    /* first in waiting
                                           queue ... */
            appendq(garage, item);      /* ... enters garage */
          }
      }
  }
```

Finally, two functions implement the queue reporting. The primitive
function *qreport* produces a labeled report listing each entry in a nominated
queue. Function *report* invokes this primitive for the two problem queues.

```
/*
**      Produce a report on the members of a single
**      queue.
*/

void qreport(name, queue)
  char            *name;
  Queue           queue;
  {
    int k, lngth, item;

    printf("%s", name);
    lngth = lengthq(queue);
    for (k = 0; k < lngth; k++)
      {
        removeq(queue, &item);
        printf("%6d", item);
        appendq(queue, item);
      }
    printf("\n");
  }

/*
**      Produce reports on the two queues -- the garage
**      queue and the waiting queue.
*/

void report(garage, waiting)
  Queue           garage, waiting;
  {
    qreport("garage :", garage);
    qreport("waiting:", waiting);
  }
```

We now consider the representation of a queue. As in the case of a stack, an array of some fixed length is used to hold the items in the queue. Two variables *front* and *rear* are required to define the limits of the queue within the array. Variable front references the array element containing the first item in the queue. Variable rear indicates the array element in which is stored the next item to be added to the queue, i.e. immediately following the last queue item.

Using this representation, the queue drifts down the array as items are added and then removed from the queue. Ultimately, the rear of the queue reaches the end of the array. Further, as items were removed from the front of the queue, some free space exists at the beginning of the array. To utilize this area, the array is considered to be circular, with the end of the array wrapping around to the beginning.

The queue is initialized with both front and rear assigned the values 1. These values denote an empty queue. However, if repeated insertions are applied to the queue until it becomes full, front and rear will both have the values 1 again, since rear will be cyclically reassigned. In fact, when front and rear are the same values, it is impossible to distinguish between a full queue and an empty queue. To achieve this, we introduce a third variable called *length*, the number of items presently in the queue. For an empty queue, length = 0, and for a full queue length = N, where N is the maximum queue size.

Since the program must support two queues, the abstraction must be capable of creating two (or more) unique queues. This is achieved dynamically using the storage management function calloc within the queue operation createq. Each queue has the parameters size, length, front and rear associated with it. This we achieve by creating an array with size + 4 integer elements having the configuration shown in Fig. 13.3.

This representation is possible since the queue (or array) has base type int. The value size is supplied as an argument to the operation createq. The

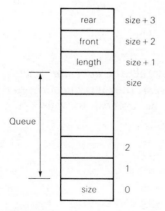

Fig. 13.3

initialization of the queue parameters takes the form:

length = 0   front = 1   rear = 1

Using the functions *getq* and *putq* (see the final listing which follows) to retrieve and store the queue parameters, function createq is programmed as:

```
/*
**      Establish a new queue with a capacity for size
**      items using the CREATEQ operator. Return TRUE if
**      successful, FALSE otherwise.
*/

Queue createq(size)
   int          size;
   {
   Queue queue;

   if ((queue = (Queue)calloc(size+4, sizeof(int))) == (Queue)NULL)
      return (NULL);
   else
      {
      putq(queue, size, 0, 1, 1);
      return (queue);
      }
   }
```

The operation *lengthq* is implemented by inspecting the value of the length parameter. Functions *emptyq* and *fullq* are also expressed in terms of length. For example:

```
/*
**      Operation FULLQ determines if the queue is full
**      or not. The logical values TRUE or FALSE are
**      returned.
*/

Boolean fullq(queue)
   Queue          queue;
   {
   int            size, length, front, rear;

    getq(queue, &size, &length, &front, &rear);
    return (size == length ? TRUE : FALSE);
   }
```

Providing that the queue is not already full, the *appendq* function places the new item in the array as indexed by rear, then increments both rear and length. The increment to rear must be cyclical to reflect the queue organization. This can be expressed by:

rear = rear = = size ? 1 : rear + 1

or more concisely by:

rear = rear % size + 1

The function appendq becomes:

```
/*
**        The APPENDQ procedure (provided the queue is not
**        full) places the new item in the array element
**        indicated by rear, and then increments both
**        length and rear. The function returns TRUE if
**        successful, and FALSE if the queue is full.
*/

void appendq(queue, item)
   Queue          queue;
   int            item;
   {
      int          size, length, front, rear;

      getq(queue, &size, &length, &front, &rear);
      *(queue + rear) = item;
      rear = rear % size + 1;
      length++;
      putq(queue, size, length, front, rear);
   }
```

Function *removeq* takes an item from the front of the queue, then increments front and decrements length. The coding is otherwise similar to appendq.

The listing which follows provides the complete implementation for the queue abstraction.

```
/*
**        File :              queue.c
**
**        Implementation of a queue of integers using an
**        array. The functions are parameterized to permit
**        a number of arrays to be processed. Arrays are
**        dynamically created by operation 'createq' for
**        some given queue length, N. The queue itself is
**        indexed by 1 to N inclusive. Array element 0
**        contains the queue size N, element N+1 is the
**        present queue length, element N+2 is the queue
**        front, and element N+3 is the queue rear. The
**        queue is organized cyclically around the array.
*/

#include <stdio.h>
#include "queue.h"

/*
**        Obtain the statistics of the given queue.
*/

static void getq(queue, size, length, front, rear)
   Queue          queue;
   int            *size, *length, *front, *rear;
   {
      *size   = *queue;
      *length = *(queue + (*size) + 1);
      *front  = *(queue + (*size) + 2);
      *rear   = *(queue + (*size) + 3);
   }

/*
**        Establish new parameters for the given queue.
*/
```

```
static void putq(queue, size, length, front, rear)
  Queue           queue;
  int             size, length, front, rear;
  {
    *queue               = size;
    *(queue + size + 1) = length;
    *(queue + size + 2) = front;
    *(queue + size + 3) = rear;
  }

/*
**      Establish a new queue with a capacity for size
**      items using the CREATEQ operator. Return TRUE if
**      successful, FALSE otherwise.
*/

Queue createq(size)
  int             size;
  {
    ...
  }

/*
**      The APPENDQ procedure (provided the queue is not
**      full) places the new item in the array element
**      indicated by rear, and then increments both
**      length and rear. The function returns TRUE if
**      successful, and FALSE if the queue is full.
*/

void appendq(queue, item)
  Queue           queue;
  int             item;
  {
    ...
  }

/*
**      Providing the queue is not already empty, operation
**      REMOVEQ takes the item from the front of the queue
**      and returns the logical indicator TRUE. FALSE is
**      returned if the queue is empty.
*/

void removeq(queue, item)
  Queue           queue;
  int             *item;
  {
    int           size, length, front, rear;

    getq(queue, &size, &length, &front, &rear);
    *item = *(queue + front);
    front = front % size + 1;
    length--;
    putq(queue, size, length, front, rear);
  }

/*
**      Operation FULLQ determines if the queue is full
**      or not. The logical values TRUE or FALSE are
**      returned.
*/

Boolean fullq(queue)
  Queue           queue;
  {
    ...
  }

/*
**      The logical value TRUE is returned if operation
**      EMPTYQ determines that there are no items in
**      the queue; FALSE otherwise.
*/
```

```
Boolean emptyq(queue)
  Queue          queue;
  {
    int          size, length, front, rear;

    getq(queue, &size, &length, &front, &rear);
    return (length == 0 ? TRUE : FALSE);
  }

/*
**      Determine the present number of items in
**      the queue.
*/

int lengthq(queue)
  Queue          queue;
  {
    int          size, length, front, rear;

    getq(queue, &size, &length, &front, &rear);
    return (length);
  }
```

13.2 Summary

1. Variable-sized data objects are used when the amount of data is not known in advance. In C, a *pointer* data type is provided and standard library functions for the dynamic allocation of storage.
2. The function *malloc* takes an argument of type unsigned integer and returns a pointer to a char that is the base of the allocated storage. Storage allocated by malloc is returned to the system for subsequent recycling by the library function *free*. It is the programmer's responsibility to ensure that the malloc operation is successful, and that memory that has been freed is not referenced.

13.3 Exercises

1. Prepare a function called string_save which dynamically allocates space sufficient to store a string given as the argument to the function. If the operation is successful, the function returns a pointer to the stored string, otherwise the function returns NULL. The function header is:

   ```
   char *string_save(s)
       char    *s;
   ```

2. No array bound checking is performed in C. To implement this feature with arrays of type int, a package array is to be constructed. The header file for the corresponding program unit is:

   ```
   /*
   ** File:    array.h
   **
   ** A package of array handling routines which
   ** support array bound checking.
   */
   ```

```
typedef int    *Array;

Array create( /* int size */ );
void assign( /* Array a, int index, int value */ );
int access( /* Array a, int index */ );
```

Function *create* dynamically establishes an integer array of *size* elements indexed from 1 to size inclusive. If the memory allocation fails, the value NULL is returned, otherwise a pointer to the array is returned. Function *assign* effectively performs the assignment 'a[index] = value'. Additionally, the function performs the necessary array bounds checking, and aborts the program if an illegal index is given. Similarly, function *access* is equivalent to 'a[index]', with once again the index checked.

Prepare the program unit using a representation similar to that of the queue given in the last case study.

## CHAPTER 14

Files

The programs we have studied have all produced some output, and in the majority of cases accepted some input. This has been achieved by using the standard files, standard input and standard output. These simple programs are unrepresentative of the majority of computer applications. Most applications involve the storage of very large volumes of permanent data. To retain the data between program execution, they are held in computer files on some auxiliary storage medium, for example, magnetic disc. In this chapter we consider the standard files and other files in some detail.

A computer file is a set of data values which is either produced by a program or is the input to a program. In general, a file is a collection of *records*. A record is the basic unit for processing. Generally, programs read and write single records from/to files. According to the application, a record may consist of a single character, or a line of text, or some other organization. Records usually consist of a number of data items known as *fields*. A record consisting of a line of text may have the words of the text as the fields. The fields themselves may be further subdivided into subordinate fields, for example, the individual letters of the words.

File organization methods define how the records of a file are organized. Four common types of file organization are:

sequential
random
indexed
inverted

In this chapter we shall consider applications employing the first two methods.

Sequential files are organized such that each record in the file, except the last, has a unique successor; and each record except the first has a unique predecessor. This ordering is a consequence of the order in which the records are written to the file when the file is created.

Many sequential files are organized so that the records maintain some ordering. A given field of the record, called the *key* field, is used to establish this ordering. Figure 14.1 shows an excerpt of a student file, where the fields

ID NUMBER	NAME	SUBJECT	GRADE
12	Brown	Pascal	4
23	Smith	Pascal	3
34	Black	Fortran	3
56	Jones	Cobol	7
67	Thomson	Fortran	5

Fig. 14.1

of each record are the student identification number, student name, subject and grade. The file is organized sequentially and is maintained in ascending sequence of the identification number. Any addition or deletion of records to/from this file must maintain the key ordering of the sequence. A new record for a student with number 45 must be inserted immediately before the record for student Jones.

Random file organization is applicable only to files held on direct access storage media. This method of access is used when the records are processed randomly with respect to their key field. Associated applications use this method to provide very fast access to the records of the file.

A random file is a set of records each identified by a unique *relative record number*. If there are N records in the file, each is distinguished by a unique integer 1, 2, 3, ..., N. When a record is stored in a random file, its location is determined by an *addressing algorithm* which transforms the record key into an integer in the range 1 to N inclusive. Retrieval of the same record from the file for the given key value employs the same addressing algorithm and computes the same relative record number. Figure 14.2 shows the records from the previous example of a sequential file held as a random file. The file contains at most 37 records (the chosen maximum number of students in a class) and the addressing algorithm is:

student-identification-number *mod* 37 + 1

where *mod* is the modulus operator.

File processing in a high-level programming language is supported by various operations performed on the file and its records. A new file is established with zero records using a *create* operator. Before processing of a file can begin, it must be opened. When processing is completed, a file must be closed properly. Files may be opened in one of a number of *modes*; e.g. input mode (the file is read but remains unchanged), output mode (new records are written to the file), and input/output mode (records are both read from and written to the file).

There are essentially two operations that apply to records of a file. A single record is retrieved from the file with a *read* operation. For a sequentially organized file, this operator causes the next record of the sequence to be read. With a random file, the record retrieved is determined by the given key value and hence the relative record number. A new record

RELATIVE
RECORD

RELATIVE RECORD NUMBER	NUMBER	NAME	SUBJECT	GRADE
1				
2				
...				
13	12	Brown	Pascal	4
...				
20	56	Jones	Cobol	7
...				
24	23	Smith	Pascal	3
...				
31	67	Thomson	Fortran	5
...				
35	34	Black	Fortran	3
36				
37				

Fig. 14.2

value is incorporated into a file with the *write* operation. For a sequential file, the record written to the file is the successor of the previous record written to the file. The record key determines where in a random file a record is written.

Reading a sequential file will ultimately cause the file to be exhausted. To determine this condition, an *end of file* operator is also required.

The standard C library contains all the functions necessary to implement these file operations. Functions *fopen* and *fclose*, respectively, open and close files. Variants of the functions which perform input/output to the standard input and standard output operate on files. Functions performing input from a file also return an end of file indicator. The position of where the next input/output operation is performed on a file is achieved with the function *fseek*. The remainder of this chapter is concerned with applications employing these file-handling functions.

14.1 File access

Before a file can be read or written it must be opened. This is performed by the standard library function fopen. The function fopen takes two arguments. The first argument is the name of the file to be opened, presented as a null-terminated string. The second argument denotes how the file is to be opened and is also given as a character string. This second argument is known as the *open mode*. A number of possible modes are supported including:

`"r"`	open an existing file for reading
`"w"`	create a new file, or truncate an existing one for writing
`"a"`	create a new file, or append to an existing one for writing
`"r + "`	open an existing file for update (both reading and writing), starting at the beginning of the file

"w + "   create a new file, or truncate an existing one, for update (both reading and writing)

"a + "   create a new file, or append to an existing one, for update (both reading and writing)

Opening a file may cause an error indicator to be set. This might arise for a number of reasons. For example, opening a file in *readonly* ("r" or "r + ") mode presupposes that the named file already exists in the file store. If it does not exist, fopen returns an error.

If a file does not exist and is opened for *writing* ("w" or "w + ") or *appending* ("a" or "a + "), then it is automatically created. If it already exists, then its original content is irretrievably lost when opened.

Once fopen has opened the specified file in the prescribed mode, it returns an internal name which is then used in subsequent input/output operations on that file. This internal name is called a *file pointer*. The data type FILE is used to hold information about a file, or more generally, a *stream*. The actual details of the data type FILE need not concern us. All the necessary definitions are provided in the standard input/output header stdio.h. The declarations for a file pointer are:

FILE *fopen( ), *fp;

and specify that the variable fp is a pointer to the derived type FILE, and that the function fopen returns a pointer to a FILE. Notice that FILE is a type name (established through a typedef statement) like any other type name.

The declaration for the function fopen is:

FILE *fopen(filename, mode)
    char   *filename, *mode;

An actual call to fopen to open for reading a file called data is:

fp = fopen("data", "r");

If there is no error when opening the file, fopen returns a file pointer assigned to the file pointer variable fp. Subsequent input operations performed on the file are in terms of fp. If there is any error, fopen returns the null pointer, NULL. NULL is also defined in the standard input/output header stdio.h. An error on opening a file is normally trapped with a conditional of the form:

if ((fp = fopen("data", "r")) = = NULL)
    printf("Cannot open data file\n");
else
    . . . . . .

When the processing performed upon a file is complete, it must be closed. The file or stream must be closed in an orderly fashion, including the emptying of any *internal buffers* held by the system. This is achieved with the function fclose:

```
int fclose(fp)
   FILE    *fp;
```

The function fclose takes the single argument fp, which should be the file pointer of a previously successfully opened file as performed by fopen. If any error is detected, fclose returns EOF. The value EOF is conventionally used to denote end of file and is a value that is not a 'real character'. In the ASCII encoding system, characters have internal codes 0 to 127 inclusive. EOF is usually the value -1. To avoid portability problems, we use the symbolic EOF which is defined in stdio.h, rather than the explicit value -1.

The following program opens, then immediately closes, a file, the name of which is given as the single command line argument. The file is not assumed to exist in the file store and should, therefore, open in write only mode. Checks are performed to ensure that the opening and closing operations are successful.

Program 14.1

```
/*
**        Program to demonstrate the operators fopen and
**        fclose. A file whose name is given as the command
**        line argument is first opened and then immediately
**        closed. The return codes from these file primitives
**        are checked.
*/

#include <stdio.h>

#define WRITEONLY        "w"

main(argc, argv)
   int     argc;
   char    *argv[];
   {
      FILE *fp, *fopen();
      int  fclose();

      if (argc != 2)
         printf("Usage: %s filename\n", argv[0]);
      else if ((fp = fopen(argv[1], WRITEONLY)) == NULL)
         printf("%s: cannot open %s\n", argv[0], argv[1]);
      else
         {
            printf("%s successfully opened\n", argv[1]);
            if (fclose(fp) == EOF)
               printf("%s: cannot close %s\n", argv[0], argv[1]);
            else
               printf("%s now closed\n", argv[1]);
         }
   }
```

14.2 The functions fgetc, feof and fputc

The function fgetc reads a single character from a file. This function's behavior is identical to the function *getchar* which we have previously encountered. The header file for the function fgetc is:

```
int fgetc(fp)
    FILE     *fp;
```

where fp is a file pointer as returned by a previous call to function fopen. Execution of the statement:

```
c = fgetc(fp);
```

has the effect of reading a single character from the stream denoted by fp. Subsequent characters are read from the same stream by making further calls to fgetc.

The function fgetc returns the value EOF when the end of file is reached. This non-existent character can be used, for example, in a loop control condition to read and process sequentially the characters in a file:

```
while ((c = fgetc(fp)) ! = EOF) . . . .
```

Care is required to ensure that the variable c used to represent the data character returned by fgetc is of type int. This is necessary to ensure that the loop operates correctly. To illustrate the difficulties, assume we are operating on a machine with 16 bit integers and the EOF value is -1. The representation for EOF is:

```
-1 (decimal) = 1111111111111111 (binary)
```

If fgetc returns EOF and this is assigned to the variable c which is erroneously declared as a character variable of, say, 8 bits, then c is assigned the low-order 8 bits returned by fgetc (EOF), namely:

```
c = 11111111 (binary)
```

The inequality test (! =) will fail to recognize the EOF value, since:

```
11111111 ! = 1111111111111111
```

evaluates to logical true. The loop would thus cycle indefinitely.

To explicitly indicate that a variable is to operate as a character variable, but is represented as an integer to correctly handle detection of EOF, we recommend that the type name *Character* be introduced. The name implies the variable type but conceals its representation as an int:

```
typedef int     Character;
```

```
Character c;
```

```
while ((c = fgetc(fp)) ! = EOF) . . . .
```

Strictly, function fgetc returns EOF either when the end of file has been detected or when an error has occurred. The function *feof* should be used to determine if the end of file has truly been reached. The function header for feof is:

```
int feof(fp)
    FILE    *fp;
```

If end of file has been detected on the specified stream, feof returns a non-zero value (representing logical true), otherwise zero (logical false) is returned. Thus, we may loop through a file character by character until the end of file is reached or until an error has occurred with the following code outline:

```
while ((c = fgetc(fp)) ! = EOF)
    {
    . . . . .
    /* process character c */
    . . . . .
    }
```

then determine whether we have an error or the true end of file:

```
if (! feof(fp))
    printf("Read error\n");
else
    /* . . . . . final processing . . . . . */
```

Function getchar, used to read a single character from the standard input, also returns the same EOF status code. So all previous programs that processed single characters read from the standard input, and searched for an explicit file-terminating character, might alternatively have detected EOF. Program 6.1 echoed characters from the standard input to the standard output. The program employed the period symbol as the unique terminator. Rewriting the program in terms of EOF and releasing the period character so that it may be a member of the input data, we arrive at Program 14.2.

Program 14.2

```
/*
**      Copy a stream of characters from the standard
**      input to the standard output. The copying
**      process terminates upon reading the end-of-file
**      on the standard input.
*/

#include <stdio.h>

typedef int             Character;

main ()
    {
    Character c;

    while ((c = getchar ()) != EOF)
        putchar (c);
    }
```

To terminate this program we must enter at the keyboard the character which corresponds to EOF. This character is very much system dependent. On most UNIX systems, EOF is represented by the control-D character.

The function *fputc* writes a single character to a file. The function's behavior is otherwise identical to the function *putchar* which we have used extensively. The header for function fputc is:

```
int fputc(c, fp)
   char      c;
   FILE      *fp;
```

If fputc is successful in writing the character to the nominated stream it returns the character as a value of type int. If an error occurs, fputc returns EOF.

With these preliminaries complete, we can now write a program called *copy* to copy the content of one file to a second file. The two file names are supplied as command line arguments with the source file named first. Note how the majority of the program consists of error checking. We shall have more to say on this subject shortly.

Program 14.3

```
/*
**       Copy the content of a source file to a destination
**       file. The two file names are given as command line
**       arguments. Full validation is performed upon
**       the file handling primitives.
*/

#include <stdio.h>


typedef int            Character;


#define READONLY       "r"
#define WRITEONLY      "w"

main (argc, argv)
   int     argc;
   char    *argv[];
   {
    FILE       *fopen (), *fpsource, *fpdestination;
    int        fclose (), fputc (), fgetc ();
    Character c;

    if (argc != 3)
      printf ("Usage: %s file1 file2\n", argv[0]);
    else
       {
        if ((fpsource = fopen (argv[1], READONLY)) == NULL)
          printf ("%s: cannot open %s\n", argv[0], argv[1]);
        else if ((fpdestination =
                      fopen (argv[2], WRITEONLY)) == NULL)
         {
          printf ("%s: cannot open %s\n", argv[0], argv[2]);
          if (fclose (fpsource) == EOF)
            printf ("%s: %s is not closed correctly\n",
                          argv[0], argv[1]);
         }
```

```
    else
      {
        while ((c = fgetc (fpsource)) != EOF)
          if (fputc (c, fpdestination) == EOF)
            {
              printf ("%s: error in writing to %s\n",
                              argv[0], argv[2]);
              break;
            }

        if (! feof (fpsource))
          printf ("%s: error in reading %s\n",
                          argv[0], argv[1]);

        if (fclose (fpsource) == EOF)
          printf ("%s: %s incorrectly closed\n",
                          argv[0], argv[1]);
        if (fclose (fpdestination) == EOF)
          printf ("%s: %s incorrectly closed\n",
                          argv[0], argv[2]);
      }
   }
 }
```

14.3 The functions fscanf and fprintf

The functions *fscanf* and *fprintf* perform analogous operations to the *scanf* and *printf* functions on a file. These new functions each take an additional argument, which is the file pointer to the required file. The function headers are:

```
int fscanf(fp, format, argument1, argument2, ... )
   FILE     *fp;
   char     *format;
```

and:

```
int fprintf(fp, format, argument1, argument2, ... )
   FILE     *fp;
   char     *format;
```

When executing fscanf the input operation may terminate prematurely. This may be due to reading end of file on the specified stream or because there is a conflict between the control string (format) and an input character. If the input reaches end of file before any conflict has occurred, then fscanf returns EOF. If the operation is terminated, fscanf returns the number of successful assignations.

A fragment of code to read two integer values from a file and perform the necessary error checking to ensure that the correct number of data items has been read and that the end of file has not been detected is:

```
status = fscanf(fpin, "%d %d", &first, &second);
if (status ! = 2)
   if (status = = EOF)
     printf("Unexpected end of file\n");
```

```
        else
            printf("Failure reading from file\n");
    else
        {
            . . . . .
            /* process the input data values */
            . . . . .
        }
```

When executing fprintf, the value returned is EOF if any error occurs; otherwise, the result is some value other than EOF. Thus, the two values read from a file by the code above may then be written to a second file by the following additions:

```
    status = fscanf(fpin, "%d %d", &first, &second);
    if (status ! = 2)
        if (status = = EOF)
            printf("Unexpected end of file\n");
        else
            printf("Failure reading from file\n");
    else if (fprintf(fpout, "%d %d\n", first, second) = = EOF)
        printf("Failure writing to file\n");
```

The error codes returned by fscanf and fprintf also apply to the functions scanf and printf respectively. The same status checking shown in the example above can also be applied to the standard input and to the standard output.

The following program is based on the previous. This time, a file of integers is copied to a second file. The source and destination file names are given as command line arguments. To avoid including checks on correct file closure, we have discarded the returned int value from fclose by simply using:

    fclose(fp);

Program 14.4

```
/*
**      Copy a series of integers from a source file to
**      a destination file. The file names are given as
**      command line arguments. The copy process
**      terminates upon reading the end of file condition
**      on the source file.
*/

#include <stdio.h>

#define READONLY        "r"
#define WRITEONLY       "w"

FILE    *fopen ();                          /* forward references */
int     fclose (), fscanf (), fprintf ();
```

```
main (argc, argv)
   int    argc;
   char   *argv[];
   {
   FILE *fpin, *fpout;
   int  data, status;

   if (argc != 3)
      printf ("Usage: %s file1 file2\n", argv[0]);
   else if ((fpin = fopen (argv[1], READONLY)) == NULL)
      printf ("%s: cannot open %s\n", argv[0], argv[1]);
   else if ((fpout = fopen (argv[2], WRITEONLY)) == NULL)
      {
         printf ("%s: cannot open %s\n", argv[0], argv[1]);
         fclose (fpin);
      }
   else
      {
         while ((status = fscanf (fpin, "%d", &data)) != EOF)
            {
               if (status != 1)
                  {
                     printf ("Failure on file read\n");
                     break;
                  }
               if (fprintf (fpout, "%d\n", data) == EOF)
                  {
                     printf ("Failure on file write\n");
                     break;
                  }
            }

         fclose (fpin);
         fclose (fpout);
      }
   }
```

14.4 The functions fgets and fputs

To read and write entire lines of data from and to files the functions *fgets* and *fputs* can be used. The function fgets takes three arguments: a string s, a count n, and a stream fp which must be opened for input:

```
char *fgets(s, n, fp)
   char    *s;
   int     n;
   FILE    *fp;
```

The argument s is assumed to point to the beginning of a character array. Characters are read from the specified stream and are stored in successive locations of the array. The reading continues until an end of file is reached, until a newline is encountered, or while the number of input characters does not exceed n. When the input is complete, an additional terminating null character is appended to the stored characters.

If the input is successful, a pointer to the array s is returned. If an error occurs during the input or the end of file is encountered, then the null pointer, NULL, is returned. Errors, therefore, are trapped in the usual way:

if (fgets(line, SIZE, fpin) = = NULL) . . . . .

The header for function fputs is:

```
int fputs(s, fp)
    char    *s;
    FILE    *fp;
```

Function fputs writes the null-terminated string s to the stream denoted by fp, which must be opened for output. If any errors occur during the writing operation, fputs returns EOF.

We have used the #include facility of the C preprocessor to assemble most of the programs in this book. In the following example, we demonstrate how we might actually implement this useful facility. The general outline of our version of include is:

```
get first line of the source file
WHILE not the end of file
DO
    IF the line starts with #include
    THEN
        include this new file
    ELSE
        output the line to the destination file
    ENDIF
    get the next line of the source file
ENDWHILE
```

If the included file contains further #include, this naturally leads to a recursive solution. Nested #include are useful and readily implemented in C.

The program is invoked with the command line:

include source-file-name destination-file-name

As described by the PDL, the lines of text are copied from the source file to the destination file. If at any time a line from the source file consisting of:

#include file-name

is met, then the include operation applies to this new source file, continuing to send the output to the same destination file as the first. When the new source file is exhausted, the copying continues with the original file or the program terminates if it is the first file.

Program 14.5

```
/*
**      Copy the content of a source file to a
**      destination file. The two file names are given
**      as command line arguments. A line of text of the
**      form:
**
**              #include filename
```

```
**
**          appearing in the source file is replaced with
**          the content of the named file. Nested include
**          statements is supported to the depth permitted
**          by the maximum number of open files allowed by
**          the host operating system.
*/

#include <stdio.h>

#define READONLY        "r"
#define WRITEONLY       "w"

#define LINESIZE        256
#define INCLUDE         "#include"

FILE    *fopen ();                       /* forward references */
int     fclose (), fputs ();
char    *fgets ();
void    file_include ();

main (argc, argv)
   int   argc;
   char  *argv[];
   {
     FILE          *fpsource, *fpdestination;

     if (argc != 3)
       printf ("Usage: %s file1 file2\n", argv[0]);
     else if ((fpsource = fopen (argv[1], READONLY)) == NULL)
       printf ("%s: cannot open %s\n", argv[0], argv[1]);
     else if ((fpdestination = fopen (argv[2], WRITEONLY)) == NULL)
       {
         printf ("%s: cannot open %s\n", argv[0], argv[2]);
         fclose (fpsource);
       }
     else
       {
         file_include (fpsource, fpdestination);
         fclose (fpsource);
         fclose (fpdestination);
       }
   }

/*
**          Perform a line by line copy of the source file
**          to the destination file. Expand all #include
**          lines. Permit nested #include's.
*/

void file_include (fpin, fpout)
   FILE *fpin, *fpout;                  /* source and destination files */
   {
     char line[LINESIZE], word1[LINESIZE], word2[LINESIZE];
     FILE *fp;

     while (fgets (line, LINESIZE, fpin) != NULL)   /* eof input? */
       if (sscanf (line, "%s %s", word1, word2) != 2) /* two words? */
         fputs (line, fpout);                       /* simple copy */
       else
         {
           if (strcmp (word1, INCLUDE) != 0)   /* #include line? */
             fputs (line, fpout);              /* no, copy */
           else
             {
               if ((fp = fopen (word2, READONLY)) == NULL)
                 printf ("Cannot open %s -- ignored\n", word2);
               else
                 {
                   file_include (fp, fpout);   /* nested include */
                   fclose (fp);
                 }
             }
         }
   }
```

14.5 Stdin, stdout and stderr

When a C program is initiated, three 'files' are automatically opened by the system and file pointers provided for them. The files are the standard input, the standard output and the standard error output. The respective file pointers are called *stdin*, *stdout* and *stderr*. These file pointers are predefined in the standard input/output library. They are constants not variables. It is, therefore, not permissible to assign values to them.

Normally, these files associate with the user's terminal. All standard I/O functions that perform input and do not take a file pointer as an argument (getchar, gets and scanf) take their input from stdin. So the example call:

    fscanf(stdin, "%d", &number);

will read the next integer value from the standard input, and is equivalent to the call:

    scanf("%d", &number);

All standard I/O functions that perform output and do not have a file pointer argument (putchar, puts and printf) deliver their output to stdout. So:

    fprintf(stdout, "My first program\n");

is equivalent to:

    printf("My first program\n");

The 'functions' which perform single character transfers on the standard input and the standard output are generally implemented as macros. The macros putc and getc are equivalent in operation to the true functions fputc and fgetc respectively. Although written as macros, they can be considered to have the following declarations:

```
int putc(c, fp)        int getc(fp)
char    c;             FILE    *fp;
FILE    *fp;
```

The 'functions' getchar and putchar can be defined in terms of getc, putc, stdin and stdout as follows:

```
#define getchar()      getc(stdin)
#define putchar(_C)    putc(_C, stdout)
```

Finally, there is the file pointer stderr. It is intended that any error messages produced by a program be written to this standard error stream. In an interactive environment, this stream is associated with the user's terminal. Stderr exists so that error messages can be logged to a device or file other than where the normal output is written. This is particularly desirable when the program's output is redirected to a file or sent down a pipe by the operating system. In the programs of this chapter, error messages should therefore have been delivered by statements of the form:

if ((fp = fopen(argv[1], READONLY)) = = NULL)
   fprintf(stderr, "%s: cannot open %s\n", argv[0], argv[1]);

using fprint and stderr instead of printf and stdout.

14.6 The function exit and error treatment

A program automatically terminates whenever the last statement in function main is executed. At times it may be desirable to force program termination when an error condition is detected. To explicitly abort a program, the function *exit* can be called. The function call:

exit(n);

has the effect of terminating the current program, flushing and closing any open files, and making the value of the integer n available to whatever process in the system was responsible for activating this program (for example, the operating system). Under UNIX, the integer value 0 conventionally denotes a successful program, and non-zero denotes a program that terminates due to some detected error condition.

All the programs of this chapter included extensive error checking which had the effect of concealing the program logic somewhat. We can go some way toward cleaning up the code by relegating the error diagnostics to a function called *syserr*. When this function is called, an error message is delivered, all open files are closed and the program is abandoned. Revisiting Program 14.3 we have the following version.

Program 14.6

```
/*
**      Copy the content of a source file to a destination
**      file. The copy process is performed character by
**      character. The source and destination file names
**      are given as command line arguments.
*/

#include <stdio.h>

typedef int             Character;              /* character input */

#define READONLY        "r"
#define WRITEONLY       "w"

FILE    *fopen ();                              /* forward references */
int     fclose (), fputc (), fgetc ();
void    syserr ();

char    *programname;
```

```
main (argc, argv)
   int    argc;
   char   *argv[];
   {
     FILE *fpsource, *fpdestination;
     Character c;

     programname = argv[0];

     if (argc != 3)
       syserr (1, "Usage: %s file1 file2\n", programname);
     else if ((fpsource = fopen (argv[1], READONLY)) == NULL)
       syserr (2, "Cannot open %s\n", argv[1]);
     else if ((fpdestination = fopen (argv[2], WRITEONLY)) == NULL)
       syserr (3, "cannot open %s\n", argv[2]);
     else
       {
         while ((c = fgetc (fpsource)) != EOF)     /* loop until done */
           if (fputc (c, fpdestination) == EOF)
             syserr (4, "error in writing to %s\n", argv[2]);

         if (! feof (fpsource))                    /* all done? */
           syserr (5, "error in reading %s\n", argv[1]);

         exit (0);
       }
   }
/*
**    --------------------------------oOo--------------------------------
**    --------------------------------oOo--------------------------------
*/

void syserr (errcode, message, argument)  /* report error, stop */
   int    errcode;                        /* program abort code */
   char   *message;                       /* format string */
   char   *argument;                      /* print argument */
   {
     fprintf (stderr, "%s [%2d]: ", programname, errcode);
     fprintf (stderr, message, argument);

     exit (errcode);
   }
```

Case study 14.1: Sequential file update

Consider a common example of file processing, *updating* a sequential file. A file of valid *transactions* is used to update a sequentially organized *master file* producing a new master file. A run chart for this processing is shown in Fig. 14.3.

Each step in the execution of the update program involves either copying

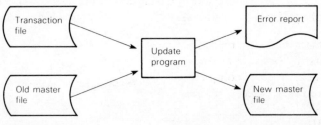

Fig. 14.3

a record from the old master file to the new master file or applying a transaction to an old master file record to create a new master file record. Three kinds of transaction are supported:

change :   alters the content of a master file record
delete :   removes a master file record
insert :   creates a new master file record

To identify any record we assume that both the master file records and the transaction file records contain a *key* and that both have been sorted into ascending order based on this key. As an example, suppose our master file contains details of students enrolled on a course. Each record has a four-digit integer key which represents the student's identification number. A sample master file is shown in Table 14.1. Note the trailer record with the unique key 9999.

The transactions shown in Table 14.2 are to be applied to this master file. After applying these transactions to the old master file, the new master file now contains the records shown in Table 14.3.

It is permissible for the transaction file to include more than one transaction for a given master file record. We allow, for example, the transactions shown in Table 14.4. Note how these two transactions are equivalent to the change transaction for Smith shown in the first example. Strictly, the change transaction is redundant because it can be accomplished by a delete followed by an insert. We choose to include it because of the convenience it affords. Our update program must be capable of correctly handling two or more transactions upon a single master file record.

During processing we must validate the transaction records against the master records. A master record can only be deleted or changed if it already exists. Equally, we cannot insert a new record if the master file already contains a record by that key.

We assume that both the transaction file and the master files are text files. The records in both are lines of text separated by newline symbols. The records and the fields in both are fixed length. The format of a record in the master file is shown in Fig. 14.4. The layout of a transaction record is shown in Fig. 14.5, where TRANS is a single character code representing the transaction, with C for change, D for delete and I for insert.

It is clear that the main processing logic will contain a loop terminating when both the old master file and the transaction file have been exhausted. The form of this logic is:

get the first old master record
get the first transaction record
WHILE neither file is complete
DO
   process one record
ENDWHILE

Table 14.1

Key	Name	Subject	Grade
1234	Brown	Pascal	4
2345	Smith	Pascal	3
3456	Black	Fortran	3
5678	Jones	Cobol	7
6789	Thomson	Fortran	5
9999	ZZZZZZZZZ	ZZZZZZZ	9

Table 14.2

Key	Transaction	Name	Subject	Grade
2345	change	Smith	Pascal	2
4567	insert	Ritchie	C	1
6789	delete			
9999	ZZZZZ	ZZZZZZZ	ZZZZZ	9

Table 14.3

Key	Name	Subject	Grade
1234	Brown	Pascal	4
2345	Smith	Pascal	2
3456	Black	Fortran	3
4567	Ritchie	C	1
5678	Jones	Cobol	7
9999	ZZZZZZZZZ	ZZZZZZZ	9

Table 14.4

Key	Transaction	Name	Subject	Grade
2345	delete			
2345	insert	Smith	Pascal	2
9999	ZZZZZ	ZZZZZZZ	ZZZZZ	9

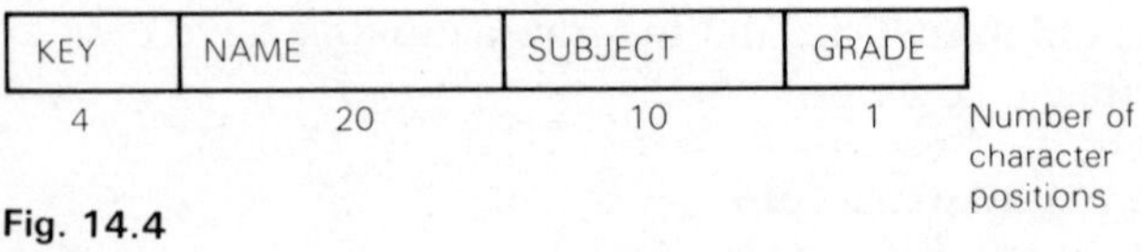

KEY	NAME	SUBJECT	GRADE	
4	20	10	1	Number of character positions

Fig. 14.4

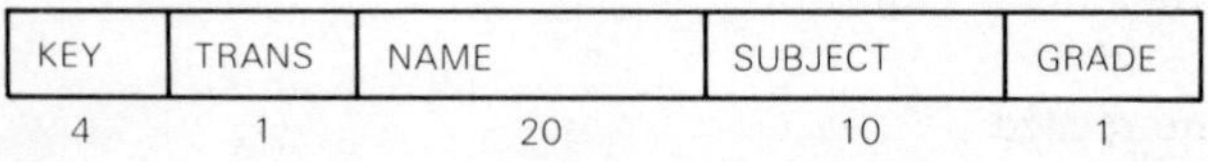

KEY	TRANS	NAME	SUBJECT	GRADE
4	1	20	10	1

Fig. 14.5

On each loop iteration, we process a single record, selected by inspecting the key value of the two records. If the old master file record has the smaller key, it is copied directly to the new master file. If the transaction file record has the lower key, the transaction *must* be an insert and the record from the transaction file is assembled and copied to the new master file. If the keys are equal, the transaction is applied to the old master record. Where the keys are equal, an insert transaction is not valid since we cannot insert a new record when one already exists. Expanding the original processing logic, we now have:

```
get the first old master record
get the first transaction record
choose the next key to process
WHILE current key is not the trailer key
DO           /* process one key */
   do initial status
   WHILE current key equals transaction key
   DO            /* process one transaction */
      apply transaction to master record
      get the next transaction record
   ENDWHILE
   do final status
   choose the next key to process
ENDWHILE
```

The body of the loop labeled 'process one key' contains the logic for updating the status of each key value. It is called repeatedly until a trailer record is found indicating end of file. The loop 'process one transaction' iterates until there are no more transactions for the current key. Process one transaction first applies the transaction to the master record, then replaces it by the next transaction. 'Initial status' attempts to retrieve the record indicated by the current key value. If it finds an active record on the old master file, it sets the Boolean indicator *allocated* to true and copies the record into the new master file record area. If an active record is not found, allocated is set to false and the content of the master file record will be ignored. 'Final status' tests the value of allocated. If it is true, the new master record is written to the file.

```
/*
**       Update of a sequential master file.
*/

#include <stdio.h>

#define READONLY        "r"
#define WRITEONLY       "w"

#define FALSE           0
#define TRUE            1
typedef int             Boolean;    /* logical values and types */
```

```
#define NAMESIZE        21          /* field sizes ... */
#define SUBJECTSIZE     11          /* including terminator */

#define TRAILER         9999        /* key sentinel, end of file */

#define INSERT          'I'         /* transaction codes */
#define DELETE          'D'
#define CHANGE          'C'

#define GET_MASTER(_F, _I, _N, _S, _G)\
            if (! get_master_record (_F, _I, _N, _S, _G))\
            syserr (10, "Error reading %s\n", "master file")
#define GET_TRANSACTION(_F, _I, _T, _N, _S, _G)\
            if (! get_transaction_record (_F, _I, _T, _N, _S, _G))\
            syserr (10, "Error reading %s\n", "transaction file")
#define PUT_MASTER(_F, _I, _N, _S, _G)\
            if (! put_master_record (_F, _I, _N, _S, _G))\
            syserr (11, "Error writing %s\n", "master file")


char    *programname;

FILE    *fopen ();                              /* forward references */
int     fclose (), fscanf (), fprintf ();

Boolean get_transaction_record ();
Boolean get_master_record ();
Boolean put_master_record ();

int choose_next_key ();
void    do_initial_status ();
void    do_final_status ();
void    apply_transaction ();
void    copy_corresponding ();

void    syserr (), error ();

main (argc, argv)
  int   argc;
  char  *argv[];
  {
    FILE        *fpold, *fptrans, *fpnew;       /* program files */
    int         current_key;
    Boolean     allocated;
    char        tran_transaction;
    int         old_identification, tran_identification,
                new_identification;
    char        old_name[NAMESIZE], tran_name[NAMESIZE],
                new_name[NAMESIZE];
    char        old_subject[SUBJECTSIZE], tran_subject[SUBJECTSIZE],
                new_subject[SUBJECTSIZE];
    int         old_grade, tran_grade, new_grade;

    programname = argv[0];

    if (argc != 4)
      syserr (1, "Usage: %s file1 file2 file3\n", programname);
    else if ((fpold = fopen (argv[1], READONLY)) == NULL)
      syserr (2, "cannot open %s\n", argv[1]);
    else if ((fptrans = fopen (argv[2], READONLY)) == NULL)
      syserr (2, "cannot open %s\n", argv[2]);
    else if ((fpnew = fopen (argv[3], WRITEONLY)) == NULL)
      syserr (2, "cannot open %s\n", argv[3]);
    else
      {
        GET_MASTER(fpold, &old_identification, old_name,
                old_subject, &old_grade);
        GET_TRANSACTION(fptrans, &tran_identification,
                &tran_transaction, tran_name, tran_subject, &tran_grade);

        current_key = choose_next_key (tran_identification,
                old_identification);
```

```
        while (current_key != TRAILER)
          {
            do_initial_status (current_key, &allocated,
                fpold, &old_identification, old_name,
                old_subject, &old_grade, &new_identification,
                new_name, new_subject, &new_grade);

            while (current_key == tran_identification)
              {
                apply_transaction (&allocated, tran_identification,
                        tran_transaction, tran_name, tran_subject,
                        tran_grade, &new_identification, new_name,
                        new_subject, &new_grade);

                GET_TRANSACTION(fptrans, &tran_identification,
                        &tran_transaction, tran_name, tran_subject,
                        &tran_grade);
              }

          do_final_status (fpnew, allocated, new_identification,
                new_name, new_subject, new_grade);

            current_key = choose_next_key (tran_identification,
                old_identification);
          }

        copy_corresponding (&new_identification, new_name,
                new_subject, &new_grade, 9999,
                "ZZZZZZZZZZZZZZZZZZZZ", "ZZZZZZZZZZ", 9);
        PUT_MASTER (fpnew, new_identification, new_name,
                new_subject, new_grade);

        fclose (fpold);
        fclose (fptrans);
        fclose (fpnew);
      }
  }

/*
** -----------------------------oOo-----------------------------
** -----------------------------oOo-----------------------------
*/

Boolean get_transaction_record (fp, identification, transaction,
        name, subject, grade)
    FILE  *fp;                  /* transaction file */
    int   *identification;      /* transaction record fields */
    char  *transaction;
    char  *name;
    char  *subject;
    int   *grade;
    {
      if (fscanf (fp, "%4d%c%20s%10s%1d", identification,
          transaction, name, subject, grade) == 5)
        return (TRUE);
      else
        return (FALSE);
    }

/*
** -----------------------------oOo-----------------------------
** -----------------------------oOo-----------------------------
*/

Boolean get_master_record (fp, identification, name, subject, grade)
    FILE  *fp;                  /* old master file */
    int   *identification;      /* master record fields */
    char  *name;
    char  *subject;
    int   *grade;
    {
      if (fscanf (fp, "%4d%20s%10s%1d", identification,
          name, subject, grade) == 4)
        return (TRUE);
      else
        return (FALSE);
    }
```

```
/*
**    ----------------------------oOo----------------------------
**    ----------------------------oOo----------------------------
*/

Boolean put_master_record (fp, identification, name, subject, grade)
  FILE  *fp;                       /* new master file */
  int   identification;           /* new master record fields */
  char  *name;
  char  *subject;
  int   grade;
  {
    if (fprintf (fp, "%4d%-20s%-10s%1d\n", identification,
        name, subject, grade) != EOF)
      return (TRUE);
    else
      return (FALSE);
  }

/*
**    ----------------------------oOo----------------------------
**    ----------------------------oOo----------------------------
*/

int     choose_next_key (transaction_key, master_key)
  int    transaction_key, master_key;
  {
    return (transaction_key < master_key ? transaction_key
                : master_key);
  }

/*
**    ----------------------------oOo----------------------------
**    ----------------------------oOo----------------------------
*/

void          apply_transaction (allocated, tran_identification,
                  tran_transaction, tran_name, tran_subject, tran_grade,
                  new_identification, new_name, new_subject, new_grade)
  Boolean       *allocated;
  char          tran_transaction;
  int           tran_identification, *new_identification;
  char          *tran_name,          *new_name;
  char          *tran_subject,       *new_subject;
  int           tran_grade,          *new_grade;
  {
    switch (tran_transaction)
      {
        case INSERT:
          if (*allocated == TRUE)
            error (INSERT, "Record already exists\n",
                      tran_identification);
          else
            {
              copy_corresponding (new_identification, new_name,
                        new_subject, new_grade, tran_identification,
                        tran_name, tran_subject, tran_grade);
              *allocated == TRUE;
            }
          break;

        case DELETE:
          if (*allocated == FALSE)
            error (DELETE, "Record does not exist\n",
                      tran_identification);
          else
            *allocated = FALSE;
          break;

        case CHANGE:
          if (*allocated == FALSE)
            error (CHANGE, "Record does not exist\n",
                      tran_identification);
          else
            copy_corresponding (new_identification, new_name,
                  new_subject, new_grade, tran_identification,
                  tran_name, tran_subject, tran_grade);
```

```
        break;
      }
  }

/*
** -------------------------------oOo-------------------------------
** -------------------------------oOo-------------------------------
*/

void        do_initial_status (current_key, allocated, fp,
              old_identification, old_name, old_subject, old_grade,
              new_identification, new_name, new_subject, new_grade)
  int         current_key;
  Boolean     *allocated;
  FILE        *fp;
  int         *old_identification, *new_identification;
  char        *old_name,            *new_name;
  char        *old_subject,         *new_subject;
  int         *old_grade,           *new_grade;
  {
    if (*old_identification == current_key)
      {
        copy_corresponding (new_identification, new_name,
              new_subject, new_grade, *old_identification,
              old_name, old_subject, *old_grade);
        *allocated = TRUE;
        GET_MASTER(fp, old_identification, old_name,
              old_subject, old_grade);
      }
    else
      *allocated = FALSE;
  }

/*
** -------------------------------oOo-------------------------------
** -------------------------------oOo-------------------------------
*/

void    do_final_status (fp, allocated, identification,
              name, subject, grade)
  FILE        *fp;
  Boolean     allocated;
  int         identification;
  char        *name;
  char        *subject;
  int         grade;
  {
    if (allocated == TRUE)
      PUT_MASTER(fp, identification, name, subject, grade);
  }

/*
** -------------------------------oOo-------------------------------
** -------------------------------oOo-------------------------------
*/

void        copy_corresponding (dest_identification, dest_name,
              dest_subject, dest_grade, sou_identification,
              sou_name, sou_subject, sou_grade)
  int    *dest_identification, sou_identification;
  char   *dest_name,            *sou_name;
  char   *dest_subject,         *sou_subject;
  int    *dest_grade,           sou_grade;
  {
    *dest_identification = sou_identification;
    strcpy (dest_name, sou_name);
    strcpy (dest_subject, sou_subject);
    *dest_grade = sou_grade;
  }

/*
** -------------------------------oOo-------------------------------
** -------------------------------oOo-------------------------------
*/
```

```
void    syserr (errcode, message, argument)
  int    errcode;
  char   *message, argument;
  {
    fprintf (stderr, "%s [%2d]: ", programname, errcode);
    fprintf (stderr, message, argument);

    exit (errcode);
  }
/*
**   ----------------------------oOo----------------------------
**   ----------------------------oOo----------------------------
*/
void    error (code, message, id)
  char   code;                        /* transaction code */
  char   *message;
  int    id;                          /* transaction identification */
  {
    printf ("%c      %30s      %4d\n", code, message, id);
  }
```

14.7 Direct access

A number of different file structures are possible and supported by functions in the standard library. The simplest file organization is the sequential file and is the type of file we have processed so far. A sequential file is constructed by writing new records to the end of the file. When the file is subsequently read, the components are input in the same order as they were originally written to the file.

A different file structure, one which permits direct access to a specified component of the file, is also supported by the standard I/O library. A direct access file can be interpreted as a number of data blocks or *record areas*. Each record area is of some fixed size measured as a number of bytes. To read (or write) a record, we must first position the reading (writing) head at the first byte of the record area. The required number of bytes is then transferred to (from) memory (see Fig. 14.6).

The function *fseek* allows random access within a file. The header for function fseek is:

```
int fseek(fp, offset, origin)
  FILE     *fp;
  long     offset;
  int      origin;
```

The first argument must be a file pointer to a file opened for input, output or both. The third argument must have the value 0, 1 or 2. If it is 0, then the position in the file is set equal to the value of the second argument considered as a byte count. The first byte of the file is numbered 0. The *origin* value 0 is used when we wish to locate the read/write head at some *absolute* position in the file. In particular, the call:

```
fseek(fp, 0L, 0)
```

will rewind the file to the beginning.

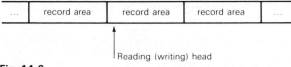

...	record area	record area	record area	...

Reading (writing) head

Fig. 14.6

If the third argument is 1, then the position in the file is set equal to the current position plus the signed *offset*. A positive offset will advance the position away from the beginning of the file, while a negative offset moves toward the beginning of the file. The origin value 1 is used for *relative* positioning within the file.

If the third argument is 2, then the position is set to the end of the file plus the signed offset. This functionality is often used to extend a file. To seek to the end of the file before, say, writing, the call is:

```
fseek(fp, 0L, 2)
```

If the operation succeeds, then fseek returns 0, otherwise it returns a non-zero value. It is usual to check this condition with a clause of the form:

```
if (fseek(fp, offset, origin) ! = 0)
    fprintf(stderr, "Seek error\n");
else
    ...
```

Once the required location in the file has been obtained with a call to fseek, subsequent reading and writing will begin at that position. The input and output can either be performed by the file I/O functions such as fscanf, fprint or by two additional functions called *fread* and *fwrite*.

The function fread reads a block of *binary* data into a specified memory buffer. The function header is:

```
int fread(buffer, size, count, fp)
    char           *buffer;
    unsigned int   size;
    int            count;
    FILE           *fp;
```

The first argument is a pointer to the first byte of the buffer. The second argument is the size of the items in the buffer; if the first argument is of arbitrary type T, then the second argument is generally computed by the expression sizeof(T). The third argument is the number of items of type T to be read. Thus, the total number of bytes read from the file is size * count. The fourth argument is a file pointer that is opened for input.

For example, to input 20 characters into an array, the call is:

```
char table[20];

fread(table, sizeof(char), 20, fp);
```

The second example reads 20 integers into an array:

```
int stack[20];

fread((char *) &stack, sizeof(int), 20, fp);
```

The first actual argument, which must be a character pointer, is obtained by taking the address of the variable stack (a pointer to an int) and coercing it to a pointer to a character. If the implementation for an integer is, say, 2 bytes, then the total number of bytes transferred is 40.

The actual number of items read is returned by function fread. Generally, this value is tested to determine if the operation has been successful. If either end of file is detected or an error occurs, fread returns 0. More typically, fread is used as in:

```
if ((nread = fread((char *) &stack, sizeof(int), 20, fp)) ! = 20)
    {
      if (feof(fp))
        fprintf(stderr, "End of file detected\n");
      else
        fprintf(stderr, "Read error\n");
      ...
      ...
    }
```

The counterpart to fread, writing a block of binary data from a memory buffer to a file, is called fwrite. The header is:

```
int fwrite(buffer, size, count, fp)
    char          *buffer;
    unsigned int  size;
    int           count
    FILE          *fp;
```

The actual number of items written to the file is returned by fwrite. If an error occurs, zero is returned.

The following program illustrates a simple use of these functions. A file, named in the command line argument to the program, consists of a number of text characters. All but the first 10 characters of the file are to be copied by the program to a second file, also given in the command line. Skipping the first 10 characters could be accomplished by simply calling fgetc ten times and discarding the result. The method would be inefficient, however, if we had to skip say the first 1000 characters of a large file. The fseek function need only be called once to position the file at the desired point to allow copying to commence.

Program 14.7

```
/*
**        Copy the content of one file to a second file,
**        discarding the first 10 characters in a header
**        of the source file. The file names are given as
**        command line arguments. The characters which are
**        removed are done so by skipping using direct
**        access operations.
*/

#include <stdio.h>

#define READONLY      "r"
#define WRITEONLY     "w"
#define SKIP          10L
#define ABSOLUTE      0

char    *programname;

FILE        *fopen();                          /* forward references */
int     fseek(), fread(), fwrite();
void    syserr();

main(argc, argv)
   int    argc;
   char *argv[];
   {
      FILE        *fpsource, *fpdestination;
      char        buff;

      programname = argv[0];
      if (argc != 3)
        syserr(1, "Usage: %s file1 file2\n", programname);

      if ((fpsource = fopen(argv[1], READONLY)) == NULL)
        syserr(2, "cannot open %s\n", argv[1]);
      if ((fpdestination = fopen(argv[2], WRITEONLY)) == NULL)
        syserr(3, "cannot open %s\n", argv[2]);

      if (fseek(fpsource, SKIP, ABSOLUTE) != 0)
        syserr(4, "fail on header in %s\n", argv[1]);

      while (fread(&buff, sizeof(char), 1, fpsource) != 0)
        if (fwrite(&buff, sizeof(char), 1, fpdestination) == 0)
          syserr(5, "fail on write to %s\n", argv[2]);

      if (! feof(fpsource))
        syserr(6, "fail on read from %s\n", argv[1]);

      fclose(fpsource);
      fclose(fpdestination);
      exit(0);
   }

void    syserr(errcode, message, argument)
   int    errcode;
   char *message, *argument;
   {
      fprintf(stderr, "%s [%2d]: ", programname, errcode);
      fprintf(stderr, message, argument);
      exit(errcode);
   }
```

Two additional functions associated with direct access files are *rewind*
and *ftell*. The function headings are:

```
void rewind(fp)        and     long ftell(fp)
    FILE    *fp;                FILE    *fp;
```

Function rewind resets a file to its beginning. The argument must be a file pointer to a file that is opened for input or output. From our previous discussion of fseek, rewind (fp) is equivalent to:

  fseek(fp, 0L, 0)

The function ftell takes a file pointer for a file that is currently open and returns the byte position in the stream. Thus:

  fseek(fp, 0L, 2);
  size = ftell(fp);

will determine the number of bytes currently in the file identified by the file pointer fp.

14.8 Summary

1. A file is a collection of records of some base type. File organization methods determine how the records of a file are processed, and include sequential and random access. A sequential file is constructed by writing new records to the end of the file. When the file is subsequently read, the elements are input in the same order as they were originally written. A direct access file can be written or read to/from any position within the file.

2. Before a file can be read or written it must first be opened. This operation is performed by the library function *fopen*, which returns an internal name (file pointer) that is then used in subsequent I/O operations. When processing of a file is complete it must be closed in an orderly manner using the function *fclose*. The library function *exit* flushes and closes any open files before terminating a program.

3. Sequential processing of a file is provided by the library functions *fgetc*, *fputc*, *fscanf*, etc. Random access within a file is provided by the functions *fseek* and *rewind*.

4. Three files automatically provided in all C programs are known by the file pointers *stdin*, *stdout* and *stderr*. Thus, for example, the function getchar reads a single character from the standard input and is effectively the call fget(stdin).

14.9 Exercises

1. Implement your own version of the library functions fgets and fputs.

2. Use the file handling functions of the standard library to double space a text file. The names of the files are given as command line arguments, with the source file named first and the target file named second.

3. Write a program to copy one file to another, removing any blank lines in the source file. The file names are given as command line arguments.

4. Write a program to number the lines in a text file. The input file name should be passed as a command line argument. The program should write to stdout.

5. Write a program called *concat*, which concatenates a set of named input files on to the standard output. One or more file names are given as command line arguments.

6. Write a program to display the content of a text file on to the standard output, 20 lines at a time. The input file is given as a command line argument. Each of the 20 lines is displayed following a return character entered from the standard input.

7. Write a program to list the content of a master file as specified in Case study 14.1.

8. Given two files of integers sorted into ascending order, write a program to merge the files into a third file of sorted integers. All three file names are given as command line arguments.

9. Write a program which reads two text files *File1* and *File2* and prints them side-by-side with the format:

    File1   File2
    . . . .
    . . . .
    . . . .
    . . . .

10. Write a program called *compare* which compares two text files and lists the places where they differ. The source files are named as command line arguments. The output consists of the line number and the two lines that differ.

11. Write a program called *find* that searches for patterns. If the command:

    find pattern filename

    is given, then the string pattern is searched in the named file. All lines containing the pattern are printed.

    Modify this program to support the command line option -n which, if present, requests that the line number should be printed as well.

12. Write a program which operates as a file printer. The program *print* is invoked with one or more file names as arguments. It prints the files with top and bottom margins on each page, and, at the top of each page the file name and the page number.

## CHAPTER 15

Structures, unions and bit fields

In Chapters 11 and 12 we introduced the array – an *aggregate* of values all of the same type. To reference an individual array element we require the name of the array and a subscript.

The C programming language also supports a second aggregate type known as a *structure*. The structure is a composite of components which are distinct and, perhaps, also of different types. Many programs in this book process calendar dates. A date may be considered as the composition of three values – the day number, the month number and the year number. We can define a structure called date consisting of the three components by:

```
struct date { int    day;
              int    month;
              int    year;
            };
```

The reserved keyword struct introduces a structure declaration, which is a list of declarations enclosed in braces. An optional name called a *structure tag* may follow the word struct (as with date here). A structure declaration, such as the one above, that is not followed by a list of variables does not allocate variable storage but acts as a *template* for the named structured type. The tag acts to name this definition that can then be used in the declaration of variables, as in:

```
struct date today, holiday;
```

This declaration introduces two variables, today and holiday, both structures of type date. The structure tag date appearing in the declaration of the variables may be substituted by the full declaration. The variable declaration is then equivalent to:

```
struct { int    day;
         int    month;
         int    year;
       } today,   holiday;
```

By not tagging the structure with a name, we cannot employ the structure elsewhere in the program. This is somewhat less useful and is relatively uncommon in programs.

Further examples of structure declarations are:

(a) struct complex { double real;
                      double imaginary;
                    };

A structure for manipulating complex numbers in a mathematical/ engineering application.

(b) enum suit { CLUBS, DIAMONDS, HEARTS, SPADES };
     struct card { enum suit soot;
                   int   rank;
                 };
For use in a card playing program.

The original implementation of C did not permit assignment between two structure variables. Most modern C compilers now support this operation, so that:

    today = holiday;

is acceptable in the more recent implementations. Where structure assignment is not supported, it can be achieved by assigning component by component.

15.1 Members

The elements named in a structure declaration are called *members* of the structure. For example, the members of the date structure, introduced in the preceding section, are called day, month and year. Like arrays, a notation is required to reference a member of a structured variable. To refer to one component of a structured variable, the variable is qualified by the member name in a construct of the form:

    variable-name.member-name

To identify the year component of the variable today, we use:

    today.year

From the structure declaration this member is of type int and can be used in any expression in which a simple integer variable might appear. For example, to set the value of member day in the variable holiday to 25, the statement is:

    holiday.day = 25;

To test the value of members we can use constructs such as:

   if (today.day = = 25 && today.month = = 12)
     printf("Merry Xmas\n");

In the construct:

variable-name.member-name

the period symbol is known as the *selection operator*. The left-hand operand is a structured variable and the right-hand operand is a member name. The selection operator has the highest (equal) priority amongst the operators. The precedence and associativity of the selection operator is shown in Appendix E.

The above discussions are incorporated into the following C program. In function main, the structure called date is established and a declaration is made for the variable today of this type. The program then proceeds to assign individual values to each member of the variable before displaying today's date with an appropriate printf function call.

Program 15.1

```
/*
**      Assign and print a date. The program demonstrates
**      simple handling of structured values. The date
**      is represented as a three-member structure.
*/

#include <stdio.h>

main()
  {
    struct date { int       day;      /* template for a date */
                  int       month;
                  int       year;
                };
    struct date today;                /* variable */

    today.day   = 27;                 /* assign */
    today.month = 9;
    today.year  = 1985;

    printf("Today\'s date is %2d/%2d/%4d\n",
        today.day, today.month, today.year);
  }
```

The usual scope rules of C apply. In particular, the structured type date is local to the main function. This means that we may not declare variables as structures of type date outside function main. For structure type date to be globally available, an external declaration is necessary.

The programmer can achieve a high degree of modularity and portability by using typedef declarations to name these derived types. This is a consequence of the abstraction of these data types through tag names and typedef statements. Applying typedef declarations to structure types can be done in a number of ways. Following a structure template such as:

```
struct date { int     day;
              int     month;
              int     year;
            };
```

the type name Date can be associated with this structure through the declaration:

```
typedef struct date     Date;
```

Thereafter, structure variables of type struct date may be declared as:

```
Date     today;
```

When using typedef declarations to name a structure type, the tag name is irrelevant. The structure's template and the type name are then introduced in a single unified declaration. The two-stage process above may also be achieved by:

```
typedef struct date { int     day;
                      int     month;
                      int     year;
                    } Date;
```

The type name Date now serves in place of the structure type. The declaration for the structured variable today appears as before. But note how the tag name date is no longer employed. The normal declaration for the above is then:

```
typedef struct { int     day;
                 int     month;
                 int     year;
               } Date;
```

Two dates are given to a program representing, respectively, the date of birth of a person and today's date. The program computes that person's age expressed as a number of years.

Program 15.2

```
/*
**      Compute a person's age expressed as a number of years
**      given the date of birth of that person and today's
**      date.
*/

#include <stdio.h>

struct date        { int        day;          /* template */
                     int        month;
                     int        year;
                   };
typedef struct date            Date;
```

```
main ()
  {
    Date        dateofbirth, today;
    int         age;

    printf ("Date of birth?: ");
    scanf ("%d/%d/%d", &dateofbirth.day,
                &dateofbirth.month, &dateofbirth.year);

    printf ("Today\'s date?: ");
    scanf ("%d/%d/%d", &today.day, &today.month, &today.year);

    if (today.month > dateofbirth.month ||
        (today.month == dateofbirth.month &&
                today.day >= dateofbirth.day))
      age = today.year - dateofbirth.year;
    else
      age = today.year - dateofbirth.year - 1;

    printf ("Age: %d\n", age);
  }
```

15.2 Name overloading

The names of structure members are defined in a special *overloading* class associated with the structure type. Member names within a structure must be distinct, but they may be the same as member names in other structures and may be the same as variable, function and type names. For example, consider the following sequence of declarations:

```
int    a;
struct x { int a; double b; } b;
struct y { int b; double a; } c;
```

The identifier a has three non-conflicting declarations; it is an integer variable, an integer member of structure x, and a double member of structure y. These three declarations are used, respectively, in the expressions:

```
a
b.a
c.a
```

The compiler determines from the context in which the name is used the association that is required.

Care is required when using name overloading, particularly when used to excess. Logic errors may easily occur due to possible confusion. Although the compiler can readily use the context to remove ambiguities, the programmer may find that the ambiguity persists, resulting in confusion.

15.3 Internal storage of structures

Structure members are stored in memory in the same order in which they are declared. However, since structures are often composed of members of

Member

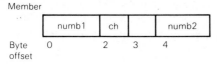

Byte offset

Fig. 15.1

different types, and since different data types often have different address alignment requirements, 'holes' may be imbedded in the actual memory space. For some hardware many multibyte data items must be located at an address that is exactly divisible by two or by four.

Consider the structure declaration:

```
struct alignment { int    numb1;
                   char   ch;
                   int    numb2;
                 } example;
```

Assume that int require alignment on a double byte boundary address (i.e. an even address), while char can be placed at any address. The structure variable *example* then occupies memory as shown in Fig. 15.1. The second integer numb2 cannot immediately follow ch because the next location is not an even byte number. Therefore, an additional byte is inserted to align numb2 as required.

From this example we see that the actual memory layout of a structure is machine dependent. Portable code should not depend on the actual numerical values of the offsets of the structure members. Always let the compiler keep track of them.

15.4 Structures and functions

Structured items may also be taken as arguments to functions and as values returned from functions. This unrestricted facility is a relatively recent feature of C. Some earlier systems only supported pointers to structures as function arguments and as function return values. We shall consider some of the difficulties associated with these restrictions in the next section.

To illustrate the use of structures with functions, consider the construction of a package of operations to be performed on *rational numbers*. A rational number is a fractional value expressed as the quotient of two positive integer values. Examples of rational numbers include 1/2, 3/4, 7/8. The elements of a rational number are the numerator and the denominator. The rational number 3/4 has numerator 3 and denominator 4. An appropriate type is:

```
typedef struct { unsigned int    numerator;
                 unsigned int    denominator;
               } Rational;
```

In our reference system structures can be passed as arguments and returned as function values. So, if two integer values num and den are to be composed into a rational value, we might employ the function *assign*:

```
Rational assign(num, den)
  unsigned int num, den;
  {
    Rational rat;

    rat.numerator   = num;
    rat.denominator = den;
    return (rat);
  }
```

The function uses the local variable rat of type Rational and assigns the two arguments to its member values. This is explicitly returned to the calling function and may be assigned there to a variable of type Rational.

We want the rational value always expressed in its simplest form. Thus, if the integer arguments given to function assign are 8 and 6 (i.e. 8/6), we should wish the function to effectively deliver the reduced rational number 4/3. To do so we must determine the highest common factor of the two arguments and divide this value into both. This is implemented with the recursive function *hcf* (see Chapter 10). Since we are to construct a package of rationals, we choose to conceal the local function hcf by giving it storage class static:

```
static unsigned int hcf(n, m)
  unsigned int n, m;
  {
    if (m > n)
      return (hcf(m, n));
    else if (m == 0)
      return (n);
    else
      return (hcf(m, n % m));
  }

Rational assign(num, den)
  unsigned int num, den;
  {
    unsigned int gcd;
    Rational     rat;

    gcd = hcf(num, den);
    rat.numerator   = num / gcd;
    rat.denominator = den / gcd;
    return (rat);
  }
```

The final revision we must make to function assign is to trap the error condition where the denominator has value zero. The rational number a/0 does not exist. The final version is then:

```
Rational assign(num, den)
  unsigned int num, den;
  {
    unsigned int gcd;
    Rational     rat;

    if (den == 0)
      {
        fprintf(stderr, "Error trap - assign (%d, %d)\n", num, den);
        exit(1);
      }
```

```
        gcd = hcf(num, den);
        rat.numerator   = num / gcd;
        rat.denominator = den / gcd;
        return (rat);
    }
```

If the floating points equivalent of the elements of a fractional number are allowed to engage in division, then the *real* value of the rational number is delivered. The rational 3/4 then reduces to 0.75. We can express this with a function having a single rational argument:

```
float real (rat)                    /* decimal equivalent */
    Rational rat;
    {
        return ((float) rat.numerator / (float) rat.denominator);
    }
```

Two rational values a/b and c/d are added by performing the following arithmetic and then reducing the result to the simplest form:

$$\frac{a}{b} + \frac{c}{d} = \frac{ad + bc}{bd}$$

```
Rational add(rat1, rat2)            /* addition */
    Rational rat1, rat2;
    {
        unsigned int num, den;

        num = rat1.numerator * rat2.denominator
                + rat2.numerator * rat1.denominator;
        den = rat1.denominator * rat2.denominator;
        return (assign(num, den));
    }
```

In function *add*, the expression to assign a value to the local variable num is difficult to read. We can shorten it and improve the clarity by introducing macros:

```
#define NUM(_R)      ((_R).numerator)
#define DEN (_R)     ((_R).denominator)
```

All the rational functions can now be recast in terms of these macros. In particular, the function add is programmed as:

```
Rational add(rat1, rat2)      /* addition */
    Rational rat1, rat2;
    {
        unsigned int num, den;

        num = NUM(rat1) * DEN(rat2) + NUM(rat2) * DEN(rat1);
        den = DEN(rat1) * DEN(rat2);
        return (assign(num, den));
    }
```

A sample package and the complementary header appears below. The package supports those already defined, together with multiply (two rational numbers), ratzero (generate rational zero: 0/1), ratunit (generate rational unity: 1/1), and a series of functions to perform relational tests on pairs of rational values.

```
/*
**        Specification part for the package of rational numbers.
*/

typedef struct  { unsigned int  numerator;       /* template */
                  unsigned int  denominator;
                } Rational;

#define NUM(_R)            ((_R).numerator)
#define DEN(_R)            ((_R).denominator)

#define ratzero()          assign(0, 1);
#define ratunit()          assign(1, 1);

#define FALSE              0
#define TRUE               1
typedef int                Boolean;

extern float real();                          /* external references */

extern Rational assign();
extern Rational add();
extern Rational multiply();

extern Boolean less();
extern Boolean greater();
extern Boolean equal();
extern Boolean unequal();
extern Boolean lessorequal();
extern Boolean greatorequal();

/*
**        Implementation package for rational numbers. Supported
**        are the operations for assignment, addition and multiplication;
**        and a series of relational operators.
*/

#include <stdio.h>
#include "rational.h"

float real(rat)                    /* decimal equivalent */
  Rational rat;
  {
    ...
  }

static int hcf(n, m)               /* highest common factor */
  unsigned int n, m;
  {
    ...
  }

Rational assign(num, den)          /* assign num/den as a rational */
  unsigned int num, den;
  {
    ...
  }

Rational add(rat1, rat2)           /* addition */
  Rational rat1, rat2;
  {
    ...
  }
```

```
.PA
Rational multiply(rat1, rat2)
  Rational rat1, rat2;
  {
    return (assign(NUM(rat1) * NUM(rat2), DEN(rat1) * DEN(rat2)));
  }


Boolean less(rat1, rat2)
  Rational rat1, rat2;
  {
    if (NUM(rat1) * DEN(rat2) < NUM(rat2) * DEN(rat1))
      return (TRUE);
    else
      return (FALSE);
  }


Boolean greater(rat1, rat2)
  Rational rat1, rat2;
  {
    return (less(rat2, rat1));
  }


Boolean equal(rat1, rat2)
  Rational rat1, rat2;
  {
    return ( ! (less(rat1, rat2) || less(rat2, rat1)));
  }


Boolean unequal(rat1, rat2)
  Rational rat1, rat2;
  {
    return ( ! equal(rat1, rat2));
  }


Boolean lessorequal(rat1, rat2)
  Rational rat1, rat2;
  {
    return ( ! greater(rat1, rat2));
  }


Boolean greatorequal(rat1, rat2)
  Rational rat1, rat2;
  {
    return ( ! less(rat1, rat2));
  }
```

We will use this package of rational numbers to develop a program to compute the partial sums of the *harmonic series*. The program will evaluate H(n) for various values of n, where:

$$H(n) = 1 + \frac{1}{2} + \frac{1}{3} + \cdots + \frac{1}{n}$$

The result of the calculation is to be expressed in the form of a rational number. The program is invoked with the command line:

harmonic n

where the integer value n is given as the argument. For example, the call:

harmonic 8

produces the output:

```
2: 3/2
3: 11/6
4: 25/12
5: 137/60
6: 49/20
7: 363/140
8: 761/280
```

Program 15.3

```
/*
**      Compute the partial sums of the harmonic series H(n)
**      for various values of n, where:
**
**      H(n) = 1 + 1/2 + 1/3 + 1/4 + ... + 1/n
**
**      The integer value n is given as a command line argument.
*/

#include <stdio.h>
#include "rational.h"

main(argc, argv)
   int     argc;
   char    *argv[];
   {
     int        k, n;
     Rational   sum, term;

     if (argc != 2)
       fprintf(stderr, "Usage: %s number\n", argv[0]);
     else
       {
         sscanf(argv[1], "%d", &n);            /* obtain n */

         sum = ratunit();                      /* sum = 1, initially */
         for (k = 2; k <= n; k++)              /* remaining terms */
           {
             term = assign (1, k);
           sum = add(sum, term);
             printf("%2d: %d/%d\n", k, NUM(sum), DEN(sum));
           }
       }
   }
```

15.5 Pointers to structures

We have shown how a pointer can be defined to point to a fundamental data type such as an int or a char. Pointers can also be defined to point to structures. Using the date structure introduced earlier:

```
struct date { int   day;
              int   month;
              int   year;
            };
```

then defining a type name Date through a type definition:

```
typedef struct date    Date;
```

we may proceed to declare a variable today of type struct date:

Date   today;

A variable declared as a pointer to a struct date variable is established in the usual way:

Date   *ptrdate;

or, by firstly introducing a type name for an object of type pointer to struct date through:

typedef Date   *Ptrdate;

and then declaring variable ptrdate by:

Ptrdate   ptrdate;

The variable ptrdate can then be used in the expected fashion. We can, for example, set it to point to the Date variable today, with the assignment:

ptrdate = &today;

Having performed the assignment, we can indirectly access any member of the date structure pointed to by ptrdate. If p is a pointer to some structured object, then the notation:

p → member-name

refers to the particular member name. Strictly, the symbol → is another C operator known as the structure operator and has precedence and associativity as shown in Appendix E. Using the pointer variable ptrdate, we may set the member day of the date structure to, say, 7 with the statement:

ptrdate → day = 7;

To test if today is the last day of the year, the statement:

if (ptrdate → day = = 31 &&
      ptrdate → month = = 12) . . . .

can be used. To read an integer value from the standard input and assign it to the member year of the object of type Date pointed to by ptrdate, the statement is:

scanf(″%d″, &ptrdate → year);

These three illustrative statements contain a mixture of operators. The assignment statement employs both the structure and assignment operators; the if statement uses the structure and equality operators and the *logical and* operator; the scanf function call employs both the address operator and the structure operator.

As always, the C programmer must be vigilant about operator precedence and operator associativity. The structure pointer operator (→) and structure member reference operator (.) have highest priorities. In the assignment:

ptrdate → day = 7;

the structure operator having precedence over the assignment operator delivers the object to receive the value before the assignment is performed. In the if statement, the operators are, in decreasing order of precedence: the structure operator, the equality operator and the logical and operator. The conditional expression is effectively evaluated as:

if (((ptrdate → day) = = 31) &&
    ((ptrdate → month) = = 12)) . . . .

In the final example:

scanf("%d", &ptrdate → year);

the address operator has low priority relative to the structure operator. Thus, the object delivered by the structure pointer has its address taken and passed to scanf so that an input value may be placed at that location.

While not really a sensible way to do things, we could write Program 15.1 in terms of pointers. We include this as Program 15.4 only for illustration.

Program 15.4

```
/*
**        Assign values to the members of a structured date,
**        then print them. The structured date value is
**        manipulated through pointers to illustrate.
*/

#include <stdio.h>

struct date      { int        day;        /* template */
                   int        month;
                   int        year;
                 };
typedef struct date              Date;      /* variable and ... */
typedef Date                     *Ptrdate;  /* pointer types */

main ()
  {
    Date        today;
    Ptrdate     ptrdate;

    ptrdate = &today;
    ptrdate -> day      = 27;
    ptrdate -> month    = 9;
    ptrdate -> year     = 1985;

    printf ("Today\'s date is %2d/%2d/%4d\n",
        ptrdate -> day, ptrdate -> month, ptrdate -> year);
  }
```

The notation:

ptrdate → day

refers to the member day of the date structure to which the pointer variable ptrdate points. Since ptrdate points to a structure, the day member could also be referred to by:

(*ptrdate).day

but pointers to structures are so frequently used that the → notation is provided as a convenient shorthand. The parentheses are necessary in (*ptrdate).day because the structure member operator '.' has higher precedence than the indirection operator '*'. The parentheses guarantee to first deliver the structured object from which the member day is obtained.

The original definition of the C language placed a number of restrictions on structures. The only operations on structures initially supported were to take its address and to access one of its members. This implied that structures could not be assigned as a unit, and that they could not be passed as arguments to functions nor returned as function values. This meant that functions such as assign and add in the package of rational numbers could not be supported.

Pointers to structures do not suffer from these limitations, however, so structures and functions can be made to operate together with these compilers which do not support the new features. Reprogrammed versions of functions assign and add appear below. The changes are two-fold. Both functions returned structures as function values. This is replaced by passing an additional argument − the address of the structure to receive the returned value. Function add also received, as input, the values of two rationals. This is now replaced with the address of the rationals from which the values can be obtained. The revisions are then:

```
#define PNUM(_R)      ((_R) -> numerator)
#define PDEN(_R)      ((_R) -> denominator)

void assign(rat, num, den)
  Rational      *rat;
  unsigned int num, den;
  {
    unsigned int gcd;

    if (den == 0)
      {
        fprintf(stderr, "Error trap -- assign (%d, %d)\n", num, den);
        exit(1);
      }

    gcd = hcf(num, den);
    PNUM(rat) = num / gcd;
    PDEN(rat) = den / gcd;
  }
void add(rat, rat1, rat2)
  Rational *rat, rat1, rat2;
  {
    unsigned int num, den;

    num = PNUM(rat1) * PDEN(rat2) + PNUM(rat2) * PDEN(rat1);
    den = PDEN(rat1) * PDEN(rat2);
    assign(rat, num, den);
  }
```

15.6 Initializing structures

Initialization of structures is similar to initialization of arrays – the values of the members are listed within a pair of matching braces, with each element separated by a comma symbol. Like arrays, only external and static structures can be initialized. Automatic structure variables cannot be initialized. To initialize the structure date variable xmas to 25 December 1986, the declaration is:

    static struct date xmas = {25, 12, 1986};

Initialization of all variables, including structure variables, can only be performed with constant values or constant expressions.

If fewer values are listed than there are members of the structure, the remaining members are assigned the default value zero. So the external declaration:

    Date beginning = {1, 1};

sets beginning.day and beginning.month to 1, but provides no explicit initializer for beginning.year. By default, its initial value is then 0.

15.7 Array members of structures

It is possible to define structures that contain arrays as members. In many applications, arrays of characters are used. For example, we might define a record type to describe the details of a person as follows:

    enum gender {FEMALE, MALE};
    typedef enum gender   Gender;

    struct person { char   surname[NAMEMAX];
                    char   forename[NAMEMAX];
                    Gender   sex;
                    int   age;
                  };
    typedef struct person   Person;

A value of type Person consists of four members – a *surname* which is an array of characters, a *forename* similarly defined, a component *sex* which is either FEMALE or MALE, and an integer *age*.

If we have the declaration:

    Person   employee;

then:

    employee   denotes a variable of type Person
    employee.forename   denotes a string of characters which might be
                        assigned, compared, or output using the usual
                        string operations

employee.surname[0] denotes the first character of the employee's surname and may be used in any way appropriate to a character variable.

The following are all permissible operations upon the structure variable employee:

```
employee.sex = FEMALE;
if (employee.age > 60) . . . .
strcpy (employee.surname, "Smith");
if (employee.forename[0] = = 'A') . . . .
```

From the previous section, initialization of non-automatic structure variables is permissible. Those members that are character arrays are initialized as shown in chapter 12, pages 223–6. If employee were, say, a variable with storage class static, then we might initialize it with:

```
static Person employee =
    { "Bloggs", "Joe", MALE, 21 };
```

15.8 Arrays of structures

A structure may occur as a component of other aggregate types. In particular, an array type may be defined whose elements are structures. Thus, the C programming language supports both members of structures which are arrays and arrays of structures. For example:

```
typedef enum {FEMALE, MALE} Gender

typedef struct { char      surname[NAMEMAX];
                 char      forename[NAMEMAX];
                 Gender  sex;
                 int        age;
               } Person;

Person        staff[STAFFSIZE];
```

defines an array called staff. Each element of the array is defined to be of type Person. For this declaration,

staff   denotes the complete array

staff[i]   denotes a variable of type Person

staff[i].forename   denotes an array of characters which may be
                     assigned, compared, or output using the usual
                     string operators

staff[i].surname[j] denotes a single character value

Further, if a function called, say, print_person exists and prints the details of an employee, then the call:

  print_person(staff[k]);

is correct, assuming that the function declaration is:

  void print_person(employee)
    Person employee;

Equally, if a function called sort arranges the staff into alphabetical order based on the surname, the call:

  sort(staff, STAFFSIZE);

would be appropriate for the function declaration:

  void sort(staff, size)
    Person staff[ ];
    int   size;

Initialization of arrays of structures is similar to the initialization of multidimensional arrays. The statement:

  static Person staff [ ] =
  { { "Bloggs", "Joe",   MALE,   21 },
    { "Smith", "John",   MALE,   30 },
    { "Black", "Mary",   FEMALE, 25 } };

declares an array of size 3. Each element is of type Person, and establishes a workforce consisting of Joe Bloggs, John Smith and Mary Black.

The sort function when applied to this workforce could be invoked with the call:

  sort(staff, NSTAFF);

The quantity NSTAFF is the number of employees in staff. Although we could enumerate this explicitly with:

  #define NSTAFF   3

it is easier and much safer to do it within the program, especially if the list is subject to change. If the size of the array and the size of an individual element are determinable, then the number of entries is:

  size-of-array/size-of-array-element

We have already met the compile time unary operator sizeof, used to compute the size of any object. The computation can then be expressed in terms of this operator and used in a #define statement to set the value of NSTAFF:

  # define   NSTAFF   (sizeof(staff))/sizeof(Person))

Let us apply all these new concepts to the following problem. A program is required to count the number of occurrences of each C keyword appearing in a program text. To simplify the processing, we assume that the programmer has created the program file in a disciplined style. This style dictates that each reserved keyword be bracketed by whitespace characters. Constructs such as "while(" with no intervening spaces are guaranteed not to occur, otherwise additional programming is required to filter out the identifier "while".

The keyword counting program is invoked with a single command line argument being the name of the program text file to be processed. After checking this argument, the main function reads the input one 'word' at a time. Each word is compared against a list of all the C keywords. If no match is found, the word is ignored. If a match is found, the associated keyword counter is incremented. This action is relegated to the subsidiary function *count*.

Program 15.5

```
/*
**        A program to count the occurrences of each C keyword.
**        The name of the text file containing the program is
**        given as a command line argument. The file is assumed
**        to have the correct format with whitespace surrounding
**        each individual token. This program listing has this
**        form and is used as the program input.
*/


#include <stdio.h>

struct wordcount { char      *keyword;        /* template */
                   int        keycount;
                 };
typedef struct wordcount      Wordcount;

static Wordcount keytable [] =
       { "auto",        0,     "break",        0,
         "case",        0,     "char",         0,
         "continue",    0,     "default",      0,
         "do",          0,     "double",       0,
         "else",        0,     "enum",         0,
         "extern",      0,     "float",        0,
         "for",         0,     "goto",         0,
         "if",          0,     "int",          0,
         "long",        0,     "register",     0,
         "return",      0,     "return",       0,
         "short",       0,     "sizeof",       0,
         "static",      0,     "struct",       0,
         "switch",      0,     "typedef",      0,
         "union",       0,     "unsigned",     0,
         "void",        0,     "while",        0
       };

#define NKEYS              (sizeof (keytable) / sizeof (Wordcount))

#define READONLY           "r"
#define WORDSIZE           128

char    *programname;

void    count (), print (), syserr ();
```

```
main ( argc , argv )
   int   argc ;
   char  * argv [] ;
   {
   FILE       * fp , * fopen ();
   char       word [ WORDSIZE ];
   int        n ;

   programname = argv [0];

   if ( argc != 2 )
      syserr ( 1, "Usage: %s filename\n", programname );
   else if (( fp = fopen ( argv [1], READONLY )) == NULL )
      syserr (2, "Cannot open %s\n", argv [1]);
   else
      {
      while ( fscanf ( fp, "%s", word ) != EOF )
         count ( word , keytable , NKEYS );
      print ( keytable , NKEYS );
      exit (0);
      }
   }


void count ( word , table , size )
   char       * word ;
   Wordcount  table [];
   int        size ;
   {
   int        n;

   for ( n = 0; n < size ; n ++ )
      if ( strcmp ( word , table [ n ] . keyword ) == 0)
         {
         table [ n ] . keycount ++;
         return ;
         }
   }

void print ( table , size )
   Wordcount  table [];
   int        size ;
   {
   int n ;

   for ( n = 0; n < size ; n ++ )
      printf ("\t%-15s %4d\n", table [ n ] . keyword ,
                         table [ n ] . keycount );
   }


void syserr ( errcode , message , argument )
   int   errcode ;
   char  * message , * argument ;
   {
   fprintf ( stderr , "%s [%2d]: ", programname );
   fprintf ( stderr , message , argument );

   exit ( errcode );
   }
```

When this program text file is processed by itself, the output is:

auto	0
break	0
case	0
char	6

continue	0
default	0
do	0
double	0
else	2
enum	0
extern	0
float	0
for	2
goto	0
if	3
int	8
long	0
register	0
return	1
short	0
sizeof	1
static	1
struct	2
switch	0
typedef	1
union	0
unsigned	0
void	4
while	1

15.9 Nested structures

Structures are allowed to occur as components of other aggregate types, including structures. It is possible, therefore, to define structures that contain another structure as one or more of its members. An application might, for instance, process details of the book stock held in a library. For each book the following information is maintained: the ISBN (International Standard Book Number), the author, the title, the publisher, the edition and the date of publication. In the context of these data, the last item is considered a single entity. In reality it is, of course, composed of three parts – a day, a month and a year. Thus, we have a nested structure based on the following declarations:

```
typedef struct { int       day;
                 int       month;
                 int       year;
               } Date;
```

```
typedef struct { char      isbn[ISBNSIZE];
                 char      author[AUTHORSIZE];
                 char      title[TITLESIZE];
                 char      publisher[PUBLISHERSIZE];
                 int       edition;
                 Date      dateofpublication;
               } Book;
```

A stock of 100 books can be established and the first entry made with the following declaration plus initialization:

```
static Book stock [100] =
  { {"0131101633", "Kernighan and Ritchie"
     "The C Programming Language", "Prentice Hall",
     1, {1, 1, 1978}}
  };
```

For this declaration:

stock	denotes the complete array
stock[i]	denotes a variable of type Book
stock[i].dateofpublication	denotes a variable of type Date
stock[i].dateofpublication.year	denotes a variable of type int

We illustrate an application of nested structures by revisiting the sequential file update in Case study 14.1. There are no structural changes in the revised program. The differences lie in the organization of the data items.

The master file records consist of four components: student identification number, name, subject and grade. These related items are encapsulated as a single structured value of type:

```
typedef struct { int       identification;
                 char      name[NAMESIZE];
                 char      subject[SUBJECTSIZE];
                 int       grade;
               } Record;
```

Such records are read from and written to the master files.

A transaction record consists of a student record together with a transaction type indicator (insert, delete or change). An appropriate type definition is then:

```
typedef struct { char      type;
                 Record    student;
               } Transaction;
```

As a consequence of these declarations, the number of arguments passed between functions is reduced. Program readability is greatly improved. The use of this typing mechanism is a powerful abstraction technique. Consider, for example, the new interface to function get_master_record:

```
Boolean get_master_record(fp, master)
    FILE    *fp;
    Record *master;
```

Given a master file pointer as an input argument, the function reads the next record from the file. The details of what constitutes a master file record are the province of the Record definition. Further, any changes to the actual content of a master file record can be implemented without affecting this interface. Below is the full version of this function. The completion of the program is left as an exercise for the reader.

```
Boolean get_master_record(fp, master)
    FILE       *fp;          /* old master file */
    Record     *master;      /* master record fields */
    {
        if (fscanf(fp, "%4d%20s%10s%1d", &master → identification,
            master → name, master → subject, &master → grade) = = = 4)
            return (TRUE);
        else
            return (FALSE);
    }
```

15.10 Files of structures

The file-handling primitives fread, fwrite and fseek consider a file as an unstructured series of byte values. The programmer may superimpose some arbitrary data structure so that the file becomes a sequence of records of some given type. Recall the structured data type Person introduced in section 15.7. A variable of type Person called, say, employee may be written to a file by the statement:

```
fwrite((char *) &employee, sizeof(Person), 1, fp)
```

The first actual argument to fwrite is the address of a character buffer, obtained by taking the address of variable employee and coercing it to a char *. The number of bytes transferred in the operation is the number of bytes in the employee record and is determined by the compile time operator sizeof (Person). The file is now interpreted as a file of Person records.

Case study 15.1: Direct access file update

In Case study 14.1 the master files were organized sequentially. Such an organization, however, imposes constraints upon the system. For instance, the actual transactions are batched together and applied to the master file at

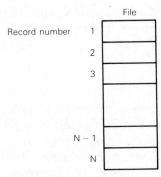

Fig. 15.2

regular intervals. As a consequence of this, the master file is only up to date immediately following an update run. Further, to perform sequential file updates, the transaction file must first be sorted, a time-consuming operation. Additionally, to access the particular record for a given student identification, the master file must be scanned sequentially until the required record is obtained.

Direct access has a number of obvious advantages. Performing an immediate update ensures that the master file is constantly up to date. The need to sort the transactions is also removed, thus saving considerable processing time.

The logical structure of a direct access file is an ordered sequence of records. Each record in the sequence is identified by a *relative record number*. If there are N records in the file, then each is addressed by a unique integer in the range 1 to N inclusive (see Fig. 15.2).

We will assume that the transaction file has been fully validated. Direct access file update is shown in the following run chart (Fig. 15.3).

The transaction file has the same layout as in Case study 14.1. The master file is fixed length binary data with fixed length fields having the format shown in Fig. 15.4. The field named *occupied* indicates whether the record area in the file contains a file record. This single character field marks the presence or absence of a data record. If occupied is the blank character, then no data record is present. If occupied is non-blank (specifically the asterisk symbol), then data exist in the record area.

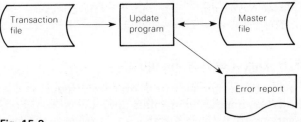

Fig. 15.3

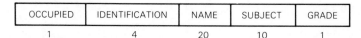

OCCUPIED	IDENTIFICATION	NAME	SUBJECT	GRADE
1	4	20	10	1

Fig. 15.4

The structure of the direct access file update follows from Case study 14.1. The transaction file is read one record ahead. The read ahead mechanism makes the program much simpler. One key value is iteratively processed until the sentinel record is found, indicating end of file. 'Process one key' contains the logic for updating the status of each key value. It calls 'process one transaction' iteratively until there are no more transactions for the current key. 'Process one transaction' first applies the transaction to the master record, then replaces it by the next transaction. The next key is always chosen as the current transaction identification.

'Initial status' attempts to retrieve the record indicated by the current key. If it finds an active record in the master file, it sets the Boolean indicator *allocated* to true. The record is read into the master record area. If an active record is not found, allocated is set to false and the content of the master record area is ignored.

'Final status' tests the value of the Boolean flag allocated. If allocated is true, it creates or replaces the record at the current key in the master file. If allocated is false, the record in the master file is tagged as unoccupied.

There are a great many ways of organizing random files, all of which are conceptually similar. In the chapter introduction it was intimated that an address function translates the record key into a relative record number 1, 2, 3, ... N, where there are at most N records in the file. If the key value itself (four decimal digits) defines the relative record number, then in this example 10000 record areas are required. The record for student 1234 is stored in record area 1234 of the file, and so on. Since the number of students on a course is likely to be small, say less than 100, the disadvantage of this addressing algorithm is that the majority of record areas in the file are unused.

To improve the utilization of the file, an addressing algorithm with values 1, 2, 3, ... N, where the total number of record areas N in the file is of the order of the actual number of data records. The addressing algorithm is referred to as a *hashing function*. A number of hashing functions can be employed. The example we shall consider divides the record key value by the prime integer immediately below the number of file record areas. For N = 100, the prime number is 97 and the hashing function is:

key *mod* 97 + 1

Thus, record key value 1234 will map on to record area number 71.

Because there are fewer record areas than possible key values, different key values can map on to the same relative record number. Key value 1234 maps on to relative record 71. Key value 2398 also maps on to the same record number:

$$2398 \bmod 97 + 1 = 71$$

This condition is known as a *collision*. If the record with key value 1234 already occupies relative record number 71, then a decision has to be made as to where to enter the record with key value 2398.

The simplest strategy we shall consider is that if the addressing algorithm specifies a record number already occupied, then a linear search of the records immediately following this record is performed until the first unoccupied record is located. In performing the search, the file is considered *cyclic* with the first record conceptually following the last record. Thus, if relative record 71 is occupied with the record having key value 1234 and a record with key value 2398 is to be entered into the file, a search is performed through records 71, 72, ... until an unoccupied record area is discovered. The record with key 2398 is then inserted and the record area is marked as occupied.

A student record has four fields: student identification number, student name, subject name and subject grade. An appropriate type definition is:

```
typedef struct { int      identification;
                 char     name[NAMESIZE];
                 char     subject[SUBJECTSIZE];
                 int      grade;
               } Record;
```

A record from the transaction file is a composite of a student record and a transaction type (insert, delete or change):

```
typedef struct { char     type;
                 Record   student;
               } Transaction;
```

A record from the master file is a student record augmented with an extra field indicating the presence or absence of a data record:

```
typedef struct { char     occupied;
                 Record   student;
               } Master;
```

Transmitting the fields of a record in a structured type reduces the number of arguments passed among functions. This improves program reliability, consistency and readability. Treating the master file as structured values of type Master simplifies the associated input/output. For example, to read a record from the master file given the relative record number, the function is:

```
int read_master_record (fp, relative_record_number, master)
   FILE        *fp;        /* old master file */
   int         relative_record_number;
   MASTER      *master;  /* master record fields */
   {
       if (fseek (fp, (long) relative_record_number * sizeof
(MASTER), ABSOL
           return (ERROR);
       else if (fread ((char *) master, sizeof (MASTER), 1, fp) ! = 1)
           return (ERROR);
       else
           return (relative_record_number);
   }
```

The full program listing is as follows.

```
/*
**         Update of a direct access master file.
*/

#include <stdio.h>

#define READONLY       "r"              /* file modes */
#define UPDATE         "r+"

#define FALSE          0
#define TRUE           1
typedef int            Boolean;         /* logical values/types */

#define NAMESIZE       21               /* field sizes ... */
#define SUBJECTSIZE    11               /* including terminator */

#define TRAILER        9999             /* key sentinel */
#define ABSOLUTE       0                /* origin in fseek */
#define PRIME          97               /* number of file records */

#define INSERT         'I'              /* transaction codes */
#define DELETE         'D'
#define CHANGE         'C'

#define ERROR          -1               /* return codes */
#define ABSENT         0

#define OCCUPIED       '*'              /* master record indicator *
#define UNOCCUPIED     ' '

#define GET_TRANSACTION(_F, _T)        if\
       (! get_transaction_record (_F, _T))\
       syserr (10, "Error reading %s\n", "transaction file")
#define GET_MASTER(_R, _F, _K, _M)     if\
       ((_R = get_master_record (_F, _K, _M)) == ERROR)\
       syserr (11, "Error reading %s\n", "master file")
#define PUT_MASTER(_R, _F, _K, _M)     if\
       ((_R = put_master_record (_F, _K, _M)) == ERROR)\
       syserr (12, "Error writing %s\n", "master file")

typedef struct { int            identification;
                 char           name[NAMESIZE];
                 char           subject[SUBJECTSIZE];
                 int            grade;
               } Record;
```

```
typedef struct { char           type;
                 Record         student;
               } Transaction;

typedef struct { char           occupied;
                 Record         student;
               } MASTER;

char    *programname;

FILE    *fopen ();                           /* forward references */
int     fclose (), fscanf (), fprintf (), fseek ();

Boolean get_transaction_record ();
int     read_master_record ();
int     write_master_record ();
int     get_master_record ();
int     put_master_record ();

int     address ();
int     choose_next_key ();
int     do_initial_status ();
void    do_final_status ();
void    apply_transaction ();
void    copy_corresponding ();

void    syserr (), error ();

main (argc, argv)
  int    argc;
  char   *argv[];
  {
    FILE          *fptrans, *fpmast;       /* program files */
    int           current_key, relative_record_number;
    Boolean       allocated;
    Transaction   transaction;
    MASTER        master;

    programname = argv[0];

    if (argc != 3)
      syserr (1, "Usage: %s file1 file2 file3\n", programname);
    else if ((fptrans = fopen (argv[1], READONLY)) == NULL)
      syserr (2, "cannot open %s\n", argv[1]);
    else if ((fpmast = fopen (argv[2], UPDATE)) == NULL)
      syserr (2, "cannot open %s\n", argv[2]);
    else
      {
        GET_TRANSACTION(fptrans, &transaction);

        current_key =
                choose_next_key (transaction.student.identification);

        while (current_key != TRAILER)
          {
            relative_record_number = do_initial_status (current_key,
                &allocated, fpmast, &master);

            while (current_key == transaction.student.identification)
              {
                apply_transaction (&allocated,
                                        &transaction, &master);

                GET_TRANSACTION(fptrans, &transaction);
              }

            do_final_status (fpmast, relative_record_number,
                allocated, &master);

            current_key =
                    choose_next_key (transaction.student.identification);
          }

        fclose (fptrans);
```

```
            fclose (fpmast);
        }
    }


Boolean get_transaction_record (fp, transaction)
    FILE          *fp;                /* transaction file */
    Transaction   *transaction;      /* transaction record fields */
    {
        if (fscanf (fp, "%4d%c%20s%10s%1d",
                       &transaction -> student.identification,
                       &transaction -> type, transaction -> student.name,
                       transaction -> student.subject,
                       &transaction -> student.grade) == 5)
            return (TRUE);
        else
            return (FALSE);
    }


int    read_master_record (fp, relative_record_number, master)
    FILE          *fp;                /* old master file */
    int           relative_record_number;
    MASTER        *master;           /* master record fields */
    {
        if (fseek (fp, (long) relative_record_number * sizeof (MASTER),
              ABSOLUTE) != 0)
          return (ERROR);
        else if (fread ((char *) master, sizeof (MASTER), 1, fp) != 1)
          return (ERROR);
        else
          return (relative_record_number);
    }


int    write_master_record (fp, relative_record_number, master)
    FILE          *fp;                /* old master file */
    int           relative_record_number;
    MASTER        *master;           /* master record fields */
    {
        if (fseek (fp, (long) relative_record_number * sizeof (MASTER),
              ABSOLUTE) != 0)
          return (ERROR);
        else if (fwrite ((char *) master, sizeof (MASTER), 1, fp) != 1)
          return (ERROR);
        else
          return (relative_record_number);
    }


int    get_master_record (fp, key, master)
    FILE          *fp;
    int           key;
    MASTER        *master;
    {
        int k, relative_record_number;

        relative_record_number = address (key);
        for (k = 0; k < PRIME; k++)
          if (read_master_record (fp, relative_record_number,
                                            master) == ERROR)
            return (ERROR);
          else if (master -> occupied == UNOCCUPIED)
            return (ABSENT);
          else if (key == master -> student.identification)
            return (relative_record_number);
          else
            relative_record_number =
                      relative_record_number == PRIME ? 1
                            : relative_record_number + 1;

        return (ABSENT);
    }
```

```
int     put_master_record (fp, key, master)
   FILE           *fp;
   int            key;
   MASTER         *master;
   {
      int         k, relative_record_number;
      MASTER      temp_master;

      relative_record_number = address (key);
      for (k = 0; k < PRIME; k++)
        if (read_master_record (fp, relative_record_number,
             &temp_master) == ERROR)
          return (ERROR);
        else if (temp_master.occupied == UNOCCUPIED)
          return (write_master_record (fp,
                          relative_record_number, master));
        else if (key == temp_master.student.identification)
          return (write_master_record (fp,
                          relative_record_number, master));
        else
          relative_record_number =
                  relative_record_number == PRIME ? 1
                      : relative_record_number + 1;

      syserr (20, "Overflow in: %s\n", "master file");
   }


int     choose_next_key (identification)
   int     identification;
   {
     return (identification);
   }


int     address (key)
   int     key;
   {
     return (key % PRIME + 1);
   }


void    apply_transaction (allocated, transaction, master)
   Boolean        *allocated;
   Transaction    *transaction;
   MASTER         *master;
   {
     switch (transaction -> type)
        {
          case INSERT:
            if (*allocated == TRUE)
              error (INSERT, "Record already exists\n",
                 transaction -> student.identification);
            else
               {
                 copy_corresponding (&master -> student,
                          &transaction -> student);
                 *allocated = TRUE;
               }
            break;

          case DELETE:
            if (*allocated == FALSE)
              error (DELETE, "Record does not exist\n",
                 transaction -> student.identification);
            else
              *allocated = FALSE;
            break;
```

```
            case CHANGE:
              if (*allocated == FALSE)
                error (CHANGE, "Record does not exist\n",
                   transaction -> student.identification);
              else
                copy_corresponding (&master -> student,
                          &transaction -> student);
              break;
        }
    }


int     do_initial_status (current_key, allocated, fp, master)
   int           current_key;
   Boolean       *allocated;
   FILE          *fp;
   MASTER        *master;
   {
     int relative_record_number;

     *allocated = FALSE;
     GET_MASTER(relative_record_number, fp, current_key, master);
     if (relative_record_number != ABSENT)
       *allocated = TRUE;
     return (relative_record_number);
   }


void    do_final_status (fp, relative_record_number,
                      allocated, master)
   FILE          *fp;
   int           relative_record_number;
   Boolean       allocated;
   MASTER        *master;
   {
     int record_number;
     if (allocated == TRUE)
       {
         if (relative_record_number != ABSENT)
           {
             master -> occupied = OCCUPIED;
             if (write_master_record (fp, relative_record_number,
                   master) == ERROR)
               syserr (21, "Error writing %s\n", "master record");
           }
         else
           {
             master -> occupied = OCCUPIED;
             PUT_MASTER(record_number, fp,
                       master -> student.identification, master);
           }
       }
     else
       {
         master -> occupied = UNOCCUPIED;
         if (write_master_record (fp,
               relative_record_number, master) == ERROR)
           syserr (22, "Error writing %s\n", "master record");
       }
   }


void          copy_corresponding (destination, source)
   Record         *destination, *source;
   {
     destination -> identification = source -> identification;
     strcpy (destination -> name, source -> name);
     strcpy (destination -> subject, source -> subject);
     destination -> grade = source -> grade;
   }
```

```
void    syserr (errcode, message, argument)
  int    errcode;
  char   *message, *argument;
  {
    fprintf (stderr, "%s [%2d]: ", programname, errcode);
    fprintf (stderr, message, argument);

    exit (errcode);
  }


void    error (code, message, id)
  char    code;                      /* transaction code */
  char    *message;
  int     id;                        /* transaction identification */
  {
    printf ("%c      %30s     %4d\n", code, message, id);
  }
```

15.11 Unions

The *union* data type in C is similar to *variant records* in other programming languages. The union data type is similar to the structure data type in that both can contain members of different types and sizes. Unlike structures, however, a union can hold at most one of its components at a time. Effectively, the members are overlaid in the storage allocated for the union. The compiler allocates sufficient storage to accommodate the largest of the specified members.

A union is a variable which can legitimately hold any one of several types. We demonstrate this in the following illustration. The notation used to declare and access members of a union is identical to that used with structures, with the keyword union replacing struct. Consider:

```
union number { int     integer;
               float   decimal;
             };
typedef union number  Number;
Number     data;
```

The variable data will be large enough to hold the largest of the two types (int or float), regardless of the machine it is compiled on. Provided the usage is consistent, any one of the types may be assigned to data and used in expressions. It is the responsibility of the programmer to maintain consistency and keep track of what type is currently stored in a union. If something is stored as one type and extracted as another, then the results are machine dependent. This is illustrated in the following program.

Program 15.6

```
/*
**       A program to illustrate how a system overlays an int
**       and a float. The program also shows how in C it is
**       the programmer's responsibility to maintain
**       consistency.
*/
```

```
#include <stdio.h>

union number {  int       integer;
                float     decimal;
             };
typedef union number      Number;

main ()
  {
   Number       data;

   data.integer = 20000;
   printf ("int: %6d, float: %f10.4\n", data.integer, data.decimal);

   data.decimal = 123.0;
   printf ("int: %6d, float: %f10.4\n", data.integer, data.decimal);
  }
```

The program demonstrates how a system overlays an int and a float. The program output, which is dependent upon the computer system in which it is run, might be:

```
20000       0.0000
31553     123.0000
```

Members of unions are accessed just as for structures. Syntactically, we use:

> union-variable.member-name

or:

> union-pointer → member-name

when using a pointer to a union variable. Unions may occur within structures and arrays and vice versa. The notation for accessing a member of a union in a structure (or for a structure in a union) is the same as that for nested structures. For example, in the structure array staff defined by:

```
#define WORDSIZE          20
#define NAMESIZE          25
#define STAFFSIZE         120

typedef union { char      word[WORDSIZE];
                int       number;
              } Word_number;

typedef struct { Word_number   day;
                 Word_number   month;
                 int           year;
               } Date;

typedef struct { char      surname[NAMESIZE];
                 char      forename[NAMESIZE];
                 Date      birthday;
               } Person;

Person          staff[STAFFSIZE];
```

in which both day and month may be expressed as either an integer or a character string, the member *number* for component *day* is referred to as:

staff[k].birthday.day.number

and the first character of the string *word* for member *month* by:

staff[k].birthday.month.word[0]

The original definition of C placed the same restrictions on unions as on structures. The only operations on unions initially supported were to take its address and to access one of its members. Later releases of C support assignment to unions, passing unions as function arguments and as return values from functions.

There is no provision in C to enquire as to which component of a union was last assigned. The programmer can, however, enclose a union in a structure that includes a *tag* component to indicate which member of a union is active. For example, we might add to the union Number:

```
typedef enum { INT, FLOAT } Tag;
typedef union {   int        integer;
                  float      decimal;
              }  Number;

typedef struct { Tag        tagged;
                 Number     value;
               } Pair;
Pair      data;
```

To assign to the union, we write either:

```
data.tagged         = INT;
data.value.integer  = 123;
```

or:

```
data.tagged         = FLOAT;
data.value.decimal  = 123.0;
```

We can then write portable functions that can discriminate among the possible values of the union. For example, we repeat the last program, including the above definitions and a function to print a Pair value, whatever it may contain.

Program 15.7

```
/*
**      Associate a tag value with a union to permit
**      descrimination among possible values of the union.
*/

#include <stdio.h>
```

```
#define INT              0
#define FLOAT            1
typedef int              Tag;

union number {  int     integer;        /* number pair template */
                float   decimal;
             };
typedef union number     Number;

struct pair  {  Tag     tagged;         /* tagged number pairs */
                Number  value;
             };
typedef struct pair      Pair;

void print_pair ();                     /* forward reference */

main ()
  {
    Pair        data;

    data.tagged        = INT;
    data.value.integer = 20000;
    print_pair (&data);

    data.tagged        = FLOAT;
    data.value.decimal = 123.0;
    print_pair (&data);
  }

void print_pair (d)
  Pair   *d;
  {
    switch (d -> tagged)
      {
        case INT:       printf ("Integer: %d\n", d -> value.integer);
                        break;

        case FLOAT:     printf ("Decimal: %f\n", d -> value.decimal);
                        break;
      }
  }
```

The output from this program is:

20000
123.0000

The print_pair function correctly discriminates between the field *integer* and *decimal* according to the value assigned to the tag.

Finally, we observe that the C language does not permit initialization of any variable of union type because there is no obvious way to specify which member is being assigned a value.

15.12 Bit fields

Systems programming activities are often required to manipulate data not only at the byte level, but also at the bit level. Bit fields are typically used in machine-dependent programs which require data structures to correspond to some fixed hardware representation. For example, data formats for interfaces to hardware devices often require the ability to access individual bits.

The C compiler allows integer numbers to be packed into spaces smaller than that ordinarily allowed. These components are called *bit fields* and are specified by following the member declarator with a colon symbol and a constant integer expression specifying the width of the field in bits:

```
struct packed {  unsigned int      a : 2;
                 unsigned int      b : 4, c : 7;
              } bits = {1, 7, 33};
```

The intent is that member a is allocated the first two bits of the structure, member b the next four bits, and finally member c the next seven bits. The two-bit field a is capable of representing the four values 0 to 3 inclusive; b is capable of storing the values 0, 1, 2, ... 15; and the seven-bit field c may represent the values 0 to 127 inclusive.

The compiler assigns in either a left-to-right or a right-to-left order of the bits in a machine word needed to store the fields. The internal representation of bit fields, therefore, is machine dependent. A machine word usually equates with the data type int, and the memory allocation for int differs among machines. Further, while the majority of machines store fields left-to-right, some store right-to-left. Assuming a two byte int and a left-to-right storage format, the memory representation for variable *bits* as declared and initialized above is shown in Fig. 15.5.

A field may not overlap an int boundary. If the bit field width would cause this to happen, the field is aligned at the next int boundary. Thus, the declaration:

```
struct filled {  unsigned int      a : 4;
                 unsigned int      b : 10;
                 unsigned int      c : 10;
              };
```

would require two 16-bit words with the fields a and b in the first word and field c in the second word.

Field members are not restricted in type, but generally implementations only support *unsigned* int. Arrays of fields are not allowed. Fields cannot be addressed directly by pointers, and the address operator cannot be applied to a bit field member.

Bit fields are likely to be non-portable and therefore should only be used in situations where memory is a scarce resource. The following program is a repeat of Program 15.2. Recognize that in a date the day number has

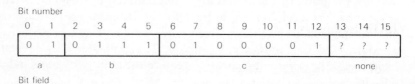

Fig. 15.5

(maximum) range 1 to 31 inclusive, month number is 1 to 12 inclusive, and the year is 0 to 99 if we discount the century. If memory is at a premium, we may choose to pack the day, month and year into, respectively, 5-bits (0 to 31 inclusive), 4-bits (0 to 15 inclusive) and 7-bits (0 to 127 inclusive) fields. The resulting program is as follows.

Program 15.8

```
/*
**       Program illustrating bit fields. The program
**       determines a person's age measured in years
**       given that person's date of birth and today's
**       date. The dates are packed into bit fields
**       of a 16-bit integer.
*/

#include <stdio.h>

struct date {   unsigned int    day : 5;
                unsigned int    month : 4;
                unsigned int    year : 7;
            };
typedef struct date         Date;

void    askfordate ();                      /* referencing declaration */

main ()
  {
    Date        dateofbirth, today;
    int         age;

    askfordate ("Date of birth?: ", &dateofbirth);
    askfordate ("Today\'s date?: ", &today);

    if (today.month > dateofbirth.month ||
        (today.month == dateofbirth.month &&
               today.day > dateofbirth.day))
      age = today.year - dateofbirth.year;
    else
    age = today.year - dateofbirth.year - 1;

    printf ("Age: %d years\n", age);
  }


void askfordate (prompt, date)
  char  *prompt;
  Date  *date;
  {
    unsigned int        d, m, y;

    printf ("%s", prompt);
    scanf ("%d/%d/%d", &d, &m, &y);

    date -> day   = d;
    date -> month = m;
    date -> year  = y;
  }
```

15.13 Summary

1. A *structure* is an example of an aggregate type consisting of a collection of subcomponents treated as a single entity. The subcomponents are called the *members* of a structure and are not necessarily of the same type.

2. Members of a structure are accessed by the structure member operator '.' or by the pointer to structure member operator ' → '. If s is structure variable and m is a member of s, then 's.m' refers to the member m of s. If p is a pointer to s, then '(*p).m', or better 'p → m', refers to the member m of s.

3. If s and t are structure variables of the same type, then the assignment s = t is supported. Also, a structure is permissible as an argument to a function and as the value returned by a function.

4. Structures may contain array members, and arrays of structure elements are supported. Additionally, structures may be members of other structures.

5. Unions have the same syntactic form as structured objects. Union members share the same storage overlaid upon each other.

6. Bit fields are members of a structure packed into a machine word. The internal representation of bit fields is highly machine dependent.

15.14 Exercises

1. Complete the sequential file update from section 15.9.

2. Define an array of structures that could be used for a telephone directory. Include the name, area code and phone number for a maximum of 40 records.

3. Define a file of records containing information on Computer Science courses. The first field of the record contains the course name. The second field contains the course number. The third field is an array of module numbers. Write a program to read this file and to print the course names which include a given module.

4. Repeat Case study 13.1, designing a suitable structure to represent the object *queue*.

5. Consider the following structure describing the information associated with a register of all persons in a country.

```
enum nationality {NATIONAL, ALIEN};
typedef enum nationality    Nationality;
struct person {  char        name[NAMESIZE];
                 Date        date_of_birth;
                 Nationality origin;
              };
```

Extend this definition to provide additional information about each person. For nationals, record their place of birth; while for aliens the country of origin and the date of entry into the country.

6. Write a program that uses bit fields to display the bit representation of the simple types int and float. The program is to operate upon a series of data values of both types.

## CHAPTER 16

Dynamic data structures

The aggregate types of array and structure permit the description of data structures whose form and size are fixed. These various data structures or information structures are accompanied by a set of algorithms that can be used for their access and manipulation, for example, sorting an array.

The data structures we shall now consider are different in that they use storage or memory *dynamically*. The amount of storage in use is directly proportional to the amount of information stored at a given stage in the computation.

The static data structures have a role to play in the creation of these dynamic data structures. The aggregates array and structure form the basic unit of storage for dynamic data structures. These basic units are commonly referred to as *nodes* of the data structure. These nodes are linked together in some way to form the structure, with the linkage information contained within each node. A given data structure is characterized by the structure imposed on the data by these linkages. Generally, there are three classes: *linear*, *hierarchical* and *graph* structures.

The linear linked list is the simplest of these categories. Normally each node has associated with it a data field and a single link field. The link associates one node with the next node in the list. The result is a chain-like structure, logically appearing as shown in Fig. 16.1.

Probably the most widely used structure from the hierarchical class is the *binary tree*. Each node in the structure can have one predecessor or *ancestor* and as many as two successors or *descendants*. Thus, each node contains data and the links to its two ancestors, as shown by Fig. 16.2.

The graph is a generalization of the tree structure which allows loops. Each node of a graph links to one or more other nodes as shown by Fig. 16.3. We shall not consider graphs in this book.

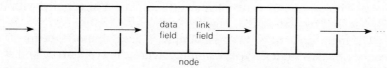

Fig. 16.1

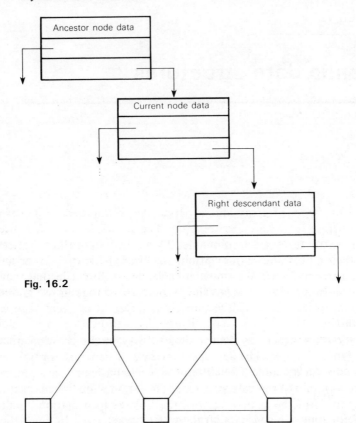

Fig. 16.2

Fig. 16.3

16.1 The linear linked list

A structure in which a member is a pointer to other such structures is known as a *self-referential structure*. The type declarations that will be needed to implement the linear linked list data structure are of the form:

```
struct node { int          data;
              struct node   *link;
            };
typedef struct node    Node;
typedef Node           *Ptrnode;
```

It is perfectly legal for a structure to contain a pointer to an instance of itself. These structures are conveniently displayed pictorially, with the links represented by arrows (see Fig. 16.4).

The member *data* is, in this example, a data item of type int. It can, of course, be any valid C type, including aggregate types array and structure. Using nested structures, a node can be made to carry a large quantity of

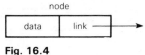

Fig. 16.4

associated data. For example, information in a node may be represented by the declaration:

    struct info { − − − − − };
    typedef struct info   Info;

and then the node by:

    struct node { Info   data;
                  struct node   *link;
                };

The member *link* is a pointer variable containing the address of another node. As a special case, this member may be the value NULL which is defined in ⟨stdio.h⟩. The pointer value NULL is used to represent the end of the list. Strictly, it is coerced to become a pointer to the node type by the cast expression (Ptrnode)NULL. Generally, NULL can be *cast* to any pointer type. However, we shall always use the explicit coercion to emphasize the required type.

Let us now declare some variables of type Node:

    Node   first, second, third;

and perform some assignments on these structures:

    first.data   = 1;
    second.data   = 2;
    third.data   = 3;

    first.link = second.link = third.link = (Ptrnode)NULL;

The result of this coding is Fig. 16.5.

A chain-like structure can be established by having the link member of *first* address the node *second*, and for its link in turn to address the node *third*. The statements are:

    first.link   = &second;
    second.link   = &third;

These pointer assignments result in linking first to second and second to third. We now have a *linear linked list* (Fig. 16.6). To reference the data

Fig. 16.5

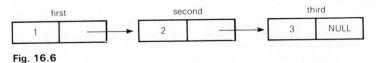

Fig. 16.6

items on this linked list there are a number of equivalent expressions. To retrieve the data item '1', the expression is:

first.data

The expression:

first.link

is an object of type pointer to a struct node. It does, of course, point to the struct node object called second. From section 15.5, a pointer to a structure permits a member of that structure to be accessed by:

structure-pointer → member-name

The expression to reference the data value '2' is:

second.data

or, indirectly:

first.link → data

The two operators, pointer to structure member reference (→) and structure member reference (.) are of equal precedence and associate left to right. Therefore, the link member of first will be determined, and then the member data of the structure addressed by this pointer.

Similarly, the member link of the object second can be referenced through:

first.link → link

and, in turn, the data item '3' by:

first.link → link → data

The essential feature here is that the members of the objects second, third and any more which may be linked into this list are accessible not only by their name (e.g. second.data) but also through the pointers which refer to them (first.link → data). Excepting first, the nodes in the linked list may be treated anonymously. Location first can also be treated this way if we have an additional variable of type Ptrnode called *head*, declared and initialized by:

Ptrnode head = &first;

to act as a pointer to the head (or first node) of the list. We then have Fig. 16.7.

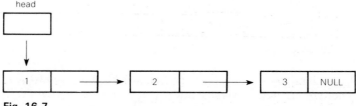

Fig. 16.7

One of the most fundamental operations on a list is list traversal in which every node of the list is visited exactly once. For each node visited, some action, such as printing the data item associated with the node, is performed. Using the list established above, Program 16.1 prints each integer in the list. List traversal is achieved by setting a pointer to the head of the list, then advancing through the list via the link pointer until the value NULL is determined, denoting the end of the list.

Program 16.1

```
/*
**       Manually establish a linear linked list then
**       perform a list traversal. Initialize a pointer
**       to the first list node, then cycle through the
**       nodes via the link member until the end of list
**       is recognized.
*/

#include <stdio.h>

struct node { int              data;
              struct node      *link;
            };
typedef struct node            Node;
typedef Node                    *Ptrnode;

main()
  {
    Node     first, second, third;
    Ptrnode head, ptr;

    first.data = 1;      first.link = &second;
    second.data = 2;     second.link = &third;
    third.data = 3;      third.link = (Ptrnode)NULL;
    head = &first;

    ptr = head;                        /* list traversal */
    while (ptr != (Ptrnode)NULL)       /* more nodes? */
      {
        printf("%d\n", ptr -> data);   /* access data */
        ptr = ptr -> link;             /* advance to next node */
      }
  }
```

Anonymous locations can be created dynamically while the program is executing. These dynamic data structures can expand and contract freely as required. The linked list offers the advantage that it can be made just as long as necessary — no more and no less. The array, by comparison, has its size fixed in advance and an arbitrary limit on the number of elements must be imposed.

Fig. 16.8

We can dispense completely with the named nodes and operate solely with anonymous nodes if each node can be created dynamically. A new region of memory can be allocated using the storage management function malloc. The function allocates a region of memory and returns a pointer to the first byte. Using the sizeof operator applied to the type name representing the dynamic data structure elements (Node) yields the number of bytes in the Node:

    sizeof(Node)

This, in turn, is given as the argument to malloc to create space for one Node:

    malloc(sizeof(Node))

Again, the value returned by malloc is a pointer to a char. For this address to be assigned to a variable of type Ptrnode, we must explicitly coerce the returned pointer into the desired type with a cast. That is, if variable ptrnode is declared as:

    Ptrnode   ptrnode;

then:

    ptrnode = (Ptrnode) malloc(sizeof(Node));

causes space for one Node to be dynamically created and for the variable ptrnode to point to it. Pictorially, we have Fig. 16.8. The members of this dynamically created node can be assigned values with expressions of the form:

    ptrnode → data = ...;
    ptrnode → link = ...;

16.2 List processing

With static data structures it is always known where the current item should be retrieved or inserted. In general, list processing applications require retrievals and insertions anywhere within a list. The list abstraction which we now develop provides the characteristics generally associated with lists.

Let us consider the range of operations to manipulate a list of items of some arbitrary type. An abstraction for a list is an ordered sequence L1, L2, L3, ... Ln (see Fig. 16.9). Presently we ignore that the list is realized through pointers and concentrate on the operations.

At any instance, only one item of the list can be under inspection. We

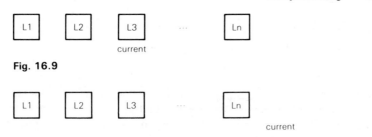

Fig. 16.9

Fig. 16.10

identify this as the *current* node. Effectively, we have a *window* through which this current node may be viewed, and no other is visible. This we depict by labeling the item current as shown in Fig. 16.9. Some list-processing operations, for example after an unsuccessful search of the list for an item with some particular property, result in no item in the window. We indicate this by positioning current immediately to the right of the list (see Fig. 16.10).

We define a list operation *active* which has the logical value TRUE when the current window is actively addressing an item in the list. If the current window is as shown in the last figure, then active delivers FALSE.

The associated operator *empty* also returns a logical value, and determines whether or not there are any items in the list. If there are no list elements, empty returns TRUE, otherwise empty returns FALSE.

We provide three operators to support positioning of the current window:

front : sets the current window over the first list item, if one exists. If the list is empty, then the operators *active* and *empty* will both return FALSE following this operation.

successor : advances to the next item in the list. If, before executing the operation, the current window is on the last item, then the effect of this operator is to cause active to subsequently deliver FALSE. If the list is empty, then successor has no effect. Similarly, if the current window is empty, then successor has no effect.

search(item) : advances the current window to the next list element containing *item*. If the present window is that item, then there is no advance. If no list element matches item, then the current window is placed beyond the last item, and active is FALSE.

The value of the list item addressed by current is obtained from the operator *content(item)*. If current does not refer to any list member, then no value is delivered. The value of the list member in the current window may be changed by the operator *replace(item)*. Again, nothing happens if current does not identify a list element.

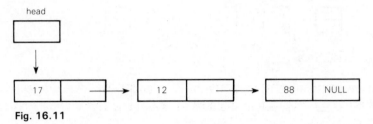

Fig. 16.11

Finally, list items may be removed or incorporated into a list with the operators *delete* and *insert*. The delete operator removes the list member in the current window. If none exists, the operator has no effect. The list member following the one deleted now inherits the current window. The insert operator establishes a new list member immediately before the current window item. The inserted item is now in the current window.

The abstraction *list* is realized using a singly chained representation. To maintain the list, three pointers are established. One points to the first item in the list and is called the list *head*. When the head does not point at anything, then the list is empty. The second pointer is called *current* and addresses the list item in the conceptual window. If no list element is in the window, then current points at nothing. Finally, the pointer *predecessor* is necessary to support insert and delete operations, and refers to the node immediately preceding that in the window. If the first list item is in the window, the predecessor points at nothing. If the window is empty, i.e. current is pointing at nothing, the predecessor is referencing the last item in the list, unless the list is empty, in which case predecessor also points at nothing. The sample list structure we shall operate upon is shown in Fig. 16.11. The data item maintained by this list is an integer value. The discussion assumes the existence of the following declarations:

```
typedef int                     Datatype;

struct node { Datatype          data;
              struct node       *link;
            };
typedef struct node             Node;
typedef Node                    *Ptrnode;

#define NIL                     (Ptrnode)NULL

#define FALSE                   0
#define TRUE                    1
typedef int                     Boolean;

Ptrnode head        = NIL;
Ptrnode predecessor= NIL;
Ptrnode current     = NIL;
```

With this representation, an empty list is denoted by the head pointer addressing no node. This is shown by the list structure shown in Fig. 16.12 and is achieved with the initialization shown earlier. Equally, the current window and predecessor pointers are also initialized to NULL, indicating

head

NULL

Fig. 16.12

that no list element is presently in the window. The two predicates empty and active are readily implemented by testing the appropriate pointer value against NULL:

```
Boolean empty()
   {
     return (head == NIL);
   }

Boolean active()
   {
     return (current != NIL);
   }
```

The operators front and successor unconditionally position the current window. The operation front places that node addressed by head into the current window and causes pointer predecessor to point at nothing. For the sample list, the result is as shown in Fig. 16.13. The effect of then executing the operator successor is to advance the window to the next node in the sequence. This is implemented by using the link pointer of the current node to reposition the window. Similarly, the predecessor pointer assumes the original value for current. Following from Fig. 16.13, the operation successor produces Fig. 16.14.

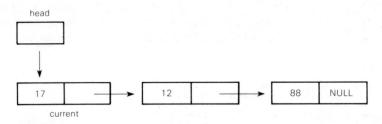

Fig. 16.13

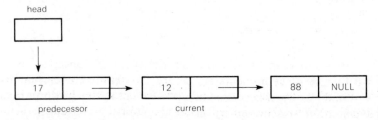

Fig. 16.14

The implementation for these operators is:

```
void front()
   {
      predecessor = NIL;
      current     = head;
   }

void successor()
   {
      if (current != NIL)
         {
            predecessor = current;
            current     = current -> link;
         }
   }
```

The operation *search* conditionally positions the current window. The window is set over the list element at or after the present position which matches the given argument. If no list member satisfies the test, then current is set to point to NULL having exhaustively searched the list (predecessor will address the last list element). The implementation is:

```
void search(item)
   Datatype     item;
   {
      while (current != NIL)
         {
            if (current -> data == item)
               break;
            predecessor = current;
            current     = current -> link;
         }
   }
```

The data item contained in the node referenced by current is obtained by the operator *content*. If no node is in the window, then the delivered value is not guaranteed to be sensible. The code is:

```
void content(item)
   Datatype     *item;
   {
      if (current != NIL)
         *item = current -> data;
   }
```

A similar piece of logic implements the *replace* operator:

```
void replace(item)
   Datatype     item;
   {
      if (current != NIL)
         current -> data = item;
   }
```

Insertions are defined in terms of the window concept. Insertion is defined to take place immediately before the item in the current window. The inserted item then becomes the new element in the window frame. The implementation is achieved by firstly dynamically creating a new node, filling its data field and then having it link to the current element (see

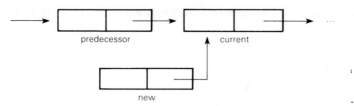

Fig. 16.15

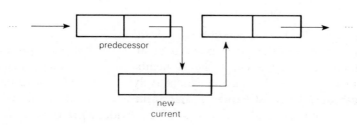

Fig. 16.16

Fig. 16.15). The predecessor addresses this new element which is then adopted as the current window element (see Fig. 16.16).

Special provision must be made for the *boundary problems* when implementing an insert operation. These are the exceptional list forms where, for example, the list is empty or the first list item is in the window. These and other cases are controlled by the following implementation:

```
Boolean insert(item)
  Datatype      item;
  {
    Ptrnode      new;

    if ((new = (Ptrnode)malloc(sizeof(Node))) == NIL)
      return (FALSE);
    else
      {
        new -> data = item;
        new -> link = current;
        if (predecessor != NIL)
          predecessor -> link = new;
        else
          head = new;
        current = new;
        return (TRUE);
      }
  }
```

The final list operator we implement is *delete*. The item deleted from the list is that in the window frame, if one exists. The element which immediately follows the deleted member is now placed in the window. Again, any boundary conditions require special processing. The implementation is:

```
Boolean delete()
  {
    Ptrnode      old;

    if (current != NIL)
      {
        old = current;
        current = current -> link;
        free((char *) old);
        if (predecessor != NIL)
          predecessor -> link = current;
        else
          head = current;
        return (TRUE);
      }
    else
      return (FALSE);
  }
```

It was observed in Chapter 7 that hierarchies of abstractions can be applied to both data and operations. If we consider a *list* as a low-level data abstraction and a *stack* as a higher-level abstraction, then the stack in the last case study may be implemented using these list operations we have defined. Provided that we ensure that the stack operators *push* and *pop* operate on a list with the current window containing the list element referenced by head, then push may be implemented using insert, and operation pop with the combination content and delete. A new implementation for the stack package is then:

```
void push(item)
  Datatype      item;
  {
    if ( ! insert(item))
      stackerror(OVERFLOW);
  }

Datatype pop()
  {
    Datatype    item;

    if ( ! content(&item))
      stackerror(UNDERFLOW);
    else
      {
        (void) delete();
        return (item);
      }
  }
```

Again we reimplement Case study 12.2 as Program 16.2. This time we have three levels of hierarchy. At the topmost level is the application program which implements a postfix expression calculator. This is supported at the intermediate level by a package of stack-handling functions, namely, push and pop. These, in turn, are realized by a package of list processing functions, specifically, insert, delete and content.

Program 16.2

```
/*
**       File:   calc.c
**
**       Reverse Polish calculator. The postfix expression
**       is presented as command line arguments, consisting
**       of a series of operands (numbers) and operators.
**       The supported operators are +, -, * and /.
*/

#include <stdio.h>
#include "stack1.h"

#define EPSILON                 1.0E-4

main (argc, argv)
  int    argc;
  char   *argv[];
  {
    int         arg;                 /* argument counter */
    Stacktype operand;               /* next operand value */

      /* ... see case study 12.2 ... */

  }
```

```
/*
**       File:   stack.h
**
**       Header file for stack handling program. The stack is
**       implemented as a linked list. All stack operations
**       take place at the list head, simulating the stack top.
**       The stack abstraction is implemented using a list
**       abstraction as a lower level hierarchy.
*/

typedef double         Stacktype;

extern void      push ();                /* external references */
extern Stacktype pop ();
```

```
/*
**       File:   stack.c
**
**       Implementation package for stacks of floating point
**       numbers.
*/

#include <stdio.h>
#include "stack1.h"
#include "list1.h"

#define UNDERFLOW         0
#define OVERFLOW          1

void    stackerror ();

void    push (item)
  Stacktype      item;
  {
    if ( ! insert (item))
      stackerror (OVERFLOW);
  }
```

```
Stacktype pop ()
  {
    Stacktype    item;

    if ( ! content (&item))
      stackerror (UNDERFLOW);
    else
      {
        (void) delete ();
        return (item);
      }
  }


static void stackerror (code)
  int    code;
  {
    switch (code)
      {
        case OVERFLOW   :
                fprintf (stderr, "Stack overflow\n"); break;
        case UNDERFLOW  :
                fprintf (stderr, "Stack underflow\n"); break;
      }

    exit (1);
  }


/*
**      Header file for a list abstraction. Each node in
**      the list carries a STACKTYPE data item. The list
**      is singly chained, and maintained by the pointers
**      head, current and predecessor.
*/

struct node { Stacktype           data;
              struct node         *link;
            };
typedef struct node                 Node;
typedef Node                        *Ptrnode;

#define NIL                         (Ptrnode) NULL

#define FALSE                       0
#define TRUE                        1
typedef int                         Boolean;

extern Boolean insert ();                      /* external references */
extern Boolean delete ();
extern Boolean content ();


/*
**      Implementation of a list abstraction.
*/

#include <stdio.h>
#include "stack1.h"
#include "list1.h"

static Ptrnode head      = NIL;
static Ptrnode current   = NIL;
static Ptrnode predecessor = NIL;

extern char *malloc ();
extern void free ();

Boolean insert (item)
  Stacktype      item;
  {
    .....
  }
```

```
Boolean delete ()
   {
       . . . . .
   }



Boolean content (item)
   Stacktype      *item;
   {
      if (current != NIL)
         {
            *item = current -> data;
            return (TRUE);
         }
      else
         return (FALSE);
   }
```

Case study 16.1: Word concordance (revisited)

Case study 12.1 produced a word concordance for some input text. The concordance consisted of an alphabetical list of all the distinct words in the text. In that implementation, the word list is realized using an array of words. A significant characteristic of this particular implementation is that movement of existing list elements is required when a new word is inserted into its correct alphabetical position in the array. Further, some predetermined limit on the number of list elements must be established at compile time.

The limitations of the array representation may be overcome by using a linked list representation. Inserting items in the list is effected by adjustments to pointers. Subject to the amount of available dynamic memory, no set limit is imposed on the length of the list.

In the original concordance program, an ordered list was maintained. In this way, the overhead of performing a sort is avoided. Ordered lists can be maintained using our existing list abstraction. The only required modification is that the search operator terminates as soon as an entry with a value greater than or equal to the search key is found. A new word is then inserted immediately before this entry.

Firstly, the program files for the list abstraction:

```
/*
**       File: list.h
**
**       Header file and interface for a singly chained
**       linked list. Each list node carries a string data
**       item.
*/

#define FALSE          0
#define TRUE           1
typedef int            Boolean;

extern Boolean empty (), active ();
extern void    front (), successor (), search (),
               content (), replace ();
extern Boolean insert ();
extern void    delete ();
```

```
/*
**        File:   list.c
**
**        Implementation of a singly chained linked list.
*/

#include <stdio.h>
#include "list2.h"
#include "wordlist.h"

struct node { char              data[TEXTSIZE];
              struct node       *link;
            };
typedef struct node             Node;
typedef Node                    *Ptrnode;

#define NIL                     (Ptrnode)NULL

static Ptrnode head = NIL;                              /* initially empty */
static Ptrnode predecessor = NIL, current = NIL;

extern char *malloc ();
extern void free ();

Boolean empty ()
  {
    return (head == NIL);
  }


Boolean active ()
  {
    return (current != NIL);
  }


void front ()
  {
    predecessor = NIL;
    current = head;
  }


void successor ()
  {
    if (current != NIL)
      {
        predecessor = current;
        current = current -> link;
      }
  }


void search (item)
  char *item;
  {
    while (current != NIL)
      {
        if (strcmp (current -> data, item) >= 0)
          break;
        predecessor = current;
        current = current -> link;
      }
  }


void content (item)
  char *item;
  {
    if (current != NIL)
      strcpy (item, current -> data);
  }
```

```
void replace (item)
  char *item;
  {
    if (current != NIL)
      strcpy (current -> data, item);
  }


Boolean insert (item)
  char   *item;
  {
    Ptrnode      new;

    if ((new = (Ptrnode) malloc (sizeof (Node))) == NIL)
      return (FALSE);
    else
      {
        strcpy (new -> data, item);
        new -> link = current;
        if (predecessor != NIL)
          predecessor -> link = new;
        else
          head = new;

        current = new;
        return (TRUE);
      }
  }


void delete ()
  {
    Ptrnode      old;

    if (current != NIL)
      {
        old = current;
        current = current -> link;
        free ((char *) old);
        if (predecessor != NIL)
          predecessor -> link = current;
        else
          head = current;
      }
  }
```

Those characteristics of the word list abstraction required by the program are the operators *insertword* and *printwords*. Where the level of abstraction is the problem domain, then the implementation details of these operators are totally removed from the application. The word list operators are realized in terms of the above list operators, giving rise to a hierarchy of levels of abstraction.

Using the list operators, printwords is implemented by first positioning the window at the front of the list. Whilst the window addresses an active cell, the content is examined and the window then advances to the next adjacent element.

To insert a word into the list, a search of the existing list is performed. If no such word is found, then a new entry is made with the correct alphabetical position. If the word already exists as a member of the list, then this new word is discarded.

The implementation is:

```
/*
**       File:   wordlist.h
*/

#define WORDSIZE        20
#define TEXTSIZE        (WORDSIZE + 1)

extern void insertword (), printwords ();


/*
**       File:   wordlist.c
*/

#include <stdio.h>
#include "list2.h"
#include "wordlist.h"

void syserr ();                             /* forward reference */

void printwords ()
  {
    char        word[TEXTSIZE];

    front ();
    while (active ())
      {
        content (word);
        printf ("%s\n", word);
        successor ();
      }
  }

void insertword (word)
  char   *word;
  {
    char        item[TEXTSIZE];

    front ();
    search (word);

    if (active ())
      {
        content (item);
        if (strcmp (item, word) != 0)
          if (! insert (word))
            syserr (100, "%s\n", "word list overflow");
      }
    else if (! insert (word))
      syserr (101, "%s\n", "word list overflow");
  }

 static void syserr (errcode, message, argument)
   int    errcode;
   char   *message, *argument;
   {
     fprintf (stderr, "[error %2d]: ", errcode);
     fprintf (stderr, message, argument);

     exit (errcode);
   }
```

Finally, the program is implemented. The program is modified from the original to read the text from a file, the name of which is given as the program command line argument. Otherwise, the logic is the same as in the original version.

```
/*
**          File:   case16.1.c
*/

#include <stdio.h>
#include "wordlist.h"

#define READONLY                "r"
#define TERMINATOR              "zzz"

main (argc, argv)
    int     argc;
    char    *argv[];
    {
        FILE        *fopen (), *fp;
        int         fclose ();
        char        word[TEXTSIZE];

        if (argc != 2)
            fprintf (stderr, "Usage: %s filename\n", argv[0]);
        else if ((fp = fopen (argv[1], READONLY)) == NULL)
            fprintf (stderr, "%s: cannot open %s\n", argv[0], argv[1]);
        else
            {
                fscanf (fp, "%s", word);
                while (strcmp (word, TERMINATOR) != 0)
                    {
                        insertword (word);
                        fscanf (fp, "%s", word);
                    }
                fclose (fp);

                printwords ();
            }
    }
```

16.3 Binary trees

In the Case study 12.1 (word concordance), the *sequential search* algorithm was used to retrieve information from an ordered array (see function insertword). The difficulty with this data structure is that it is very costly to maintain if frequent insertions and deletions are required. The linked list data structure used in the revised version (Case study 16.1) avoids these difficulties but still only supports sequential searching. The more efficient *binary search* is preferred if a suitable data structure can be found.

Since sequential searching is costly for long lists, it is desirable to have a data structure that implements efficient insertions and deletions and can also be searched efficiently. The linked data structure that meets these requirements is the *binary tree*. The binary tree data structure has nodes each having two links or pointers associated with it, one pointing to the root of its left subtree and the second pointing to the root of its right subtree. This is shown in Fig. 16.17.

In particular, an *ordered* binary tree is a finite set of nodes which is either empty or consists of a root node as the ancestor of two disjoint binary trees called the left subtree and the right subtree. Nodes of the left subtree satisfy the ordering relation (e.g. alphabetical or numerical) when compared with nodes of the right subtree. At any level in the tree, it is permissible for either

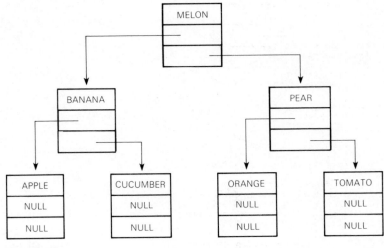

Fig. 16.17

or both of the subtrees to be empty. Fig. 16.17 is then an instance of an ordered binary tree.

The characteristic of the binary tree is that its definition is *recursive*. Each tree node has two descendants associated with it, both of which are the roots of disjoint subtrees. The necessary definitions to describe a binary tree of Datatype values are:

```
struct node {   Datatype        data;
                struct node     *left;
                struct node     *right;
            };
typedef struct node             Node;
typedef Node                    *Ptrnode;
```

The members *left* and *right* are pointer variables containing the addresses of other tree nodes. As a special case, these members may be the coerced value (Ptrnode)NULL, denoting no further descendants.

Let us now declare some variables of type Node:

```
Node                    top,
            left,                   right,
    leftleft, leftright,    rightleft, rightright;
```

and perform some assignments on these structures:

```
top.data         = 40;
left.data        = 20;
leftleft.data    = 10;
leftright.data   = 30;
right.data       = 60;
rightleft.data   = 50;
rightright.data  = 70;
```

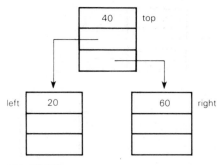

Fig. 16.18

We assume in this instance that Datatype is defined as:

typedef int   Datatype;

A tree structure can be established by having the *left* member of *top* address the node *left*, and the *right* member of *top* address the node *right*. The statements are:

top.left   = &left;
top.right   = &right;

Pictorially, the effect of these pointer assignments is as shown in Fig. 16.18. Continuing with these pointer assignments:

left.left   = &leftleft;
left.right   = &leftright;
right.left   = &rightleft;
right.right   = &rightright;
leftleft.left   = (Ptrnode)NULL;
leftleft.right   = (Ptrnode)NULL;
leftright.left   = (Ptrnode)NULL;
leftright.right = (Ptrnode)NULL;
rightleft.left   = (Ptrnode)NULL;
rightleft.right = (Ptrnode)NULL;
rightright.left = (Ptrnode)NULL;
rightright.right = (Ptrnode)NULL;

we ultimately construct the binary tree in Fig. 16.19.

To reference the data items in this tree, there are several equivalent expressions. To retrieve the data item '40', we use:

top.data

The expression:

top.right

is an object of type pointer to a struct node. It does, of course, point to the node called right. From section 15.5, a pointer to a structure permits a

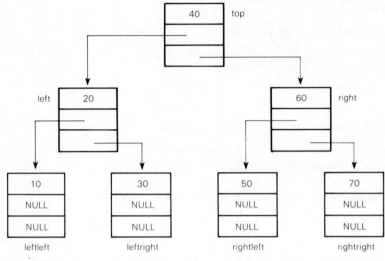

Fig. 16.19

member of that structure to be accessed. Two expressions to reference the data value '60' are:

  right.data

or:

  top.right → data

Similarly, the data item '30' can be accessed by:

    leftright.data
  or: left.right → data
  or: top.left → right → data

The essential feature here is that members of the objects immediately below the top node are accessible not only by their name (e.g. leftright.data) but also anonymously through the pointers which refer to them (e.g. top.left → right → data). If we have a variable of type Ptrnode called *root*, declared and initialized by:

  Ptrnode root = ⊤

then the complete tree is accessible through root and its pointers.

We can dispense completely with the named nodes and operate solely with anonymous nodes if each node can be created dynamically. Like linear linked lists, this is achieved with the standard library function malloc. If ptrnode is declared as:

  Ptrnode   ptrnode;

then:

ptrnode = (Ptrnode) malloc(sizeof(Node));

causes space for one tree Node to be dynamically created and addressed by the variable ptrnode. The node can then be attached to the tree structure at some appropriate point.

16.4 Binary tree processing

There are numerous ways to systematically examine all the nodes of a binary tree exactly once. Several *traversal* methods are important because of the order superimposed on the data stored in the tree. A common task is to print in order the data items held in an ordered binary tree. Consider the example tree of the previous section. The numerical ordering of this data set is:

10, 20, 30, 40, 50, 60 and 70

When data items are stored in an ordered binary tree and printed in order, the tree traversal is called *inorder*.

To perform this inorder traversal of the tree, we initially start with a pointer to the root node. The data item at the node addressed by the variable root is the value 40. Before we can print this value in its correct sequential order, we must first print all the data items in the subtree immediately to the left of the root node (data values 10, 20 and 30). All the nodes in the right subtree (data values 50, 60 and 70) are printed after the root data item. The printing order is therefore:

(a) print all the data items in the left subtree of root;
(b) print the data item at the root;
(c) print all the data items in the right subtree of root.

This sequence suggests that recursion can be used to perform the task, since as we move from the root to the left subtree, we actually apply the *same* process to the root of this subtree. Similarly with the right subtree. To construct a recursive function we refine steps (a) and (c) and determine the termination condition for the recursive calls. Consider that the recursive function is called inorder and has the declaration:

void inorder(r)
    Ptrnode r;

The argument r represents the root of the tree to be printed, and would initially be called by:

inorder(root);

for the tree.

Step (a) of the process amounts to making a recursive call on inorder applied to the root of the subtree to the left of r:

    inorder(r → left);

Similarly, the recursive call:

    inorder(r → right);

descends to the root of the right subtree of the current node. The statements we have in our recursive implementation of inorder are then:

    inorder(r → left);
    printf("%d\n", r → data);
    inorder(r → right);

A series of these recursive calls follow the left subtrees until we encounter the node containing the data item '10'. When we reach this point, it is found to have no left subtree. It follows that when we process a subtree whose root is NULL the recursive process terminates. The three statements are then guarded by a suitable conditional. The completed version of inorder is then:

```
void inorder(r)
   Ptrnode r;
   {
      if (r ! = (Ptrnode)NULL)
         {
            inorder(r → left);
            printf("%d\n", r → data);
            inorder(r → right);
         }
   }
```

Traversing a binary tree using this function is illustrated in the following program. The example binary tree is first established as shown above, then the function is called to traverse the tree printing the data items in ascending order.

Program 16.3

```
/*
**        Establish an ordered binary tree of height
**        two and demonstrate an inorder traversal of the
**        structure.
*/

#include <stdio.h>

typedef int                        Datatype;
struct node { Datatype             data;
              struct node          *left;
              struct node          *right;
            };
typedef struct node                Node;
typedef Node                       *Ptrnode;
#define NIL                        (Ptrnode)NULL
```

```
void inorder();                      /* forward reference */

main()
  {
    Node           top, left, right,
                   leftleft, leftright, rightleft, rightright;
    Ptrnode        root;

    root = &top;
    top.data = 40;         top.left = &left;
        top.right = &right;
    left.data = 20;        left.left = &leftleft;
        left.right = &leftright;
    right.data = 60;       right.left = &rightleft;
        right.right = &rightright;
    leftleft.data = 10; leftleft.left = leftleft.right = NIL;
    leftright.data = 30;leftright.left = leftright.right = NIL;
    rightleft.data = 50;rightleft.left = rightleft.right = NIL;
    rightright.data =70;rightright.left = rightright.right = NIL;

    inorder(root);
  }


void inorder(root)
  Ptrnode          root;                    /* of subtree */
  {
    if (root != NIL)                        /* a further subtree? */
      {
        inorder(root -> left);              /* left side first */
        printf("%d\n", root -> data);       /* root node data item */
        inorder(root -> right); /* then traverse right side */
      }
  }
```

Two other methods for binary tree traversal are called *preorder* and *postorder*. They differ from each other and from inorder traversal in the order in which they visit the roots with respect to the left and right subtrees. We leave implementing these two traversals as exercises.

The fundamental operations performed on an ordered binary tree are similar to those for a linked list and include:

empty   :determine whether or not there are any nodes in the tree. Return TRUE or FALSE

active   :determine if the current window is actively addressing a tree node

setwindow   :position the window on the root node of the tree if it exists

search(item)   :position the window to the tree node containing item. If no member matches, then active is FALSE

insert(item)   :establish a new tree node containing item (unless item is a duplicate) such that the data ordering is maintained

inorder(root)   :visit and print the data items in
preorder(root)   the tree in some prescribed order.
postorder(root)

Using the binary tree containing the integer data items 10, 20, 30, etc., we have the following definitions:

```
typedef int                         Datatype;
struct node { Datatype              data;
              struct node  *left;
              struct node  *right;
            };
typedef struct node                 Node;
typedef Node                        *Ptrnode;

#define NIL                         (Ptrnode)NULL
```

To manipulate such a tree, three tree pointers are maintained. They are *root* (a pointer to the root node of the tree), *current* (a pointer to the tree node in the current window) and *predecessor* (a pointer to the tree node which is the immediate ancestor of the node in the current window). The pointer values NIL report special cases. The declarations are:

Ptrnode root   = NIL;
Ptrnode current   = NIL;
Ptrnode predecessor = NIL;

The two predicates empty and active are easily implemented by comparing the correct pointers against NULL:

```
Boolean empty()
   {
      return (root == NIL);
   }

Boolean active()
   {
      return (current != NIL);
   }
```

The unconditional operator *setwindow* places the current window on the root node of the tree. If this node does not exist because the tree is empty, then current is set to NULL. In either case, predecessor is set to NULL.

```
void setwindow()
   {
      predecessor = NIL;
      current     = root;
   }
```

In common with many recursively defined data structures such as trees, recursive programming offers a direct and natural mechanism to implement data structured algorithms. For example, the operation search can be implemented by a recursive function which inspects the value at the node. If this node does not contain the required value, the function calls itself recursively to search either the left or the right subtree.

As might be expected, there are many similarities between the binary search algorithm on an ordered data set and the search of a linked binary tree. The binary search first operates by comparing the search key with the middle entry of the set. This is equivalent to comparing the search key with the data item at the binary tree root. If the search key does not match the middle entry, the comparison performed in the binary search determines whether now to search the first half or the second half of the data set. With the ordered binary tree, the equivalent is to process the left or right subtrees. The algorithm is:

IF search key does not match data item at current root
THEN
  IF search item before data item at current root
  THEN
    search in left subtree of current root
  ELSE
    search in right subtree of current root
  ENDIF
ENDIF

The resulting recursive function can be programmed immediately from this logic:

```
void search(item)
  Datatype      item;
  {
    if (current != NIL)
      if (item != current -> data)
        {
          predecessor = current;
          current     = item < current -> data ?
                        current -> left :
                        current -> right;

          search(item);
        }
  }
```

The tree insertion algorithm is similar to that performing an insertion to a linked list. First, the tree insert algorithm must determine where in the tree the inserted item is to be placed, and can be obtained by applying the search

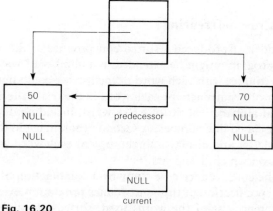

Fig. 16.20

algorithm. Second, the insertion is achieved by adjusting the necessary pointers.

To illustrate, consider inserting the data value 55 into the example tree. Function search sets current to NULL, indicating that no such entry presently exists in the tree. The pointers within the tree fragment are as shown in Fig. 16.20. The node containing the new data value links to that referenced by predecessor. The relationship to this node is governed according to whether the data value to be inserted is numerically before or after 50. This relationship determines whether the new node links to the left or the right of the node addressed by predecessor.

```
Boolean insert(item)
   Datatype       item;
   {
      Ptrnode          new;

      setwindow();
      search(item);

      if (current == NIL)
         if ((new = (Ptrnode) malloc(sizeof(Node))) == NIL)
            return (FALSE);
         else
            {
               current = new;
               new -> data = item;
               new -> left = new -> right = NIL;
               if (predecessor != NIL)
                  {
                     if (item < predecessor -> data)
                        predecessor -> left = new;
                     else
                        predecessor -> right = new;
                  }
               else
                  root = new;

               return (TRUE);
            }
      return (TRUE);
   }
```

Case study 16.2: Cross referencing

Case studies 12.1 and 16.1 produced a sorted concordance of the words in an input text. This program might be extended in a number of ways. If we associate an integer counter with each word in the list, we could maintain a count of the number of occurrences of each word in the text. Alternatively, we might produce an alphabetical list of every word, including duplicates, together with an associated line number. A second program could then read the output from the latter and display a single copy of each word with a list of the line numbers on which it appears.

We shall extend the concordance case study by a combination of the last two proposals. The specification of the concordance program is extended to produce a cross-reference list of the words used, sorted into alphabetical

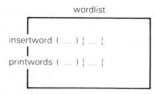

<blockquote>
wordlist

insertword (...) { ... }

printwords (...) { ... }
</blockquote>

Fig. 16.21

order, and including a list of the line numbers, in ascending order, on which each word appears.

In this new problem, there are two abstractions operating:

(a) a stream of words and associated line numbers extracted from the input file, one word at a time;
(b) a list of the unique words maintained in dictionary order together with the line number list for every word.

We shall consider the input stream abstraction later. To implement the program, the word list abstraction must support operations to:

(a) record a word and its line number in the list;
(b) print the entire word list content with a line number list for every word.

Following the organization of Case study 16.1, and using our usual notation, an outline of the associated module is given in Fig. 16.21. The word list abstraction can be realized as an ordered binary tree. The insertword operation can be implemented as we described for a general binary tree insertion. The operation printwords follows the logic for inorder traversal of a binary tree.

To complete the program implementation, we must also consider the line number list. The necessary operations are:

(a) record a new line number in the list for a given word;
(b) print the entire line number list content in numerical order for a given word.

Since these operations are subsumed by the operations insertword and printwords, they are hidden functions in the word list module (see Fig. 16.22).

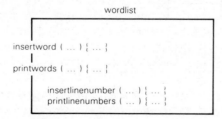

Fig. 16.22

A second abstraction is now identified − the list of occurrences or line numbers associated with each word. Because this list will grow dynamically and because its length is indeterminate, the list is represented as a singly chained linked list. Each new line number inserted into the list is appended on to the end of the list. If each occurrence of a word appears on different lines, then as the lines are read sequentially, appending on to the end of the list maintains line number order. If the inserted line number is the same as the final entry in the list, then we have a duplicate of a word appearing on the same line, and the inserted line number will be ignored.

The only outstanding problem is how to associate a list of line numbers with one of the words in the word list. The word list is maintained as an ordered binary tree. The line number list is a linked list with new entries appended on to the end of the list. The association between a word in the word list tree and a list of line numbers is achieved by two auxiliary pointers from the tree node of the word list to the line number list. The two pointers address the first and last line number nodes. The last line number pointer is reserved so that appending new line numbers can be done efficiently. The pointers are known as *head* and *tail*. If, for example, the input word 'the' associates with line numbers 1 and 3, then a possible fragment of this data structure might contain the data shown in Fig. 16.23.

In the original version, no account was taken of the whitespace characters between the input words, other than as separators. In this new problem we must identify all occurrences of newline symbols to maintain the correct line count. The second program abstraction is thus a stream of input characters formed into words and separated by whitespace. The separators may include newline symbols which must be correctly processed. The operator

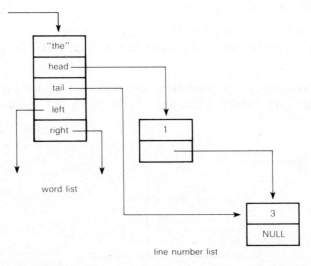

word list

line number list

Fig. 16.23

is:

nextword   :   which delivers the next input word and its source text
line number. If the end of file is determined, an empty
word is returned.

The program listings follow:

```
/*
**       File:    case16.2.c
**
**       Produce a cross reference list of the words
**       in a file. The list is alphabetically printed
**       one word per line, with each word followed by
**       a list of the line numbers on which that word
**       occurs. Duplicate appearances on a line are
**       reported once.
*/

#include <stdio.h>
#include "word16.2.h"
#include "list16.2.h"

#define READONLY                "r"

main (argc, argv)
  int    argc;
  char   *argv[];
  {
    FILE           *fopen (), *fp;
    int            fclose ();
    char           word[TEXTSIZE];
    unsigned int   linenumber;

    if (argc != 2)
      fprintf (stderr, "Usage: %s filename\n", argv[0]);
    else if ((fp = fopen (argv[1], READONLY)) == NULL)
      fprintf (stderr, "%s: cannot open %s\n", argv[0], argv[1]);
    else
      {
        while ( nextword (fp, word, &linenumber),
                        strcmp (word, "") != 0)
          {
          if ( ! insertword (word, linenumber))
              {
                fprintf (stderr, "Insufficient memory\n");
                exit (1);
              }
          }

        fclose (fp);
        printwords ();
      }
  }



/*
**       File:    word16.2.h
**
**       Input stream abstraction. The end of file
**       status is determined by the standard library
**       function. The next word from the input stream
**       together with text line number is returned by
**       function nextword.
*/

extern void nextword ();
```

```
/*
**        File:    word16.2.c
**
**        Implementation module for the input stream
**        abstraction. Function nextword obtains the next
**        word and its linenumber from the nominated file.
*/

#include <stdio.h>

#define BLANK            ' '
#define TAB              '\t'
#define NEWLINE          '\n'
typedef int              character;

#define FOREVER          for(;;)

static unsigned int linenumber = 1;      /* first line */

static character nextchar ();            /* forward reference */

void nextword (fp, word, lineno)
  FILE          *fp;
  char          *word;
  unsigned int  *lineno;
  {
    character ch;

    *word = NULL;
    FOREVER
      {
        ch = nextchar (fp);
        if (ch == EOF)
          return;
        if (ch != BLANK && ch != TAB)
          break;
      }

    *lineno = linenumber;
    *word++ = ch;
    FOREVER
      {
        ch = nextchar (fp);
        if (ch == BLANK || ch == TAB)
          break;
        *word++ = ch;
      }

    *word = NULL;
  }




static character nextchar (fp)
  FILE  *fp;
  {
    character ch;

    ch = agetc(fp);
    if (ch == EOF)
      return (EOF);
    else if (ch == NEWLINE)
      {
        linenumber++;
        return (BLANK);
      }
    else
      return (ch);
  }
```

```
/*
**         File:     list16.2.h
**
**         List of words abstraction. The two supported
**         operations are insertword and printwords.
*/

#define FALSE               0
#define TRUE                1
typedef int                 Boolean;

#define WORDSIZE            20
#define TEXTSIZE            (WORDSIZE + 1)

extern void printwords ();
extern Boolean insertword ();


/*
**         File:     list16.2.c
**
**         Implementation of the word list abstraction.
**         The implementation is in two parts: one for the
**         word list and one for the line number list.
**         Both are represented as ordered binary trees
**         and hence the coding is repeated.
**
**         PART ONE         LINE NUMBER LIST
*/

#include <stdio.h>
#include "list16.2.h"

struct linenode { unsigned int          linenumber;      /* template */
                  struct linenode        *link;
                };
typedef struct linenode                 Linenode;
typedef Linenode                        *Ptrlinenode;

#define LINENIL                         (Ptrlinenode)NULL


static Ptrlinenode     lineroot, linecurrent, linepredecessor;


extern char *malloc ();

static void lineprint (root)             /* perform a traversal */
  Ptrlinenode    root;                   /* of the linenumber list */
  {                                      /* printing the values */
    if (root != LINENIL)                 /* an empty list? */
      {
        printf("%6d", root -> linenumber); /* first, the left node */
        lineprint(root -> link);           /* then the right list */
      }
  }


static Ptrlinenode lineinsert (lineno, tail) /* insert a linenumber */
  unsigned int   lineno;                 /* into ordered linked */
  Ptrlinenode    tail;                   /* list for current word */
  {
    Ptrlinenode new;

    if (tail != LINENIL)
      {
        if (tail -> linenumber == lineno)
          return (tail);                      /* ignore duplicate */
        else if ((new =
                (Ptrlinenode) malloc(sizeof(Linenode))) == LINENIL)
          return (LINENIL);                        /* no room */
```

```
        else
          {
            new -> linenumber = lineno;            /* append to tail */
            new -> link = LINENIL;
            tail -> link = new;
            return (new);
          }
      }
    else if ((new =
              (Ptrlinenode) malloc(sizeof(Linenode))) == LINENIL)
      return (LINENIL);
    else
      {
        new -> linenumber = lineno;                /* first list node */
        new -> link = LINENIL;
        return (new);
      }
  }


/*
**       PART TWO         WORD LIST ABSTRACTION
*/

struct wordnode { char                word[TEXTSIZE];
                  Ptrlinenode         head;
                  Ptrlinenode         tail;
                  struct wordnode     *left;
                  struct wordnode     *right;
                };
typedef struct wordnode               Wordnode;
typedef Wordnode                      *Ptrwordnode;

#define WORDNIL                       (Ptrwordnode)NULL


static Ptrwordnode      wordroot = WORDNIL, wordcurrent,
                        wordpredecessor;


static void wordprint(root)        /* inorder tree traversal */
  Ptrwordnode    root;             /* printing each node and the */
  {                                /* line numbers */
    if (root != WORDNIL)           /* another subtree? */
      {
        wordprint(root -> left);
        printf("%-20s:", root -> word);
        lineprint(root -> head);
        putchar('\n');
        wordprint(root -> right);
      }
  }


void printwords()
  {
    wordprint(wordroot);
  }


static void setword()                      /* initialize current and */
  {                                        /* predecessor to the word */
    wordpredecessor = WORDNIL;             /* tree root */
    wordcurrent     = wordroot;
  }

static void wordsearch(newword)
  char   *newword;
  {
    int compare;
```

```
        if (wordcurrent != WORDNIL)            /* another subtree? */
          if ((compare = strcmp(newword, wordcurrent -> word)) != 0)
            {
              wordpredecessor = wordcurrent;        /* advance */
              wordcurrent = compare < 0 ?
                                  wordcurrent -> left :
                                  wordcurrent -> right;
              wordsearch(newword);
            }
    }


Boolean insertword(newword, newline)      /* insert a word and */
  char           *newword;                /* line number into list */
  unsigned int    newline;
  {
    Ptrwordnode new;

    setword();
    wordsearch(newword);

    if (wordcurrent != WORDNIL)            /* existing word? */
      {
        if ((wordcurrent -> tail =
                lineinsert(newline, wordcurrent -> tail)) != LINENIL)
          return (TRUE);
        else
          return (FALSE);
      }
    else if ((new =
                (Ptrwordnode) malloc(sizeof(Wordnode))) == WORDNIL)
      return (FALSE);                       /* no room! */
    else
      {
        wordcurrent = new;
        strcpy(new -> word, newword);
        new -> left = new -> right = WORDNIL;

        wordcurrent -> head =
                wordcurrent -> tail = lineinsert(newline, LINENIL);
        if (wordcurrent -> tail == LINENIL)
          return (FALSE);

        if (wordpredecessor != WORDNIL) /* ancestor? */
          {
            if (strcmp(newword, wordpredecessor -> word) < 0)
              wordpredecessor -> left = new;
            else
              wordpredecessor -> right = new;
          }
        else
          wordroot = new;

        return (TRUE);

      }
  }
```

16.5 Summary

1. Static data objects are used to build dynamic data structures. These static objects, or *nodes*, contain pointers to other such nodes and are known as *self-referential* structures. The nature of the linkages reflects the underlying data structure.
2. A singly chained linked list is a dynamic data structure composed of one or more nodes chained together by single pointers. Variations on singly

chained lists include the *circular* list (see Exercise 7) and the *doubly linked* list (see Exercise 5).
3. A tree is a non-linear data structure with a root node that points to zero or more subtrees. In particular, in a binary tree, each parent may have at most two descendants.

16.6 Exercises

1. Write a function that determines the length of a singly chained linked list of the form shown in section 16.2.

2. Write a C function *merge* which merges two ordered lists. The function header is:

   Ptrnode merge(p1, p2)
     Ptrnode p1, p2;

   where p1 and p2 are pointers to the first node of each list. The function should dynamically create the result list and return a pointer to its first element as the function value.

3. Write a C function *reverse*:

   Ptrnode reverse(p)
     Ptrnode p;

   which reverses the order of the nodes in a singly chained list pointed to by p, and returns a pointer to the resulting list.

4. Write a function to sort a list into ascending order.

5. A *doubly linked* list is one in which each node contains a pointer to the preceding node in the list as well as a pointer to the next in the list. Provide an appropriate structure definition for such a list and give implementations for the list abstraction of section 16.2.

6. In Program 16.2, a stack was realized as a singly chained linked list. In a similar manner, show how a *queue* (see Case study 13.1) would be realized by a similar structure.

7. A *circular* list is one in which the final node of a singly chained list is made to point to the first node in the list. Show how a circular list is used to implement a queue.

8. Provide functions preorder and postorder that are the counterparts of the function inorder given in section 16.4.

9. Write a function that counts the number of leaf nodes in a binary tree.

10. Two binary trees are said to be equal if they have the same structure and if the contents of the data fields of the corresponding nodes in the tree are the same. Write a C function of two tree arguments that traverses each tree in preorder and determines if they are equal.

Operations on bits

It was remarked in Chapter 1 that C was originally conceived as a systems programming language to implement the UNIX operating system. A particular feature of this activity is the processing of individual bit patterns within a computer word. These facilities are supported in C by the provision of a number of *bitwise operators*.

17.1 Bitwise operators and expressions

In addition to the bit fields associated with structured values, C also supports six operators to manipulate bit values of integral types. The six bitwise operators are shown in Table 17.1.

Like all C operators, the bitwise operators have rules of precedence and associativity which determine how expressions involving these and other operators are evaluated. Further, all these bitwise operators, except the unary complement, operate in conjunction with the assignment operator. The full table of operators is given in Appendix E.

All the bitwise operators apply to integer types only. Thus these operators may not be applied to types float and double. We will restrict our discussion to a machine with a 16-bit, 2s complement representation for a standard-sized int. Other architectures are processed similarly.

The bitwise *complement operator* ˜, also known as the 'one's complement operator', computes the bitwise negation of its single operand. The usual

Table 17.1

Category	Bitwise operator	Symbol
Bitwise operators	(Unary) bitwise complement	˜
	Bitwise and	&
	Bitwise or	¦
	Bitwise exclusive or	^
Shift operators	Left shift	《
	Right shift	》

Table 17.2

x	y	x & y	x ¦ y	x ^ y
0	0	0	0	0
0	1	0	1	1
1	0	0	1	1
1	1	1	1	0

unary conversions apply to the operand. Every bit in the binary representation of the result is the inverse or complement of the operand. If the integer variable t has decimal value 12, the binary representation for this value is:

0000000000001100

then ~t has the binary representation:

1111111111110011

This 2s complement value equates to decimal -13.

The bitwise operators *and* (&), *or* (¦) and *exclusive or* (^) are binary operators. Each operand is treated in terms of its binary representation. Each bit of the result is computed by applying the operators *and*, *or* or *exclusive or* to the corresponding bits of both operands. The semantics of these three operators are given by Table 17.2.

In the context of the following declarations and initializations:

int p = 123, q = -17;

Table 17.3 shows a series of expressions, the binary representation of the result of evaluating the expression, and the corresponding decimal value.

A *mask* is used to extract the desired bit pattern from an expression. For example, the int constant 3 has the binary representation:

0000 0000 0000 0011

and can be used in conjunction with the bitwise *and* operator to determine the low-order 2 bits of an int expression value. For example, the expression:

y = x & 3;

assigns to y the rightmost (least significant) 2 bits of the integer variable x. If x has the value 17 (binary: 0000000000010001), then y has the value 1 (binary: 0000000000000001). To find the value of a particular group of bits in an expression, a mask with 1 in those bit positions and 0 elsewhere is used. Thus, the hexadecimal constant 0x30 is a mask for bits 5 and 6 from the right.

To clear the low-order byte of a 16-bit integer, the mask 0xFF00 can be used. To allow the code to work properly, independent of the size of an

Table 17.3

p	0000 0000 0111 1011	123
q	1111 1111 1110 1111	− 17
p & q	0000 0000 0110 1011	107
p ¦ q	1111 1111 1111 1111	− 1
p ˆ q	1111 1111 1001 0100	− 108

integer, the bitwise complement can be used to construct the necessary mask:

high_byte = word & (˜0xFF)

Finally, there are the *shift* operators. Both are binary operators with two integral operands. The right operand is converted to an int. The type of the expression result is that of its left operand. The *left* shift operator ⟨⟨ shifts the binary representation of its left operand the number of places to the left as specified by the right operand. The low order bits are zero filled. The *right shift* operator ⟩⟩ shifts the binary representation of its left operand the number of places to the right as specified by its right operand. The bits shifted in from the left are machine dependent. If the left operand is unsigned, then zeros are shifted in from the left. If the left operand is a signed operand, then whether zeros or ones are shifted in is at the discretion of the implementor. On some implementations, zeros are always shifted in; on others the leftmost sign bit is regenerated as the shifted in bit. Right shifting a signed value is, therefore, highly non-portable and should be avoided. Table 17.4 shows a number of expressions, the binary representation after evaluating the result, and the corresponding decimal value. The integer variable p is assumed to have the decimal value 123.

Bitwise expression can be used for data compression, making useful savings in program storage requirements. For example, on a machine with 32-bit unsigned int, four bytes may be packed into one int. The function *pack* uses the bitwise operators to perform byte-by-byte packing:

```
unsigned int pack(a, b, c, d)
  char a, b, c, d;
  {
    unsigned int packed;

    packed = a;
    packed = (packed ⟨⟨ 8) ¦ b;
    packed = (packed ⟨⟨ 8) ¦ c;
    packed = (packed ⟨⟨ 8) ¦ d:

    return (packed);
  }
```

Table 17.4

Expression	Binary representation	Decimal value
p	0000 0000 0111 1011	123
p ⟪ 4	0000 0111 1011 0000	1968
p ⟫ 2	0000 0000 0001 1110	30
(p ⟫ 2) & 0xF	0000 0000 0000 1110	14

The four bytes in a packed unsigned integer can be recovered with the function *unpack*:

```
#define MASK      0xFF

void unpack(p, a, b, c, d)
   unsigned int p;
   char *a, *b, *c, *d;
   {
     *d = p & MASK;
     *c = (p ⟫ 8) & MASK;
     *b = (p ⟫ 16) & MASK;
     *a = (p ⟫ 24) & MASK;
   }
```

Program 15.8 used bit fields to pack the elements of a date. We repeat the same problem in Program 17.1, this time using the bitwise operators to perform the packing and unpacking.

Program 17.1

```
/*
**      The program determines a person's age measured
**      in years given that person's date of birth and
**      today's date. The dates are packed into 16 bits
**      and stored left to right as day (5 bits), month
**      (4 bits) and year (7 bits).
*/

#include <stdio.h>

typedef unsigned int          Date;   /* packed representation */

#define DAY(_D)               ((_D) >> 11)
#define MONTH(_D)             (((_D) >> 7) & 0xF)
#define YEAR(_D)              ((_D) & 0x7F)

void askfordate();                     /* forward reference */

main()
   {
   Date         dateofbirth, today;
   int          age;

   askfordate("Date of birth?: ", &dateofbirth);
   askfordate("Today\'s date?: ", &today);
```

```
      if (MONTH(today) > MONTH(dateofbirth) ||
          MONTH(today) == MONTH(dateofbirth) &&
             DAY(today) > DAY(dateofbirth))
        age = YEAR(today) - YEAR(dateofbirth);
      else
        age = YEAR(today) - YEAR(dateofbirth) - 1;

      printf("age: %d\n", age);
    }
  void askfordate(prompt, date)
    char  *prompt;
    Date  *date;
    {
      unsigned int d, m, y;

      printf("%s", prompt);
      scanf("%d/%d/%d", &d, &m, &y);

      *date = (((d << 4) | m) << 7) | y;
    }
```

Case study 17.1: Sets

A college offers ten courses in Mathematics, Physics, Chemistry, Biology, English, French, German, Italian, Accounting and Economics. Each student's enrolment is recorded in a text file, one record per line. The student's surname appears in columns 1–20 inclusive. Each course taken by a student is shown by the presence of the letter X in columns 21–30, representing, respectively, the ten courses. Design and write a program which reads the enrolment file and prints a class list for every course. It can be assumed that there are not more than 80 students.

The problem is most naturally expressed in terms of the set concept. Each student record consists of the student's name and the set of courses on which that student is enrolled. As each student record is input, each occurrence of the letter X in columns 21–30 causes the corresponding course to be included in the set of courses that the student attends. Producing a class list for a given subject is expressed by determining whether the course is a member of the set of courses attended by a student.

A set is fundamental to modern mathematics. A set is a collection of objects of some type. In Case study 11.2 a set of integers was implemented. In this application, the base type for the set is the courses. We can define the enumeration type:

typedef enum { MATHEMATICS, PHYSICS, CHEMISTRY,
               BIOLOGY, ENGLISH, FRENCH, GERMAN,
               ITALIAN, ACCOUNTING, ECONOMICS } Course;

Variables of type Course are declared and assigned in the usual way. For example:

Course enrolled = MATHEMATICS;

These courses can be mixed in any combination to form the set of courses on which a particular student is matriculated. For example, a student enrolled for MATHEMATICS, ENGLISH and ACCOUNTING would be denoted by:

{ MATHEMATICS, ENGLISH, ACCOUNTING }

using { and } to denote a set (do not confuse with the C syntactic tokens { and }). If a student has enrolled on no courses, this is shown as the empty set:

{ }

The *union* of two sets is a set containing the members of both sets. The value of:

{ MATHEMATICS } *union* { ENGLISH, ACCOUNTING }

is the set shown above. The *intersection* of two sets is a set containing only the objects which are members of both sets. The value of:

{ MATHEMATICS, ENGLISH, ACCOUNTING }
    intersection { PHYSICS, MATHEMATICS }

is the set:

{ MATHEMATICS }

The *difference* of two sets is a set containing all the members of the first set which are not members of the second set. The value of:

{ MATHEMATICS, ENGLISH, ACCOUNTING }
    difference { PHYSICS, MATHEMATICS }

is the set:

{ ENGLISH, ACCOUNTING }

The operator *ismember* delivers TRUE or FALSE according to whether the left operand is a member or not a member of the second operand. The value of:

enrolled *ismember* { MATHEMATICS, ENGLISH, ACCOUNTING }

for the value of the Course variable as declared above, is TRUE.

Using our usual notation, we consider a package of set-handling functions. The set base type is Course as defined above. The type name Setofcourses is assumed to have been defined in a typedef statement to denote an abstraction for these sets (see Fig. 17.1).

Function ismember has two arguments and returns a Boolean value according to whether the first argument of type Course is a member of the

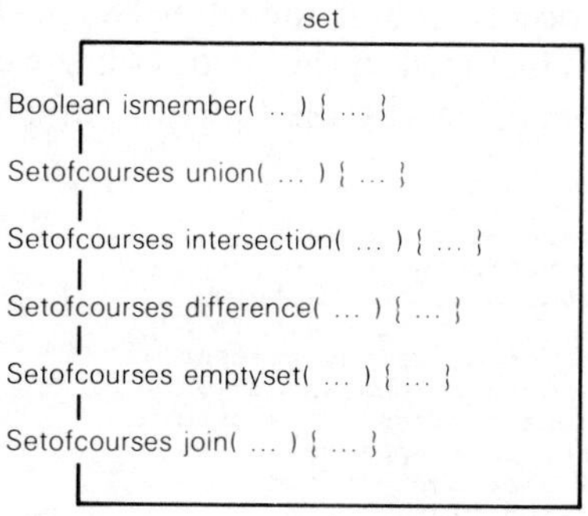

set

```
Boolean ismember( ... ) { ... }
    |
Setofcourses union( ... ) { ... }
    |
Setofcourses intersection( ... ) { ... }
    |
Setofcourses difference( ... ) { ... }
    |
Setofcourses emptyset( ... ) { ... }
    |
Setofcourses join( ... ) { ... }
```

Fig. 17.1

set obtained from the second argument. The function header is:

    Boolean ismember(element, set)
        Course   element;
        Setofcourses set;

The function header for *join* is:

    Setofcourses join(element, set)
        Course   element;
        Setofcourses set;

and adds the single item *element* to the set returning a new set as the function value.

The problem naturally divides into two parts. The first phase builds the array of student records. Each record contains the student's name and the set of courses for which that student is enrolled. The second phase produces a class list for each subject.

The internal data structure for the problem is an array of student records. Appropriate declarations are:

```
#define NAMESIZE    20
#define TEXTSIZE    (NAMESIZE+1)
#define CLASSSIZE   80

typedef struct { char          name[TEXTSIZE];
                 Setofcourses  matriculated;
               } Student;

Student      students[CLASSSIZE];
```

An external file of unknown length contains each student record, one per line. Each record is read from the file and stored in consecutive elements of the array. The reading continues until the end of file is reached. A student's record is read in two parts. First, the 20 character name is input. Second, the 10 character course selection is read and stored in the Setofcourses member *matriculated*. This set variable is initialized to the empty set using the *emptyset* operation. For each occurrence of the letter 'X' in the input stream, the corresponding course is included in the set of courses using the join operation. The coding is accomplished by the function input:

```
/*
**      Read a series of student records from the
**      specified file. Continue until the end of
**      file is reached. Each student record is held
**      as a single line of text. The first field is 20
**      characters long and is the name of the student.
**      The next field is 10 characters long and is an
**      encoding for the 10 college courses. If a student
**      is enrolled on the course, an X appears in the
**      corresponding column. If a student is not
**      enrolled, the column remains blank.
*/

void input(fp, students, number)
    FILE            *fp;
    Student         students[];
    int             *number;
    {
      Setofcourses          enrolled;
      Course                subject, successor();
      char                  ch;
      int                   k;

      *number = 0;
      while (fscanf(fp, "%20s", students[*number].name) != EOF)
        {
          for (k = strlen(students[*number].name); k < NAMESIZE; k++)
            fscanf(fp, "%c", &ch);          /* ignore trailing blanks */
          enrolled = emptyset();
          for (subject = MATHEMATICS; subject != TRAILER;
                  subject = successor(subject))
            {
              fscanf(fp, "%c", &ch);
              if (ch == 'X')
                enrolled = join(subject, enrolled);
            }
          students[*number].matriculated = enrolled;
          (*number)++;
        }
    }
```

The program output is a class list for each of the ten subjects. The data structure is nested. The outer loop cycles through all the subjects, while the inner loop cycles through all the students. If the named subject is a member of the set of courses on which the student is enrolled, that student's name is printed. The coding is:

```
/*
**      Produce a class list for every college course.
**      The list is presented in subject order, with
**      each enrolled student tabulated under the
**      course name.
*/

void output(students, number)
    Student         students[];
    int             number;
    {
      Course          subject, successor();
      int             k;
      void            printcourse();
```

```
      for (subject = MATHEMATICS; subject != TRAILER;
              subject = successor(subject))
        {
          printcourse(subject);
          for (k = 0; k < number; k++)
            if (ismember(subject, students[k].matriculated))
              printf("\t%s\n", students[k].name);
        }
    }
/*
**      Print the course title.
*/

static *coursename[] = { "MATHEMATICS", "PHYSICS", "CHEMISTRY", "BIOLOGY",
                         "ENGLISH", "FRENCH", "GERMAN", "ITALIAN",
                         "ACCOUNTING", "ECONOMICS" };

void printcourse(subject)
  Course         subject;
  {
    printf("\n\n\n\n%s\n", coursename[(int) subject]);
  }
```

In Case study 11.2 the integer set was realized by an array of int. This solution was appropriate, given the number of possible values in the set and also given that an integer value may be any from the range of possible integers.

In this problem, we can take advantage of two known attributes. First, the maximum set size is 10. There can be no more than ten subjects on which a student is enrolled. Further, the values of the set elements are known; they are the values from the enumeration type Course. If, as the C compiler does, we encode each subject with MATHEMATICS = 0, ... ECONOMICS = 9, then bit position 0 of an unsigned int can represent MATHEMATICS, bit position 1 can represent PHYSICS, and so on. The abstraction Setofcourses can be realized with an unsigned int value, such that if bit position 0 is value 1, MATHEMATICS is a member of the set, and if bit position 0 is value 0, MATHEMATICS is not a member of the set. The definition we have is then:

typedef unsigned int   Setofcourses;

If on our particular machine the bits are numbered right to left, then the set denoted by:

{ MATHEMATICS, ENGLISH, ACCOUNTING }

is recorded in the unsigned int value as shown in Fig. 17.2. The empty set is readily constructed from a binary pattern of ten zeros, i.e. decimal zero. The function emptyset yields the empty set and is established by:

#define emptyset()   ((Setofcourses) 0)

Note how this and all the other set 'functions' are written as macros. It would be possible to write then as true functions, but they are so concise

Bit position	9	8	7	6	5	4	3	2	1	0
	0	1	0	0	0	1	0	0	0	1

Fig. 17.2

Bit position	9	8	7	6	5	4	3	2	1	0
	0	0	0	1	0	0	0	0	0	0

Fig. 17.3

Bit position	9	8	7	6	5	4	3	2	1	0
	0	1	0	1	0	1	0	0	0	1

Fig. 17.4

that macros suffice. Further, there is no function call overhead, and the implementation is therefore efficient. Macro emptyset has no arguments and the null parameter list () may be omitted. We choose to retain this redundancy to provide compatibility with the other 'functions'. Outwardly, they will all appear as C functions.

The operation join is implemented by setting the bit which corresponds to the subject encoding. To join PHYSICS to any set involves setting bit position 1. To join GERMAN, bit position 6 assumes the value 1. Consider the set denoted by:

{ MATHEMATICS, ENGLISH, ACCOUNTING }

with representation as shown in Fig. 17.2. To join GERMAN to this set, bit 6 must change to value 1, while the remaining bits are unchanged. This we achieve by creating a bit pattern containing all zeros, except in bit position 6 (see Fig. 17.3), then performing a bitwise OR operation between the two patterns. The resulting set is given in Fig. 17.4.

The coding for this operation is:

```
#define join(_ELEM, _SET) ((Setofcourses)1
   << (int)(_ELEM) | (_SET))
```

The argument _ELEM will be an enumeration value for the type Course. This value is coerced to type int by the explicit cast to produce the course encoding. A binary 1 is then left-shifted that number of places to create the mask which is then OR'ed with the original set argument.

The other operators are implemented in a similar manner. As noted above, all the operators are coded as macros rather than as pure functions. The listing for this program unit and the remainder of the program appears below.

```
/*
**       File :           case17.1.c
**
**       A college offers a range of 10 courses. Produce
**       a class list of the students enrolled on each
**       of the courses.
*/

#include <stdio.h>
#include "set.h"

#define READONLY        "r"

#define NAMESIZE        20
#define TEXTSIZE        (NAMESIZE+1)
#define CLASSSIZE       80

typedef struct { char          name[TEXTSIZE];
                 Setofcourses  matriculated;
               } Student;

void     input(), output();                 /* forward references */

main(argc, argv)
  int    argc;
  char   *argv[];
  {
    FILE        *fp, *fopen();
    Student     students[CLASSSIZE];
    int         number;

    if (argc != 2)
      fprintf(stderr, "Usage: case17.1 filename\n");
    else if ((fp = fopen(argv[1], READONLY)) == NULL)
      fprintf(stderr, "case17.1: cannot open %s\n", argv[1]);
    else
      {
        input(fp, students, &number);
        fclose(fp);
        output(students, number);
      }
  }


void input(fp, students, number)
  FILE          *fp;
  Student       students[];
  int           *number;
  {
    .....
  }


void output(students, number)
  Student       students[];
  int           number;
  {
    .....
  }

static *coursename[] = .....

void printcourse(subject)
  Course        subject;
  {
    printf("\n\n\n\n%s\n", coursename[(int) subject]);
  }

/*
**      Determine the next subject, from the enumeration
**      of subjects.
*/
```

```
Course successor(subject)
  Course        subject;
  {
    return ((Course) ((int)subject + 1));
  }

/*
**      File :          set.h
**
**      A set package, suitable for sets of small
**      integers. The integers are abstracted as course
**      names in the context of the application.
*/

typedef enum { MATHEMATICS, PHYSICS, CHEMISTRY, BIOLOGY,
               ENGLISH, FRENCH, GERMAN, ITALIAN,
               ACCOUNTING, ECONOMICS, TRAILER } Course;

typedef unsigned int            Setofcourses;

#define emptyset()                      ((Setofcourses) 0)

#define ismember(_ELEM, _SET)\
    ((Setofcourses)1 << (int)(_ELEM) & (_SET))

#define join(_ELEM, _SET)\
        ((Setofcourses)1 << (int)(_ELEM) | (_SET))

#define union(_SET1, _SET2)     ((_SET1) | (_SET2))

#define intersection(_SET1, _SET2)      ((_SET1) & (_SET2))

#define difference(_SET1, _SET2)        ((_SET1) ^ (_SET2))
```

17.2 Summary

1. Bitwise expressions allow storage compaction and operations on the machine-dependent bit representation of integral data values. Bitwise operations are highly machine-dependent and make programs difficult to port. Where appropriate, consideration should be given to portability aspects when using bitwise operators. In particular, code should be conditionally compiled for a number of architectures.
2. Packing is the name given to placing bit patterns into integral data values. Unpacking is used to access these bit patterns. Masks are used to perform these operations.

17.3 Exercises

1. Develop a C function called *rotate* which rotates a bit pattern a given number of places. The function header is:

   unsigned int rotate(value, n)
       unsigned int value;
       int   n;

   The process of rotation is similar to shifting, except that when a value is rotated to the left the bits that are shifted out of the high order bits are shifted back into the low order bits. Similarly with a right rotation. Left and right shifts are denoted by positive and negative values for n respectively.

2. Write a function called *getbits* which delivers the value of the bit pattern contained in the argument *value* between bits p and q inclusive:

    unsigned int getbits(p, q, value)
      unsigned int p, q, value;

The corresponding function *putbits* places the bit pattern represented by the argument *patt* into bits p through q of value. The remaining bits of value are left undisturbed.

3. Write a function that reverses the bit representation of a byte. For example:

    10101110 yields 01110101 when reversed.

4. One possible method of representing numbers in a computer is called the *binary coded decimal* notation, or BCD. In this system two digits of a number can be packed into a single byte. For example, the number 93 is represented as the byte value 10010011.

Write a program unit that supports BCD arithmetic. Functions should be included to convert from BCD to int and back, to add (multiply) two BCD values producing a BCD value, to read and print a BCD value, etc.

## CHAPTER 18

Advanced topics

This is the final chapter, and one in which we introduce further features of C. Many programs can be written without the constructions presented in this chapter. They do, however, provide more functionality. *Generics* establish templates for functions to be written that apply to more than one data type. Functions as arguments generalize the processing performed by functions. Though strictly not an advanced subject, the *goto* statement is introduced here. It is no accident that all the programs we have written have been developed without using the goto statement. Programs can be written without it. The problems associated with it and its possible limited uses are discussed below.

18.1 Generic program units

As we functionally decompose software systems into modules, we usually find subprograms (functions) that are similar in purpose. For example, in Program 11.3 we developed a function to sort an array of integers. This operation is easily provided in C and is applicable to arrays of any size. The following function header may be assumed:

```
void isort(itable, size)
   int    itable[ ];
   int    size;
```

To sort an array of some other component type, we must create a separate function. This is because the rules of C require us to specify the type of array elements. Thus, we might be forced to write the additional function:

```
void fsort(ftable, size)
   float   ftable[ ];
   int     size;
```

This is an undesirable situation since we must explicitly create separate versions of functions with identical algorithms, but which process objects of different types. What is needed is the ability to create templates of program units tailored to a particular type at compile time. This is achieved through the use of generic program units.

To create a generic program unit, we simply take a package or subprogram and include a prefix that defines the generic parameters. For example, a function that exchanges two elements of type int is:

```
void iswap(first, second)
   int      *first, *second;
   {
      int temp = *first;

      *first = *second;
      *second = temp;
   }
```

If it is required to exchange other types of element, it is not necessary to create a new function for every situation. Since in each case the algorithm is identical, we may factor out this operation by adding a generic prefix to the function header:

```
#ifdef INT
#       define SWAP      iswap
        typedef int       Type;
#endif

#ifdef FLOAT
#       define SWAP      fswap
        typedef float     Type;
#endif

#ifdef CHAR
#       define SWAP      cswap
        typedef char      Type;
#endif

void SWAP(first, second)
   Type      *first, *second;
   {
      Type temp = *first;

      *first = *second;
      *second = temp;
   {
```

Note that the algorithm expressed in the body of this function is identical to that for *iswap*, except for the data types. In the generic part, we declare the data type Type and the function name which forms the parameters for the program template. We conceptually substitute the parameter Type for every occurrence of the int type.

We may submit this program unit for compilation. To do so, we need to match the generic arguments (SWAP and Type) with the actual quantities. This can be achieved in a number of ways. If we edit the program file and insert the definition:

#define INT

at the beginning of the file, then during compilation an instance of the generic unit is created. Specifically, we recreate the function iswap. Inserting an alternative definition, either:

#define FLOAT

or:

#define CHAR

other swap functions may be established.

Alternatively, we make use of the compiler arguments (see Appendix G). To compile this generic program unit, selecting to create the function *fswap*, the command line is:

cc−c−DFLOAT swap.c

where the generic program file is swap.c.

Case study 11.1 developed a sort function based on the quicksort algorithm. Specifically, an array of type int is sorted into ascending order. By establishing the array type as a generic parameter, different instantiations of quicksort can be created. We demonstrate this in Program 18.1. As illustrated above, by defining either INT, FLOAT or CHAR, different quicksort functions can be produced.

Program 18.1

```
/*
**       Sort a sequence of integer values using the quicksort
**       algorithm. The set of integer data values is preceded
**       by the integer N representing the number of items.
*/

#include <stdio.h>

#define MAXTABLE        1000

#define CHAR

#ifdef INT
#       define TYPE     int
#endif
#ifdef FLOAT
#       define TYPE     float
#endif
#ifdef CHAR
#       define TYPE     char
#endif

#define SWAP(_X,_Y)     { TYPE Z; Z = (_X); (_X) = (_Y); (_Y) = Z; }
void     input(), output();        /* referencing declarations */
void     quicksort(), rquick();
```

```
  main ()
    {
      TYPE table[MAXTABLE];                 /* data items */
      int number;                           /* number of values */

      input(table, &number);               /* read the data */
      if (number <= MAXTABLE)              /* check sizes */
        {
          quicksort(table, number);        /* apply algorithm */
          output(table, number);           /* print results */
        }
      else
        printf("Too many data items\n");
    }


void input(table, number)
  TYPE  table[];                           /* data destination */
  int   *number;                           /* count of data items */
    {
      int k;

      scanf("%d", number);
      if (*number > MAXTABLE)
        return;

      for (k = 0; k < *number; k++)
#ifdef INT
        scanf("%d", &table[k]);
#endif
#ifdef FLOAT
        scanf("%f", &table[k]);

#endif
#ifdef CHAR
        scanf("%c", &table[k]);
#endif
    }

void output(table, number)
  TYPE  table[];                           /* data values */
  int   number;                            /* count */
    {
      int k;

      for (k = 0; k < number; k++)
#ifdef INT
      printf("%d\n", table[k]);
#endif
#ifdef FLOAT
      printf("%f\n", table[k]);
#endif
#ifdef CHAR
      printf("%c", table[k]);
#endif
    }


void quicksort(table, number)
  TYPE  table[];                           /* items to be sorted */
  int   number;                            /* number of values */
    {
      rquick(table, 0, number-1);          /* recursive quicksort */
    }


void rquick(table, lo, hi)
  TYPE  table[];                  /* data values */
  int   lo, hi;                   /* subset of table (indices) */
    {
      int low, high;
      TYPE pivot;
```

```
low = lo;
high = hi;
if (low < high)
  {
    pivot = table[high];
    do {
      while (low < high && table[low] <= pivot)
        low++;
      while (high > low && table[high] >= pivot)
        high--;
      if (low < high)                  /* out of order pair */
        SWAP(table[low], table[high]);
    } while (low < high);
    SWAP(table[low], table[hi]);     /* move pivot to low */
    rquick(table, lo, low-1);
    rquick(table, low+1, hi);
  }
}
```

18.2 Pointers to functions

Objects of type *function* may be introduced in only one of two ways. First, a *function declaration* creates a function object, defines the type of the arguments and return value, and provides the body of the function. For example, *square* is a function object:

```
int square(x)
  int    x;
  {
    return (x * x);
  }
```

Second, a *referencing declaration* is used to introduce a function declared elsewhere. A referencing declaration for function square is:

```
extern int square( /* int x */ );
```

The C language provides for values of one type to be automatically converted to values of other types under several circumstances. This *unary* conversion determines whether and how a single operand is converted before an operation is performed. We know that an expression of type 'array of T' for some arbitrary type T is converted to a value of type 'pointer to T'. Similarly, an expression of type 'function returning T' for some type T is converted to value of type 'pointer to a function returning T' by substituting a pointer to the function for the function itself. The only expression that can have type 'function returning T' is the name of a function. A function identifier by itself and not in the context of a function call (the function identifier followed immediately by ″(″) is converted to the type 'pointer to function returning ...'. Thus, in the usual way, we may declare a variable of type 'pointer to a function returning ...' and assign to it the name of a function. In the context of the declaration:

```
int (*fp)();
```

the identifier fp is declared as a 'pointer to a function returning an int'. We may then assign to fp any 'pointer to a function returning an int'. The latter is delivered by the name of a suitable declared function. For example:

    fp = square;

Variable fp is a pointer to the function object known in the program as square. The function call:

    y = square(x);

can also be achieved indirectly with the indirection operator applied to an expression of type 'pointer to function returning int'. An equivalent call is:

    y = (*fp)(x);

It is especially useful to consider the declaration:

    int i, *pi, f( ), *fpi( ), (*fi)( );

which declares an integer i, a pointer to an integer pi, a function returning an integer f, a function returning a pointer to an integer fpi, and a pointer to a function returning an integer fi. The declaration should be studied with some care. The construct:

    int .... , (*fi)( );

says that fi is a pointer to a function returning an int. The first set of parentheses are necessary. Without them:

    int .... , *fi( );

would declare fi to be a function returning a pointer to an int (like fpi), which is quite different.

The use of fp in the statement:

    y = (*fp)(x);

is consistent with the declaration. The variable fp is a pointer to a function, *fp is the function, and (*fp)(x) is the call to that function. The parentheses are necessary so that the components correctly associate.

The following program illustrates the use of this construct. The pointer to function variable *func* is first assigned to the function object *square* which in turn is called indirectly to determine 5 squared. The process is then repeated using the function *cube*.

Program 18.2

```
/*
**      Determine the square and the cube of the value 5.
**      The squaring and cubing functions are called
**      through indirect function calls.
*/

#include <stdio.h>
```

```
int square(), cube();                    /* forward references */

main()
  {
    int y, x = 5;
    int (*func)();                       /* pointer to function */

    func = square;                       /* not a call to square !! */
    y = (*func)(x);                      /* indirect call on square */
    printf("Square of %d is %d\n", x, y);

    func = cube;
    y = (*func)(x);
    printf("Cube of %d is %d\n", x, y);
  }
int square(x)
  int x;
  {
    return (x * x);
  }

int cube(x)
  int x;
  {
    return (x * x * x);
  }
```

The syntax of the C language in handling function pointers makes the program text somewhat obscure. The typedef statement can improve matters by introducing a suitable type name. For example, the definition:

typedef int   (*Pfi)();

introduces Pfi as a pointer to a function returning an integer. The declaration for a variable of this type is then:

Pfi func;

Were it not for typedef statements, the obscurity can become much worse when we recognize that a 'pointer to a function returning ...' object can be used as array types, members of structures and even arguments to functions. For example, an array of pointers to functions returning integers is declared by:

int (*apfi[4])();

Using the typedef statement introduced above, we can increase the clarity of this declaration by:

Pfi apfi[4];

Thus, *apfi* is an array, with each element of type Pfi. In turn, Pfi is a pointer to a function returning an int. Finally, apfi is an array of pointers to functions returning int.

In many programming problems we invoke one of a number of functions selected by the current value of some integer variable. For example, consider a program that displays a menu of options numbered 0, 1, 2 and 3. According to the value entered by the user, the program invokes a subsidiary function to service that choice. One possible program fragment might be:

```
display_menu( );
scanf("%d", &choice);
switch (choice)
    {
       case 0 : do_zero( );   break;
       case 1 : do_one( );    break;
       case 2 : do_two( );    break;
       case 3 : do_three( );  break;
     default : printf("Unknown selection\n");
     }
```

Alternatively, we might consider establishing an array of pointers to these service functions, and activate the appropriate one by using the integer variable *choice* as an index into the array. The program constituents now are:

```
void do_zero( ), do_one( ), do_two( ), do_three( );
typedef void      (*Pfv)( );
Pfv do_choice[ ] = {do_zero, do_one, do_two, do_three};

display_menu( );
scanf("%d", &choice);
if (0 <= choice && choice <= 3)
   (*do_choice[choice])( );
else
   printf ("Unknown selection\n");
```

These concepts are demonstrated in the following program. A menu of four options is available to the user. The choices are numbered 0 to 3 inclusive. Selection 1 invites the user to enter a date in the form DD/MM/YYYY. Selection 2 prints the date in the same format, and selection 3 prints the day of the week for the input date. After selecting 1, 2 or 3 the menu is redisplayed and the process repeats until the choice 0 is entered and the cycle terminates.

Program 18.3

```
/*
**      Demonstration of a menu-driven program. Each
**      menu option is serviced by a function. The
**      selection made by the user is used to determine
**      the function to call. An array of function
**      pointers is indexed by the user choice to
**      invoke the support function.
*/

#include <stdio.h>

#define FOREVER        for (;;)
```

```
typedef struct { int      day;
                 int      month;
                 int year;
               } Date;

typedef void              (*Pfv)();  /* pointer to a function ... */
                                     /* ... returning void */

void    abort(), date_in(), date_out();
void    day_out(), menu();
int     zeller();

Pfv selection[] = {abort, date_in, date_out, day_out};

main()
   {
     Date          date;
     int           choice;

     FOREVER
       {
         menu(&choice);
         if (0 <= choice && choice <= 3)
           (*selection[choice])(&date);
         else
           printf("\n\nUnknown selection\n");
       }
   }


/*
**      Prompt the user and read the entered date.
*/

void date_in(date)
  Date  *date;
  {
    printf("\n\nEnter the date as DD/MM/YYYY: ");
    scanf("%d/%d/%d", &date -> day, &date -> month, &date -> year);
  }


/*
**      Print the present value of the date.
*/

void date_out(date)
  Date  *date;
  {
    printf("\n\nEntered date is: %d/%d/%d\n", date -> day,
              date -> month, date -> year);
  }


/*
**      Print the day name of the present date.
*/

void day_out(date)
  Date  *date;
  {
    static char *day_name[] = {
        "Sunday", "Monday", "Tuesday", "Wednesday",
        "Thursday", "Friday", "Saturday" };

    printf("\n\nDay is: %s\n", day_name[zeller(date)]);
  }


/*
**      Apply Zeller's congruence to a valid date
**      expressed as DD/MM/YYYY.
*/
```

```
int zeller(date)
   Date  *date;
   {
      int k, y, m, d, c, z;

      k = date -> day;
      y = date -> year;
      if (date -> month < 3)
         {
            m = date -> month + 10;
            y = date -> year -1;
         }
      else
         m = date -> month -2;
      d = y % 100;
      c = y / 100;

      z = (26 * m - 2)/10 + k + d + (d/4) + (c/4) - 2*c;
      return (z % 7);
   }

/*
**       Terminate the program.
*/

void abort(dummy)
   Date  *dummy;                                  /* unused */
   {
      printf("\n\nProgram closing\n");
      exit(0);
   }

/*
**       Main menu. A menu selection is displayed and
**       the user is invited to make a choice. The
**       selected value is returned to the main function,
**       validated, and the appropriate service
**       function called.
*/

void menu(choice)
   int   *choice;
   {
      int k;

      for (k = 0; k < 24; k++)
         printf("\n");                       /* clear screen */

      printf("\t\t\tMAIN MENU\n\n\n");
      printf("\t\t\t0 Exit\n");
      printf("\t\t\t1 Date in\n");
      printf("\t\t\t2 Date out\n");
      printf("\t\t\t3 Day out\n\n\n\n\n");

      printf("Enter selection: ");
      scanf("%d", choice);
   }
```

18.3 Functions as arguments

We have written programs in which one function invokes another. Indeed, without this facility, large programs would be very difficult to write. We sometimes encounter circumstances in which we wish to write a function that will invoke another function whose effect is not determined until program execution time. This is achieved by passing a pointer to a function as a formal function argument. The specification for this formal argument indicates a function pointer and the value returned by the function. For example, the declaration:

```
void ppp(...., f, ....)
    .....
    int (*f)();
    .....
    {
        int x, y;
        .....
        y = (*f)(x);
        .....
    }
```

introduces a function *ppp* with a formal function argument f which returns an int. Within the body of ppp, f is used like any other pointer to a function returning an int. When the function ppp is called, the actual parameter corresponding to f must be the identifier of a function with the same argument requirements and the same result type. A legal call to ppp would be:

```
ppp( ...., square, ....);
```

with function square as defined in the previous section.

Consider the function *tabulate* to generate a succession of values for x, as determined by the arguments *lower*, *upper* and *increment*, and to evaluate and print f(x). Function tabulate takes f as a function argument. The function declaration is:

```
void tabulate(f, lower, upper, increment)
    double (*f)(), lower, upper, increment;
    {
        double x;
        for (x = lower; x < = upper + 0.5*increment; x + = increment)
            printf("%6.2f %10.4f\n", x, (*f)(x));
    }
```

The function call:

```
tabulate(f1, 0.0, 1.0, 0.1);
```

would cause the values of x and f1(x) to be tabulated for x in the range 0.0 to 1.0 at intervals of 0.1. Function f1 should possess one *double* argument and return a value of type double. The program which follows employs function tabulate to display x and x*x for x = 0.0, 0.1, 0.2, ..., 2.0.

Program 18.4

```
/*
**        Demonstration of a pointer to function argument.
**        A series of values are tabulated for some
**        given function. The tabulation function
**        receives the function as one of its arguments.
*/

#include <stdio.h>

double square();                            /* forward references */
void   tabulate();

main()
  {
    tabulate(square, 0.0, 2.0, 0.1);
  }

void tabulate(f, lower, upper, increment)
  double (*f)(), lower, upper, increment;
  {
    .....
  }

double square(x)
  double x;
  {
    return (x * x);
  }
```

Functions as arguments are very useful for constructing general-purpose functions, such as function tabulate. The facility must be used with great care since the effect of one function which receives another as an argument is not always immediately obvious. Programs using functions as arguments are often difficult to both understand and debug. Their strength, however, is in the functionality afforded by their use.

Case study 18.1: Quicksort (revisited)

The quicksort algorithm developed in Case study 11.1 sorted an array of int into ascending order. The sort procedure consists of three distinct elements – the *sort* algorithm which orders the array elements by a series of comparisons and exchanges; the *comparison* by which the ordering of any pair of array elements is determined; and an *exchange* which reverses the order of two array members.

The sort algorithm has already been established. It is independent of the operations that perform the comparisons and the exchanges. By passing different comparison functions to the sort routine, and by generalizing the exchange operation, we can arrange to sort different types.

The function we shall now develop is called quicksort. The header to the function definition is described as:

```
void quicksort(base, nelements, nbytes, compare)
  char   *base;
  int    nelements, nbytes, (*compare)();
```

When the function is called, the first argument is a pointer to the base of the data. The second argument is the number of elements in the array to be sorted. The third argument is the number of bytes required by each array element. The final argument is the name of the comparison function to be used, returning the int value -1, 0 or $+1$ according to whether the two values being compared are less than, equal to or greater than each other.

To sort the integer array *table* declared as:

    int table[20];

the function call is:

    quicksort((char *)&table, 20, sizeof(int), intcmp)

where function *intcmp* compares two integer values accessed through character pointers from the data according to:

```
int intcmp(x, y)
  char *x, *y;
  {
    int first, second;

    first = *((int *)x);
    second = *((int *)y);

    if (first < second)
      return (-1);
    else if (first > second)
      return (1);
    else
      return (0);
  }
```

Similarly, we can develop functions *charcmp* and *realcmp* to compare, respectively, characters and doubles. The standard library function strcmp is already available to compare strings.

The program listing appears below. It is heavily parameterized to permit different instantiations of the program to be generated. Compiling the program with INT defined, produces a sort of an array of integers. Recompiling with, say, STRING defined sorts an array of strings.

```
/*
**      Reimplementation of the quicksort algorithm
**      generalized to perform a sort on any
**      fundamental type. Details of the base type
**      and the comparison function are passed
**      to this implementation.
*/

#include <stdio.h>

#ifdef INT
```

```
#define TYPE            int
#define NAME            intcmp
#define TABLE           itable
#define FORMAT          "%6d\n"
#define QUICKSORT quicksort((char *)itable, 5, sizeof(int), intcmp)
int itable[] = {14, 7, 2, 10, 21};

#endif


#ifdef CHAR

#define TYPE            char
#define NAME            charcmp
#define TABLE           ctable
#define FORMAT          "%c\n"
#define QUICKSORT       quicksort(ctable, 5, sizeof(char), charcmp)
char ctable[] = {'q', 'w', 'e', 'r', 't'};

#endif


#ifdef DOUBLE

#define TYPE            double
#define NAME            doubcmp
#define TABLE           dtable
#define FORMAT          "%10.4f\n"
#define QUICKSORT\
  quicksort((char *)dtable, 5, sizeof(double), doubcmp)
double dtable[] = {12.6, 8.2, 1.2, 9.1, 7.4};

#endif


#ifdef STRING

#define NAME            strcmp
#define TABLE           stable
#define FORMAT          "%s\n"
#define QUICKSORT       quicksort((char *)stable, 5, 6, strcmp)
char stable[][6] = {{"one  "}, {"two  "}, {"three"},
                    {"four "}, {"five "}};

#endif


#define PRINT(_L, _F, _T) { int K; for (K = 0; K < (_L); K++) \
                            printf(_F, _T[K]); }

int     NAME();                         /* forward references */
void    quicksort();

main()
   {
   QUICKSORT;
   PRINT(5, FORMAT, TABLE);
   }

/*
**      Quicksort algorithm.
**      The first argument is a pointer to the base of
**      the data expressed as a character address. The
**      second argument is the number of elements to be
**      sorted, and represents the array size. The third
**      argument is the number of bytes required by each
**      array element. The fourth argument is the name
**      of the comparison function to be used, returning
**      the int value -1, 0 or +1 according to whether
**      the two values being compared are less than, equal
**      to or greater than each other.
*/
```

```
void quicksort(base, nelements, nbytes, compare)
  char *base;                     /* base address of the data */
  int   nelements;                /* number of array elements */
  int   nbytes;                   /* number of bytes per element */
  int   (*compare)();             /* comparison function */
  {
    void        rquick();         /* forward reference */

    rquick(base, nelements, nbytes, compare);
  }

/*
**      Recursive implementation of the quicksort
**      algorithm.
*/

void rquick(base, nelements, nbytes, compare)
  char *base;
  int   nelements, nbytes, (*compare)();
  {
    char          *low, *high, *lo, *hi, *pivot;
    void          swapbytes();                /* forward reference */

    lo = low = base;
    hi = high = base + (nelements - 1) * nbytes;

    if (low < high)
      {
        pivot = high;
        do {
          while (low < high && (*compare)(low, pivot) <= 0)
            low += nbytes;
          while (high > low && (*compare)(high, pivot) >= 0)
            high -= nbytes;
          if (low < high)
            swapbytes(low, high, nbytes);
        } while (low < high);

        swapbytes(low, hi, nbytes);
        rquick(lo, (low-lo)/nbytes, nbytes, compare);
        rquick(low+nbytes, (hi-low)/nbytes, nbytes, compare);
      }
  }

/*
**      Interchange the nbytes in the byte arrays
**      b1 and b2.
*/

void swapbytes(b1, b2, nbytes)
  char *b1, *b2;
  int   nbytes;
  {
    int k;
    char byte;

    for (k = 0; k < nbytes; k++)
      {
        byte = *b1;
        *b1++ = *b2;
        *b2++ = byte;
      }
  }

#ifndef STRING

/*
**      Comparison function for the base types int,
**      float and char. The comparison function used
**      to compare strings is the library function
**      strcmp.
*/
```

```
int NAME(first, second)
  char   *first, *second;
  {
    TYPE          tfirst, tsecond;

    tfirst = *((TYPE *) first);
    tsecond = *((TYPE *) second);

    if (tfirst < tsecond)
      return (-1);
    else if (tfirst > tsecond)
      return (1);
    else
      return (0);
  }

#endif
```

18.4 The goto statement

We conclude our discussion of the C programming language by introducing the only remaining C statement. The *goto* statement permits unconditional transfers of control from one part of a function to another. The goto statement follows the syntax:

   goto label;

where label is an identifier and goto is a reserved keyword. Labels are not declared in the sense of program variables. The label identifier in a goto statement must be the same as a named label associated with some statement in the current function. Labels are effectively declared on the statement with which they associate. A labeled statement is preceded by a label identifier immediately followed by a colon symbol, as in:

   label : statement;

When a goto statement is executed, control passes immediately to the statement prefixed with the corresponding label. Examples of labeled statements include:

   sum : a = b + c + d;
   but : printf("Execution error\n");

Statements may be multiply labeled, permitting one statement to be referenced by different named labels. Thus, we might have:

   but : recover : abort : exit(1);

The free format of C would permit this last example to also appear as:

   but :
   recover :
   abort : exit(1);

the null statement may be labeled, so that we have:

   dummy : /* null statement */ ;

All the programs presented in this book were solved satisfactorily using the control structures of sequence, selection and iteration. Together with the simple statement forms, they are combined into major statement groupings. Nevertheless, situations arise which make certain aspects of the program design awkward to solve using only these three control structures. A typical example of this problem is input data validation. Consider a function to read the elements of a three-dimensional integer array from a file. Without performing any validation, the function might appear as:

```
void input3d(fp, matrix, rows, columns, planes)
   FILE    *fp;
   int     matrix[][COLUMNS][PLANES];
   int     rows, columns, planes;
   {
     int i, j, k;
     for (i = 0; i < rows; i++)
       for (j = 0; j < columns; j++)
         for (k = 0; k < planes; k++)
           fscanf(fp, "%d", &matrix[i][j][k]);
   }
```

A robust program will check its input data and take the necessary action upon detecting an error. In our example, one possible check we may wish to perform is to detect the end of file condition. Function fscanf returns EOF upon encountering the end of file. Using this value, a logical flag, and additional conditions in the for statement, we have a revised version for this function. If the end of file is detected, an error message is generated and the program terminates.

```
void input3d(fp, matrix, rows, columns, planes)
   FILE    *fp;
   int     matrix[][COLUMNS][PLANES];
   int     rows, columns, planes;
   {
     int     i, j, k;
     Boolean eof_flag = FALSE;

     for (i = 0; i < rows && !eof_flag; i++)
       for (j = 0; j < columns && !eof_flag; j++)
         for (k = 0; k < planes && !eof_flag; k++)
           eof_flag = fscanf(fp, "%d", &matrix[i][j][k]) == EOF;

     if (eof_flag)
       {
         fprintf(stderr, "Unexpected eof\n");
         exit(1);
       }
   }
```

Because of the incorporation of additional conditional checks, the solution is somewhat clumsy. A more graceful exit is achieved by simply using a goto statement from within the nested loops to a point in the function where the error action can take place:

```
void input3d(fp, matrix, rows, columns, planes)
   FILE    *fp;
   int     matrix[][COLUMNS][PLANES];
   int     rows, columns, planes;
   {
     int i, j, k;

     for (i = 0; i < rows; i++)
       for (j = 0; j < columns; j++)
         for (k = 0; k < planes; k++)
           if (fscanf(fp, "%d", &matrix[i][j][k]) == EOF)
             goto abort;
     return;

abort :
     fprintf(stderr, "Unexpected eof\n");
     exit(1);
   }
```

C permits a goto statement to transfer control to any other statement within the function in which it is used. Certain kinds of branching can be especially confusing and should be avoided. For example, transferring control into the middle of a compound statement from outside it bypasses any initialization of variables declared at the head of the compound statement:

```
    . . . . . . . . . .
    . . . . . . . .
    goto middle;
    . . . . . . . . .
    . . . . . . . .
    {
        int sum = 0, divisor = 1;
        . . . . . . . . .
        . . . . . . . .
    middle :
        . . . . . . . . .
    }
```

Other restrictions that should also apply to the use of the goto statement include:

(a) branching into the 'then' or 'else' parts of an *if* statement from outside the if statement;
(b) branching into the body of a *switch* statement;
(c) branching into the body of an *iteration* statement.

Indiscrimate use of the goto statement must be avoided. The fact that both the selection and repetition control structures can be emulated using only if and goto statements does not mean that they should be used as substitutes. The keywords *while*, *for* and *do* signify repetition; *if* and *switch* denote selection. Their appearance in a program immediately indicates the desired control flow. By way of comparison, consider Program

18.5 which repeats the processing in Program 6.14. Note how the repetition is now implemented using a combined if and goto. Further, the tests are conducted with the same pairing. Overall, the program logic is much less obvious.

Program 18.5

```
/*
**      A piece of text consists of a character sequence
**      spanning a number of lines and terminated by a period
**      symbol. Count the number of 'words' in the text,
**      where a word is defined as any character string
**      delimited by whitespace (blank, tab or newline)
**      symbols.
*/

#include <stdio.h>

#define PERIOD          '.'
#define BLANK           ' '
#define TAB             '\t'
#define NEWLINE         '\n'

#define FALSE           0
#define TRUE            1

main()
    {
    char c;                         /* data character */
    int  words = 0;                 /* word counter */
    int  inword = FALSE;            /* word indicator */

loop:
    c = getchar();                  /* get next character */
    if (c == PERIOD)                /* terminator? */
      goto finish;                  /* yes - complete program */

    if (c == BLANK || c == TAB || c == NEWLINE) /* whitespace? */
      {
      inword = FALSE;               /* outwith a word */
      goto loop;                    /* go fetch next character */
      }

    if (! inword)                   /* within a word? */
      {
      inword = TRUE;                /* now in a word */
      words++;                      /* increment counter */
      }

    goto loop;                      /* cycle for next character */
finish:
    printf("Number of words is %d\n", words);
    }
```

The freedom to destroy the program structure provided by the while, if, etc., is what makes the goto statement a dangerous facility, and hence a topic for advanced study. The goto statement should only be used in exceptional circumstances, when the required control cannot be reasonably expressed by the control flow primitives introduced in Chapter 6. Most times this is so rare that the goto statement can virtually be ignored. This way, the difficulties associated with its use can be avoided.

18.5 Summary

1. *Generic* program units are templates of programs that can be tailored to a particular type at compile time. Generics establish reusable items of code from which we can create separate versions.
2. The C language supports the type 'pointer to function returning ...' which can be used as array elements, members of structures, function arguments, etc. Functions to arguments are useful for constructing general-purpose functions whose effect is not determined until execution time.
3. The goto statement violates the principles of structured programming. The goto statement permits unconditional transfer of control and results in unmanageable code. In the majority of cases, the structured control structures should be used. There are, however, a number of situations when the occasion demands the use of the goto statement.

18.6 Exercises

1. Write the function *max*:

   ```
   double max(f, a, b)
     double (*f)( ), a, b;
   ```

   to find the maximum of f(x) over the interval a $<=$ x $<=$ b.

2. Write the function *integrate*:

   ```
   double integrate(f, a, b)
     double (*f )( ), a, b;
   ```

   which returns an approximation of the integral of f(x) over the interval a to b inclusive.

3. Write two equivalent versions of a program, one with goto statements and one without. Try to choose a problem that makes the version with the goto simpler and shorter.

Hardware characteristics

Table A.1 summarizes the hardware properties of the basic data types of a C program on two typical configurations.

Table A.1

	INTEL 8088/86	DEC VAX*
char	8 bits (0, 255)	8 bits
short	16 bits (− 32768, + 32767)	16 bits
int	16 bits	32 bits (− 2147483648, + 2147483647)
long	32 bits	32 bits
unsigned	16 bits (0, 65535)	32 bits (0, 4294967295)
float	32 bits (range: 10e − 38, 10e + 38) (accuracy: approximately 7 significant digits)	32 bits
double	64 bits (range: 10e − 38, 10e + 38) (accuracy: approximately 17 significant digits)	64 bits

*VAX is a registered trademark of Digital Equipment Corporation

ASCII character set

Table B.1 lists the American Standard Code for Information Interchange (ASCII) character codes in hexadecimal, octal and decimal and the associated character symbol. The ASCII code is a 7-bit code with the range 0 to 127 inclusive. Character codes 0 through 31 inclusive, and decimal 127 are the non-printing characters or control characters.

Table B.1

ASCII character	Hexadecimal code	Octal code	Decimal code
NUL (CTRL SPACE)	00	000	0
SOH (CTRL A)	01	001	1
STX (CTRL B)	02	002	2
ETX (CTRL C)	03	003	3
EOT (CTRL D)	04	004	4
ENQ (CTRL E)	05	005	5
ACK (CTRL F)	06	006	6
BEL (CTRL G)	07	007	7
BS (CTRL H or BACKSPACE)	08	010	8
HT (CTRL I or TAB)	09	011	9
LF (CTRL J or LINEFEED)	0A	012	10
VT (CTRL K)	0B	013	11
FF (CTRL L)	0C	014	12
CR (CTRL M or RETURN)	0D	015	13
SO (CTRL N)	0E	016	14
SI (CTRL O)	0F	017	15
DLE (CTRL P)	10	020	16
DC1 (CTRL Q)	11	021	17
DC2 (CTRL R)	12	022	18
DC3 (CTRL S)	13	023	19
DC4 (CTRL T)	14	024	20
NAK (CTRL U)	15	025	21
SYN (CTRL V)	16	026	22
ETB (CTRL W)	17	027	23
CAN (CTRL X)	18	030	24

continued

Table B.1 (*continued*)

ASCII character		Hexadecimal code	Octal code	Decimal code
EM	(CTRL Y)	19	031	25
SUB	(CTRL Z)	1A	032	26
ESC	(CTRL [or ESC)	1B	033	27
FS	(CTRL \)	1C	034	28
GS	(CTRL])	1D	035	29
RS	(CTRL ^)	1E	036	30
US	(CTRL ?)	1F	037	31
	(space)	20	040	32
!		21	041	33
"		22	042	34
#	(hash symbol)	23	043	35
$		24	044	36
%		25	045	37
&	(ampersand)	26	046	38
'	(quote)	27	047	39
(		28	050	40
)		29	051	41
*	(asterisk)	2A	052	42
+		2B	053	43
,		2C	054	44
−		2D	055	45
.		2E	056	46
/		2F	057	47
0		30	060	48
1		31	061	49
2		32	062	50
3		33	063	51
4		34	064	52
5		35	065	53
6		36	066	54
7		37	067	55
8		38	070	56
9		39	071	57
:		3A	072	58
;		3B	073	59
<		3C	074	60
=		3D	075	61
>		3E	076	62
?		3F	077	63
@	(at symbol)	40	100	64
A		41	101	65
B		42	102	66
C		43	103	67
D		44	104	68
E		45	105	69
F		46	106	70
G		47	107	71
H		48	110	72
I		49	111	73
J		4A	112	74
K		4B	113	75
L		4C	114	76

continued

Table B.1 (*continued*)

ASCII character		Hexadecimal code	Octal code	Decimal code
M		4D	115	77
N		4E	116	78
O		4F	117	79
P		50	120	80
Q		51	121	81
R		52	122	82
S		53	123	83
T		54	124	84
U		55	125	85
V		56	126	86
W		57	127	87
X		58	130	88
Y		59	131	89
Z		5A	132	90
[		5B	133	91
\	(backslash)	5C	134	92
]		5D	135	93
^	(circumflex)	5E	136	94
_	(underscore)	5F	137	95
`	(grave)	60	140	96
a		61	141	97
b		62	142	98
c		63	143	99
d		64	144	100
e		65	145	101
f		66	146	102
g		67	147	103
h		68	150	104
i		69	151	105
j		6A	152	106
k		6B	153	107
l		6C	154	108
m		6D	155	109
n		6E	156	110
o		6F	157	111
p		70	160	112
q		71	161	113
r		72	162	114
s		73	163	115
t		74	164	116
u		75	165	117
v		76	166	118
w		77	167	119
x		78	170	120
y		79	171	121
z		7A	172	122
{		7B	173	123
|	(stick symbol)	7C	174	124
}		7D	175	125
~	(tilde)	7E	176	126
delete		7F	177	127

Reserved keywords

The following is a list of reserved keywords – identifiers used by the C programming language. They may not be used as programmer-defined identifiers.

auto
break
case
char
continue
default
do
double
else
enum
extern
float
for
goto
if
int
long
register
return
short
sizeof
static
struct
switch
typedef
union
unsigned
void
while

Further, some implementations have additionally reserved the three keywords asm, fortran and entry to reference non-C facilities. Additionally, the ANSII C standard has assigned the keywords const, signed and volatile.

Identifiers

An identifier is created according to the following rule:

> An identifier is a combination of letters and digits, the first of which must be a letter. The underscore symbol (_) is permitted in an identifier and is considered to be a letter.

An identifier may be any length. However, many C compilers consider only the first eight characters as significant. The ninth and subsequent characters in an identifier are ignored. Further, identifiers for external objects are processed by systems software other than compilers (such as linking loaders), and they have their own limitations on the length of identifiers. Frequently, only the first six characters are significant. These linkers may not be case-sensitive and fail to distinguish between two identifiers treated as unique by the C compiler.

Operators

The C programming language supports an extensive list of operators. Table E.1 provides the full list. The table presents the symbol(s) used to represent the operator, a description of the operator, and the operator associativity. The operators are listed in non-increasing order of precedence. Thus, the operators addition (+) and subtraction (−) have equal precedence, and both have higher precedence than the equality (= =) operator. The addition and subtraction operators associate left to right. The precedence and associativity are used to determine how an expression is evaluated. The general rule is that operators with highest precedence are evaluated first. An expression involving operators of equal precedence is eveluted according to the associativity of the operators.

Operands in a C expression are subject to a number of conversions. Any data item not one of the preferred types is automatically converted or promoted. A data item of a lower type is promoted to one of a higher type. Table E.2 shows these automatic promotions. Thus, following these promotions, an expression can only involve data items of types int, unsigned, long and double.

In a mixed expression, binary conversions determine whether and how operands are further converted before a binary operation is performed. When two values are to be operated upon in combination, they are first converted to a single common type. The result after applying the operation is also of that same common type. The ordered sequence of conversions that applies is:

If either operand is a *double,* the other is converted to a *double* and that is the type of the result.

If either operand is a *long,* the other is converted to a *long* and that is the type of the result.

If either operand is an *unsigned*, the other is converted to an *unsigned* and that is the type of the result.

Otherwise, both operands must be of type *int,* and that is the type of the result.

C also specifies certain adjustments in the types of function arguments. These adjustments are made in two places: on the actual argument types at the point of the function call, and on the formal argument type in the function definition.

If a formal argument is declared to be of type char, short or float, then the compiler automatically promotes them as described above. When an expression appears as an argument in a function call, it is subject to the usual conversions that apply to all expressions. The types of the actual argument should then match the type of the corresponding formal argument (following its promotion).

Table E.1

Operator	Description	Associativity
( )	Function call	Left to right
[ ]	Array element reference	
→	Pointer to structure member reference	
.	Structure member reference	
−	Unary minus	Right to left
+ +	Increment	
− −	Decrement	
!	Logical negation	
˜	One's complement	
*	Pointer reference (indirection)	
&	Address	
sizeof	Size of an object	
(type)	Type cast (coercion)	
*	Multiplication	Left to right
/	Division	
%	Modulus	
+	Addition	Left to right
−	Subtraction	
⟨⟨	Left shift	Left to right
⟩⟩	Right shift	
<	Less than	Left to right
< =	Less than or equal	
>	Greater than	
> =	Greater than or equal	
= =	Equality	Left to right
! =	Inequality	
&	Bitwise AND	Left to right
ˆ	Bitwise XOR	Left to right
¦	Bitwise OR	Left to right
&&	Logical AND	Left to right
¦ ¦	Logical OR	Left to right
? :	Conditional expression	Right to left
=	Assignment operators	Right to left
* = / = % =		
+ = − = & =		
ˆ = ¦ =		
⟨⟨ = ⟩⟩ =		
,	Comma operator	Left to right

Table E.2

Original type	Promoted type
char, short	int
float	double

The standard C library

Many C facilities are provided by C libraries. The facilities are categorized by their functionality and belong to a particular library. The capabilities detailed in this appendix are partitioned into five groupings:

Operations on characters
Operations on strings
Storage management operations
Input/output procedures
Mathematical functions.

To use a function from one of these libraries, the appropriate #include command is needed to provide the relevant library declarations. Many functions, particularly those that provide operations on characters, are macros. All of the facilities we discuss are described as if they were functions to permit detailing the number and type of the arguments.

F.1 Character functions

The standard header file *ctype.h* contains a set of macros that are used to process single characters. The macros fall into two categories: test a single character, and convert a single character. The macros are made accessible by the preprocessor statement:

#include ⟨ctype.h⟩

The macros which test a single character return an int value that is non-zero (logical TRUE) or zero (logical FALSE), according to whether the test succeeds or not. All these functions are distinguished with the prefix 'is', for example, isdigit. The macros which perform character translation have the prefix 'to' (e.g. toupper) and return an int representation of some character.

isalnum

    int isalnum(c)
        char   c;

Returns non-zero if c represents an alphanumerical character; otherwise returns zero. The alphanumerical character is any one of 0–9, a–z and A–Z inclusive.

isalpha

```
int isalpha(c)
    char    c;
```

Returns non-zero if c represents an alphabetic character; otherwise returns zero. The alphabetical characters are a–z and A–Z inclusive.

isascii

```
int isascii(c)
    char    c;
```

Returns non-zero if c represents any character from the standard ASCII character set; otherwise returns zero. According to Appendix B, c is any value in the range 0x00 to 0x7F inclusive.

iscntrl

```
int iscntrl(c)
    char  c;
```

Returns non-zero if c represents a control character; otherwise returns zero. The control characters are the 'non-printing' characters. From the standard ASCII set, the control characters are 0x00 to 0x1F, inclusive, and also 0x7F.

isdigit

```
int isdigit (c)
    char    c;
```

Returns non-zero if c represents a decimal digit character; otherwise returns zero. The decimal digits are 0 to 9 inclusive.

isgraph

```
int isgraph(c)
    char    c;
```

Returns non-zero if c represents a graphics character; otherwise returns zero. From the standard ASCII character set, the graphics characters are those with codes 0x21 to 0x7E inclusive.

islower

```
int islower(c)
    char    c;
```

Returns non-zero if c represents a lower-case alphabetic character; otherwise returns zero. The lower-case alphabetics are a–z inclusive.

isprint

```
int isprint (c)
    char    c;
```

Returns non-zero if c represents a printable character; otherwise returns zero. From the standard ASCII character set, the printable characters are those with codes 0x20 to 0x7E inclusive.

ispunct

```
int ispunct(c)
    char    c;
```

Returns non-zero if c represents a punctuation symbol; otherwise returns zero. From the standard ASCII character set, the punctuation characters are:

```
!   "   #   $   %   &   '   (
)   *   +   ,   -   .   /   :
;   <   =   >   ?   @   [   \
]   ^   _   `   {   |   }   ~
```

as well as the space character.

isspace

```
int isspace(c)
    char    c;
```

Returns non-zero if c represents a whitespace character; otherwise returns zero. The whitespace characters from the standard ASCII character set are horizontal tab (0x09), newline (0x0A) and space (0x20).

isupper

```
int isupper(c)
    char    c;
```

Returns non-zero if c represents an upper-case alphabetic character; otherwise returns zero. The upper-case characters are A–Z inclusive.

tolower

```
int tolower(c)
    char    c;
```

If c represents an upper-case alphabetic character, then tolower returns the corresponding lower-case character; otherwise c is returned unchanged.

toupper

```
int toupper(c)
    char    c;
```

If c represents a lower-case alphabetic character, then toupper returns the corresponding upper-case character; otherwise c is returned unchanged.

F.2 String processing

A string in C is an array of characters terminated by the ASCII null character (' \0'). String constants in a program are automatically constructed in this form by the C compiler.

The standard header file *string.h* contains a series of external referencing declarations to the string-handling functions. Generally, there are two classes of functions. The first category is concerned with varieties of string copying. The functions usually return a character pointer result. When characters are transferred to a destination string, no checks are performed to ensure that the destination string is sufficiently large. Possible array overflow can then occur and corrupt other program variables. The second class of functions perform tests and return a non-zero value representing TRUE or zero for FALSE.

strcat

```
char *strcat(s1, s2)
   char    *s1, *s2;
```

Appends the content of the string s2 to the end of the string s1. The first character of s2 overwrites the null character which terminates s1. A pointer to the first character of s1 is returned.

strchr

```
char *strchr(s, c)
   char *s, c;
```

The string s is searched for the first occurrence of the character c. If c is found, the function returns a pointer to c in s; otherwise NULL is returned. This function may be known as *index* on some systems.

strcmp

```
int strcmp(s1, s2)
   char    *s1, *s2;
```

Compares the two strings s1 and s2. If s1 is less than s2, the function returns a negative value. If s1 equals s2, zero is returned. If s1 is greater than s2, a positive value is returned. Two strings are equal if they have the same length and have identical contents. String s1 is less than string s2 if: (a) their content is identical to some character and then the next character from s1 is less than the next from s2 according to the character set encoding; or (b) string s2 is longer than string s1 and the contents of s1 and s2 up to the length of s1 are identical.

strcpy

```
char *strcpy(s1, s2)
   char    *s1, *s2;
```

Overwrites the original content of the string s1 with the content of the string s2. A pointer to the first character of s1 is returned.

strlen

```
int strlen(s)
    char    *s;
```

Returns the number of characters in the string s, not including the terminating null character.

strncat

```
char *strncat(s1, s2, n)
    char    *s1, *s2;
    int     n;
```

Appends the first n characters from the string s2 to the end of the string s1. If s2 contains fewer than n characters, only these are appended. A pointer to the first character of s1 is returned.

strncmp

```
int strncmp(s1, s2, n)
    char    *s1, *s2;
    int     n;
```

Compares up to n characters of the two strings s1 and s2. Returns a negative integer if s1 is less than s2; zero if s1 equals s2; and a positive integer if s1 is greater than s2 (see: strcmp). If either string contains fewer than n characters, the entire string is used.

strncpy

```
char *strncpy(s1, s2, n)
    char    *s1, *s2;
    int     n;
```

Overwrites the original content of string s1 with the first n characters of string s2. If s2 contains fewer than n characters, the entire string is used. A pointer to the first character of s1 is returned.

strrchr

```
char *strrchr(s, c)
    char    *s, c;
```

The string s is searched for the last occurrence of the character c. If c is found, the function returns a pointer to c in s; otherwise NULL is returned. The function is also known as *rindex*.

F.3 Storage management functions

The storage management functions support the dynamic allocation and deallocation of memory space. A region of memory which is deallocated is recycled by the storage manager for further allocation requests. A pointer to the region of memory is returned by the allocation functions and is required as an argument by the deallocation functions. A pointer to a char is returned and may be coerced to any other pointer type.

calloc

```
char *calloc(n, size)
   unsigned int n, size;
```

Allocates a region of memory of n elements, each of size bytes. A pointer to the first character of this region is returned by the function. If the requests cannot be satisfied, NULL is returned.

cfree

```
void cfree (ptr)
   char     *ptr;
```

Deallocates a region of memory previously allocated by calloc. The argument is a pointer to a char previously returned by calloc.

free

```
void free(ptr)
   char     *ptr;
```

Deallocates a region of memory previously allocated by malloc. The argument to free is pointer to a char previously returned by malloc.

malloc

```
char *malloc(n)
   unsigned int n;
```

Allocates a region of memory of n bytes. A pointer to the first character of this region is returned by the function. If the request cannot be satisfied, NULL is returned.

F.4 Standard I/O functions

The header file *stdio.h* should be included in any program that uses one of the standard I/O library functions. The file contains external referencing declarations for those functions from this library; macros for a number of character functions; definitions for symbolic constants such as EOF and NULL; type declarations for the type name FILE; and definitions for the constant file pointers *stdin, stdout* and *stderr.*

clearerr

```
void clearerr(fp)
   FILE *fp;
```

Resets any error indication on the file identified by the file pointer fp (see also ferror).

fclose

```
int fclose(fp)
   FILE    *fp;
```

Closes the file identified by the file pointer fp. All internal data buffers are emptied and freed. If an error occurs, fclose returns EOF; otherwise zero is returned.

feof

```
int feof(fp)
   FILE    *fp;
```

Returns non-zero if the file identified by the file pointer fp is truly at the end of file; otherwise returns zero.

ferror

```
int ferror(fp)
   FILE    *fp;
```

Returns non-zero if an error condition has occurred while reading or writing the file identified by the file pointer fp; otherwise returns zero. Function clearerr can be used to reset the error condition.

fflush

```
int fflush(fp)
   FILE    *fp;
```

Flushes any internal data buffers for the file identified by the file pointer fp. The file should have been opened for output. Function fflush returns EOF if an error is detected; otherwise zero is returned.

fgetc

```
int fgetc(fp)
   FILE    *fp;
```

Returns the next character from the file identified by the file pointer fp, which must be opened for input. If an error occurs or the end of file condition is determined, fgetc returns EOF.

fgets

```
char *fgets(buffer, n, fp)
   char     *buffer;
   int      n;
   FILE     *fp;
```

Characters are read from the file identified by the file pointer fp which must be opened for input. The reading continues until the end of file is reached, until a newline character is read, or until n − 1 characters have been input. The characters are stored in successive locations of the character array buffer, and a terminating null character is appended.

If a newline character is read, then it is stored in the array. If the end of file is encountered before any characters have been read or an error occurs, then the function returns the NULL pointer. If the input operation succeeds, then a pointer to the first character of buffer is returned.

fopen

```
FILE *fopen(filename, mode)
   char   *filename, *mode;
```

Function fopen opens the named file according to the indicated access mode. If the function is successful, then a FILE pointer is returned and used in subsequent I/O operations; otherwise the value NULL is returned. Both arguments to fopen are null-terminated character strings. Permissible values for the mode argument are:

"r"   open an existing file for reading
"w"   truncate an existing file or create a new file for writing
"a"   create a new file or append to an existing file for writing
"r + " open an existing file for both reading and writing, positioned at the beginning of the file
"w + " truncate an existing file or create a new file both for reading or writing, positioned at the beginning of this empty file
"a + " create a new file or append to an existing file both for reading or writing, positioned at the end of the file

fprintf

```
int fprint(fp, format, argument1, argument2, ...)
FILE   *fp;
char   *format;
```

Performs formatted output to the file identified by the file pointer fp. For details see: printf.

fputc

```
int fputc(c, fp)
   char   c;
   FILE   *fp;
```

Writes the character c to the file identified by the file pointer fp. Function fputc returns c if successful; otherwise it returns EOF.

fputs

```
int fputs(s, fp)
   char   *s;
   FILE   *fp;
```

Writes the characters in the null-terminated string s to the file identified by the file pointer fp. If any errors occur, fputs returns EOF; otherwise a value other than EOF is returned.

fread

```
int fread(buffer, size, n, fp)
   char          *buffer;
   unsigned int  size;
   int           n;
   FILE          *fp;
```

Reads a block of binary data from the file identified by the file pointer fp into buffer. The number of data items read is n, each of size bytes. The actual number of items read is returned by fread. If this value is positive and less than n, then that number of items was read before encountering the end of file. If fread returns 0, either the immediate end of file or an error has occurred.

freopen

```
FILE *freopen(filename, mode, fp)
   char    *filename, *mode;
   FILE    *fp;
```

Closes the file presently associated with the file pointer fp and opens a new file with name filename and mode (see: fopen). If the call to freopen is successful, the fp is returned; otherwise NULL is returned.

fscanf

```
int fscanf(fp, format, argument1, argument2, ...)
   FILE    *fp;
   char    *format;
```

Performs formatted input from the file identified by the file pointer fp. For details see: scanf.

fseek

```
int fseek(fp, offset, origin)
   FILE    *fp;
   long    offset;
   int     origin;
```

Positions the file identified by the file pointer fp to a point that is offset bytes relative to some place dependent upon the value of origin. If origin is 0, then the position is relative to the beginning of the file. If origin is 1, the position is relative to the current file position. If origin is 2, then the position is relative to the end of the file. If the operation is successful, fseek returns zero; otherwise it returns non-zero.

ftell

```
long ftell(fp)
   FILE    *fp;
```

Returns the relative offset in bytes of the current position in the file identified by the file pointer fp.

fwrite

```
int fwrite(buffer, size, n, fp)
    char            *buffer;
    unsigned int    size;
    int             n;
    FILE            *fp;
```

Writes a block of binary data from buffer to the file identified by the file pointer fp. The number of data items written is n, each of size bytes. The actual number of items written is returned by fwrite. If an error occurs, fwrite returns zero.

getc

```
int getc(fp)
    FILE    *fp;
```

Reads and returns the next character from the file identified by the file pointer fp. The value EOF is returned if the end of file is reached or if an error occurs. Usually implemented as a macro.

getchar

```
int getchar( )
```

Reads and returns the next character from the standard input file stdin. The value EOF is returned if the end of file is reached or if an error occurs. Normally implemented as a macro.

gets

```
char *gets(buffer)
    char    *buffer;
```

Reads characters from the standard input file stdin into buffer until a newline is read or the end of file is reached. If an error occurs, or if no characters are read because the end of file is immediate, then function gets returns NULL; otherwise buffer is returned. If the input is terminated because the newline symbol is read, the newline character is not stored in the buffer (see also: fgets).

printf

```
int printf(format, argument1, argument2, ...)
    char    *format;
```

Writes the arguments to the standard output stream stdout according to the format string. Function printf returns EOF if an error occurs; otherwise it returns the number of characters written.

The argument list is composed of comma-separated expressions. The expressions are evaluated and converted according to the conversion specifications in the format string. The conversion specifications should agree in number and type with the arguments. Characters in the format string which are not part of a conversion specification are copied unaltered to the output. A conversion specification is

Table F.1

Character	Action
c	The argument is displayed as a single character
d	Signed decimal conversion of an *int* or a *long*
e, E	Signed decimal floating point conversion in scientific notation
f	Signed decimal floating point conversion
g, G	Signed decimal floating point conversion using either e (or E) or f conversion whichever requires the least space
o	Unsigned octal conversion
s	The argument is displayed as a string
u	Unsigned decimal conversion of an *unsigned*
x, X	Unsigned hexadecimal conversion using a–f or A–F as appropriate

introduced by the percent symbol (%). Following the percent sign, a conversion specification is constructed from:

flag characters
field width
precision
long size specification
conversion operation

Only the percent sign and the conversion operation are obligatory. The remaining elements are optional modifiers but should appear in the given order, if present. The permissible conversion operations are the single characters c, d, e, E, f, g, G, o, s, u, x, X or %. The conversion operation % is used as the literal representation for the percent sign, which is otherwise reserved. The effect of these conversion operations is summarized in Table F.1, then detailed later in this section.

When an argument is printed, the place where it is output is called its *field*. The number of characters in the field is called the field *width*. If the optional field width in the conversion specification is omitted, the minimum number of character places is used in the conversion. To demonstrate some simple uses of printf, consider the following declarations and calls. In these and further examples, the output characters are delimited by the symbols [and] to indicate the extent of the field.

```
int     j = 45, k = - 123;
float   x = 12.34;
char    c = 'W';
char    *m = "Hello";
```

```
printf("No arguments")        No arguments
printf("Tax is 10%%")         Tax is 10%
printf("[%d]", j)             [45]
printf("[%d]", k)             [- 123]
printf("[%f]", x)             [12.340000]
printf("[%c]", c)             [W]
printf("[%s]", m)             [Hello]
```

Table F.2

Modifier	Description
−	The value to be displayed is left justified in the field
+	The value will always be displayed with a numeric sign (only for the conversion operations d, e, E, f, g and G)
space	Non-negative numbers are to be preceded by a blank space (only for the conversion operations d, e, E, f, g and G)
#	Integers displayed in octal format are preceded by a leading 0. Integers displayed in hexadecimal format are preceded by a leading 0x (or 0X). Floating point conversions always guarantee that the decimal point is displayed
0 (zero)	The zero character is used as the padding to the left of the converted value, rather than with leading spaces
field width	The minimum field width, expressed as a decimal integer constant. If this minimum field width is insufficient to display the value, then that which is necessary is used. If this field width is specified by an asterisk symbol (*), the field width is given by the next argument to printf, which should be an integer
.precision	The precision is expressed as a decimal integer constant and is used to indicate the maximum number of digits to the right of the decimal point in an e, E, f, g or G conversion. When used with an s conversion, the precision determines the maximum number of characters to be displayed. If the precision is specified by an asterisk symbol, then the precision is provided by the next argument to printf which should be an integer
l or L	The long size specification is used in conjunction with the conversion operations d, o, u, x and X and indicates that the argument is a *long*

The optional modifiers in a conversion specification affect the meaning of the main conversion operation. They are summarized in Table F.2. If no modifiers are present, certain defaults occur. For example, the format %f always defaults to six decimal places of output. These defaults and the effect of the modifiers are detailed with the conversion operations.

The main conversion operations are now discussed in detail. The illustrative examples use the symbol ƀ to represent blanks (spaces) in the output.

Conversion operation c
An int or unsigned int argument is printed as a single character which should represent a symbol from the valid character set. The minimum field width and ' − ' modifiers can be meaningfully employed with this conversion (see Table F.3).

char c = 'W';

Table F.3

Function call	Output
printf("[%c]", c)	[W]
printf("[%3c]", c)	[ƀƀW]
printf("[% − 4c]", c)	[Wƀƀƀ]

Conversion operation d

One argument of integral type (*long* if the long size specification is given) is consumed. A signed decimal conversion of the value is performed. A sequence of decimal digits representing the number is displayed. If no field width is given, the default is the least number of characters necessary. If the value requires fewer positions than that given by the field width, it is right-justified in the field and padded on the left with spaces. If a field width is insufficient to display the converted value, then the default field width is assumed. The conversion modifier '0' uses leading zeros rather than spaces. The ' − ' modifier left-justifies the value in the field. The ' + ' modifier ensures that a plus or minus symbol is output (see Table F.4).

    int   j = 45, k = − 123;
    long int jj = 1234567890;

Table F.4

Function call	Output
printf("[%d]", k)	[− 123]
printf("[%4d]", j)	[ƀƀ45]
printf("[% − 5d]", j)	[45ƀƀƀ]
printf("[%05d]", j)	[00045]
printf("[%2d]", k)	[− 123]
printf("[% + 4d]", j)	[ƀ + 45]
printf("[%1d]", jj)	[1234567890]
printf("[% + 05d]", j)	[+ 0045]

Conversion operations e and E

Signed decimal floating point conversion is performed on an argument of type double. An argument of type float is automatically converted to type double in the usual way. Thus, these conversion operations are equally applicable to variables of types float and double. The conversion produces a value in scientfic notation form − d.dddddde + dd (for e conversion) or − d.ddddddE + dd (for E conversion). The leading minus sign is optional. The precision specifies the number of decimal digits following the decimal point. If no precision is given, a default value of 6 is assumed. If the precision is given as 0, no fractional value is present nor is the decimal point (unless the ' # ' modifier is used). The exponent is always signed and consists of at least two decimal digits (see Table F.5).

    float   x = 12.345;
    double y = − 678.9;

Table F.5

Function call	Output
printf("[%e]", x)	[1.234500e + 01]
printf("[%E]", x)	[1.234500E + 01]
printf("[%14.4e]", x)	[ƀƀƀƀ1.2345e + 01]
printf("[% − 12.1E]", y)	[− 6.8E + 02ƀƀƀƀ]
printf("[% + 12.2E]", x)	[ƀƀƀ + 1.24E + 01]
printf("[%.2e]", y)	[− 6.79e + 02]
printf("[%10.0e]", x)	[ƀƀƀƀƀ1e + 01]
printf("[% # 10.0e]", x)	[ƀƀƀƀ1.e + 01]

Conversion operation f

A signed decimal floating point conversion is performed on a value of type double (or float). The output value consists of a sequence of decimal digits with an imbedded decimal point. At least one digit appears before the decimal point. The number of digits in the fractional part is determined by the precision. If no precision is given, the default is 6 decimal places. If the precision is given as 0, no fractional value is present in the output nor is the decimal point (unless the '#' modifier is used) (see Table F.6).

```
float    x = 12.345;
double   y = -678.9;
```

Table F.6

Function call	Output
printf("[%f]", y)	[-678.900000]
printf("[%-10.2f]", x)	[12.35ƀƀƀƀƀ]
printf("[%+8.1f]", x)	[ƀƀƀ+12.4]
printf("[%.2f]", y)	[-678.90]
printf("[%08.2f]", x)	[00012.35]
printf("[%+06.1f]", x)	[+012.4]
printf("[%#4.0f]", x)	[ƀ12.]

Conversion operations g and G

A signed decimal floating point conversion is performed on a value of type double (or float). The conversion is as for either the f or e (or E when G is used) conversion, whichever is the shorter (see Table F.7).

```
float    x = 12.345;
double   y = -234567.89;
```

Table F.7

Function call	Output
printf("[%g]", x)	[12.345000]
printf("[%G]", x)	[12.345000]
printf("[%.1g]", y)	[-2.4e+05]
printf("[%.1G]", y)	[-2.4E+05]

Conversion operation o

The argument, which should be of integral type, is output as an unsigned octal value. The value is displayed as a sequence of octal digits in a minimum field, unless the field width specification is given. No leading 0 prefixes the octal value unless the '#' modifier is used (see Table F.8).

```
int            k = 45;
unsigned int j = 0123;
```

Table F.8

Function call	Output
printf("[%o]", j)	[123]
printf("[%5o]", k)	[ƀƀƀ55]
printf("[% # 6o]", j)	[ƀƀ0123]
printf("[% − 4o]", k)	[55ƀƀ]

Conversion operation s
The argument is printed as a string of symbols. The argument is expected to be of type pointer to char. If no field width is specified, the string is displayed without change, otherwise the string is displayed right-justified in the field. If a precision specification p is given, then the first p characters of the string or the string itself, whichever is the shorter, is displayed. The only appropriate modifier is ' − ' which left-justifies the string in the field (see Table F.9).

char *mess = "Hello";

Table F.9

Function call	Output
printf("[%s]", mess)	[Hello]
printf("[%8s]", mess)	[ƀƀƀHello]
printf("[% − 8s]", mess)	[Helloƀƀƀ]
printf("[%6.2s]", mess)	[ƀƀƀƀHe]
printf("[% − 10.6s]", mess)	[Helloƀƀƀƀƀ]

Conversion operation u
The u operation performs unsigned decimal conversion of an unsigned int. A sequence of decimal digits representing the value of the argument is displayed. The field is as short as possible, unless a field width modifier is present (see Table F.10).

unsigned int t = 123;

Table F.10

Function call	Output
printf("[%u]", t)	[123]
printf("[%6u]", t)	[ƀƀƀ123]
printf("[% − 4u], t)	[123ƀ]

Conversion operations x and X
An argument of integral type is printed as an unsigned hexadecimal value. The conversion operation x uses the hexadecimal digits 0–9 a–f, while the X operation

Table F.11

Function call	Output
printf("[%x]", k)	[f4]
printf("[%X]", k)	[F4]
printf("[%6x]", k)	[ƀƀƀƀf4]
printf("[% #6X], k)	[ƀƀ0XF4]

uses the hexadecimal digits 0–9 A–F. If the '#' modifier is used, then the prefix 0x for the x operation (or 0X for the X operation) is prepended (see Table F.11).

    int k = 0xf4;

putc

    int putc(c, fp)
        char   c;
        FILE   *fp;

Writes the single character c to the file identified by the file pointer fp. If an error occurs, putc returns EOF; otherwise the value of the written character is returned.

putchar

    int putchar(c)
        char   c;

Writes the single character c to the standard output. If an error occurs, putchar returns EOF; otherwise the value of the written character is returned. Normally, putchar is implemented as a macro.

puts

    int puts(buffer)
        char   *buffer;

Writes the null-terminated character string in buffer to the standard output. A newline symbol is automatically written following the last character in the buffer (see also: fputs). If an error occurs, puts returns EOF; otherwise a value other than EOF is returned.

rewind

    void rewind(fp)
        FILE *fp;

Resets the file indicated by the file pointer fp back to the beginning of the file.

scanf

    inf scanf(format, argument1, argument2, ...)
        char   *format;

Function scanf reads items from the standard input according to the format string. The arguments after the format string must all be pointers. Converted values read from the standard input are stored in the locations referenced by the pointers. Function scanf returns the number of successful assignments. If this number is less than the number of arguments given to scanf, the input operation has prematurely terminated either because end of file has been reached or because an error has occurred. If end of file occurs before any assignments have been performed, scanf returns EOF.

The format string is a picture of the expected input, and may contain the following:

1. Whitespace characters, which match optional whitespace characters in the input stream. One or more whitespace characters in the format string are considered as one. This equivalent single whitespace character matches any number of whitespace characters in the input. The first non-whitespace character remains in the input as the next character to be read.
2. Non-whitespace characters, other than the percent symbol (%), which must match exactly the next input character. If there is no match, the operation is terminated and the failed input character remains in the input stream as the next available character.
3. A conversion specification which is introduced by a percent symbol (%). A conversion specification is constructed from:

    percent symbol
    assignment suppression symbol
    field width
    short or long size specification
    conversion operation

Only the percent symbol and the conversion operation are obligatory. The remaining modifiers are optional but should appear in the given order, if present. The conversion operations are, with one exception, a single character

Table F.12

Character	Action
c	Read and assign one or more characters
d	Signed decimal conversion and assignment to a *short*, *int* or a *long*
e, E, f, g and G	Signed decimal floating point conversion and assignment to a *float* or a *double*
o	Unsigned octal conversion and assignment to a *short*, *int* or a *long*
s	Read and assign a string
u	Unsigned decimal conversion and assignment to an *int*
x, X	Unsigned hexadecimal conversion and assignment to a *short*, *int* or a *long*
%	A percent symbol is expected in the input
[	A string of characters from the input stream is read and assigned. The permissible set of scanned characters is enclosed between the [and a matching] symbols

from: c, d, e, E, f, g, G, o, s, u, x, X, % or [. The exception is the operation [, which is followed by a series of characters ending in]. The effect of all these conversion operations is summarized in Table F.12.

Except for character input and the [conversion operation, an input field consists of a sequence of non-whitespace characters, appropriate to the conversion operation. The first inappropriate character terminates the field or the field width is exhausted (if specified), whichever comes first. Except for the same two exceptions, a field may be preceded by a sequence of whitespace characters.

The optional modifiers in a conversion specification alter the meaning of the main conversion operation. The effect of these modifiers is summarized in Table F.13.

The main conversion operations are now discussed in detail. Each subsection discusses the operation and the effect of any modifier. The symbol b is used in the examples to denote a blank or space symbol.

Table F.13

Modifier	Description
*	The *assignment suppression flag*. Characters are read from the input and processed in the normal way for the conversion operation, but no assignment is performed. No argument to *scanf* is used
field width	The maximum field width, expressed as an unsigned decimal integer constant which is not zero
size specification	The size specification is either the character 'h' (meaning *short*), or the character 'l' (meaning *long*). The character 'h' may be used in conjunction with the d, o, x or X conversions, and specifies that the argument is a pointer to a *short*. The character 'l' specifies that the argument is a pointer to a *long*. When used with the e, f or g conversions, the character 'l' specifies that the argument is a pointer to a *double* rather than a pointer to a *float*

Conversion operation c

One or more characters are read and stored at the location(s) addressed by the pointer to char argument. Note that the c conversion does not skip over any initial whitespace characters. If no field width is given, then that number of characters are read and stored. The pointer argument is considered to be the address of an array of characters in which the input is stored. Note that no null terminator is appended to the stored input characters (see Table F.14).

    char ch1, ch2, text[6];

Table F.14

Function call	Input	Effect
scanf("%c", &ch1)	ABC123	ch1 = 'A'
scanf("%c%c", &ch1, &ch2)	AbBC	ch1 = 'A', ch2 = ' '
scanf("%*4c")	ABC123	skip ABC1
scanf("%2c", text)	ABC123	text[0] = 'A', text[1] = 'B'
Note no address operator with *text*		

Conversion operation d
Signed decimal conversion and assignment to an int or to a short (if h size specification is given) or to a long (if l size specification is given). On some systems, conversion D is available and is equivalent to ld (see Table F.15).

```
short  sx;
int    xx;
long   lx;
```

Table F.15

Function call	Input	Effect
scanf("%d", &xx)	ƀƀƀ123ƀ	xx = 123
scanf("%2d", &xx)	1234	xx = 12
scanf("%*2d%d", &xx)	1234ƀƀ	xx = 34
scanf("%hd", &sx)	ƀƀ − 12A	sx = − 12
scanf("%ld", &lx)	ƀ + 123ƀ	lx = 123
scanf("%d/%ld", &xx, &lx)	12/34ƀƀ	xx = 12, lx = 34

Conversion operations e, E, f, g and G
Signed decimal floating point conversion. The conversions e and f expect an argument which is a pointer to a float. The same conversions preceded with the long size modifier l (le and lf) and the conversions E and G expect a pointer to a double argument. All these operations accept a floating point value. The form of a floating point value is an optional sign, zero or more decimal digits, an optional decimal point, and zero or more decimal digits. These formats may then be followed by the letters 'e' or 'E', an optional sign and zero or more decimal digits (see Table F.16).

```
float  x;
double y;
```

Table F.16

Function call	Input	Effect
scanf("%f", &x)	ƀƀ12.34ƀ	x = 12.34
scanf("%lf", &y)	+ 1.23AB	y = 1.23
scanf("%*f%e", &x)	ƀƀ − 6.2ƀƀ1e + 1	x = 10.0
scanf("%f", &x)	ƀƀ2ƀ	x = 2.0
scanf("%2f%E", &x, &y)	1234A	x = 12.0, y = 34.0
scanf("%le", &y)	1.ƀ = 1.0	y = 1.0
scanf("%2f%lg", &x, &y)	1.79ƀ	x = 1.0, y = 79.0

Conversion operation o
Unsigned octal conversion and assignment to an int or to a short (if h size specification is given) or to a long (if l size specification is given). On some systems,

Table F.17

Function call	Input	Effect
scanf(" %o", &xx)	ƀƀƀ17ƀ	xx = 15
scanf(" %2o%h2o", &xx, &sx)	1234ƀ	xx = 10, sx = 28
scanf(" %*3o%lo, &lx)	74117A	lx = 15

conversion O is available and is equivalent to lo. A leading zero in the input stream is not necessary (see Table F.17).

    short sx;
    int   xx;
    long   lx;

Conversion operation s
Reads a string of characters and assigns to the argument which must be of type pointer to char. Any leading whitespace characters in the input are ignored. Non-whitespace characters are input until the first occurrence of a whitespace character, or until the maximum number of characters has been read if a field width is specified. The characters are stored in the array and terminated with the null character (see Table F.18).

    char t1[10], t2[12];

Table F.18

Function call	Input	Effect
scanf(" %s", t1)	ƀƀABCƀ	t1 = "ABC"
scanf(" %s %s", t1, t2)	ƀABƀƀCDEƀ	t1 = "AB", t2 = "CDE"
scanf(" %4s", t1)	ƀƀABCDEF	t1 = "ABCD"
scanf(" %*4s%s", t2)	ƀƀABCDEFƀ	t2 = "EF"
scanf(" %1s", t1)	ƀƀXYZƀ	t1 = "X"

Conversion operation u
Performs unsigned decimal conversion and assigns to an argument which must be of type pointer to unsigned. Leading whitespace symbols are ignored. Characters are read until the first occurrence of a non-digit or until the maximum field width has been read (see Table F.19).

    unsigned int ux;

Table F.19

Function call	Input	Effect
scanf(" %u", &ux)	ƀƀ123ƀƀ	ux = 123
scanf(" %2u", &ux)	ƀƀ123ƀƀ	ux = 12
scanf(" %*2u%u", &ux)	ƀƀ123ƀƀ	ux = 3

Conversion operations x and X

Unsigned hexadecimal conversion and assignment to an int or to a short (if h size specification is given) or to a long (if l size specification is given). The x and X operations are identical. Both accept 0–9a–fA–F as valid hexadecimal digits. Leading whitespace is ignored. Hexadecimal digits are read until a non-hexadecimal digit appears in the input, or until the maximum field width has been used. Leading 0x or 0X is not necessary, but if present is counted toward the field width (see Table F.20).

    int xx;

Table F.20

Function call	Input	Effect
scanf("%x", &xx)	␢␢␢1F␢	xx = 31
scanf("%2X", &xx)	␢FFF␢	xx = 255
scanf("%*2x%x", &xx)	␢FFF␢	xx = 15

Conversion operation [

Reads a string of characters and assigns to the argument which must be of type pointer to char. The input characters are stored in the array and null terminated. The set of characters between [and the matching] denotes those that may read as part of the input. The first input character not a member of the set terminates the input operation. Leading whitespace characters are *not* skipped by this operation. If the first character following the [is the circumflex symbol, ^, then the input is any character other than those in the set (see Table F.21).

    char t1[10], t2[12];

Table F.21

Function call	Input	Effect
scanf("%[ABC]", t1)	ABAB␢	t1 = "ABAB"
scanf("%[ABC]", t1)	␢␢ABAB␢	t1 = ""
scanf("%[ABC]", t2)	ABACD	t2 = "ABAC"
scanf("%[^ABC]", t1)	ABAB␢	t1 = ""
scanf("%[^ABC]", t1)	␢␢ABAB␢	t1 = "␢␢"

sprintf

    int sprintf(buffer, format, argument1, argument2, ...)
        char   *buffer, *format;

The values of the arguments are converted according to the format string (see: printf) and are placed in the character array pointed to by buffer. The character string in buffer is null terminated. Otherwise, the function operates in a manner similar to printf (see Table F. 22).

    int jj = 45;
    char *m = "Hello";
    char text[80];

Table F.22

Function	Effect
sprintf(text, "[%d]", jj)	text = "[45]"
sprintf(text, "[% − 8s]", m)	text = "[Helloбɓɓ]"

sscanf

```
int sscanf(buffer, format, argument1, argument2, ...)
   char    *buffer,  *format;
```

Values as specified by the format string are input from the character array buffer and stored in the arguments. Otherwise, function sscanf operates in a manner similar to scanf (see Table F23).

```
int jj;
char *m = "Hello";
char t1[10];
```

Table F.23

Function call	Effect
sscanf("45", "%d", &jj)	jj = 45
sscanf("first second", "%s", t1)	t1 = "first"
sscanf(m, "%2s", t1)	t1 = "He"

ungetc

```
int ungetc(c, fp)
   char    c;
   FILE   *fp;
```

The character c is pushed back on to the file identified by the file pointer fp. The next call to getc will then return this same character. Only one character may be put back into a file. Between two calls to ungetc, there must be at least one read operation on that file. Function ungetc returns the character c if successful; otherwise ungetc returns EOF.

F.5 Mathematical functions

The mathematical functions are declared by the library header file *math.h*. All the functions, except three, take arguments of type double and return a value of type double. Two of these functions have two arguments, the remainder have only one. The three exceptions all operate with values of type int.

The functions which operate with integers are:

int abs(x)   the absolute value of the integer argument x
int rand( )   pseudo random number generator of integer values between 0 and
                  the largest positive integer

void srand (x)   initialize the pseudo random number generator with the unsigned int value x

The functions which operate on a single argument of type double and return a value of type double are:

acos(x)   trigonometric arc cosine of x, the result expressed in radians between 0 and π

asin(x)   trigonometric arc sine of x, the result π expressed in radians between $-\pi/2$ and $\pi/2$

atan(x)   trigonometric arc tangent of x, the result expressed in radians between $-\pi/2$ and $\pi/2$

ceil(x)   returns the floating point equivalent of the integer value not less than x

cos(x)   trigonometric cosine of x, where x is expressed in radians

cosh(x)   hyperbolic cosine of x

exp(x)   exponential of x

fabs(x)   absolute value of x

floor(x)   returns the floating point equivalent of the largest integer not greater than x

log(x)   natural logarithm

log10(x)   logarithm of x to the base 10

sin(x)   trigonometric sine of x, where x is expressed in radians

sinh(x)   hyperbolic sine of x

sqrt(x)   square root of x

tan(x)   trigonometric tangent of x, where x is expressed in radians

tanh(x)   hyperbolic tangent of x

Two functions operate with two arguments of type double. Each function returns a value of type double. These functions are:

atan2(x, y)   trigonometric arc tangent of x/y, with the result expressed in radians between $-\pi$ and π

pow(x, y)   x raised to the power y

Compiling under UNIX

A C program is composed of one or more program text files. The files can be either *header* files or *program unit* files. Normally, header files have the suffix '.h' in the filename and program units have the suffix '.c'. Under UNIX, program files are compiled with the cc command. Strictly, cc is not the C compiler proper, but a driver program that initiates the phases associated with macro preprocessing, compiling, linking and loading. The general form of the cc command is:

cc option file1 file2 . . . .

The options are distinguished by a leading hyphen (-). They alter the effect of the cc command.

A program that is created as one source file, say prog.c, is compiled with the command:

cc prog.c

Any errors that appear in the program are reported on the standard error output stream. A program with no errors produces no report. The command translates the C source code into an executable object program in the file a.out. This executable program image can be run by entering the command:

a.out

Normally, compiled programs are retained in files with the same name as the program source file name but with the '.c' suffix removed. The object filename is given to the compiler command with the option '-o':

cc -o prog prog.c

The '-o' option is followed by the filename of the destination file, as opposed to a.out which is the default. These arguments may be given in any order to the cc command. It is perfectly valid to enter:

cc prog.c -o prog

The executable program image in file prog is now executed by entering the command:

prog

Consider now a program split over two files (say, prog1.c and prog2.c). The two files can be compiled and combined to produce an executable program file called prog with the command:

cc -o prog prog1.c prog2.c

The cc command actually does its work in a number of stages. The source program file prog1.c is processed up to and including the compilation phase. An object file called prog1.o is created. Similarly, an object file prog2.o is created for the second file. The two object files are then linked together to produce the executable program file prog. The two '.o' files are automatically deleted after the linking phase.

In a typical edit/compile/run cycle, we can retain the '.o' object files by using the '-c' option. If a program resides in two '.c' files, say main.c and file.c, then each may be separately compiled to produce the object files main.o and file.o. The commands are:

cc -c main.c
cc -c file.c

The two object files are linked to produce the executable program file prog with the command:

cc -o prog main.o file.o

Note that both the named files have '.o' suffixes. The cc command recognizes these as object file names and does not attempt to recompile them. This last example simply executes the linking phase of the cc command.

If a later change is made to, say, the source file file.c, then it alone may be recompiled by:

cc -c file.c

then relinked with the unchanged main.o using the previous command. Alternatively, the source file file.c may be compiled then linked with the original main.o file with a mix of file types in the command:

cc -o prog main.o file.c

The '-D' option provides a compile time macro definition. This option has two forms:

     -Dname
or   -Dname = def

The first form has the effect of including the preprocessor statement:

 #define name

in the source program file. In the second form, the statement effectively incorporates into the program text:

 #define name   def

The first example might be used to define a macro name which is the subject of an #ifdef or #ifndef preprocessor statement. The second example establishes a definition for a macro name. Two practical examples are:

cc -c -DVAX code.c
cc -c -DBITS = 16 interp.c

The cc command automatically searches the standard C library during the linking phase. The library functions referenced in the program file (for example, printf) are copied from the library and linked with the program to produce the object code. The '-l' option permits other libraries to be specified. The command:

    cc -o prog statistics.c -lm

compiles the program statistics.c and links it with functions from the mathematical library. The program would be expected to reference one or more math library functions (e.g. sqrt) and incorporate an #include ⟨math.h⟩ preprocessor statement. It is important that the '-lm' option is placed after the program filename. This is because the linker searches only for those functions referenced by program source files named preceding the '-l' option in the cc command. The general form for the '-l' option is:

    -lname

where 'name' is the name of the library to be searched. No intervening space appears between '-l' and the library name.

G.1 Lint: a C program checker

Lint examines C source programs, detecting a number of bugs and obscurities. Lint enforces the type rules of C more strictly than the C compiler. Lint may also be used to enforce a number of portability restrictions involved in moving programs between different machines. Another option detects a number of wasteful, or error prone, constructions which, nevertheless, are strictly legal.

The separation of functionality between lint and C compilers has both historical and practical rationale. The compilers turn C programs into object files both rapidly and efficiently. This is possible in part because the compilers do not perform sophisticated type checking, especially between separately compiled program units. Lint takes a more global, leisurely view of the program, looking more carefully at the compatibilities.

Lint accepts multiple input files and library specifications and checks them for consistency. Suppose there are two C source files, file1.c and file2.c, which are ordinarily compiled and loaded together. The command:

    lint file1.c file2.c

produces messages describing inconsistencies and inefficiencies in the programs. The command:

    lint -p file1.c file2.c

produces additional messages relating to portability of the programs. Replacing the option -p by -h produces messages about various wasteful constructions which, strictly speaking, are not bugs. Saying -hp gets the whole works. A collection of other options are used to select or to cancel the reports produced by lint.

The messages produced by lint fall into a number of classes. Lint complains about variables and functions which are defined but not otherwise mentioned. This frequently occurs as programs evolve and develop. These errors rarely cause working programs to fail but they are a source of inefficiency and make programs harder to understand and change. In a similar vein, lint attempts to detect cases where a variable is used before it is set, or set then never used.

Lint also attempts to analyze the program flow of control. It complains about unlabeled statements immediately following goto, break, continue, or return statements. An attempt is made to detect loops which can never terminate and loops which cannot be entered at the top. Sometimes functions return values which are never used; sometimes programs incorrectly use function values which are never returned.

Lint enforces the type checking rules of C more strictly than the C compiler. The additional checking is in four major areas: across certain binary operators and implied assignments, at the structure selector operators, between the definition and use of functions, and in the use of enumerations. The type checking provided by lint is comparable to that provided by an Algol 68 compiler, a strongly typed language.

Many of the facts which lint requires may be impossible to discover from the source text. For example, whether a function ever gets called may depend upon the input data. Most of the lint algorithms are thus a compromise. If a function is never mentioned, it can never be called. If a function is mentioned, lint assumes it can be called. This is not always necessarily so but in practice is quite reasonable.

Lint tries to give information with a high degree of relevance. Messages are only acceptable if the majority are relevant. If the ratio of real bugs to misinterpretations is too small, the messages lose their credibility and serve merely to clutter up the output, obscuring the important messages.

G.2   Make: maintaining computer programs

It is common practice to divide large programs into smaller, more manageable pieces (see Chapter 7). The pieces may require different treatments: some may be run through a macro processor, and others may be processed by a sophisticated program generator. The outputs from these utilities may have to be compiled with special options and with certain definitions and declarations. The code may then need to be loaded with certain libraries under the control of particular options. Unfortunately, it is very easy for the programmer to forget which files depend upon which others, which files have been modified recently, and the exact sequence of operations needed to make a new version of the program. One may easily lose track of which files have been changed and which object modules are still valid. Forgetting to compile a routine that has been changed or that uses changed declarations usually results in a program that will not work, and a bug that is very difficult to identify. On the other hand, recompiling everything just to be safe is very wasteful.

Make mechanizes many of the activities of program development and maintenance. Make provides a simple mechanism for maintaining up-to-date versions of programs. This is achieved by telling make the sequence of commands that create certain files and the list of files that require other files to be current before the operations can be performed. Whenever a change is made in any part of the program, make will create the files simply, correctly and with the minimum of effort.

The basic operation of make is to update a target file by ensuring that all the files on which it depends exist and are up to date. To illustrate, consider a simple example: a program named prog is made by compiling and loading three C-language files x.c, y.c and z.c with the lm library. By convention, output of the C compilations is found in the files named x.o, y.o and z.o. Assume that the files x.c and y.c share some common declarations in a file named defs, but that z.c does not. That is, x.c and y.c have the line:

#include "defs"

The following text describes the relationships and operations:

prog: x.o y.o z.o
   cc -o prog x.o y.o z.o -lm

x.o y.o: defs

If this information is stored in a file named makefile, the command:

make

would perform the operations needed to recreate prog after any changes had been made to any of the source files x.c, y.c, z.c or defs.

Make operates using three sources of information: the user-supplied description file (as above), file names and time stamps from the file system, and built in rules. In the example, the first line states that prog depends on three '.o' files. Once these object files are current, the second line describes how to create prog. The final line says that x.o and y.o depend on the file defs. From the file system, make discovers that there are three '.c' files corresponding to the required '.o' files, and uses built-in knowledge to generate the object files from the source files (that is, it issues a cc -c file command).

If none of the source or object files had changed since the last time prog was created, all of the files would be current, and the make command would announce this fact and stop. If, however, the defs file had been changed, x.c and y.c (but not z.c) would be recompiled and then prog created from the new '.o' files.

G.3 SCCS: source code control system

A large software system may involve hundreds of program units and thousands of lines of code produced by many programmers. A number of different versions of the system, tailored to different environments, may have to be produced. Major problems of large software systems include keeping track of the development and maintenance of program units, determining the interdependence of components, and ensuring the consistency of code common to different versions of the system.

SCCS is a system for recording changes to a system module. Each time a program unit is changed, that change is recorded and stored in a *delta*. Subsequent changes to a unit are also recorded as deltas. The latest version of a system is then created by SCCS by applying all the deltas in turn to the original code. A series of deltas D1, D2, ... is shown in Fig. G.1. SCCS permits generation of any version in the chain. Systems at different stages of the development can thus be produced. For example, a customer using version 1.2 may report a bug. In the meantime, development is presently working on version 1.3. To identify the source of the user bug, version 1.2 may be recreated and the fault diagnosed.

Fig. G.1

An extension of this feature is the ability to freeze development of a system at any point in the chain. For example, the customer-released version may be to V1.3. Further system development may continue in parallel, with new deltas constituting a new release of the system, for example, delta D2.1 may apply to V1.3 producing V2.1. To produce release 1 of the system, the SCCS user requests that those deltas pertaining to release 1 are applied. Further, additional deltas can be introduced to version 1 while development to release 2 is in progress.

ANSII standard C

The C programming language already has a de facto standard taken from B. Kernighan and D. Ritchie's book (*The C Programming Language,* Prentice Hall, 1978). The considerable investment in the C programming language and the availability of compilers over a wide spectrum of machines creates pressure for the adoption of a new standard. The evolving ANSII standard for the C programming language proposes a number of additions and changes. These proposals will greatly enhance the portability of programs, provide a language definition for compiler implementors, and allow C to develop in an orderly fashion. This Appendix considers some of the proposals.

The preprocessor (see Chapter 8) has always been part of the C language. Its definition has, however, lacked the same rigor as the remainder of the language, and has resulted in many implementation interpretations. The standardization committee has now specified it more fully, and included revisions that have been available in some compilers.

Simple #define directives are unchanged. However, one change is the adoption of two new preprocessor operators # and # #, both of which have to do with macros and strings. In section 8.1 we noted that macro expansions take place outwith string literals. Thus, in:

```
#define WRITE(X)      printf("X = %d", X)
```

the source program statement:

```
WRITE(abc);
```

is replaced with:

```
printf("X = %d", abc);
```

Some implementations, however, replaced the occurrence of a formal argument within a string with the actual argument. To support both features the operators # and # # are introduced. A # when followed by the name of a macro formal argument is replaced by the actual macro argument and enclosed in quotes. Thus in:

```
#define DISPLAY(X)      printf(#X " = %d", X)
```

the program statement:

```
DISPLAY(abc);
```

is replaced with:

   printf("abc" " = %d", abc);

The result introduces another new feature. Two or more adjacent string literals are concatenated into one string. Hence, the last statement is equivalent to:

   printf("abc = %d", abc);

The # # is the token concatenation operator. In a macro expansion, following all replacements, each # # is removed and the tokens surrounding the operator are concatenated. For example, in:

   #define DEBUG(S, T)   printf("x" #S " = %d, x" #T
                          " = %s", x # # S, x # # T)

the call:

   DEBUG(1, 2);

results in:

   printf("x1 = %d, x2 = %s", x1, x2);

We noted in section 15.4 that a relatively recent extension to C allowed structured items to be taken as arguments to functions and as values returned from functions (and hence assigned). This has now been incorporated into the new standard.

The original definition of C specified that all components in all structures were drawn from the same name class. This meant that no two distinct structures could have members with the same name. Thus:

   struct s {int a; float b;};
   struct t {char c; int a; };

would be illegal because of the a member. The problem is made worse by the exception to the rule which permitted this situation when the member had the same type and same relative position in the structure. The example:

   struct u { int a; float b; };
   struct v { int a; char c; };

would have been acceptable. This interpretation is now anachronistic and has been removed. Member names may now possess the same identifier in different structures.

Five new keywords have been introduced into the new standard. They are *void, enum, const, signed* and *volatile*. The keywords void and enum have already been described. Additionally, void has another role and this is discussed later. The type modifier signed can be used anywhere that the type modifier unsigned is allowed. This allows the programmer to be specific in the declaration of a variable. It also eliminates the problem when a char is unsigned and a program cannot receive a signed character value between -128 and $+127$ (see section 14.2).

The keyword const is a type specifier that defines an object that cannot be modified by the compiler's code, for example, data that are to be resident in read-only memory. Data identified as const can be checked by the compiler if the programmer tries to modify its value. Volatile is a compiler directive to ensure that every read and write operation on a data object must take place as specified. The compiler must not optimize out reads or writes to such objects. Usually, volatile objects are I/O objects such as memory-mapped locations, or a shared memory location modified by another process as in a semaphore.

Function prototypes are a significant new addition to the language. Using them will improve program documentation, improve compiler error detection, and enhance program portability. A function prototype is an expansion of the old extern functionname( ) syntax. For example, the library function *fseek* has three arguments and returns an int value. In usage, the referencing declaration is given as:

    extern int fseek( );

This form is still valid and will continue to be supported. The function prototype declaration is:

    extern int fseek(FILE *file, long position, int mode);

and informs the compiler that this function has three arguments of the given types (see Program 7.3). Any call to fseek not containing three arguments is a compilation error. The function prototype also converts the actual argument values to the specified types. When, for example, the second actual argument is an int, it is automatically promoted to a long. Thus, instead of having to say:

    ... fseek(..., (long) 12, ...)...

we may now simply write:

    ... fseek(..., 12, ...)...

The names in the function prototype are optional. They are included as documentation. Without them a prototype appears as:

    extern int fseek(FILE *, long, int);

The type void is also useful in the context of function prototypes. Many existing compilers support void type functions. Practically, they are procedures that have some operation but do not return a value (see section 5.4). An example is:

    extern void rewind(FILE *);

Void pointers can be used when the pointer type is application dependent. This gives rise to a form of generic pointer type. For example, the memory allocation routine malloc has the referencing declaration:

    char *malloc( );

To return a pointer of the required type an explicit coercion is required, as in:

    int *px;

    px = (int *) malloc(20);

To permit malloc to return a pointer of the required type, its new prototype declaration is:

    void *malloc(unsigned);
    void free(void *);

The assignment can then be presented as:

    px = malloc(20);

Similarly, when the memory deallocation routine *free* is called the pointer argument may be of any type and does not need a cast. A generic pointer type is thus formed using the void type as the base type.

To declare a function with no arguments the keyword void is used as the argument list in the prototype. For example, function *convert* in Program 5.5 should have the referencing declaration:

    void convert(void);

This function declaration states that convert should never be called with any arguments nor assigned to any variable.

Finally, C is almost unique in its ability to handle functions that take a variable number of arguments. The old external function declaration is used to denote such a function. For example:

    extern int print( );

declares printf to have a variable number of arguments. An improved version notes that the first argument must be a character string:

    extern printf(char *,);

With this declaration, the first argument must be a string but all subsequent arguments (including none) may be of any type.

Index of symbols

+ addition operator 6, 19, 25
& address operator 39, 69
= assignment operator 6, 25

\ backslash 14
\\ backslash escape sequence 14
\b backspace escape sequence 14
& bitwise and operator 386
^ bitwise exclusive or operator 386
¦ bitwise or operator 386
{ brace 5, 7
} brace 5, 7

, comma operator 31
/* comment delimiter 7
*/ comment delimiter 7
−c compiler option 450
−D compiler option 450
−l compiler option 451
−o compiler option 449
2's complement 12
~ complement operator 385
+ = compound assignment operator 27
− = compound assignment operator 27
%= compound assignment operator 27
?: conditional operator 89
% conversion specification 36
%% conversion 36
%[conversion 36, 40, 437, 443, 446
%c conversion 437, 443
%d conversion 6, 36, 37, 40, 438, 444
%e conversion 36, 40, 438, 444
%E conversion 36, 40, 438, 444
%f conversion 36, 38, 40, 439, 444
%g conversion 37, 40, 439, 444
%G conversion 37, 40, 439, 444
%o conversion 36, 40, 439, 444
%s conversion 36, 38, 40, 227, 440, 445
%u conversion 36, 40, 440, 445
%x conversion 36, 40, 440, 445
%X conversion 36, 40, 440, 445

/ division operator 19

" double quote 7, 15
\" double quote escape sequence 14

e power 13
E power 13
= = equality operator 86

\f formfeed escape sequence 14

> greater than operator 84
>= greater than or equal operator 84

* indirection operator 70
! = inequality operator 86

<< left shift operator 387
< less than operator 84
<= less than or equal operator 84
&& logical and operator 88
! logical negative operator 88
¦¦ logical or operator 88
l long integer suffix 12
L long integer suffix 12

% modulus operator 19
* multiplication operator 19

\n newline escape sequence 5, 14
\0 null character 15

(parenthesis 5, 7
) parenthesis 5, 7
−> pointer to structure member
    reference 323
− − pre/post decrement operator 29
+ + pre/post increment operator 28
# preprocessor character 76, 164, 455
# # preprocessor character 455
\ preprocessor continuation 167

\r return escape sequence 14
>> right shift operator 387

; semicolon 5, 7, 45

' single quote 14
\' single quote escape sequence 14
− subtraction operator 19

\t tab escape sequence 14

_ underscore symbol 16

General index

abs 447
absolute file position 306
abstraction 142
access mode, file 285, 433
acos 448
actual argument 62
addition operator + 6, 19, 25
address operator & 39, 69
addressing algorithm 284
aggregate types 193, 312
Algol 5
algorithm 53
allocator, storage 265
ambiguity, if-else 111
ANSII standard C 455
apostrophe 14
argc, argument count 250
argument: command line 250;
   conversion 66; function 407; pointer
   69
arguments 5
argv, argument vector 250
arithmetic: conversions 22; expression
   19; operators 19; overflow 25
array: character 223; declaration 193;
   function arguments 199; initialization
   202, 223; multi-dimensional 197;
   name argument 199; pointers 204;
   referencing 209; size, determination
   202; typedef declarations 209
arrays 192; of pointers 243–5; of
   structures 327
ASCII 14, 419
asin 448
assignment 6; conversion 26; multiple
   26; operator = 25; suppression flag
   443
associativity of operators 20
atan 448
atan2 448
atoi 241
atol 242
automatic: storage class 55, 147:
   variables 54, 148

automatics, initialization 150

B 1
backslash: symbol \ 14; escape sequence
   \\ 14
backspace escape sequence \b 14
basic type 11
BCPL 1
binary: arithmetic operators 19;
   conversions 22; search 367; tree 349,
   367; tree processing 371
bit fields 345
bitwise: and operator & 386; exclusive
   or operator 386; operators 385; or
   operator ¦ 386
block 45, 148
bound 149
boundary problems 359
braces { } 5, 7
break statement 125, 133
bubble sort 196, 200–1

%c conversion 36, 40, 437, 443, 446
call by value 62
calling sequence 58, 62
calloc, storage allocator 268, 431
case keyword 123
case labels 124
cast operator () 30
cc command 8
ceil 448
cfree 431
character: array 223; array initialization
   223; constant 14; functions 426;
   string 5, 223; type 11
class 144
clearerr 431
COBOL 3
collisions 336
comma 7; operator , 31
command: line 164; line arguments 249
comment 7; nested 7
compile time errors 8
compiling 8, 449

complement operator ~ 385
compound: assignment operators 27;
    statement 45, 148
condition 84
conditional: compilation 170; operator
    ?: 89
const keyword 456
constant: expression 157, 171, 173;
    pointer 224
constants 11
continue statement 136
control expression 91
conversion: of array name 204; of
    function 402; operation 36; rules 22;
    specifications 35
conversions, binary 22
cos 448
cosh 448

%d conversion 6, 36, 37, 40, 438, 444
dangling else 111
data structure, recursive 365, 368
data structures: dynamic 264, 349;
    linear 350; variable sized 264
data structuring capabilities 1
decimal: integer constants 11; point 13
declaration 6; referencing 60
decouple 144
decrement operator – – 29
default keyword 123
#define 76, 164
demotion 26
denotations 11
derived data types 1
direct access file 306; update 333
directives 164
division operator / 19
do statement 103
double quote " 7, 15; escape sequence
    \" 14
double type 11, 13
dynamic data structures 264, 349

%e %E conversion 36, 40, 438, 444
EBCDIC 14
#else 171
else keyword 108
end of file record 91
#endif 171
enum keyword 182
enumeration: constant 182; tag 182;
    types 182
EOF 288
equal symbol = 6
equality operator = = 86
errors: compile time 8; logic 9; run time
    9
escape sequence 14
executable program 8

exp 448
exportable 145
exported 152
expressions 6, 11
extern storage class 146, 151
external: array referencing 209;
    functions 2; objects 151; referencing
    declarations 151; static 159
externals, initialization of 156
exit 297

%f conversion 36, 38, 40, 439, 444
fabs 448
false logical value 85
fclose 285, 287, 432
feof 289, 432
ferror 432
fflush 432
fgetc 287, 432
fgets 293, 432
fields 283, 345
FILE 286
file: access mode 285, 443; inclusion
    170; modes 284; pointer 286; position
    306; update, direct access 333
files 283; indexed 283; inverted 283;
    random 283, 284; sequential 283, 298;
    of structures 333
float type 11
floating point constant 13
floor 448
flow control primitives 1
fopen 285, 286, 433
for statement 100
formal argument 62
format string 35, 39
formfeed escape sequence \f 14
FORTRAN 3
fprintf 291, 433
fputc 290, 433
fputs 294, 433
fread 307, 434
free 267; format 3
freopen 434
fscanf 291, 434
fseek 306, 434
ftell 309, 434
function: argument 5, 61, 407;
    argument agreement and conversion
    66; body 5; call statement 5, 49, 52;
    definition 45, 58, 62; invocation 49;
    name 45; parameter 61; point of call
    50; prototypes 457; returning pointer
    208; value 57
functional decomposition 48
functions 4
fwrite 308, 435

%g %G conversion 37, 40, 439, 440

generic program units 398
getc 435
getchar 41, 435
gets 435
global 154
goto statement 413
graph data structures 349
greater than operator > 84
greater than or equal operator >= 84

hardware characteristics 418
harmonic series 321
hashing function 335
header files 77
hexadecimal: digit 12; integer constant
   11
hierarchical data structures 349
hiding, information 143

identifier 16, 423
#if 171
#ifdef 171
#ifndef 171
if-else ambiguity 111
if statement 108, 110; nested 109
implicit: function type 58; return 53
imported 152
#include 77, 170
increment operator ++ 28
index 193
indexed files 283
indirect: addressing 71; recursion 191
indirection operator * 71
inequality operator != 86
infinite loop 99, 101
infix notation 255
information hiding 143
initialization 57; of arrays 202, 223; of
   automatics 150; of externals 156; of
   multidimensional arrays 202; of
   pointers 254; of statics 159; of
   structures 326
initializing pointer arrays 254
inorder tree traversal 371
int 6
integer: constant 6, 11; precision 12;
   qualifier 18; type 11
internal static 159
inverted files 283
isalnum 426
isalpha 427
isascii 427
iscntrl 427
isdigit 427
isgraph 427
islower 427
isprint 427
ispunct 428
isspace 428

isupper 428
iteration 84
itoa 242

key field 283
keywords 17, 422

librarian manager 16
libraries 4
#line 174
line numbering 174
linear: data structures 349; linked list
   350
linked list 350
linker 16
lint 2, 66, 451
list 350; processing 354
left shift operator << 387
less than operator < 84
less than or equal operator <= 84
local variables 55
locality, multilevel 146
log 448
log10 448
logic errors 9
logical: and operator && 88; negation
   operator ! 88; operators 88; or
   operator ¦¦ 88
logical value: false 85; true 85
long integer: constant 12; suffix 12
long qualifier 18
loop, infinite 99, 101
loops, nested 98

machine oriented languages 1
macro 76; arguments 166; body 164;
   definition 164; expansion 168;
   invocation 166; processor 164
macros, redefining 169
main function 4
make 452
malloc 265, 431
mask 386
master file 298
math.h 78
mathematical functions 78, 447
middle level language 1
mixed expression 23
modes 284
modular programming 2
modules 142
modulo arithmetic 19
modulus operator % 19
multidimensional arrays 197;
   initialization 202
multifunction programs 49
multilevel locality 146
multiple assignment 26
multiplication operator * 19

name overloading 181, 316
names 3
narrowing 26
negative operator − 11
nested: comment 7; if statement 109;
    loops 98; structures 331
newline 5; escape sequence \n 5, 14
NUL 15
null: character \0 15; statement 102
NULL pointer 286

%o conversion 36, 40, 439, 444
octal digits 12
octal integer constant 11, 12
one's complement operator ⁻ 385
open mode 285
operands 11
operator 6, 11; associativity 20;
    precedence 20
ordered binary tree 367
overflow 25
overloading, name 181, 316

packages 142
parameter, function 61
parentheses () 5, 7; free notation 255
Pascal 4
PDL 48
percent character %o 6
permanent 154, 158
plus symbol + 6
point of call 50
pointer 69; argument 69; arithmetic 205;
    arrays, initialization 254; to structure
    member reference 323
pointers: array of 244, 245; and arrays
    204; and function arguments 69; to
    functions 402; initialization of 254; to
    pointers 248
post-decrement operator − − 29
postfix notation 254
post-increment operator + + 28
post-order tree traversal 373
pow 448
power of ten 13
precedence of operators 20
pre-decrement operator − − 29
pre-increment operator + + 28
pre-order tree traversal 373
preprocessor 75, 164; character # 76,
    164, 455; character # # 455
printf 4, 35, 435
privacy 158
private 143, 147, 158; variables 56
problem oriented languages 1
procedures 4
program: design language 48; statements
    4; units 142
promotion 22, 67

public 143
putc 441
putchar 41, 441
puts 441

qualified integer constants 12
qualifier 18, 19
quicksort 210, 409

rand 447
random files 283, 284
rational numbers 317
read ahead mechanism 93
record areas 306
records 283
rectangular arrays 197
recursion, indirect 191
recursive: data structures 365, 368;
    external functions 2; functions 187
redefining macros 169
refinement, stepwise 48
referencing declaration 60
register storage class 160
relational: expression 85; operators 84
relative: file position 307; record
    number 284, 334
representation change 22
reserved identifiers 17, 422
return: escape sequence \r 14; statement
    52
rewind 309, 441
right shift operator > > 387
robustness 97
rounding 27
run time errors 9

%s conversion 36, 38, 40, 227, 440, 445
scanf 39, 441
SCCS 453
scientific notation 13
scope 55, 148; effect 144
selection 54
self-referential structures 350
semicolon 5, 7, 46
sentinel 91
sequence 84
sequential: files 283, 298; processing 54
Shell sort 201, 246
shift operators 387
short qualifier 18
signed keyword 457
sin 448
sinh 448
single quote ' 14
single quote escape sequence \' 14
sizeof operator 266, 328
sprintf 243, 446
sqrt 448
srand 448

sscanf 243, 447
standard: error 34; input 34; I/O
   functions 431; library 34; output 34
statements 4
static: external 159; internal 159;
   storage class 146, 158
statics, initialization of 159
stderr 296
stdin 296
stdio.h 35
stdout 296
stepwise refinement 48
storage: allocator 265; class, automatic
   55, 147; class, register 160; class,
   static 146, 158; classes 2, 55;
   management 264; management
   functions 430; mapping function 199
strcat 232, 429
strchr 429
strcmp 231, 429
strcpy 232, 429
string 5; comparison 226; constants 15;
   conversions 241; handling functions
   231, 429; input 227
strings 223
strlen 232, 430
strncat 430
strncmp 430
strncpy 430
strongly typed language 2
strrchr 430
structure: array members 326;
   initialization 326; members 313;
   nested 331; pointer operator − > 323;
   pointers 322; storage 316; tag 312
structures 193, 312; array of 327; file of
   333; self-referential 350
stylistic conventions 4, 5
subroutine 1, 4
subscripted variable 194
subscripts 193
subtraction operator − 19
suppression flag, assignment 443
switch statement 123
symbolic constant 76, 165

tab escape sequence \t 14
tan 448
tanh 448
template 182, 312
token string 76, 164
tokens 164
tolower 428
toupper 428
transaction file 298
tree, binary 349, 367, 371
tree traversal, inorder 371
true logical value 85
truncation 27
type 11; cast operator () 30; conversion
   22; definition 179; specifier 17
typedef declaration 179; array 209
typeless programming language 1

%u conversion 36, 40, 440, 445
unary: conversion 22; negative operator
   11, 13, 20
#undef 169
undefining macros 168
underscore symbol _
ungetc 447
unions 193, 342
UNIX 1, 8, 9
unsigned qualifier 19

variable: declaration 17; sized data
   structures 264
variables 6, 11, 17
variant records 342
visibility of variables 56, 149
void keyword 59, 77
volatile keyword 456

while statement 90
whitespace 7
widening 26

%x %X conversion 36, 40, 440, 445

Zeller's congruence 116